Collective Killings in Rural China during the Cultural Revolution

The violence of Mao's China is well known but its extreme form is not. In 1967 and 1968, during the Cultural Revolution, collective killings were widespread in rural China in the form of public executions. Victims included women, children, and the elderly. This book is the first to systematically document and analyze these atrocities, drawing data from local archives, government documents, and interviews with survivors in two southern provinces. This book extracts from the Chinese case lessons that challenge the prevailing models of genocide and mass killings and contributes to the historiography of the Cultural Revolution, in which scholarship has mainly focused on events in urban areas.

Yang Su is Associate Professor of Sociology at the University of California, Irvine. A social movement scholar, he has published work on social movements in the United States and in China. His research has appeared in flagship journals, including *American Sociological Review*, *Law and Society Review*, *Journal of Asian Studies*, and *China Quarterly*. A native of Guangdong, China, he holds a Ph.D. from Stanford University.

Cambridge Studies in Contentious Politics

Ronald Aminzade et al., *Silence and Voice in the Study of Contentious Politics*
Javier Auyero, *Routine Politics and Violence in Argentina: The Gray Zone of State Power*
Clifford Bob, *The Marketing of Rebellion: Insurgents, Media, and International Activism*
Charles Brockett, *Political Movements and Violence in Central America*
Christian Davenport, *Media Bias, Perspective, and State Repression*
Gerald F. Davis, Doug McAdam, W. Richard Scott, and Mayer N. Zald, *Social Movements and Organization Theory*
Jack A. Goldstone, editor, *States, Parties, and Social Movements*
Joseph Luders, *The Civil Rights Movement and the Logic of Social Change*
Doug McAdam, Sidney Tarrow, and Charles Tilly, *Dynamics of Contention*
Sharon Nepstad, *War Resistance and the Plowshares Movement*
Kevin J. O'Brien and Lianjiang Li, *Rightful Resistance in Rural China*
Silvia Pedraza, *Political Disaffection in Cuba's Revolution and Exodus*
Eduardo Silva, *Challenging Neoliberalism in Latin America*
Sarah Soule, *Contention and Corporate Social Responsibility*
Sidney Tarrow, *The New Transnational Activism*
Ralph Thaxton, Jr., *Catastrophe and Contention in Rural China: Mao's Great Leap Forward Famine and the Origins of Righteous Resistance in Da Fo Village*
Charles Tilly, *Contention and Democracy in Europe, 1650–2000*
Charles Tilly, *Contentious Performances*
Charles Tilly, *The Politics of Collective Violence*
Stuart A. Wright, *Patriots, Politics, and the Oklahoma City Bombing*
Deborah Yashar, *Contesting Citizenship in Latin America: The Rise of Indigenous Movements and the Postliberal Challenge*

Collective Killings in Rural China during the Cultural Revolution

YANG SU
University of California, Irvine

CAMBRIDGE UNIVERSITY PRESS
Cambridge, New York, Melbourne, Madrid, Cape Town,
Singapore, São Paulo, Delhi, Mexico City

Cambridge University Press
32 Avenue of the Americas, New York, NY 10013-2473, USA

www.cambridge.org
Information on this title: www.cambridge.org/9780521173810

First published 2011
Reprinted 2012

A catalog record for this publication is available from the British Library.

Library of Congress Cataloging in Publication Data

Su, Yang, 1964–
Collective killings in rural China during the cultural revolution / Yang Su.
p. cm. – (Cambridge studies in contentious politics)
Includes bibliographical references and index.
ISBN 978-0-521-19808-0 (hardback) – ISBN 978-0-521-17381-0 (paperback)
1. China – History – Cultural Revolution, 1966–1976. 2. Genocide – China – History – 20th century. I. Title.
DS778.7.S817 2011
951.05´6–dc22 2010045698

ISBN 978-0-521-19808-0 Hardback
ISBN 978-0-521-17381-0 Paperback

To my teachers, past and present

Contents

List of Figures		*page* xi
List of Tables		xiii
Preface and Acknowledgments		xv
1	Kill Thy Neighbor	1
2	On the Record	35
3	Community and Culture	68
4	Class Enemies	95
5	Mao's Ordinary Men	125
6	Demobilizing Law	156
7	Framing War	188
8	Patterns of Killing	221
9	Understanding Atrocities in Plain Sight	242
Appendix: Methodological Issues and Statistical Analyses		265
References		271
Index		291

List of Figures

2.1 Comparing timing of mass killings and founding of revolutionary committees. *page* 51
3.1 Guangdong and Guangxi Provinces in China. 80
8.1 The geography of collective killings, Guangdong Province, 1967–1968. 231
8.2 The geography of collective killings, Guangxi Province, 1967–1968. 232
9.1 A sociological model of collective killings. 259

List of Tables

2.1 Examples of Counties That Under-Reported the Number of Deaths in the *Xianzhi* *page* 47
2.2 Frequencies of Reported Collective Killings in Three Provinces 49
2.3 Victimization in Three Periods of the Cultural Revolution 52
2.4 Cultural Revolution Violence in Three Provinces Compared to National Figures 55
2.5 Reported Deaths per County and Average Length of Accounts in the County Gazetteers by Province 56
2.6 Counties Reporting 1,000 or More Deaths by Province, Deaths, and Length of Account 57
2.7 County Characteristics and Mass Killings in Guangxi and Guangdong Provinces 63
2.8 Profiles of Victims of Collective Killings, Selected Jurisdictions 64
3.1 Size of Subethnic Han Groups in Guangdong and Guangxi Provinces 82
3.2 Administrative Units in Selected Counties 88
3.3 Average Number of Deaths in Guangxi Province: Comparison between Minority and Han Counties 91
3.4 Average Number of Deaths in Guangdong Province: Comparison between Hakka and Mixed Counties 92
3.5 Average Number of Deaths in Guangxi Province: Comparison between Counties with and without a Significant Hakka Population 92

4.1 Class Composition and Land Ownership before and after the Land Reform, Xingning County, Guangdong Province, 1950–1953 104
4.2 Counter-Revolutionary Crimes in China, 1956–1965 and 1977–1980 122
5.1 Stagnation of State-Building prior to the Cultural Revolution: Cadres in China, 1949–1971, by Status (in thousands) 135
5.2 Changes in Total Population and Nonagricultural Population in Xin-Feng County, 1949–1966 136
5.3 Promotions to and Demotions from Cadre Rank in Guangdong Province, 1949–1971 137
5.4 Promotions to and Demotions from Cadre Rank in Guangxi Province, 1949–1971 137
6.1 Civil and Criminal Cases in China, 1950–1965 166
6.2 Types of Criminal Cases in China, 1950–1965 167
6.3 Campaigns in China: 1950–1969 169
6.4 Reported Armed Battles and Related Deaths in Guangdong and Guangxi Provinces 175
8.1 Deaths, Injuries, and Numbers Persecuted per County in Three Provinces 227
8.2 Average County Death Tolls in Two Types of Provinces 228
8.3 County Characteristics and Collective Killings (Guangxi and Guangdong Provinces) 232
8.4 Comparing Means of Collective Killing Deaths by Selected County Characteristics 234
8.5 Odds Ratio of Selected Measures from Poisson Regression Models Predicting Collective Killing Deaths in Guangdong and Guangxi Provinces 237
8.6 Differing Average Scores in Key Predictors of Collective Killings in Guangxi and Guangdong Provinces 239

Preface and Acknowledgments

This book presents and explains a chapter in human history of extreme suffering inflicted by extreme cruelty. The specifics are very Chinese but the lessons behind them are not. This writing coincides with the world community's anguish for the events raging on in Darfur and its most significant attempt to intervene yet: the indictment of Sudanese president Omar al-Bashir for genocide. Only the future will tell whether this is an effective course of action, although some scholars and humanitarian groups have already complained that, in fact, the indictment may alienate a government whose cooperation must be sought.[1] Since the United Nations adopted its convention on genocide in 1948, the record of intervention has not been encouraging.[2]

One of the lessons I attempt to extract from the Chinese case is that collective killing, mass killing, or genocide is, according to Scott Straus, "a massively complex social phenomenon." This understanding requires us to look beyond the "genocidal policy," if there is any, of a rogue state. Short of regime change, it may be more effective to engage the government at issue than to alienate it because the government is the most capable agent of affecting other social factors that have implications on the outcome. In his groundbreaking work on the Rwanda genocide, Straus writes: "Genocide is ultimately about how ordinary people come to see fellow citizens, neighbors, friends, loved ones, and even children as

1 For a forceful criticism of the indictment, see Julie Flint and Alex de Waal, "Justice Off Course in Darfur," *Washington Post*, A15, June 28, 1998. For more discussion, see a list of blogs at www.ssrc.org/blogs/darfur/ocampo-v-bashir/, accessed May 23, 2009.

2 Samantha Power, "*A Problem from Hell*": *America and the Age of Genocide* (New York: Harper Perennial, 3rd ed., 2003).

'enemies' who must be killed."[3] However expedient legally and politically, merely laying the blame for genocide on a few state leaders may not lead to the outcome we desire. The dynamics that turn "ordinary people" into perpetrators must be appreciated and then altered. To adapt the benign saying: "It takes a village" – or a community – to kill collectively.

The seeds of this research project were sowed in my childhood memories. As an elementary school student during the waning years of Mao's rule in China in the 1970s, I had no problem embracing the political education of the time. However, not every aspect of the indoctrination conquered this child's mind. In violent struggle rallies in which humiliation and beating unfolded on stage, I would forget that I was supposed to see the targets as "class enemies." Instead, I saw them just as human beings: a neighbor, a classmate's father, or someone's grandmother. As a raucous day gave way to the dead of the night, I could not remove the victim's image from my thoughts. More troubling, however, was that grown-ups did not seem to have the same concerns. Toiling in the collectively owned rice paddies, they would converse casually about the previous day's events. More often than not, a rally with struggle targets was considered more worthy of attending than one without them. Violence seemed to excite the adults. The conversations generated enormous confusion in me, for these were people with whom I was intimate and whom I knew to be otherwise kind and gentle. These early memories began to present the question of how ordinary people could lose their sympathy with the weak, a natural capacity that had remained in a child.

That the political system was at fault became evident to those of us who came of age in the 1980s – a time of awakening prompted by Chinese intellectuals. The enlightenment culminated as our bid for a clean break from the Maoist past in the 1989 Tiananmen Square Movement. Only in my graduate studies in sociology, however – first in China, then in the United States – did I begin to grasp the intellectual tools needed to comprehend the incomprehensible, starting with the concept of "social construction of reality" articulated by Berger and Luckmann.[4] It dawned on me that my fellow villagers in the Mao years perceived a different

[3] Scott Straus, *The Order of Genocide: Race, Power and War in Rwanda* (Ithaca, NY: Cornell University Press, 2006), p. 2.

[4] Peter L. Berger and Thomas Luckmann, *The Social Construction of Reality: A Treatise on Sociology of Knowledge* (Garden City, NY: Anchor Books, 1967).

reality from what I did as a child, although how their reality was constructed was yet to be explored.

Training to be a social movement scholar, I chose as my dissertation topic the mass movements in the Chinese Cultural Revolution. I collected data from *xianzhi*, or county gazetteers, as part of a larger project directed by Andrew Walder at Stanford University. I then discovered the fact of collective killings in Guangdong and Guangxi Provinces, a widespread phenomenon yet barely known to scholars. After I graduated and took a teaching position, Andrew Walder, one of my advisors, suggested that I expand one of my dissertation chapters on the collective killings into a book manuscript. For this purpose, I co-taught a graduate seminar on genocide and mass killings with David Snow at the University of California, Irvine (UC Irvine). After surveying the literature on the subject, I decided that the Chinese case had much to offer to existing scholarship, potentially with fresh lessons for policy making. In the meantime, I made field trips to China to interview survivors and witnesses. Over the years, I also obtained key government documents: some through my informants and some leaked to the public by exiled dissidents. I hope that this book provides a small voice for the victims in my village, in China, and beyond. I also hope that readers with childlike sympathy for human suffering find these pages informative and thought-provoking.

Acknowledgments

Writing a first book after graduation is not unlike writing a second dissertation thesis. In my case, not only did I have one of my former advisors direct me to a topic, I also enjoyed the encouragement and, at times, the verbal prodding from my other former mentors, John McCarthy and Doug McAdam. This book is rooted in the groundwork of my earlier apprenticeship with these scholars and their continuous support. Most crucial of all, I found a new mentor in Edwin Amenta, a senior colleague at UC Irvine. Without Professor Amenta as advisor, enforcer, reader, and editor, the writing of this book would never have been completed. Ed read and edited every line of all nine chapters. If the book does not appear to be written by a nonnative English speaker, he is the reason. Whenever I e-mailed him a new chapter, he would interrupt his vacation, with his extended family witnessing a book in the making. An accomplished scholar and author of three books, Ed also guided me through the publication process. To acknowledge his level of support, I find no appropriate language that does justice to my gratitude. As a Chinese saying goes: "No word of gratitude should be bestowed to a grand benevolence." For these reasons, I dedicate this book to these teachers and many before them, including Chen Foguang, Chen Jian, Yang Xiaolian, and Yang Yuanxiang, four village teachers who many years ago saw me off to see the world.

The Department of Sociology at UC Irvine provided a supportive and nurturing environment for junior faculty members. Chair Wang Feng, following his predecessors Judy Stepan-Norris and Calvin Morrill, took special measures to guard our research time against possible distractions. Wang Feng, David Snow, and Calvin Morrill took me to many lunches that sizzled with advice and guidance. I thank them for uplifting my spirit and sharpening my intellect. I am also grateful for friendship from other colleagues in the department, particularly Stan Bailey, Nina Bandelj, David Frank, Ann Hironaka, Jennifer Lee, David Meyer, Andrew Noymer, Francesca Polletta, Evan Schofer, and Judy Stepan-Norris. My special thanks go to Wang Feng for his camaraderie, brotherhood, and generosity.

I thank my informants in Guangxi and Guangdong Provinces and those who made possible my acquaintance with them. I regret that I cannot list their actual names, but I hope the following pages do justice to their kind assistance and their courage to speak out. I would like to acknowledge the institutional support of the University Services Centre at the Chinese University of Hong Kong. The Centre, which was under the leadership of Jean Hung during my research, has been the most professional and researcher friendly of the research centers with which I have been associated.

I thank Lew Bateman of Cambridge University Press and Elisabeth Wood, a coeditor of the Cambridge Studies in Contentious Politics series, for their insight and support. In their reviews for the Press, Yang Guobin and an anonymous reader, as well as Professor Wood, provided extensive criticism and suggestions that made the manuscript a better book. Xin He, Junling Ma, Doug McAdam, David Snow, Andrew Walder, and Dingxin Zhao also read an early draft and offered invaluable comments.

Xin He provided expertise on the legal system in Mao's China; Chapter 6, "Demobilizing Law," bears his contribution. Song Yongyi shared one of the important leaked documents with me. Ting Jiang and Feng Shizheng assisted me with the notes. Yong Cai created the maps. Support and assistance from the following individuals are also acknowledged:

Thomas Burstein, Amy Grubb, Su Jing, Liu Junqiang, Haining Li, Li Qiulan, Li Renqing, Lian Siying, and Ma Zengsheng.

I thank June ShuangShuang Su, Brooke JiuJiu Su, and Mingchen Zhang for inspiration and purpose. The preciousness of these children deepened my appreciation of the emotional dimension of my subject matter, and it reminded me every day of the urgency for understanding the origins of similar human tragedies. Finally, my deepest gratitude goes to Junling Ma; in the course of this book project and beyond, she sustains me with faith, sacrifice, and, above all, love.

The following permissions are acknowledged.

- Cambridge University Press permitted me to reprint some tables from "The Cultural Revolution in the Countryside: Scope, Timing and Human Impact," by Andrew Walder and Yang Su, *China Quarterly* 173, no. 3 (2003), pp. 74–99.
- Stanford University permitted me to reprint tables from "Mass Killings in the Cultural Revolution: A Study of Three Provinces," by Yang Su, in Joseph Esherick, Paul Pickowicz, and Andrew Walder (eds.), *China's Cultural Revolution as History* (pp. 96–123) (Stanford, CA: Stanford University Press, 2006).

1

Kill Thy Neighbor

Around the time of the traditional moon festival in the autumn of 1967, Sha Kaichu was rounded up by militiamen from his village, his own neighbors. He was denounced and roughed up in a "struggle" rally in the town square in Xiaojiang Village in Hunan. The next morning, he and five others were escorted to the commune's headquarters. Sha implored them to allow higher officials to hear his case: "I fought the war for our country. Please consider the efforts I have made. . . . "

Sha, thirty-seven and a father of three, had been the head of his family since his early twenties. His father, a landlord, was killed during the Land Reform movement of 1952. Sha joined the Chinese Voluntary Army to fight in the Korean War. After his discharge he worked in his village as a tractor driver. Sha had committed no crime but now was being singled out as the son of a landlord. A few days before his apprehension, his loved ones pleaded with him to hide; rumors of killings had come from other villages. He was too proud and confident to do so, citing his contribution to the country.

Sha considered himself to be safer than the other five male descendants of landlords being marched to the headquarters, but he was wrong. The village leader and the militia had decided to kill all of them at the roadside, 4 *li* (1 li equals 0.5 kilometers) shy of their destination. Zheng Mengxu, Sha's executioner who bludgeoned him to death, was no stranger. The Shas and Zhengs had been next-door neighbors since the Land Reform. Sha's father's house had been confiscated and granted to Zheng, who at the time was a shiftless drifter from another village. Zheng was not sorry about the murder. He yelled joyously, "*Tai hao le! Tai hao le!*" ("This is great! This is great!"), as he returned to the village.[1]

The story of Sha, his fellow victims, and his neighbor–executioner was, sadly, far from unique. During the Cultural Revolution, tens of thousands like Sha – at least four hundred thousand and possibly as many as three million – were killed in the countryside villages by neighbors like Zheng.[2] The victims' only crime was their political label as a "class enemy." There were no army, Red Guards, or systematic bureaucratic machinery of genocide; rather, neighbors killed neighbors. Days of rage in the squares brought rivers of sorrow that still flow through the villages today.

Nearly four decades after Sha's death, I visited his first cousin Sha Kaiping and his wife Ms. Li, both in their late seventies, in the suburban subdivision of University Hills in California, a neighborhood basking in sunshine and enjoying an ocean breeze. The house is provided by the University of California, Irvine, where their son is a member of the faculty. Sha's death happened thirty-eight years ago in faraway China, but when I sat with Sha and Li in their backyard, I was startled by the vividness and urgency in their voices. Li was spared due only to a technicality: Although she was the daughter of a former landlord, her husband's family was classified as "middle peasant" and therefore so was she.[3]

Archival records and field-research interviews unmistakably document events similar to the one in Xiaojiang Village in Hunan in the provinces of Guangdong and Guangxi, which I label as episodes of "collective killing." During the Cultural Revolution, previous categorizations and designations that resulted in discrimination were used to justify wholesale extermination. Hunan experienced killings in late summer 1967; mass killings lasted into late 1968 in the province of Guangxi. Here, I cite examples from the *Chronology of the Cultural Revolution in Guangxi*,

1 Personal interviews with Sha Kaiping and his wife, Ms. Li, 2005. I use pseudonyms throughout to protect the informants' identity; but I keep the real names of persons or places if they are already published or otherwise available in official records.

2 Andrew Walder and Yang Su, "The Cultural Revolution in the Countryside: Scope, Timing and Human Impact," *The China Quarterly* 173 (2003), pp. 75–99.

3 When I conducted field research in China, I did not obtain official records about the Xiaojiang Village killings. However, *Jianghua County Gazetteer* published in 1994 listed an entry that recorded a wave of "illegal killings" in 1967, resulting in 743 deaths in the county. That number may include the six Xiaojiang villagers. Similar to other county gazetteers, which I introduce in more detail in Chapter 2, the gazetteer was compiled and published by the local government.

based on government-sponsored post–Cultural Revolution investigations, which was officially published in 1995:

- October 2–4, 1967; Quanzhou County: Seventy-six members of the so-called Four-Type families in a village were killed.
- November 1967; Rongxian County: Sixty-nine people were killed in Licun Village.
- April 30, 1968; Ningming: One hundred eight people were killed in a siege.
- July 24, 1968; Binyang County: Mass killings occurred in every commune; 3,681 people were killed.
- August 18, 1968; Fengshan County: 1,331 people were killed.

Puzzles about Collective Killings

In his book, *Love Thy Neighbor,* Maass writes about the Bosnian ethnic cleansing in the early 1990s: "What intrigued me most about Bosnia was the question it posed about human beings – how could they do such monstrous things? How could a man wake up one morning and shoot his neighbor in the face and perhaps rape the neighbor's wife for good measure? How could they forget, as though it never existed, the commandment to love thy neighbor?"[4] I repeatedly encountered the same vividness and urgency that I heard in Li's and Sha's voices when I interviewed other witnesses and survivors in China; their stories never failed to move me. I strove to understand what constituted their extraordinariness and to formulate appropriate research questions for a historical and sociological inquiry.

The first extraordinary dimension of such killings concerns selection of the victims. They were killed not for any crime or for their current class position but rather for their family background. Many were children of former landlords or rich peasants. When Sha Kaichu's family was classified as landlords during the Land Reform, he was barely an adult. He could not have committed the crime of "exploitation" of the poor; in any case, his father had already been killed for that crime. During the Cultural Revolution, labels such as "landlord" and "rich peasant" reflected no economic reality because the land had been confiscated and redistributed fifteen years earlier. Neither did these descendants of landlords or rich

[4] Peter Maass, *Love Thy Neighbor: A Story of War* (London: Papermac, 1996), p. 14.

peasants pose any source of resistance to the government: They had been deprived of all political rights and were under surveillance. Therefore, selection of victims recalls genocide and mass killing: Individuals were singled out to be killed – along with their family members – for their kinship ties.

The second extraordinary dimension is the sheer rawness of the killings. The weapons were ad hoc and primitive – farming tools are the most commonly cited. In the killing of Sha and the five other victims, only one rifle was available and the killers were reluctant to spend bullets. Among the six dead, five were bludgeoned with a hardwood club. In another community, Liu Xiangyuan's perpetrators pushed him and his two children off a cliff.[5] Such a primitive method of killing seems to have been typical. Informants in the Hakka counties in Guangdong and Guangxi mostly used the word *bo/* – in Hakka dialect it means *strikes that produce a dull impact* – to describe the killings in those months. As a child, I once watched buffalos being butchered. An old buffalo would first be trapped and then a group of men would advance with large hammers to *bo/* until it lost consciousness. It was a horrifying scene.

One is also struck by the intimacy of the killings, which is the third extraordinary dimension: They took place in familiar neighborhoods, often among friends and acquaintances. In Hunan, Zheng Mengxu lived next door to his victim Sha Kaichu. In Guangxi, Liu Xiangyuan, before being ordered to jump to his death with his children, addressed his killer Huang Tianhui by his first name, "Tianhui."[6] The execution sites – riverbanks and roadsides – were part of a familiar setting.[7] Together, the primitiveness and intimacy underscore the fact that the killers were ordinary civilians rather than institutional state agents, such as soldiers, police, or professional executioners. State agents kill because of their institutional role; ordinary civilians kill for their own reasons. To borrow Goldhagen's memorable phrase, Chinese perpetrators were Mao's "willing executioners."[8] A village or township was turned into a willing community during those extraordinary days of terror in the Cultural Revolution,

[5] GXWGDSNB *Guangxi wenge dashi nianbiao* 广西文革大事年表 [The Chronology of Main Events of Guangxi's Cultural Revolution], unpublished document.

[6] GXWGDSNB.

[7] Personal interview with Du Zhengyi, 2006.

[8] Daniel Jonah Goldhagen, *Hitler's Willing Executioners: Ordinary Germans and the Holocaust* (London: Little, Brown and Co., 1996).

for the killers inflicted the atrocities in the name of their community, with other citizens tacitly observing.

The fourth extraordinary dimension is that the killing of neighbors was a public enterprise. In a normal community, a killer often becomes a fugitive after a murder, fleeing from the crime scene to avoid capture. With political killings, it is the potential victims who are on the run. Two of my informants took extraordinary measures to escape: One hid in the wilderness for months, the other had himself committed to prison.[9] In the Xiaojiang Village case, Zheng happily announced that he had killed his neighbors. He made a point of standing in the neighborhood with a rifle hanging around his neck, chanting to broadcast the deaths. The publicity of the killings says as much about the bystanders as the killer; that is, the killings appeared to be undertaken on behalf of the entire community. The tragedies usually unfolded in the open for days or months at a time.

In one way or another, these extraordinary dimensions echo other historical events in which neighbors collectively and publicly murdered their neighbors. The most notorious for American readers may be the Salem witch-hunts of 1692. Teenagers and housewives from respected families publicly accused their neighbors of being "witches" or "wizards," knowing that the crime would be punished by death. A few months into the wave of accusations, trials, and imprisonments, twenty-two people had been hanged or stoned to death, including church members, a successful merchant, and a priest.[10] On a summer day in 1941 in the village of Jedwabne in Poland, half of the town murdered the other half: sixteen hundred men, women, and children – all but seven of the town's Jews. In that case, what designated the victims is unmistakable: being a Jew. This event occurred during World War II in which Nazi Germany slaughtered six million Jews. Instead of a gas chamber or a killing field operated by soldiers, the Jedwabne pogrom took place in an intimate community.[11] The 1994 Rwanda genocide did not involve advanced

9 Personal interviews with Du Zhengyi and DuJianqiang.

10 Marion Lena Starkey, *The Devil in Massachusetts: A Modern Enquiry into the Salem Witch Trials* (Garden City, NY: Doubleday & Co., 1969); Paul S. Boyer and Stephen Nissenbaum, *Salem Possessed: The Social Origin of Witchcraft* (Cambridge, MA: Harvard University Press, 1974); Mary Beth Norton, *In the Devil's Snare: The Salem Witchcraft Crisis of 1692* (New York: Alfred A. Knopf, 2002).

11 Jan Tomasz Gross, *Neighbors: The Destruction of the Jewish Community in Jedwabne, Poland* (Princeton, NJ, and Oxford, England: Princeton University Press, 2001). The

weaponry or professional personnel. Using machetes, ordinary Hutus turned against their Tutsi neighbors in their homes and churches, on the hillsides, and in the sugar fields. In one hundred days, eight hundred thousand Tutsis were killed.[12]

Central to all of these events is the fact that the community was willing. The collective murders described previously were carried out in the name of the community. Past research tends to treat collective murders (e.g., genocide and mass killing) by focusing on the perpetrators and analyzing their motives, psychology, and resources.[13] Recognizing a willing community expands the focus to include not only the perpetrators but also the bystanders and, indeed, the entire community. When communities kill, they define the target as either an unredeemable criminal or an enemy. Although the killing may not be committed by the majority of the community, the entire community is involved in the process of defining or, to use a social-movement term, framing.[14]

A community willing to kill collectively exists in the context of state institutions. The state, by definition, is responsible for order, given its supposed monopoly on violent means. Therefore, large-scale killings can be seen to result from the state's sponsorship, acquiescence, or simple failure to stop them, or some combination of the three. At one extreme, there may be an endorsement by the state apparatus. For example, in the summer of 1793, the French Revolution was threatened by internal enemies and conspirators as well as foreign powers. The new government passed legislation that stipulated mass executions. The "Reign of Terror" lasted ten months, taking the lives of as many as forty thousand people, and is a clear example of state-sponsored public terror.[15]

exact number is disputed in later accounts, especially forcefully by a report from a group of Polish historians. See Antony Polonsky and Joanna B. Michlic, *The Neighbors Respond: The Controversy over the Jedwabne Massacre in Poland* (Princeton, NJ, and Oxford, England: Princeton University Press, 2004).

12 Philip Gourevitch, *We Wish to Inform You That Tomorrow We Will Be Killed with Our Families: Stories from Rwanda* (New York: Farrar, Straus and Giroux, 1998).

13 Michael Mann, *The Dark Side of Democracy: Explaining Ethnic Cleansing* (New York: Cambridge University Press, 2005).

14 To be elaborated upon later.

15 David Andress, *The Terror: The Merciless War for Freedom in Revolutionary France* (New York: Farrar, Straus and Giroux, 2006); David Andress, *The Terror: Civil War in the French Revolution* (London: Abacus, 2006). The example may not be clearcut, however; some argue that the bloodshed was caused by various competing factions radicalizing one another.

At the other extreme, however, killings may result from the incapacity of the state. A case in point is the lynching of blacks in the United States, which took place in communities that are often portrayed as "lawless" or "extralegal." A typical lynching event consisted of a sequence of interactions between state law enforcement and the lynching mob. Here, the state, which usually played the role of protector of the black victim, was too weak to succeed. The leaders of the lynch mob would outmaneuver a sheriff and his deputies, kidnap the prisoner, and execute him before a gathering crowd.[16]

The Chinese collective killings appear to fall between these two extremes. On the one hand, they were highly organized and carried out in the name of the state. On the other hand, the acts were committed by ordinary citizens with considerable autonomy. In this book, I address the following questions: Why did such an extreme form of killing appear in the time and place it did? How did state sponsorship induce ordinary citizens to become killers? Was there an extermination policy sent down from the Center or provincial authorities? Alternatively, was it a phenomenon of local improvisation? Could it represent a failure of control at the state's weakest reaches of society? In summary, the paradox of the primitive nature of the killings and their high level of organization warrants our attention.

Limits of The State-Policy Model

Killing civilians in large numbers is an age-old phenomenon.[17] Since World War II, its conceptualization has been shaped by the enormity of the Holocaust, in which Hitler and the Nazi regime killed more than six million Jews. In 1948, the United Nations (UN) passed the "Convention on the Prevention and Punishment of the Crime of Genocide." Lemkin and other framers clearly had the Holocaust in mind when they

[16] Despite such a usual sequence of parallel actions for and against the lynching, few would take it that the occurrence of lynching is due only to the state failure. Instead, the state is culpable in many ways – its support of white domination in the South, its agents' "incompetence," and its failure to persecute the perpetrators for future deterrence. See James R. McGovern, *Anatomy of a Lynching* (Baton Rouge: University of Louisiana Press, 1982); W. Fitzhugh Brundge, *Lynching in the New South: Georgia and Virginia, 1880–1930* (Urbana: University of Illinois Press, 1993).

[17] Chalk and Jonassohn provide a litany of episodes since the early history of humanity. Frank Robert Chalk and Kurt Jonassohn, *The History and Sociology of Genocide: Analyses and Case Studies* (New Haven, CT: Yale University Press, 1990). Also see Mann, *The Dark Side of Democracy.*

defined *genocide* as an act of a nation-state to eliminate an ethnic or national group.[18] Other conceptions of genocide also are preoccupied by central state policies, state-led exterminations, and institutionalized state killers. Later scholars expanded the concept to include cases in which victims are defined other than by ethnic, national, or religious characteristics. Valentino uses the term *mass killing* instead, and defines it as "the intentional killing of a massive number of noncombatants."[19] Other concepts such as *politicide*, *democide*, and *classicide* were developed to address killings in communist countries.[20]

Despite myriad variations and endless debates, the essential elements originated in the UN definition survive to this day. One element is the persistence of the idea of eliminationist policy intent at the central-state level. Related to this is the perspective that the killings are orchestrated by a fully functional state bureaucracy. In his three-volume classic, *The Destruction of the European Jews*, Hilberg wrote:

> Established agencies relied on existing procedures. In his daily work the bureaucrat made use of tried and tested formulas with which he was familiar and which he knows to be acceptable to his superiors, colleagues, and subordinates. The usual practices were applied also in unusual situations. The Finance Ministry went through condemnation proceedings to set up Auschwitz complex, and the German railroads billed the Security Police for the transport of the Jews, calculating the one-way fare for each deportee by the track kilometer.[21]

18 Essays in two anthologies provide a comprehensive review on the concept of "genocide" and its variants. See Chalk and Jonassohn, *The History and Sociology of Genocide*; George J. Andreopoulos and Harold E. Selesky, *The Aftermath of Defeat: Societies, Armed Forces, and the Challenge of Recovery* (New Haven, CT: Yale University Press, 1994). Also see Samantha Power, *A Problem from Hell: America and the Age of Genocide* (New York: Basic Books, 2002).

19 Benjamin Valentino, *Final Solutions: Mass Killing and Genocide in the Twentieth Century* (Ithaca, NY: Cornell University Press 2004), pp. 10–11.

20 Barbara Harff and Ted Robert Gurr, "Toward Empirical Theory of Genocides and Politicides: Identification and Measurement of Cases since 1945," *International Studies Quarterly* 32, no. 3 (1988), pp. 359–371; Barbara Harff, "No Lessons Learned from the Holocaust? Assessing Risks of Genocide and Political Mass Murder since 1955," *The American Political Science Review* 97, no. 1 (2003), pp. 57–73; R. J. Rummel, *China's Bloody Century: Genocide and Mass Murder since 1900* (New Brunswick, NJ: Transaction Publishers, 1991); R. J. Rummel, *Never Again: Ending War, Genocide, & Famine through Democratic Freedom* (Coral Springs, FL: Lumina Press, 2005); Mann, *The Dark Side of Democracy*.

21 Raul Hilberg, *The Destruction of the European Jews* (New York: Holmes & Meier, 1985), pp. 994–995.

Similarly, Arendt's famous concept of the "banality of evil" greatly contributed to the intellectual prominence of the state-policy model.[22] This state-policy model – that is, genocide and mass killing conceived as state policy and carried out through bureaucratic operation by state officials – has been the baseline for scholars introducing other cases of genocide or mass killing.

Building from the state-policy model of genocide and mass killing, some scholars explore the reasons for "obedience" in such an evil undertaking. Kelman and Hamilton use the My Lai Massacre as an empirical anchor point and conceptualize the authority structure in which the "crime of obedience" is likely to be committed. The authors define the My Lai Massacre – a mass murder of 347 to 504 unarmed Vietnamese civilians, mostly women and children, by the U.S. Army on March 16, 1968 – as a "sanctioned massacre," suggesting a command structure and subordination. According to them, soldiers follow such brutal orders because of an authority structure and prior processes of routinization and dehumanization.[23]

The state-policy model's influence remains strong in recent comparative studies. In Harrf and Gurr's massive project on political violence, *Minority at Risk*, the unit of analysis is the nation-state. The main criterion they employ to judge whether a case is genocide or politicide is the central state's intent in its policy.[24] Valentino also argues that mass killing is mainly a result of the strategic choice of a small number of elites in authority positions. In his qualitative comparison of various cases of mass killing, his unit of analysis is also the nation-state.[25]

However, the state-policy model hinders academic inquiry into collective killings. To prove their association to alleged state policies, the perpetrator's association to the state becomes an exclusive focus. Because it is treated as a state-policy decision, the social processes between the alleged policy and the eliminationist outcome fall outside the scope of inquiry as if, once the policy were set, everything else would follow

[22] Hannah Arendt, *Eichmann in Jerusalem: A Report on the Banality of Evil* (London: Penguin, 2006).

[23] Herbert C. Kelman and V. Lee Hamilton, *Crimes of Obedience: Toward a Social Psychology of Authority and Responsibility* (New Haven, CT, and London: Yale University Press, 1989), pp. 1–20.

[24] Harff, "No Lessons Learned from the Holocaust?" Barbara Harff and Ted Robert Gurr, "Toward Empirical Theory of Genocides and Politicides: Identification and Measurement of Cases since 1945."

[25] Valentino, *Final Solutions*.

automatically. Inquiries of this sort are generally not interested in explaining the variations in mass killings across communities within the same country.

Moreover, as other studies have shown, the state-policy model's empirical base is weak. Among thousands of cases of civilian killings in human history, the Holocaust may be the only true fit. The majority of civilian-killing cases, however, lack some of the model's essential ingredients, such as centralized commands and official killers. Even in the case of the Holocaust, the state-policy model may miss a major part of the story, as recent scholars have argued. For one thing, historians have found documentation for the so-called Final Solution policy to be elusive. It is unclear how much of the Holocaust was due to top-down command.[26] For another, the perpetrators acted more on individual conviction and initiative than their trial testimony tried to present. Recent scholars such as Goldhagen and Mann focus squarely on the perpetrators' anti-Semitic ideology and all manner of personal initiatives unprompted by bureaucratic roles and state-policy directives.[27] The thrust of their argument is that the perpetrators may be members of the state bureaucracy, but they take on a self-constituted identity in the act of killing.

A second group of studies that veer from the state-policy model includes detailed accounts of more recent genocide and mass killings. In the 1994 Rwandan case, the killers were Hutus from all walks of life instead of a well-organized state army or even a nationally coordinated militia. According to Gourevitch, the only way to coordinate different parts of the country was via a radio station.[28] Straus found that in many local communities, the previous government administration was overtaken by a newly self-constituted militia leadership that oversaw the genocide, and that the severity of violence differed from one hamlet to another.[29] Even in the case of Cambodia in the 1970s, many killings took place despite explicit orders to stop.[30] The Jedwabne

26 Raul Hilberg, *The Destruction of the European Jews* (New York: Holmes & Meier, 1985).

27 Goldhagen, *Hitler's Willing Executioners.*

28 Gourevitch, *We Wish to Inform You That Tomorrow We Will Be Killed with Our Families.*

29 Straus, *The Order of Genocide.*

30 George J. Andreopoulos and Harold E. Selesky, *The Aftermath of Defeat: Societies, Armed Forces, and the Challenge of Recovery* (New Haven, CT: Yale University Press, 1994).

pogrom was the work of Polish villagers, and Gross reports that at the time, only two Gestapo soldiers were stationed at the edge of the village.[31]

A third line of scholarship that challenges the state-policy model includes psychological work on the situational nature of inhumane human actions. This line of research and thinking includes the oft-cited experiments by Shrief, Milgram, and Asch, as well as the Stanford Prison experiment conducted by Zimbardo.[32] Some interpret the results of these experiments as individuals succumbing to authority (e.g., the experimenter's instruction in the Milgram experiment) or institutional pressure (e.g., role-playing in the prison experiment). However, recent work by Ross and Nisbett suggests that a more plausible interpretation of these results relies on the question of information. Individuals take cues from their fellow humans in a particular situation, giving rise to action that would be unthinkable in other circumstances – that is the power of the situation. As I argue in the next section, mass killing may be cued by one or more of three conditions: (1) a pending threat that requires immediate action; (2) targets who are deemed subhuman or dangerous enemies; and (3) knowing that the killings will go unpunished.[33]

A Community Model

I provide an alternative, the *community model,* which breaks with the state-policy model in three basic ways. First, I treat eliminationist killings as emergent events in extraordinary situations, as opposed to resulting from premeditation and planning. A state policy of extermination may or may not exist, but I consider that as an empirical question rather than a premise or presumption. More important, I do not rely on a "master plan" to explain collective killing. The killings may not be extensive even with a master plan or they may take place nonetheless without one. In the

[31] Gross, *Neighbors.*

[32] The first three are reviewed by Ross and Nisbett in their book. Lee Ross and Richard Nisbett, *The Person and the Situation: Perspectives of Social Psychology* (Philadelphia, PA: Temple University Press, 1991). For the Stanford Prison experiment, see K. Musen & P. G. Zimbardo, *Quiet Rage: The Stanford Prison Study* (videorecording) (Stanford, CA: Psychology Department, Stanford University, 1995).

[33] Lee Rose and Richard Nisbett, *The Person and the Situation: Perspectives of Social Psychology* (Philadelphia, PA: Temple University Press, 1991).

emergent situation, actors – including perpetrators, bystanders, and victims – take on what McAdam, Tarrow, and Tilly call "newly constituted identities."[34] This also applies to those whose work is related to the state (e.g., leaders, bureaucrats, prison wardens, and militia members) as well as those who have no official association with the state. Being a member of a state machine is not a sole explanation for the act of eliminationist killings.

Second, like scholars adhering to the state-policy model, I consider the state to be essential, but I argue that the effect of the state is usually indirect. A national government may be engaged in mobilization processes that have implications for producing eliminationist killing incidents. It may help promote hatred and generate categories of human beings deemed subhuman or menacing or both; the label may be "Jews," "enemy combatants," "infidels," "class enemies," or "terrorists." It may also organize – or at least acquiesce in the organization of – avenging vigilantes, which can undermine the legal system and forfeit the justice function to mob violence. Finally, it can frame a wartime situation in peacetime, with domestic groups framed as the enemy. A government may be engaged in one or more such mobilizations to different degrees, and at the macro level help produce the climate in which eliminationist killing is more likely to occur. This conception of the state is in contrast to the state-policy model of genocide and mass killing, in which the state hands down direct orders and carries out the policy through state bureaucratic machinery. Recognizing the indirect effect of the state allows us to examine the interaction between state policy and local conditions. Only then can we explain the variations among collective killings within a country where collective killings occur.

Third, my unit of analysis is the *community* instead of the state. I stress the subnational level communities, such as province, county, township, and village. The theoretical underpinning of such a treatment is the simple fact of geographical variations within countries that suffer from mass killings: Some communities are unmolested, some are slightly affected, and some are gravely afflicted. This is because the killing of a large number of civilians requires an extraordinary level of mobilization of local actors. Local conditions differentiate communities in terms of defining "enemies" and carrying out killings. A community that is

[34] Doug McAdam, Sidney G. Tarrow, and Charles Tilly, *Dynamics of Contention* (New York: Cambridge University Press, 2001), pp. 7–8.

engaged in mass killing consists of the perpetrators, the victims, and the bystanders. The mobilization within a community creates a situation in which the most extreme elements possess the largest share of organizing capacity, who become the perpetrators, including enablers, organizers, and killers (see Chapter 5); the rest of the community – victims as well as bystanders – are deprived of the means to resist or even to protest. To what extent the majority of the community members – that is, the bystanders – are supportive or acquiescent is an empirical question. However, in most cases, even if they are against the killings, they find themselves lacking a public forum in which to express their opposition. In short, the perpetrators "hijack" the will of the community and kill in its name. Eliminationist killing does not result merely from a leader's decision making, nor a perpetrator's; instead, it is an outcome of a collective definition of the situation by all community members: perpetrators, victims, and bystanders. The focus has to be switched from individual leader or individual perpetrator to the community as a whole – that is, how the community defines the situation as one of wartime, in which extensive killing is made legitimate and how the community loses its legal and moral constraints.

In another conceptual departure from standard scholarship, I use the term *collective killing* as opposed to *genocide* or *mass killing*. This concept shares three basic premises with genocide or mass killing. First, the criteria for becoming a victim are not about deeds but rather with membership in a group. Second, the killing must be intentional, which is distinct from acts of endangerment that carry no goal of killing in the first place. Using torture to elicit confessions, for example, may cause significant numbers of deaths. Third, the number of victims must reach a certain level. This aspect is very much related to the first premise regarding membership: Individuals are rounded up because they are members of a particular group, which by definition results in a collective of victims. I replace the word *mass* with *collective*, for the analyses of units smaller than a country as a whole, for example, county. Collective killings may occur in smaller areas without meeting the criteria suggested by Valentino of "at least fifty thousand intentional deaths over the course of five or fewer years."[35] With this more fine-grained conceptual approach, it is also possible to compare collective killings across counties, townships, and villages.

[35] Valentino, *Final Solutions.*

The community model considers five related processes to be crucial for collective killing to take place. The first process concerns "collective ethnic categorization" shaped by a community's history, tradition, and culture.[36] In any given community, there are myriad ways of classifying its members – class, religion, skin color, language, clan lineage, and so on. However, a history of prior conflicts often renders one way as particularly salient and is easily evoked as a salient fault line for new conflict, which provides a potential cultural source for building new collective identities in a time of mobilization. The historical legacy of anti-Semitism in Europe and prior conflicts between Hutus and Tutsis in Rwanda are two examples. But contrary to writings that claim to have "explained" mass killing by cataloging such preexisting divisions, recent scholarship rightly points out that group divisions are poor predictors simply because they are universal whereas mass killings are rare. Indeed, the historical legacy of group demarcations leads to mass killing only through the other processes described herein.

To explain the Chinese collective killings, I trace the long history of south-bound immigration to southern provinces and highlight the group identities based on surname lineage or family clan. I point out that such identities are more salient in some communities than others due to differing ecological conditions. Three points are particularly noteworthy in this Chinese case of "collective categorization." First, group boundaries were drawn within the Han ethnic population rather than between ethnic or subethnic groups. Second, they served as the starting point for imagining out-group members as potential targets of violence – an image sharpened by violent clan conflicts in the competition for community resources. Third, they took on an "ethnic" dimension in the sense that opponents in the conflict were judged by blood relations as opposed to the deeds of individuals. This tradition set the stage for revenge or punishment to be extended to an entire family or clan.

The second process generates potential victims in the community. Although there is no central command to designate potential victims, the state may have long-standing policies that encourage discrimination and abuse. Such policies, in Helen Fein's words, place a segment of the

[36] I borrow the term from Scott Straus, *The Order of Genocide: Race, Power and War in Rwanda* (Ithaca, NY: Cornell University Press, 2006), p. 9.

population outside "the universe of obligations."[37] In the Chinese case, the land reform and subsequent campaigns generated a class of vulnerable individuals, known as Four Types, to be subject to scapegoating under the most fanatic circumstances.

The third process generates potential killers in the community. Valentino suggests that mass killing is a rational, strategic decision by a few top leaders facing political or military dilemmas.[38] Left unanswered, however, is the question of how the top leaders' decisions, if any, translate into lethal action on the ground. Without a disciplined army to carry out an order, how do local citizens in a community turn themselves into cold-blooded killers? My solution is to address strategic tendencies not of the top leaders, who are distant from the community, but rather of actors within the community. In the case of collective killings in China, the actors included the county, township, and village cadres and the militia members under their leadership. If "attacking class enemies" was a general policy of the time, only those willing zealots performed eliminationist killings. It is the local actors' strategic choices – motivated by their fear of being deemed politically lapse or by their ambition for career advancement – that explain why some communities were involved in collective killings and others were not.

The fourth process is the demobilization of legal constraints in a community. If eliminationist killing is a national policy sent downward, as believed to be the case with Nazi Germany, then the legal issue is moot because killers are not expected to be punished; the responsibility for killing rests solely with the policy makers. When such a policy is absent, however, the killers' lack of fear of state-sanctioned punishment warrants explanation, and there are three possibilities. First, the leaders and the state may lack the will to enforce existing laws because the political terror generated by the killings helps to accomplish the political task of the time. This possibility is consistent with Valentino's strategic model, in which the top leaders consciously take advantage of terror. Second, the leaders and the state may be unable to enforce existing laws;

[37] Helen Fein, *Accounting for Genocide: National Responses and Jewish Victimization during the Holocaust* (New York: Free Press, 1979). Also see, e.g., Leo Kuper, *Genocide: Its Political Use in the Twentieth Century* (New Haven, CT: Yale University Press, 1981); Leo Kuper, *The Prevention of Genocide* (New Haven, CT: Yale University Press, 1985), p. 182; Florence Mazian, *Why Genocide?: The Armenian and Jewish Experiences in Perspective* (Ames: Iowa State University Press, 1990).

[38] Valentino, *Final Solutions*.

hence, collective killing in local communities may result from state failure rather than state sponsorship. This possibility arises often, I argue, particularly when a country is fighting external enemies or experiencing internal turmoil. Third, a suspension of punishment for illicit killing may be merely a misperception of the killers rather than the reality, based on informational cues conveyed to the community. I argue that the Chinese case of demobilizing legal restraints resulted from the combination of the three possibilities, with the latter two playing the largest roles.

The fifth process is the demobilization of moral constraints by framing war in a peacetime community. Typically, killing is morally justifiable only when applied to unredeemable criminals (i.e., in a law and punishment setting) or to enemy combatants (i.e., in a battlefield setting). As discussed previously, victims of collective killings meet their fate not for their deeds but rather for who they are. That is, they are not killed as criminals but rather as enemy combatants, supporters of foreign enemies during war, or guerrilla insurgents. Well-known cases include victims in the Armenian genocide (i.e., Christian civilians accused of aiding outside enemies); the Rwandan genocide (i.e., Tutsi civilians accused of aiding Tutsi guerrilla forces based in a bordering country); and the Japanese "three-all" (i.e., burn all, kill all, and loot all) policy in China during World War II (i.e., civilians accused of providing sanctuary for communist guerrillas). In 1967–1968, the continuing street battles in Chinese cities created a wartime domestic climate, and the Four Types in the countryside were portrayed as the class base for urban resistance.

Although I use the term *community model*, I do not neglect the momentous force of state policy and institutions in these five processes. Indeed, the latter four describe how state institutions take root in local communities. Calling it a community model is a departure from the top-down perspective of the state-policy models, and a call for a new perspective that is more sensitive to local conditions. The political system at the nation-state level can powerfully engage the community to undergo each process, but the response can be superficial or substantive depending on local conditions.

Thus theorized, the community model explains two types of variations: one temporal, the other cross-sectional. Documenting history in light of these processes explains why the same political system commits collective killings in a particular moment but not, most of the time, before or after it. In the Chinese case, although Maoist rule was violent throughout, collective killings in which family members were targeted along with class enemies took place only in 1967 and 1968. The answer becomes clear in my documentation of the events of the Cultural Revolution starting in 1966 and including the previous seventeen years of political campaigns.

Although the first four of the five processes had been long in the making, only in the years 1967 and 1968 did they all converge in some rural communities, with the war-framing rhetoric drumbeating imminent threat. None of these processes alone would have led to collective killing; they worked together interactively. To predict whether collective killing takes place in a community, the presence of each process must be determined. This reasoning is inspired by Smelser's "value-added" model of collective behavior. This discussion also follows Mazian, who posits a value-added or cumulative interacting set of determinants of genocide.[39] Recent scholars have demonstrated the utility of this research logic in predicting mobilization outcomes. For example, Amenta et al. find that the cumulative effects of local conditions can be used to account for a state government's adoption of the federal old-age policy in the 1930s. Cress and Snow demonstrate that the outcome of collective action among homeless people differs according to the combination of a set of factors.[40]

Delineating these processes also sets the stage for explaining cross-unit variations. Notable among these variations are the facts that collective killing was invariably a rural phenomenon, that Guangxi and Guangdong were by far the bloodiest provinces, and that – even within these two provinces – there was significant variation in whether localities engaged in killings and the degree to which they did. The five processes explain

39 Neil J. Smelser, *Theory of Collective Behavior* (New York: Free Press, 1962); Florence Mazian, *Why Genocide?: The Armenian and Jewish Experiences in Perspective* (Ames: Iowa State University Press, 1990).

40 Edwin Amenta, Neal Caren, and Sheera Joy Olasky, "Age for Leisure? Political Mediation and the Impact of the Pension Movement on U.S. Old-Age Policy," *American Sociological Review* 70, no. 3 (2005), pp. 516–538; Daniel M. Cress and David A. Snow, "The Outcomes of Homeless Mobilization: The Influence of Organization, Disruption, Political Mediation, and Framing," *American Journal of Sociology* 105, no. 4 (2000), pp. 1063–1104. This line of argument echoes the configurational causation championed by Charles Ragin; see Charles C. Ragin, *The Comparative Method: Moving beyond Qualitative and Quantitative Strategies* (Berkeley: University of California Press, 1987); Charles C. Ragin, *Fuzzy-Set Social Science* (Chicago: University of Chicago Press, 2000).

the timing of the killings and establish the rationale for the cross-unit analysis. For example, I show that the five processes were much more advanced in rural than in urban communities.

A key question regarding cross-unit variations is why did Guangdong and Guangxi – the two provinces that are the focus of this study – suffer the highest death tolls from collective killing in the country? Of the five processes that lead to collective killing, the two provinces shared a similar experience with others in three of them: designating the class enemy, motivating potential killers, and demobilizing law. However, the two provinces stood out in terms of the other two processes. Because of their immigration history, the populations in the two provinces were more immersed in the culture of clan identities and competition than Chinese elsewhere. This provided a particularly strong base for the influence of the other processes. Another factor that was more prominent in the two provinces was the depth and salience of the war-framing. Factional violence in Guangdong and Guangxi was particularly drawn out, and the Party Center was unhappy with the delay in establishing revolutionary committees. To end the violence and speed up the creation of a new provincial governmental authority, the country's top leaders ratified and reinforced the conspiracy claims manufactured by the leading faction to slander its opponents. The campaign to root out bogus conspirators and their alleged supporters hence took on extraordinary ferocity.

Explaining these provincial differences also has a temporal component. Elsewhere in the country, where revolutionary committees had already been established, war-framing had less resonance and fewer repercussions. In Guangdong and Guangxi, these processes were probably exacerbated by the unusual political trajectories during the Cultural Revolution. Due to their strategic locations as border provinces, the Party Center permitted them – along with the other three provinces – to retain their pre–Cultural Revolution leaders, which made the two provinces less representative and particularly repressive.

Analysis of why the killings in Guangxi and Guangdong were so horrendous sets the stage for the analysis of variations in killings across county jurisdictions in these two provinces. Even within provinces, there was great divergence in collective killings. A series of factors derived from my community model explains these differences. By highlighting the salient collective identities built on clan rivalry, I compare communities that are deeper in their legacy of clan conflict with others in terms of their collective killings. Establishing war-framing as a process that contributed to the killings explains why a remote community is more likely to suffer collective killings. Establishing a phony threat was more likely to occur in a community insulated from competing information. Similarly, counties experiencing factional fighting made the war-framing of the Center resonate more and were associated with significantly more killings.

Mobilization or Breakdown, or Both?

The term *collective killing* is modeled in part on the concept of collective action; indeed, collective killing can be seen as a special form of collective action. Collective action is emergent and situational – or, in the term used by McAdam, Tarrow, and Tilly, *transgressive* in comparison to standard "contained" politics.[41] The community model distinguishes collective killing from the imagery of a routine, bureaucratic operation in the same way that collective action is distinct from typical politics. Readers familiar with social-movement literature may see parallels in the community-model discussion. The five processes outlined previously echo four of the major theoretical perspectives: collective identity, resource mobilization, political-opportunity structure, and framing.[42] My community model benefits greatly from this literature; however, this study also provides a critique and a new synthesis. Contemporary movement theories tend to formulate collective action – including its features and outcomes – as a result of strategic mobilization. However, the qualitative nature of collective action – in this case, eliminationist killing in a public place – is often as much an outcome of conscious mobilization as an unintended result of a structural breakdown in the mobilization apparatus.

41 McAdam, Tarrow, and Tilly, *Dynamics of Contention*, pp. 4–8.

42 The latter three have gained canonical prominence in the field. See the most comprehensive review and synthesis in Doug McAdam, John D. McCarthy, and Mayer N. Zald, *Comparative Perspectives on Social Movements: Political Opportunities, Mobilizing Structures, and Cultural Framings* (New York: Cambridge University Press, 1996); Sidney G. Tarrow, *Power in Movement: Social Movements, Collective Action and Politics* (New York: Cambridge University Press, 1994); Sidney G. Tarrow, *Power in Movement: Social Movements, Collective Action, and Politics* (Cambridge: Cambridge University Press, 1998); and McAdam, Tarrow, and Tilly, *Dynamics of Contention*. Research on collective identity has a long tradition, with new impetus propelled by "identity movements" in recent years such as the gay–lesbian movement. For the latest summary of this research, see Francesca Polletta and James M. Jasper, "Collective Identity and Social Movements," *Annual Review of Sociology* 27 (2001), pp. 283–305.

My inquiry into the preexisting group identities and the origins of the victims is informed by research on collective identity. Two dimensions are particularly important in collective identity: group boundaries (or fault lines) and saliency. Theorists have proposed three main categories of independent variables: the cultural framework of interpretation; structural factors, such as daily interaction networks and formal organization affiliations; and situational factors, such as critical events.[43] This conceptual framework has guided my inquiry into the origins of the "killable" category and the collective identities of other community members that emerged.

My discussion on how the perpetrators – that is, organizers and killers – came into being is informed by the resource-mobilization model pioneered by Tilly, McCarthy, and Zald with its emphasis on formal organization and mobilizing structures. I also follow their theoretical starting point of actors making strategic choices.[44] Being in the position within or close to the party–state machine enabled the actors to convene rallies, including those with a public display of extreme violence. Their career considerations, shaped by preexisting mobility ladders, motivated the actors to be active in political matters, including inflicting harm on fellow human beings.

The discussion about legal constraints and collective killing is informed by theories of political-opportunity structure articulated by McAdam, Tarrow, and Meyer and others. Particularly relevant are two of the dimensions of the opportunity structure: the openness of the system and the strength of state repression.[45] With regard to openness, the Maoist society was intrinsically violent with its class-struggle doctrine. Physical

[43] Polletta and Jasper, "Collective Identity and Social Movements," *Annual Review of Sociology* 27 (2001), pp. 283–305; David A. Snow, *Collective Identity and Expressive Forms* (Irvine, CA: Center for the Study of Democracy, 2001); Roger V. Gould, *Insurgent Identities: Class, Community, and Protest in Paris from 1848 to the Commune* (Chicago: University of Chicago Press, 1995).

[44] John D. McCarthy and Mayer N. Zald, "Resource Mobilization and Social Movements: A Partial Theory," *American Journal of Sociology* 82, no. 6 (1977), pp. 1212–1241; John D. McCarthy, "Constraints and Opportunities in Adopting, Adapting, and Inventing," in Doug McAdam, McCarthy, and Zald (eds.), *Comparative Perspectives on Social Movements*, pp. 141–151; Doug McAdam, *Political Process and the Development of Black Insurgency, 1930–1970* (2nd Edition) (Chicago: University of Chicago Press, 1999); Sidney G. Tarrow, *Power in Movement: Social Movements, Collective Action and Politics* (New York: Cambridge University Press, 1994).

[45] Doug McAdam, "Political Opportunities: Conceptual Origins, Current Problems, Future Directions," in McAdam, McCarthy, and Zald (eds.), *Comparative Perspectives on Social Movements,* pp. 24–40; Tarrow, *Power in Movement.*

abuse in the struggle rallies was a staple of political life, but eliminationist killing was in no way endorsed by the system. It occurred nonetheless, attesting to a damaged state capacity to prevent it. Close examination of the institutional logic reveals that the constructed enemy class was for the community to keep, not eliminate. The existence of such an enemy class provided a reality base for treating other political conflicts in class terms. In high-profile killing events, the government sent in army to suppress killings, although with uneven levels of success.

Finally, the discussion on the creation of a bogus wartime situation is informed by framing-analysis theories pioneered by scholars such as Snow and Gamson.[46] Facing the mass conflict persistent in cities, the leaders framed the problem as class struggle, a master frame commonly understood in Mao's China. For a swift solution, the leaders transformed this master frame into a frame of war by inventing conspiracy networks. However, the leaders completed only two of the three key tasks of framing – diagnosis and attribution – leaving the third task, framing action, to local community cadres. Some communities then cast the blame on the labeled individuals and their families, and taking up collective killing as a legitimate course of action.

The community model is constructed on a foundation provided by the social-movement literature, but it is necessary to move beyond these theories to explain collective killing in China. Strategic mobilization – the central tenet of these theories[47] – explains only half of the story; the other half concerns structural breakdowns within the mobilization apparatus. Collective killing originated from a paradox between mobilization and breakdown. Mobilization theories, as McAdam admits, can better explain the emergence of rather than the development or outcome of a social

[46] For the original formulation of frames and framing analysis, and transformation between frames, see David A. Snow, E. Burke Rochford, Jr., Steven K. Worden, and Robert D. Benford, "Frame Alignment Processes, Micromobilization, and Movement Participation," *American Sociological Review* 51, no. 4 (1986): 464–481. For the concept of master frame, see David A. Snow and Robert D. Benford, "Master Frames and Cycles of Protest," in A. D. Morris and C. M. Mueller (eds.), *Frontiers in Social Movement Theory* (New Haven, CT: Yale University Press, 1992), pp. 133–155. For a comprehensive review of research and debates, see Robert D. Benford and David A. Snow, "Framing Processes and Social Movements: An Overview and Assessment," *Annual Review of Sociology* 26, (2000), pp. 611–639.

[47] In her critique of the contemporary social-movement literature, Cohen considered models represented by the resource mobilization a "strategic paradigm." See Jean L. Cohen, "Strategy or Identity: New Theoretical Paradigms and Contemporary Social Movements," *Social Research* 52 (1985), pp. 663–716.

movement.[48] Whereas collective-action scholarship concerns mostly how many individuals appear in a public place at the same time – that is, why collective coordination becomes possible – a collective-killing scholar has to explain why the public gathering takes such an extreme form of human action. In other words, it is not whether a gathering occurs that matters but rather whether it will result in mass murder that needs to be explained. Traditional models are successful in predicting emergence in strategic terms: building identities, amassing resources, seeking opportunities, and framing problems. When it comes to the features of collective action, they have much less to say. For example, how do these models distinguish gatherings that end violently from those that end peacefully? Can strategic mobilization explain anomalies within the mobilization machine? The character of a collective-action event often is precisely defined by such anomalies.

The extensive literature on collective violence does not entirely address the issue because, in recent decades, it has been dominated by the same strategic paradigm.[49] Indeed, among the pioneers who set the tone, Gamson and McAdam make protest strategy almost synonymous with disruptiveness, which in most cases means violence.[50] Older psychological breakdown models were discredited, with voluminous evidence suggesting that rioters are no less integrated in mainstream social structures than peaceful participants.[51] Observers such as McPhail et al. testified that violence is usually committed by the few who harbor "the dark side of purpose."[52] Gradually, research on collective violence merged with

[48] Doug McAdam, "Political Opportunities: Conceptual Origins, Current Problems, Future Directions," in McAdam, McCarthy, and Zald (eds.), *Comparative Perspectives on Social Movements*, pp. 24–40.

[49] A phrase used by Cohen in 1985. See Jean L. Cohen, "Strategy or Identity: New Theoretical Paradigms and Contemporary Social Movements," *Social Research* 52 (1985), pp. 663–716.

[50] William A. Gamson, *The Strategy of Social Protest* (Homewood, IL.: Dorsey Press, 1975); Doug McAdam, "Tactical Innovation and the Pace of Insurgency," *American Sociological Review* 48, no. 6 (1983), pp. 735–754.

[51] For an excellent review of this literature, see Clark McPhail, "The Dark Side of Purpose: Individual and Collective Violence in Riots," *The Sociological Quarterly* 35, no. 1 (1994), pp. 1–32. For rejoinders, see David L. Miller, Kenneth J. Mietus, and Richard A. Mathers, "A Critical Examination of the Social Contagion Image of Collective Behavior: The Case of the Enfield Monster," *Sociological Quarterly* 19, no. 1 (1978), pp. 129–140; Frances Fox Piven and Richard A. Cloward, *Poor People's Movements: Why They Succeed, How They Fail* (New York: Pantheon Books, 1977); Bert Useem, "Disorganization and the New Mexico Prison Riot of 1980," *American Sociological Review* 50, no. 5 (1985), pp. 677–688.

[52] Clark McPhail, "Civil Disorder Participation: A Critical Examination of Recent Research," *American Sociological Review* 36, no. 6 (1971), pp. 1058–1073; Clark

research on collective action in general, using similar mobilization models. In his synthesis of a new generation of research, Rule makes no distinction between collective action and "civil violence."[53]

I contend that although mobilization provides an opportunity for collective violence to occur, anomalies result from the failure of the mobilization's control over disparate elements. If a protester charges the stage and grabs the microphone from the speaker, the act is better explained by lapses of the event's security marshals rather than by any conscious decision on the part of the organizers. McAdam sees the wave of riots in U.S. cities in the late 1960s as the last round of "tactical innovations," yet evidence is weak for linking the movement leaders to any such strategic planning.[54] Once a mobilization apparatus is unleashed, its elements are neither necessarily coherent nor easily subject to central control.

This point is particularly germane to the case of the Chinese Cultural Revolution. Here, I refer to the mobilization apparatus as the vast network of party–state personnel and mass activists. Leaders at various levels – central, provincial, county, township, and village – had conflicting interests and, as important, they could not communicate clearly with one another. For coherence and consistency, upper-level authorities exerted two types of control – organizational and informational – over lower-level actors.[55] Some local communities took to heart the promoted frames of class struggle and war, which was successful informational control; however, they failed to anticipate punishment for extreme violence, which only organizational control could bring about. Moreover, in the heat of the Cultural Revolution, the two controls contradicted one another because the war rhetoric undermined law-and-order organizational procedures. Indeed, the perpetrators of the killings were not punished until ten years later, after the Cultural Revolution.[56] The killers need not be those isolated from the state machine; to the contrary, to the extent that

McPhail and David Miller, "The Assembling Process: A Theoretical and Empirical Examination," *American Sociological Review* 38, no. 6 (1973), pp. 721–735; Clark McPhail, "The Dark Side of Purpose: Individual and Collective Violence in Riots," *The Sociological Quarterly* 35, no. 1 (1994): 1–32.

53 James B. Rule, *Theories of Civil Violence* (Berkeley: University of California Press, 1988).

54 McAdam, "Tactical Innovation and the Pace of Insurgency."

55 This is inspired by Franz Schurmann's 1968 classic depiction of the party–state as consisting of organization and ideology. See Franz Schurmann, *Ideology and Organization in Communist China* (Berkeley: University of California Press, 1968).

56 To use an example familiar to U.S. readers, the rhetoric "enemy combatants" in the war on terror by the Bush administration was taken to the heart by soldiers, a success of informational control. That helped created incidents as failure of organizational control such as the Abu Ghraib prisoner abuses and the Haditha civilian killings during the war in Iraq.

individuals were close to the party–state, they were more likely to identify with the Central Party's frames. Therefore, the breakdown I refer to herein is structural rather than psychological.[57] In summary, the community model falls between strategic mobilization and structural breakdown. From the vantage point of the state, collective killing is a result of both state sponsorship and state failure.

This line of reasoning presents a twofold critique of the traditional state-policy model of eliminationist killing. First, contrary to the image of policy deliberation in routine politics in the traditional model, I contend that such killings are emergent events in the realm of extra-institutional politics. It is true that state apparatuses play a key role, but collective killings represent a moment in an extraordinary campaign of mobilization that involves social actors who did not have previous positions in the bureaucracy. Collective killings do not result from the original policy intent of elimination but rather from the extent to which ordinary citizens heed the call. Even when the state does not have an eliminationist intent, nongenocidal policies nonetheless may lead to genocidal outcomes, albeit indirectly.

Second, by recognizing the dimension of structural breakdown that contributes to eliminationist killings, I reject the assumption of a well-oiled state machine delivering a prescribed outcome. To the contrary, even when the state does not subscribe to an eliminationist goal, collective killings nonetheless could take place. In other words, collective killings may not be a rational outcome of a strong bureaucracy but rather result from the organizational pathology built into the system. Organizational-behavior theorists have long reminded us of "decoupling" – that is, organizational behavior deviating from formal rules – a phenomenon ubiquitous in the most advanced industrial societies.[58] I now apply this insight to our analyses of those bureaucracies that are deemed "rogue states."

The Cultural Revolution in New Perspective

In addition to providing a sociological argument about collective killing, I offer a historical narrative that contrasts with standard accounts. Existing

[57] See Chapter 9 for an elaboration of this point.

[58] John W. Meyer, John Boli, George M. Thomas, Francisco O. Ramirez, "World Society and the Nation-State," *The American Journal of Sociology*, vol. 103, no. 1 (July 1997), pp. 144–181; Stanley Baiman, Paul E. Fischer, and Madhav V. Rajan, "Performance Measurement and Design in Supply Chains," *Management Science*, vol. 47, no. 1, *Design and Development* (January 2001), pp. 173–188.

scholarship on the Cultural Revolution mass movement has three biases. First, it focuses on the first two years, 1966 and 1967.[59] The early scholarship on Red Guard factionalism served an agenda-setting role by proposing interesting and provocative research questions for many studies to follow. The interest-group divisions behind the early rebellions were debated, then repeatedly reexamined.[60] Second, existing scholarship focuses on events taking place in urban centers; some even erroneously asserts that "the Cultural Revolution was evidently an urban phenomenon."[61] Third, the research is biased toward hidden interests and ideals behind the mass action, at the expense of social consequences that such actions produced.[62] A result of these three biases is an underappreciation of the violent nature of the Cultural Revolution mass movement. The more staggering human impact in the countryside after 1967 is more or less undocumented and its implications for understanding

59 For the most authoritative review of the Cultural Revolution literature to date, see Joseph Esherick, Paul Pickowicz, and Andrew G. Walder, *The Chinese Cultural Revolution as History* (Stanford, CA: Stanford University Press, 2006), pp. 1–28.

60 See Hong Yung Lee, *The Politics of the Chinese Cultural Revolution: A Case Study* (Berkeley: University of California Press, 1978); Anita Chan, Richard Madsen, and Jonathan Unger, *Chen Village: The Recent History of a Peasant Community in Mao's China* (Berkeley: University of California Press, 1984); Andrew G. Walder, "Beijing Red Guard Factionalism: Social Interpretations Reconsidered," *Journal of Asian Studies* 61, no. 2 (2002), pp. 437–471. There are new studies on major cities that followed the entire period of the Cultural Revolution. See Keith Forster, *Rebellion and Factionalism in a Chinese Province: Zhejiang, 1966–1976* (Armonk, NY, and London: Sharpe, 1990); Elizabeth J. Perry and Xun Li, *Proletarian Power: Shanghai in the Cultural Revolution* (Boulder, CO: Westview, 1997); Shaoguang Wang, *Failure of Charisma: The Cultural Revolution in Wuhan* (Hong Kong: Oxford University Press, 1995); Guobin Yang, 2000. *China's Red Guard Generation: The Ritual Process of Identity Transformation, 1966–1999*. Ph.D. dissertation, New York University.

61 Richard Baum, "The Cultural Revolution in Countryside: Anatomy of a Limited Rebellion," in Thomas W. Robinson and R. Baum (eds.), *The Cultural Revolution in China* (Berkeley: University of California Press, 1971), pp. 367–476. Also see Jonathan Unger, "Cultural Revolution Conflict in the Villages," *The China Quarterly* 153 (1998), pp. 82–106. For a forceful rejoinder, see Walder and Su, "The Cultural Revolution in Countryside"; Yang Su, "State Sponsorship or State Failure? Mass Killings in Rural China, 1967–68" (Irvine, CA: Center for the Study of Democracy, University of California, 2003); Yang Su, "Mass Killings in the Cultural Revolution: A Study of Three Provinces," in Joseph W. Esherick, Paul G. Pickowicz, and Andrew G. Walder (eds.), *China's Cultural Revolution as History* (Stanford, CA: Stanford University Press, 2006).

62 I follow the criticism by Walder. See Andrew G. Walder, "Cultural Revolution Radicalism: Variations on a Stalinist Theme," in William Joseph, Christin Wong, and David Zweig (eds.), *New Perspectives on the Cultural Revolution, Harvard Contemporary China Series* (Cambridge, MA: Council on East Asian Studies, Harvard University, Harvard University Press, 1991), pp. 41–61.

the Maoist society are unexplored.[63] The aim of this book is to fill this gap.

The Cultural Revolution in official parlance is defined as "ten years of turmoil" between 1966 and 1976; however, the extensive mass campaigns and reorganization of local bureaucracy took place from 1966 through 1969.[64] This book is concerned with only the first four years, dividing the period into three stages. The political campaign was first launched in early 1966 in cultural and educational sectors. The earliest wave of mass action, known as the Red Guard movement, took place in high schools and universities in major cities; the targets included teachers, writers, and other intellectuals, as well as those labeled as politically problematic in earlier campaigns. Later in the year, however, party and government officials were accused of implementing a "bourgeois reactionary line," thus becoming the main and more lasting targets. They were believed to exist throughout the system – from the center down to the lowest administrations, from universities, factories to rural communes. Soon afterward, mass movements spread into every corner of society. By January 1967, mass organizations captured the authority and organizational resources previously controlled by local party–state administrations. The conflict over new leadership started an unprecedented period of political turmoil.

At the end of January 1967, the Cultural Revolution entered a second stage as the masses all over the country formed warring factions to contest the power positions vacated by disgraced "power holders." In each jurisdiction, this process was like a perpetual election dispute, except that the

[63] However, see Walder and Su, "The Cultural Revolution in Countryside"; Su, "State Sponsorship or State Failure?"; and Su, "Mass Killings in the Cultural Revolution."

[64] For general history of the movement, see Wang Nianyi 王年一. *Da dongluan de niandai* 大动乱的年代 [The Era of Great Turmoil] (Henan: Henan renmin chubanshe, 1988). For accounts about major cities, see Hong Yung Lee, *The Politics of the Chinese Cultural Revolution: A Case Study* (Berkeley: University of California Press, 1978); Elizabeth J. Perry and Xun Li, *Proletarian Power: Shanghai in the Cultural Revolution* (Boulder, CO: Westview, 1997); Wang Shaoguang, *Failure of Charisma: The Cultural Revolution in Wuhan* (Hong Kong: Oxford University Press, 1995); Hai Feng 海枫. *Guangzhou diqu wen'ge licheng shulue* 广州地区文革历程述略 [Mapping the Cultural Revolution Trajectory in Guangzhou Area] (Hong Kong: Youlian yanjiu chubanshe, 1972). For the Cultural Revolution in the countryside, see Richard Baum, "The Cultural Revolution in Countryside: Anatomy of a Limited Rebellion," in Thomas W. Robinson and Richard Baum (eds.), *The Cultural Revolution in China* (Berkeley: University of California Press, 1971), pp. 367–476; Walder and Su, "The Cultural Revolution in Countryside"; and Su, "State Sponsorship or State Failure?" The next several paragraphs are based on these accounts.

outcome was not decided by ballots but by mass action. The way to show one's strength was to wage collective action in the street; poster displays, rallies, parades, and demonstrations were daily routines. As conflict escalated, factions began to sabotage one another's activities. Mass factions formed militant groups, secured weapons, built barricades, and fought street battles. Death and injury from street battles were commonplace. Mao and the party then decided to restore order, by violent means if necessary.

The third stage of the movement began as new governments were established in late 1967 and early 1968, and lasted for approximately two years. In some locales, the new government was a result of factional struggles; in many places, however, new local authorities were imposed by the central authorities. The Party Center encouraged provinces to side with one mass faction against another. Most collective killings reported in this study took place not in the heat of extensive factional street battles of the second stage but rather in this third stage of demobilization and restoration of order. As defined herein, the Cultural Revolution began to wind down by the end of 1968, when mass organizations were effectively disbanded by the newly established administrations. The waves of collective killings that swept local communities also came to an end as urban centers began to stabilize.

The countryside was not as involved as urban centers in the first and second stages.[65] Peasants had few prospects of upward social mobility; hence, they had less at stake regarding who was in charge. Villages were relatively quiet in the early stages.[66] In the third stage, however, state cadres and their rural surrogates forced peasants into the fray as onlookers and rally participants. The policy took the form of the time-honored rhetoric of class struggle, and the class base of resistance was believed to be the former propertied classes residing in the countryside. The Four Types became victims, and those close to the state cadres joined the local militia as tormenters and executioners. This change in policy led to the slaughter of hundreds of thousands in the countryside.

As is made clear in the chapters that follow, in the entire 1966–1969 period, mass action and violence were a result of the combination of state mobilization, state failure, and popular initiation. Specifically, collective killings stemmed from the interaction of a willing community and the

65 Walder and Su, "The Cultural Revolution in Countryside."

66 Jonathan Unger, "Cultural Revolution Conflict in the Villages," *The China Quarterly* 153 (1998), pp. 82–106; Baum, "The Cultural Revolution in Countryside."

state-directed wartime rhetoric. This understanding challenges the prevailing historic view, which makes a distinction between a "mobilization and rebellion" period and a later "restoration" period. To Unger and other scholars, the early years of mass action were rooted in preexisting social cleavages and were spontaneous; victimizations in later years were a result of government repression.[67] My data show that the extreme violence beginning in late 1967 was not simply a matter of government repression.

Guangxi and Guangdong were not the only provinces that experienced collective killings. High-profile cases were reported in other regions, including Beijing, Hunan, Inner Mongolia, Yunnan, and Qinghai.[68] However, as demonstrated herein, the two provinces were among the most severe in terms of the Cultural Revolution's human toll. Because they were frontline regions of the Cold War – that is, they bordered Vietnam, which was at war with the United States, and Hong Kong, a British colony – Mao and the Party Center devised a different policy for the two provinces of Guangxi and Guangdong. In the majority of provincial jurisdictions, the Center sided with a rebel mass faction and entirely reorganized the provincial governments. In Guangdong and Guangxi, however, the Center endorsed the provincial heads – two party secretaries who were also army generals and who relied on the progovernment mass faction to form the new government.

This created a unique political landscape in which the new government and its mass surrogates enjoyed an unquestionable mandate. The state persecution machine, unshaken during the entire movement, was emboldened to adopt any means it saw fit, including unspeakable terror. Meanwhile, in urban centers such as Nanning and Guangzhou, rebel mass factions were no less formidable than their counterparts in other provinces, for Mao and the Party Center had been equivocal in adjudicating disputes between progovernment and antigovernment factions until late in the Cultural Revolution. Urban street battles plagued the two capitals even after the new provincial revolutionary committees were established. To demobilize mass organizations and pacify armed conflicts in urban centers, the Center and the provincial authorities ratcheted up long-existing class-struggle rhetoric. The disorder was deemed the work

[67] Jonathan Unger, "The Cultural Revolution at the Grassroots," *The China Journal*, no. 57, January 2007, pp. 109–137.

[68] Song Yongyi 宋永毅, editor. *Wen'ge datusha* 文革大屠杀 [Massacres during the Cultural Revolution] (Hong Kong: Kaifang zazhishe, 2002).

of widespread counter-revolutionary conspiracy networks. Local cadres turned such policies into "reality" by rounding up village Four Types based on fabricated crimes or merely accusing them to be members of an enemy class base responsible for the urban melee. Collective killings ensued.

That many villagers could turn into killers of their neighbors is without a doubt extraordinary, possible only in an extraordinary time, but the logic behind this transformation had been evolving since Mao's 1949 revolution. In other words, the extraordinary moment had its roots planted in less extraordinary times. In this study, I situate the collective killings in the entire history of Mao's China. Understanding the collective killings advances our understanding of Mao's era in its entirety. Moreover, using extreme violence to bring an end to a social crisis is by no means an approach exclusive to Mao's regime; examining this extraordinary moment in Chinese history has implications for understanding similar moments elsewhere.

In the spirit of Boyer and Nissenbaum, I use the extraordinary events to shed light on a historical epoch. In their 1974 classic, *Salem Possessed: The Social Origins of Witchcraft*, they noted: "We have tried to use the interaction of the two – the 'ordinary' history and the extraordinary moment – to understand the epoch which produced them. We have, in other words, exploited the focal events of 1692 somewhat as a stranger might make use of a lightning flash in the night: better to observe the contours of the landscape which it chances to illuminate."[69] This book uses the years 1967 and 1968 in rural China to illuminate the Maoist era.

Research Design and Sources of Evidence

I draw on two types of variation: temporal and geographical. Put differently, I explore why collective killing occurred in 1967 and 1968 but not at other times and why it occurred in some communities but not in others. Temporal development is described in my historical narrative, which begins with the Land Reform movement of the 1950s. Despite its violent nature and other waves of mass executions, Mao's regime did not commit eliminationist killings until the second year of the Cultural Revolution. The violent abuses against the Four Types in the countryside started with the Land Reform movement; since then,

[69] Paul S. Boyer and Stephen Nissenbaum, *Salem Possessed: The Social Origins of Witchcraft* (Cambridge, MA: Harvard University Press, 1974), p. xii.

the system rewarded organizers and perpetrators with political accolades and career prospects. Only when the Cultural Revolution overhauled local governments, however – and particularly when it created an equivalent of domestic war – did violent practices escalate to killings that included the victims' family members. The cause was a combination of the long-standing institutional practice with the situational factors that exacerbated it.

As discussed herein, previous studies tend to examine collective killings only at the level of a country as a whole. In my research design, I pinpoint where the most extreme collective killings occurred.[70] I explain why some communities were the site of staggering deaths whereas others were unaffected, despite there being the same overall national policy. It is unambiguous that the nation was not uniform when it turned to collective killing. In Guangdong and Guangxi, collective killing were widespread. Hubei Province – where, according to the county gazetteers, there was virtually no eliminationist killing – is used for comparison. I attribute the difference to the diverging trajectories of the Cultural Revolution mass movement in the two types of provinces. Collective killings occurred below the county-level jurisdiction in townships and villages, not in major cities or county seats. At the county level, only about half of the counties in Guangdong and Guangxi experienced collective killings. Within a county, collective killings were concentrated in a small number of townships and villages. These geographical patterns, combined with the fact that organizers and killers were neighbors rather than uniformed soldiers, raise doubts about the state-policy model but support my community model. In later chapters, I use county-level data to test a series of hypotheses derived from these two models. For example, if the state-policy model holds true, collective killing would be more likely in counties with a higher density of party membership and located closer to political centers.

[70] Although cross-unit analysis is rare in genocide research (exceptions including Fein, *Accounting for Genocide*, and Straus, *The Order of Genocide*), it is a long-standing scholarly tradition in studies of collective violence to conduct quantitative analysis across subnational regions. My research was informed by pioneering studies such as Charles Tilly, *The Vendee* (Cambridge, MA: Harvard University Press, 1964); John Markoff, "The Social Geography of Rural Revolt at the Beginning of the French Revolution," *American Sociological Review* 50 (1985), pp. 761–781; *The Abolition of Feudalism: Peasants, Lords and Legislators in the French Revolution* (University Park, PA: Pennsylvania State University Press, 1997); and recent studies such as Stathis N. Kalyvas, *The Logic of Violence in Civil War* (New York: Cambridge University Press, 2006); and Elisabeth J. Wood, *Insurgent Collective Action and Civil War in El Salvador* (New York: Cambridge University Press, 2003).

I use three major sources of evidence for this book, which is based on archival research and interviews. The first is the systematic (albeit sparse) county-level records of historic events from county gazetteers (i.e., *xianzhi*). I report Cultural Revolution violence, in various forms, in more than 1,500 counties. I also use the records of 182 counties in the three provinces of Guangdong, Guangxi, and Hubei to further examine the issue of collective killings in 1967–1968. Records from *xianzhi*, officially compiled and published, unequivocally establish that collective killings were a common phenomenon in Guangdong and Guangxi.

The data on collective killings in Guangdong and Guangxi are augmented by a series of internal documents, mostly unpublished. Like entries in the published *xianzhi* volumes, the information was initially generated during post–Cultural Revolution investigations. Whereas *xianzhi* are restrained in their approach to describing the atrocities, the internal documents contain blow-by-blow accounts. Collective killings were recorded including details on the victims, locations, and perpetrators, as well as the manner of killing. The records suggest not only that the scale of violence was grossly underestimated in the *xianzhi* but also that these documents shed light on the dynamics of events that led to the killings.

The third source of evidence is the interviews I conducted in 2006 and 2007. I visited the two provinces three times, meeting approximately thirty informants from Mengshan and Cangwu in Guangxi and from Xingning and Wuhua in Guangdong. The interviewees ranged from former county leaders, *xianzhi* compilers, and party and militia members to survivors of landlord families. My questions were not limited to their experiences during the Cultural Revolution in the 1960s; rather, I encouraged them to recall their experiences since 1949. Their stories provided the background about rural communities from the Land Reform movement to the Cultural Revolution.[71]

[71] In addition to these three main sources, I consult other published materials, the most important among them including a detailed account on collective killings in Hunan Province by Zhang Cheng and a document known as *Guangxi wenge dashi nianbiao* 广西文革大事年表 [The Chronology of Main Events of Guangxi's Cultural Revolution]; unpublished documents. For the Cultural Revolution events in Guangdong's provincial capital, I refer to Hai Feng 海枫. *Guangzhou diqu wen'ge licheng shulue* 广州地区文革历程述略 [Mapping the Cultural Revolution Trajectory in Guangzhou Area] (Hong Kong: Youlian yanjiu chubanshe, 1972). For comparison, I refer to Wang Shaoguang, *Failure of Charisma: The Cultural Revolution in Wuhan* (Hong Kong: Oxford University Press, 1995).

The Book in Summary

I devote two chapters to directly describing the collective killings that occurred during the Cultural Revolution. In the intervening chapters, I provide a comprehensive historic narrative, delineating the five processes that led to the collective killing. These intervening chapters cover a long span, starting as early as the Qin Dynasty two thousand years before the Cultural Revolution. However, the narration accelerates to the eve of the collective killings, with more details describing the years under Mao after 1949 and the days and months after the Cultural Revolution that started in 1966.

In Chapter 2 (On the Record), I establish the extent of collective killings based on *xianzhi* data and internal documents. Beginning in October 1967, unarmed civilians – mostly the Four Types – were executed in public, often along with their family members. Hundreds of thousands died. I first document the scale of the collective killings through the *xianzhi*, which are less than forthcoming. I then cite internal documents that provide a more extensive account. I also report on how the victimization information came into being. Following the third Plenum of the Eleventh Party Congress in late 1978, Guangdong and Guangxi (as elsewhere in the nation) conducted thorough investigations of the "innocent, false, and wrongful" cases in the Cultural Revolution. Deaths were meticulously tallied, compensation was awarded to surviving family members, and the culpable were punished. Although the investigations were largely covered up in the *xianzhi*, many documents survived that attest to the extent of the killings. Using both sets of documents, I unveil a series of empirical puzzles about when and where victims were found. In some provinces and localities, the killings were more extensive than others.

In Chapter 3 (Community and Culture), I introduce the survivors and witnesses in four rural counties. After interviewing local officials for a UN rural-development project, I was able to compile a list of informants to record oral histories of their experiences during the months of terror. I also examine traditional clan identities: their historic origins and their contemporary significance. The long history of ethnic competition among the subethnic Han groups sharpened clan identities, which provided a cultural basis for individuals to perceive out-group members antagonistically. Clan competition and a long-standing culture of violence were local conditions that facilitated political violence after 1949, as villagers "sugar-coated" long-standing group antagonism with new class rhetoric. My data show that the depth of immersion in the culture of clan competition significantly explains variations in the Cultural Revolution collective killings across subethnic groups.

In Chapter 4 (Class Enemies), I examine the social construction of class enemies in the early years after 1949 and subsequent political campaigns. The evidence points to a connection between inciting class rhetoric and mass mobilization. Contrary to the view that communist victimization is a result of a class-elimination ideology, or classicide, Chapter 4 shows that collective killings were a result of manufacturing an artificial class divide.

In Chapter 5 (Mao's Ordinary Men), I identify the organizers, killers, and enablers and then explore their motives. I also examine social mobility in rural communities. The importance of a political-performance system resulted in over-compliance, and local officials and militia leaders initiated collective killings as a strategic choice. An organizational pathology in the Maoist system contributed to the failure of upper-level authorities to contain increasing radicalization at the lower levels.

In Chapter 6 (Demobilizing Law), I explore the collapse of legal constraints in rural communities. The right to kill was typically in the hands of the state; however, in some political campaigns, boundaries between the state and the masses became blurred. The tendency was to reframe the issue of social order from a crime-and-punishment routine to a life-and-death class struggle. I examine the transformation from a rule-of-law approach to a "mobilization regime" in the early years of the People's Republic of China (PRC). I then examine the events of the Cultural Revolution mass movement that dismantled and reorganized local governments. The mass killings took place in the void of law and in the heat of class struggle.

In Chapter 7 (Framing War), I document how a wartime atmosphere emerged in 1967–1968 in the two provinces of Guangdong and Guangxi. This development stripped the rural communities of moral constraints on killing. The state policy to end mass armed conflict in urban centers adopted a language of war, calling for attacks on imagined enemies. Such a call was rendered as reality as local cadres organized slaughters of the rural Four Types, who were considered the default class base for alleged conspiracy groups and insurgent activities.

In Chapter 8 (Patterns of Killing), I document the patterns of collective killings. I address the questions of why killings were invariably rural occurrences, why Guangxi and Guangdong were the bloodiest provinces, and why the province of Hubei was not involved in the the killings. From there, I analyze the patterns of killings at the county level. The systematic data on the counties of the three provinces are augmented by information available in the *xianzhi*, which allowed me to develop a set of variables measuring the county's demographic, social, and political characteristics. Hence, I was able to chart the social geography of the collective-killing events, and the revealed patterns answer important questions. For example, were the killings more likely in urban centers or in remote reaches of society? Did the density of party membership have any impact on the likelihood of their occurrence?

In Chapter 9 (Understanding Atrocities in Plain Sight), the concluding chapter, I summarize the previous chapters and discuss human relations in Mao's China, as well as the theoretical implications of this episode in history for understanding genocide and mass killings in general.

2

On the Record

Although a complete and accurate assessment of the death toll from the Cultural Revolution is not possible until the Chinese government opens its archives, available publications and documents indicate unambiguously that there were extensive collective killings.[1] In the years immediately after the Cultural Revolution, during a major political shift, local governments conducted extensive investigations of the atrocities. The reports were quickly locked up and classified due to a yet newer and more restrictive political climate, but not before statistics and event descriptions found their way into various official publications.

The most systematic among these publications are the county gazetteers (*xianzhi*) and province gazetteers (*shengzhi*). These materials tend to be circumspect because they were highly censored. The compilers of these reports were given specific orders to record "sparsely" the "negative side" of past political campaigns, and for the most part they did so. However, the documents are nonetheless extremely valuable. The data, mainly gathered in the mid-1980s, cover almost all of China, and here I use statistics that were derived from these reports as the baseline estimate of the number of collective killings. There are more revealing documents but, unfortunately, they are not readily available to the public or academic institutions. However, some documents occasionally were leaked to researchers.

[1] That may not happen soon because the authorities, soon after the investigations, guarded them as state secrets and put great limits on research and discussion.

In this chapter, I establish the case of collective killings through these two types of written materials: local gazetteers and leaked documents. The main source, the *xianzhi* – which most counties published in the late 1980s or early 1990s – provides a systematic picture with timing, scale, victim identities, and sequence of events. It is clear from this source that collective killings were widespread across the country and especially in the main focus of this study, the two provinces of Guangdong and Guangxi. More than half of the counties in both provinces reported collective killings. Also, using the gazetteers, it is possible to analyze the timing of collective killings, which was not considered classified information. This helps to establish that the majority of deaths in the Cultural Revolution were killings rather than battle-related and to determine patterns in their timing. Nevertheless, the true severity of collective killings is undercounted in the gazetteers.

The leaked documents provide a partial remedy. These internal documents came to light by various accidents of fate. Some slipped through the cracks of government censorship and wound up in my possession; others were later leaked to me by informants who had been involved in the post–Cultural Revolution investigations. Interviews with the informants also gave me needed context to understand the reports. These documents cover only a few jurisdictions, however, and cannot be used to construct a systematic picture like the one using the *xianzhi*. Taken together, however, the documents significantly help us to understand a great deal about the collective killings in the countryside during the Cultural Revolution. The *xianzhi* provide a sense of how widespread collective killing was; the internal documents give us a glimpse into the depth of the tragedy.

Part of the focus of this chapter is how the extensive investigations into the Cultural Revolution deaths found their way – in a highly edited form – to official county gazetteers. However, the juxtaposition of censored sources and less-circumspect government documents makes it possible to derive reasonable estimates about how many were killed, when and where they were killed, for what reasons, and who the victims were. I have drawn a fairly complete portrait of the numbers, types, and timing of these staggering acts of murder, including detailed examinations of the killings in Guangdong and Guangxi. What happened in those two bloody provinces is compared to events in Hubei, a province in which collective killings were not nearly as widespread.

The Big Picture

Based on 1,530 volumes of *xianzhi*, Andrew Walder and I estimated the number of deaths in the countryside during the Cultural Revolution to be between 492,000 and 1,970,000.[2] National estimates of the violence can also be found in one of the less guarded reports, a book credited to the Party History Research Institute of the Party Center: "In May 1984, after a two-year-and-seven-month thorough investigation and verification, the Central Committee of the Communist Party's new tally of the Cultural Revolution's related statistics is as follows: 4,200,000 were detained and investigated; 1,728,000 killed, among which 13,500 were executed as a counter-revolutionary; 237,000 died in the mass factional armed battles; 7,030,000 were severely injured; 71,200 families were destroyed in their entirety."[3] Thus, at least one official document indicates that approximately 1.5 million Chinese were killed neither in battle nor through legal punishments. As shown herein, most of the deaths can be identified as collective killings in the countryside. Furthermore, beginning in late 1967, the majority of collective killings occurred in the third phase of the Cultural Revolution, coincident with the establishment of "revolutionary committees," or new local governing regimes, in the countryside.

Other published reports show that the two provinces had especially extensive collective killings. According to the *Guangxi Province Gazetteer* (i.e., Guangxi *shengzhi*) published in 1998, the number of those "persecuted to death or randomly killed" in the province during the Cultural Revolution was eighty thousand, not including three thousand who died in street battles between mass factions.[4] In Guangdong, "42,237 died of unnatural causes due to random beatings, random killings, random detentions and random struggles," according to the *Guangdong Province Gazetteer* published in 2004.[5] These aggregate numbers – 80,000 killings

[2] Andrew G. Walder and Yang Su, "The Cultural Revolution in the Countryside: Scope, Timing and Human Impact," *The China Quarterly* 173 (2003), pp. 74–99, (see p. 95).

[3] Zhonggong Zhongyang dangshi yanjiushi deng 中共中央党史研究室等合编 [Party History Research Institute, Communist Party Central Committee]. *Jianguo yilai lishi zhengzhi yundong shishi* 建国以来历史政治运动史实 [Historical Facts on Political Campaigns Since Founding the Republic], cited in Li Zijing 黎自京, 1996, "Zhonggong an cheng Mao baozheng haiguo yangmin: er qian liu bai wan ren cansi" 中共暗承毛暴政害国殃民:二千六百万人惨死 (The Damage County and Victimized People by the Violent Communist Regime Under Mao), *Cheng Ming* 争鸣 228: 14–17.

[4] *Guangxi shengzhi: Main Events Volume* 广西省志.大事记, guangxi renmin chupanshe (广西人民出版社), 1998: 393.

[5] GXWGDSNB *Guangdong shengzhi*: *General Summary* 广东省志.通志, Guangdong renmin chubanshe, 广东人民出版社, 2004: 106–107.

in Guangxi, 42,237 in Guangdong, and 1.5 million in the entire country – are staggering but they still likely underestimate the true scale of Cultural Revolution carnage.

As will become apparent, in Guangdong and Guangxi and most likely elsewhere, the recorded deaths from "unnatural causes" were primarily the result of collective killings in the countryside in 1967 and 1968. In an earlier study based on the *xianzhi,* Walder and I established that deaths from early persecutions before the power-seizure campaign in January 1967 were rare, and the number of deaths from armed battles prior to the establishment of county revolutionary committees was insignificant.[6] Two ratios reflected in the quoted numbers – that is, 3,000 armed-battle deaths to 80,000 total deaths in Guangxi, and 237,700 armed-battle deaths to 1,728,000 deaths for the entire country – also show that the number of deaths in armed battles was dwarfed by those due to other reasons. Those reasons comprise almost entirely what I call collective killings, a type of murder – not simply severe legal punishments, byproducts of overzealous public-humiliation "struggle" sessions, or deadly results of battles. If this reasoning holds true, then the official national estimate of collective killings is approximately 1.5 million – that is, the overall Cultural Revolution death toll minus the armed-battle death toll (i.e., 1,728,000 – 237,700 = 1,490,300).

Documenting Collective Killings with the *Xianzhi*

Before further analysis of the collective killings, some distinctions between them and other deaths prominent in the Cultural Revolution are worth making. Building on Valentino's concept of mass killing, I define *collective killing* as "the intentional killing of a significant number of the members of any group (as a group and its membership is defined by the perpetrator) of noncombatants."[7] The elements of this definition warrant discussion. First, the identification of a victim is based on supposed "membership" in

[6] See Walder and Su, "The Cultural Revolution in the Countryside: Scope, Timing and Human Impact," *The China Quarterly* 173 (2003), pp. 74–99. We report that deaths prior to the revolutionary committees were at least ten times fewer than those after the revolutionary committees. However, I should point out that in some counties in Guangxi, collective killings had started a few months before. When this point is taken into consideration, the contrast is even starker.

[7] Benjamin Valentino, *Final Solutions: Collective killing and Genocide in the Twentieth Century* (Ithaca, NY: Cornell University Press, 2004), pp. 1–90.

a certain group as opposed to immediate threat to the perpetrator. During the Cultural Revolution, membership in a target group was based largely on alleged political crimes or family background. Second, the perpetrator must intend to kill; this separates collective killing from other causes of death during the Cultural Revolution, such as beating during a public struggle session (the intent of which was mainly symbolic humiliation) and torture during the course of interrogation (for which obtaining a confession was the main purpose). Third, the toll does not include deaths from armed battles widespread between factions in an earlier phase of the Cultural Revolution. However, if victims were disarmed captives taken prisoner after armed combat, I consider them noncombatants because they no longer posed a threat to the perpetrators. Finally, the criterion of "a significant number" indicates a concentration in terms of time and space. I use ten deaths as an initial cutoff point. The most prevalent type of collective killing was what I call the pogrom against the Four Types, but there were two other significant sources of killing as well: political witch-hunts and murder of captives.[8]

It is useful to quote from the more explicit *xianzhi* reports – those in which the gazetteers did not document as sparsely as others – for a sense of the collective killings and the circumstances under which they occurred. The following record from Quanzhou County, Guangxi, is typical among the minority of county gazetteers that used unequivocal language to describe collective killings:

> October 3, [1967]. In Sanjiang Brigade, Dongshan Commune, the militia commander Huang Tianhui led [the brigade militia] to engage in a massacre. They pushed off a cliff and killed 76 individuals of the brigade – former landlords, rich peasants, and their children – in the snake-shaped Huanggua'an canyon.... From July to October, [another] 850 individuals [in the county] – the Four-Type elements (landlords, rich peasants, counter-revolutionaries, and bad elements) and their children – were executed with firearms.[9]

This is one of the most devastating examples of collective killings. In terms of demography, governing structure, and recent history, Quanzhou was otherwise a typical county. In 1966, about 93 percent of its

[8] See Note 13.

[9] This quotation and others that follow are quoted directly from the gazetteers listed herein. Translations are mine. Tang Chuying 唐楚英 (ed.), *Quanzhou xianzhi* 全州县志 [Quanzhou County Gazetteer] (Nanning: Guangxi renmin chubanshe, 1998), p. 17.

population of 485,000 was rural and organized in three levels of government: county, commune (i.e., township), and brigade (i.e., village). In the Land Reform movement of the early 1950s, 10,110 families were classified as landlords and 3,279 families as rich peasants.[10] In subsequent political campaigns, the ranks of these "class enemies" were enlarged by two other classes, labeled "counter-revolutionaries" and "bad elements." Together, these segments of the population – including their family members – were known as Four Types (*silei fenzi*). Whenever class-struggle rhetoric was provoked, they were instant targets for harassment and persecution. The tragedy reached a climax in the Cultural Revolution: By 1971, when the most violent period of the Cultural Revolution had ended, 2,156 men, women, and children of Quanzhou County had died "unnatural deaths,"[11] like those in the example quoted previously.

Brief though it is, an account like this provides information on the timing, location, identities of victims and perpetrators, and way in which the deaths occurred. These accounts also represent one of the major types of collective killing, which I call pogrom against the Four Types. Most other county gazetteers provide less explicit information about the manner of killing; however, based on the time period specified in the record and the large number of deaths, collective killings clearly occurred.

In the following example from Lingui County, Guangxi, the Four Types comprise the majority of victims, but also included among the killed are members of an alleged conspiracy. This suggests a second type, which I call killings in a political witch-hunt:

> In the name of "cleansing the class ranks" and "mass dictatorship," indiscriminate killings took place across the county. Between mid-June and August [of 1968], 1,991 people were killed as members of "Assassination Squads," "Anti-Communist Army of Patriots," and other "black groups." Among them were 326 cadres, 79 workers, 53 students, 68 ordinary urban residents, 547 peasants, and 918 Four-Type elements and their children. Among the 161 brigades [of the county], only Wenquan in Huixian and Dongjiang in Wantian did not indiscriminately detain and kill.[12]

Unlike a pogrom against the Four Types, the identities of victims in a political witch-hunt were constructed from events of the Cultural Revolution and based on the accuseds' supposed association with alleged

[10] Ibid., p. 147.

[11] Ibid., p. 565.

[12] *Lingui xianzhi* 临桂县志 (Beijing: Fangzhi chubanshe, 1996), p. 492.

conspiracy groups such as an "Assassination Squad" and an "Anti-Communist Army of Patriots." Although 918 victims were family members of Four Types, most of those noted in the report as being killed were not in this category: cadres, workers, ordinary peasants, and urban residents. As discussed in later chapters, these two types of collective killings overlapped one another because previously labeled class enemies were considered the class base for conspiracy groups.[13]

I should mention those counties for which I was unable to establish in the reports that collective killings occurred. My initial reading of these conservative reports is conservative as well. Even for those counties whose gazetteers mention a substantial number of deaths, I do not include the county as experiencing collective killings in the estimates if (1) substantial numbers of deaths are only implied rather than explicitly recorded; or (2) recorded deaths were due to armed battles, not imposed on unarmed civilians.[14]

[13] A third type of collective killings prevalent during the Cultural Revolution was the summary execution of captives. Limited cases are reported only in Guangxi Province. Because this type took place mostly in urban areas and is related to combatants, I excluded it from the scope of this book, which focuses on civilian killings in the countryside. The victims were disarmed after a factional battle and thus were no longer armed combatants; later, they were killed. Killings of this type occurred after one alliance (or faction) already had defeated the other. The following example vividly illustrates the nature of this type of event. After a joint meeting attended by public security officers of a few counties on August 18, 1968,

"... the People's Armed Forces Department (人民武装部 *renmin wuzhuangbu*) in each county went ahead to carry out the 'order.' About 4,400 (a number that exceeded what had been stipulated in the meeting) armed individuals of the 'United Command' (联指 *lianzhi*) 1 besieged the members of '7.29' [a dissenting mass organization] who had fled to Nanshan and Beishan of Fengshan County [Guangxi]. More than 10,000 were detained (the county population was then 103,138). During the siege and the subsequent detentions, 1,016 were shot to death, making up more than 70 percent of the total Cultural Revolution deaths of the county" (GXWGDSNB, p. 117).

Although summary executions of captives constituted the largest source of deaths in this county, in my overall analyses, this type of killing was less prevalent than the other two.

[14] Quotations from three counties illustrate, respectively, these two scenarios:

"On the evening of March 20 [1968], the militia of Huangqiao Brigade, Xinlian Commune indiscriminately killed people on the pretext of quelling the 'Pingmin Party.' Afterwards indiscriminate killings *frequently* occurred across the county and were particularly severe in Youping and other places." See Mengshan xianzhi bianzuan weiyuanhui 蒙山县志编纂委员会, *Mengshan xianzhi* 蒙山县志 [Mengshan County Gazetteer] (Nanning: Guangxi renmin chubanshe, 1993), p. 27.

"March 3 [1968]. The two [mass] factions engaged in armed battles in Liantang, resulting in 144 deaths." See Hengxian xianzhi bianzuan weiyuanhui 横县县志 编纂委员会 *Hengxian xianzhi* 横县县志 [Hengxian County Gazetteer] (Nanning: Guangxi renmin chubanshe, 1989), p. 19.

Behind the Official Numbers

There was once reason to believe that collective killings in the countryside during the Cultural Revolution would be officially publicized and made known to the world. In 1978, the Third Plenum of the Tenth Central Committee of the Communist Party called for rehabilitation of victims in "false," "innocent," and "wrongful" cases in the Cultural Revolution.[15] This policy was heeded by local provinces. Twice – in 1979 and again in 1983 – the government in Guangxi and Guangdong, for instance, set up special committees in every county and conducted systematic investigations into what were referred to delicately as "remaining historical questions." According to a chief compiler of the Cangwu County *xianzhi*, in Guangxi, the first wave of investigations in that province following the 1978 Third Plenum was utterly incomplete. Leaders at both provincial and county levels who rose to power during the Cultural Revolution not surprisingly treated the task perfunctorily. After more pointed directives from Central Party leaders such as Hu Yaobang and Zhao Ziyang in 1983, however, the province commenced investigating the Cultural Revolution in earnest. In each county, a "Resolving Remaining Historical Problems Committee" was formed, headed by top party leaders.[16]

The labor expended in these investigations was far from negligible. Cangwu *xianzhi*, one of the more revealing volumes, detailed the bureaucratic efforts behind the post–Cultural Revolution investigations:

> In April 1983, upon instructions from the above, Cangwu County commenced its work of resolving the remaining problems from the Cultural Revolution. In June, the County Party Committee formed the "Resolving Remaining Problems" leadership group with offices at the lower jurisdictions, led by deputy secretary and mayor Huang Jiyuan, director of People's Congress Tao Yuepan, and vice mayor Lu Yaoshan.

In the first quotation, the Mengshan County gazetteer reports "indiscriminate killings" on March 20, 1968, and afterwards. From the text, we can discern that the number of deaths must be substantial, but because no specific number is provided, I do not count those events as collective killings. In the second quotation from Hengxian, 144 deaths are recorded on March 3, 1968, alone; but because these deaths were a result of armed conflict, I do not count this as a collective killing.

15 "Zhongguo gongchandang shiyi jie zhongyang weiyuanhui disanci quanti huiyi gongbao" 中国共产党十一届中央委员会第三次全体会议公报 [Communiqué of the Third Plenum of the Eleventh Central Committee of the Chinese Communist Party], December 22, 1978, in Song Yongyi (ed.), *The Chinese Cultural Revolution Database* (CD-ROM) (Hong Kong: Universities Service Centre for China Studies, Chinese University of Hong Kong, 2002).

16 Interview with Mr. Zhao, 2006.

The efforts enlisted 516 county and commune cadres as work-team members, and 600 brigade cadres to assist.... By November 1985, the county exonerated the wrongful cases of "5. 16 Group," "Wuxiu Group," and "Anti-Communist Party Patriotic Army," and reinstated 2,006 cadres and mass members implicated by these cases."[17] Mengshan County also experienced a similar two-stage post–Cultural Revolution investigation. The second wave that started in 1983 was well organized and manned: "The leadership group called up 496 cadres to join the work-teams, and thoroughly investigate the remaining Cultural Revolution problems. 1,263 individuals were reinstated from the wrongful cases. 273,000 *yuan* was used as burial fees and child support funds for those individuals who were killed."[18]

The investigation in Guangdong counties also was apparently vigorous, as a *xianzhi* indicates:

> Following Third Plenum of the Eleventh Communist Party Congress, Xingning County Committee quickly started the investigations on various cases taking place before 1978.... The Committee established a leadership group with offices set in lower jurisdictions in August 1978. Then special offices were set up to reinstate the Rightists, reinvestigate criminal cases, and handle cases of unnatural deaths during the Cultural Revolution.... [The offices] reinvestigated 661 unnatural deaths caused by the Cultural Revolution, and rendered them with proper conclusions. The County Committee and its related agencies held 63 reinstatement rallies and 2 memorials, to clear names for those wrongfully persecuted or killed.... In 1983, [the county] established "Implementing Policy Offices" one more time to further resolve remaining issues."[19]
> In Wuhua County, "between October [1983] and the end of 1985, the county reinvestigated 1,265 cases, among which 1,253, or 99%, were concluded. Among them, the original conclusion of 1,193 cases was overturned.[20]

That these investigations resulted in a wide range of punishment for many culpable individuals – some quite powerful – attests to the

[17] Cangwu xianzhi bianzuan weiyuanhui 苍梧县志编纂委员会, *Cangwu xianzhi* 苍梧县志 [Cangwu County Gazetteer] (Nanning: Guangxi remin chubanshe, 1997), p. 483.

[18] Mengshan xianzhi bianzuan weiyuanhui 蒙山县志编纂委员会, *Mengshan xianzhi* 蒙山县志 [Mengshan County Gazetteer] (Nanning: Guangxi renmin chubanshe, 1993), p. 129.

[19] Xingning xian difang zhi bianxiu weiyuanhui 兴宁县地方志编修委员会 *Xingning xianzhi* 兴宁县志 [Xingning County Gazetteer] (Guangzhou: Guangdong renmin chubanshe, 1998), 505.

[20] Wuhua xian difang zhi bianzuan weiyuanhui 五华县地方志编纂委员会 *Wuhua xianzhi* 五华县志 [Wuhua County Gazetteer] (Guangzhou: Guangdong renmin chubanshe, 1998), pp. 379–380.

seriousness of the crimes. A leader of the Cangwu County investigations told me that in 1983 his work-team conducted exhaustive information-gathering on every instance of killing. They encouraged confessions and interviewed as many eyewitnesses as possible, as well as victims' surviving family members or relatives. "We did not want to create remaining problems for the future in resolving remaining historic problems," he said.[21] In his county, 633 individuals were investigated regarding their responsibilities during the Cultural Revolution. Among the 572 who were disciplined, 501 were Party Center members. Each level of government was reorganized following the investigations.[22] In Mengshan County, 819 cadres, workers, and peasants were found responsible; among them, 303 were expelled from the Party, 55 were stripped of government employment, and 29 were convicted of crimes, which resulted in 2 death sentences and 1 life sentence.[23]

The central policy and local investigations generated valuable and detailed information regarding collective killings during the Cultural Revolution, most of which was later documented and published – in a much abbreviated form, however – by the county gazetteers. The *xianzhi*, with few exceptions, have a "Major Events" section that, among other historical events in a county, records key events during the Cultural Revolution. The records also include death and injury statistics. In 1966, there were about 2,250 county-level jurisdictions in China.[24] In 1988, there were 1,936 counties (*xian*) in China, virtually all of which are considered rural for the purposes of this study. In addition, there were 248 "county-level cities," the majority of which were labeled counties and considered rural in 1966.[25] By 2001, the vast majority of the jurisdictions published

[21] Interview with Mr. Zhao, 2006.

[22] Cangwu xianzhi bianzuan weiyuanhui 苍梧县志编纂委员会 *Cangwu xianzhi* 苍梧县志 [Cangwu County Gazetteer] (Nanning: Guangxi remin chubanshe, 1997), p. 483.

[23] Mengshan xianzhi bianzuan weiyuanhui 蒙山县志编纂委员会, *Mengshan xianzhi* 蒙山县志 [Mengshan County Gazetteer] (Nanning: Guangxi renmin chubanshe, 1993), p. 129.

[24] Zhonghua renmin gongheguo minzheng bu 中华人民共和国民政部 [Ministry of Civil Affairs, People's Republic of China] (ed.), *Zhonghua renmin gongheguo xingzheng quhua, 1949–1997* 中华人民共和国行政区划, 1949–1997 [Administrative Jurisdictions of the People's Republic of China, 1949–1997] (Beijing: Zhongguo shehui chubanshe, 1998).

[25] Yan Chongnian 阎崇年 (ed.). *Zhongguo shi xian da cidian* 中国市县大辞典 [The Encyclopedia of Chinese Cities and Counties], (Beijing: Zhonggong zhongyang dangxiao chubanshe, 1991), p. 1. In addition to the three cities directly under the national government, there were 183 "prefectural-level" cities (地级市 *diji shi*). Unless otherwise specified, this is the source for all information in this chapter about the location and boundaries of counties.

their newly compiled gazetteers, covering the history of their county until 1985, the year that localities began this project.[26]

The Universities Service Centre Library at the Chinese University of Hong Kong has one of the largest collections of county documents outside Beijing and which is easily accessible. When Andrew Walder's research team from Stanford University in California began photocopying and coding relevant sections in 1996, there were approximately 900 documents on the shelves; by the summer of 2005, there were close to 1,850.[27] Our aim was to create a database of basic information, including the sources, which was essential for evaluating variations in the quality of information provided about the Cultural Revolution. We assigned codes to each province and county, recorded the year of publication, and counted the number of characters devoted to the description of Cultural Revolution political events in three separate sections of the gazetteer: the chronicle of events (*dashiji*); a specialized section on the Cultural Revolution (if any); and "other" sections (e.g., Party-building, political movements, and legal and judicial affairs). Local compilers of these publications faced a serious political dilemma: How should they treat the "errors" and "mistakes" of the Mao period? Most sensitive was how to treat the Cultural Revolution. Shortly after local writing groups were established in the early 1980s to collect materials and draft sections of the gazetteers, a lively debate erupted about the way the Cultural Revolution should be handled. Some local scholars and functionaries assigned to work on these sections wanted to detail local events with honesty and accuracy. Others, however, felt that full accounts could create serious embarrassment for local political incumbents and perhaps exacerbate nascent factional tensions.[28]

[26] See Eduard B. Vermeer, "New County Histories: A Research note on Their Compilation and Value," *Modern China* 18, no. 4 (1992), pp. 438–467. Historians have long used the term *gazetteer* to designate the fangzhi of the imperial and republican eras. See also Stig Thogersen and Soren Clausen, "New Reflections in the Mirror: Local Chinese Gazetteers (*Difangzhi*) in the 1980s," *The Australian Journal of Chinese Affairs* 27 (1992), pp. 161–184 (see p. 162).

[27] The library at the Chinese University of Hong Kong has an online catalog that permits a user to list currently cataloged holdings of *difangzhi* (地方志) by province. Available at www.usc.cuhk.edu.hk.

[28] See Vermeer, "New County Histories," pp. 445–446. See also Qu Jiang, "Da xianzhi bangongshi, "Jixu 'wenhua da geming' yi xi buyi cu" 记叙 '文化大革命' 宜细不宜粗 [The "Cultural Revolution" should be narrated in detail, not in broad strokes], *Sichuan difangzhi tongxun* 四川地方志通讯 [Sichuan Local Gazetteers Newsletter], no. 1 (1982), pp. 7–9; Xuan Ping, Chongqing shi shuili zhi bianji shi 重庆市水利志编辑室, "Zhide shensi

The latter group won. The debate was seemingly settled in favor of circumspection with the promulgation of national guidelines in 1985. The guidelines specified the principle of "recording in broad strokes, not in detail" (*yi cu, bu yi xi*) when dealing with politically sensitive subject matter.[29] This more conservative approach was embodied in the slogan "three proper [methods]": (1) past political mistakes should be dealt with in "broad strokes" but not in "detail"; (2) coverage should be distributed throughout different sections of the gazetteer; and (3) the account should be brief. "Politically negative movements" and "political mistakes" were to be dealt with by the local Party, not the compilers of local gazetteers.[30]

As is often the case in China, however, the interpretation and implementation of these general regulations were primarily a matter for local authorities. Early drafts of the county gazetteers were subjected to nervous scrutiny by local officials who demanded extensive cuts before publication. In one case, the document was already at the printers when orders came down from the province to stop the presses and implement further cuts.[31] The process of political vetting of local gazettes later became regularized and professionalized in an attempt to ensure evenhanded local censorship of drafts and also the uniformity of the product.[32]

The conservative spirit of the 1985 guidelines is reflected primarily in the final county gazetteers. Indeed, most accounts are brief and provide few details about the Cultural Revolution. Most of the gazetteers that do provide information about the events of this period distribute it throughout different parts of the publication, including the standard "chronicle of major events" (*dashiji*) and separate sections on Party-building, government, legal and criminal affairs, and political movements; in some cases, there is a separate section on the Cultural Revolution. But because there was remarkably broad latitude exercised by provincial authorities in deciding how exactly to define "broad strokes" and "brevity," there is

de yipian wenzhang – 'Jixu "wenhua da geming" yi xi buyi cu'" 值得深思的一篇文章 – "记叙'文化大革命'宜细不宜粗" [An essay worth pondering – "The 'Cultural Revolution' should be narrated in detail, not in broad strokes"], ibid., no. 5 (1982), pp. 40–41.

29 Thogersen and Clausen, "New Reflections in the Mirror," (p. 166).

30 Vermeer, "New County Histories," (p. 455). See also Zheng Zhengxi, Guangxi tongzhi guan 广西通志馆, "'Cu' ji 'wenge' yu fenshi 'taiping'" "粗"记"文革"与粉饰"太平" [Recording the "Cultural Revolution" in broad strokes, and "presenting a false picture of peace and prosperity"], *Sichuan difangzhi* 四川地方志 [Sichuan Local Gazetteers], no. 2 (1988), pp. 13–14.

31 Vermeer, "New County Histories," pp. 451–452.

32 Thogersen and Clausen, "New Reflections in the Mirror," pp. 169–170.

TABLE 2.1. *Examples of Counties That Under-Reported the Number of Deaths in the* Xianzhi

Provinces	County	Other Sources	*Xianzhi*
Guangxi	Binyang[1,2]	3,951 dead	40 dead
Guangxi	Mengshan[1]	850 dead	9 dead
Guangxi	Shanglin[1]	1,906 dead	171 dead
Guangxi	Wuxuan[1]	524 dead	526 dead
Guangxi	Zhongshan[1]	625 dead	63 dead
Hunan	Daoxian[3]	4,519 dead	7 dead
Jiangsu	Taicang[4]	7,500 dead	2,027 dead
Jiangxi	Dingnan[5]	7 dead	0 dead
		396 victims	144 victims
Shaanxi	Hua xian[6]	217 dead	0 dead
		1,929 victims	0 victims
Shaanxi	Tongguan[7]	16+ dead	0 dead
		3,343 victims	3,348 victims
Shanxi	Xiyang[8]	141 dead	0 dead
Yunnan	Xinping[9]	22,000 victims	9,368 victims

Sources: (1) Internal reports in county archives cited by Zheng Yi, *The Scarlet Memorial* (Boulder, CO: Westview, 1996), pp. 7–14, 24, 39, 51, 71. (2) *Guangxi wenge dashi nianbiao* (*Chronology of the Cultural Revolution in Guangxi*) (Nanning: Guangxi renmin chubanshe, 1990). (3) Zhang Cheng, "The Great Dao County Massacre" (see n. 36); (4) *Renmin ribao*, 15 March 1979; figures refer to only one case. (5) *Jiangxi ribao*, 18 December 1978; figure refers to only one case. (6) *Hua xianzhi: "wenhua da geming" zhi huaxian, Shaanxi*, mimeographed, no date, 50 pp.; figures are overall totals for the entire period. (7) *Shaanxi ribao*, 30 December 1978; figures refer to only one campaign. (8) *Renmin ribao*, 13 August 1980. (9) *Renmin ribao*, 23 July 1978.

wide variation in the amount of material about the Cultural Revolution contained in county gazetteers.[33]

All the same, any estimates of deaths based on the *xianzhi*, even relatively forthcoming data, must be considered incomplete minimums. As shown in Table 2.1, the number of deaths reported by the *xianzhi* is in some cases significantly smaller than reported in other sources. For example, the death toll in Daoxian County, Hunan, is notorious, with one estimate prior to the cover-up putting the number at 4,591. However, the Daoxain *xianzhi* only has this much to say about its "illegal killings": "Between August 13 and October 17 [1967], a group of people were illegally killed, which shocked the entire nation. On 22nd of the same month, the 6950 Brigade of PLA entered Daoxian... and ordered

33 Walder and Su, "The Cultural Revolution in the Countryside: Scope, Timing and Human Impact," *The China Quarterly* 173 (2003), pp. 74–99.

an end to the illegal killings."[34] The *xianzhi* of Binyang County, Guangxi, reported only forty deaths, most of which occurred in armed battles earlier in 1967. Regarding the 1967–1968 collective killings, the *xianzhi* shies away from reporting the death toll: "Between the end of July and the beginning of August [1968], [the county] implemented the July 3rd Notice from the Party Center, State Council, the Central Military Committee and the Cultural Revolution Leadership Group and waged attacks against 'class enemies,' causing deaths of innocent cadres and masses."[35] However, an independent source revealed the county as one of the more atrocious in Guangxi, with 3,951 deaths.[36]

Patterns of Killings across Counties and over Time

The *xianzhi* provide valuable information, which often may be checked against their sometimes less-circumspect counterparts and documents written before the clampdown on information about the Cultural Revolution. For the scale and timing of collective killings in Guangxi and Guangdong, I present more detailed analyses based on 122 volumes of *xianzhi*.[37] The numbers of deaths *as reported* in the county gazetteers should be considered minimum figures.[38] In some instances, as I show, descriptions of collective killings are unaccompanied by figures. Nonetheless, in addition to providing a baseline of estimated killings, these accounts also provide an outline of when they occurred and for

34 Hunan sheng Daoxian xianzhi bianzuan weiyuanhui 湖南省道县县志编纂委员会, *Daoxian zhi* 道县志 [Dao County Gazetteer] (Beijing: Zhongguo shehui chubanshe, 1994), p. 33.

35 Binyang xianzhi bianzuan weiyuanhui 宾阳县志编纂委员会 *Binyang xianzhi* 宾阳县志 [Binyang County Gazetteer] (Nanning: Guangxi renmin chubanshe, 1987), pp. 12, 162.

36 Internal reports cited by Zheng Yi, 1996. Zheng Yi 郑义, 1997. "Liangge wen'ge chuyi" 两个文革雏议 [On Two Cultural Revolutions]. *Huaxia wenzhai* [华夏文摘], no. 83 (Supplement Issue): 1–14. Available at www.cnd.org, accessed September 30, 2004.

37 For further discussion of the data collection, see Zhang Cheng 章成, 2001. "Daoxian da tusha" 道县大屠杀 [The Daoxian Massacre]. *Open Magazine* 开放杂志 (2001) July, August, September, and December issues, Hong Kong: Xianggang zhongwen daxue chubanshe. See also Yang Su, "Tumult from Within: State Bureaucrats and Chinese Mass Movements, 1966–1971" (Ph.D. dissertation, Stanford University, 2003); and Andrew G. Walder and Yang Su, "The Cultural Revolution in the Countryside: Scope, Timing and Human Impact," *The China Quarterly* 173 (2003), pp. 74–99.

38 A previous analysis of more than 1,400 counties showed that the numbers of victims (the persecuted, injured, and dead) correlate with the number of words devoted to the Cultural Revolution in a county's gazetteer. When compared with reports from other sources for twelve counties, the under-reporting of casualties was substantial. See Andrew G. Walder and Yang Su, "The Cultural Revolution in the Countryside: Scope, Timing and Human Impact," *The China Quarterly* 173 (2003), pp. 74–99, especially Table 2.8 on p. 94.

TABLE 2.2. *Frequencies of Reported Collective Killings in Three Provinces*

	Guangxi	Guangdong	Hubei
Total counties with data (percent)	65 (100)	57 (100)	65 (100)
Counties with collective killings (percent)	43 (66.2)	28 (49.1)	4 (6.2)
Counties with 500 or more deaths (percent)	27 (41.5)	10 (17.5)	0 (0.0)
Median deaths (among counties with mass killings)	526	278	46.5
Largest number of deaths in one county	2,463	2,600	115

what supposed reasons. These outlines often can be filled in with details from the more forthcoming reports and documents. I obtained relatively complete information about the three provinces that I analyzed closely: the *xianzhi* reports from sixty-five of the eighty-three counties of Guangxi, fifty-seven of eighty counties in Guangdong, and sixty-five of seventy-two counties in Hubei, ranging from 71.3 to 90.2 percent of the total.

If the undercounting were relatively consistent across counties, which we will assume for the moment, then the most severe collective killings took place in Guangxi Province. Of sixty-five counties for which I have gazetteers, forty-three (66 percent) reported collective killings (Table 2.2) and fifteen counties reported more than one thousand deaths. Wuming County had the highest death toll: 2,463, with 1,546 victims killed in one campaign from mid-June through early July of 1968.[39] Guangdong Province exhibited a similar pattern: Twenty-eight of fifty-seven counties (49 percent) experienced collective killings; in six counties, the number of deaths exceeded one thousand.[40] The most severe toll was in Yangchun County, with 2,600 deaths between August and October of 1968. Table 2.2 indicates clearly that collective killings were a widespread phenomenon in Guangxi and Guangdong Provinces.

The statistics also reveal the timing of the collective killings. Whereas the earliest known episode occurred in August 1966 in the Beijing suburban county of Daxing,[41] collective killings did not occur in this study's

[39] Wuming xianzhi bianzuan weiyuanhui 武鸣县志编纂委员会 *Wuming xianzhi* 武鸣县志 [Wuming County Gazetteer] (Nanning: Guangxi renmin chubanshe, 1998), p. 30.

[40] These counties include Yangchun 阳春, Wuhua 五华, Meixian 梅县, Lianjiang 连江, Guangning 广宁, and Lianxian 连县.

[41] Zhang Lianhe 张连和, "Wu jin Macun quan ting sha" 五进马村劝停杀 [Five Visits to Ma Village to Dissuade Killings], in Zhe Yongping 者永平 (ed.), *Nage niandia zhong*

three provinces until late 1967 or 1968, shortly before or after the establishment of a revolutionary committee or new local government. Figure 2.1 compares the dates of the founding of the county-level revolutionary committee with the dates of the collective killings in Guangxi, Guangdong, and Hubei. The data clearly show that the collective-killing peaks closely followed the founding of the revolutionary committee.

Both in Guangxi and Guangdong, collective killings peaked in July 1968, soon after most counties had established their revolutionary committees. In the same month, the Party Center issued two well-publicized directives to ban armed battles and to disband mass organizations.[42] In Guangxi, the provincial revolutionary committee was not yet established, and the opposition mass alliance – known as the April 22nd Faction (FTT) – led insurgencies in all major cities. Provincial authorities implemented the two directives to crack down on the opposing faction, forcing some members to flee to rural counties. At the same time, the newly established governments at the lower levels were called to "preemptively attack class enemies."[43]

Some local governments, particularly communes (i.e., townships), zealously responded to this call, whether or not there was significant organized resistance in the jurisdiction. In Guangdong, although the provincial government had been established only in February, organized defiance represented by the so-called Red Flag faction persisted. The Guangdong provincial government used the two directives from the Center as a weapon in its faceoff with the Red Flag faction. As in Guangxi, policy pronouncements from Beijing and the provincial capital that targeted organized resistance translated into a climate of terror in lower-level jurisdictions (i.e., counties, communes, and brigades), whether or not organized resistance was widespread. Collective killings took place in that climate.

de women 那个年代中的我们 [We as in That Era] (Huhehot, Inner Mongolia: Yuanfang chubanshe, 1998), pp. 398–404; Yu Luowen 遇罗文, "Beijing Daxingxian canan diaocha" 北京大兴县惨案调查 [An Investigation of the Beijing Daxin Massacre], in Song Yongyi 宋永毅 (ed.), *Wen'ge da tusha* 文革大屠杀 [Massacres in the Cultural Revolution] (Hong Kong: Kaifang zazhishe, 2002), pp. 13–36.

42 The Party Center issued directives on July 3 and July 24, 1968, calling for mass organizations to be disbanded and for punishment of those who persisted in armed conflict. See CRRM, *Zhongguo renmin jiefanjun guofang daxue dangshi dangjian zhenggong jiaoyanshi* 国防大学党史党建政工教研室, *Wenhua da geming yanjiu ziliao* 文化大革命研究资料 (中) [The Cultural Revolution Research Materials, CRRM], vol. 2 (Beijing: Zhongguo renmin jiefanjun guofang daxue dangshi chubanshe, 1988), pp. 138–139, 152–153.

43 GXWGDSNB.

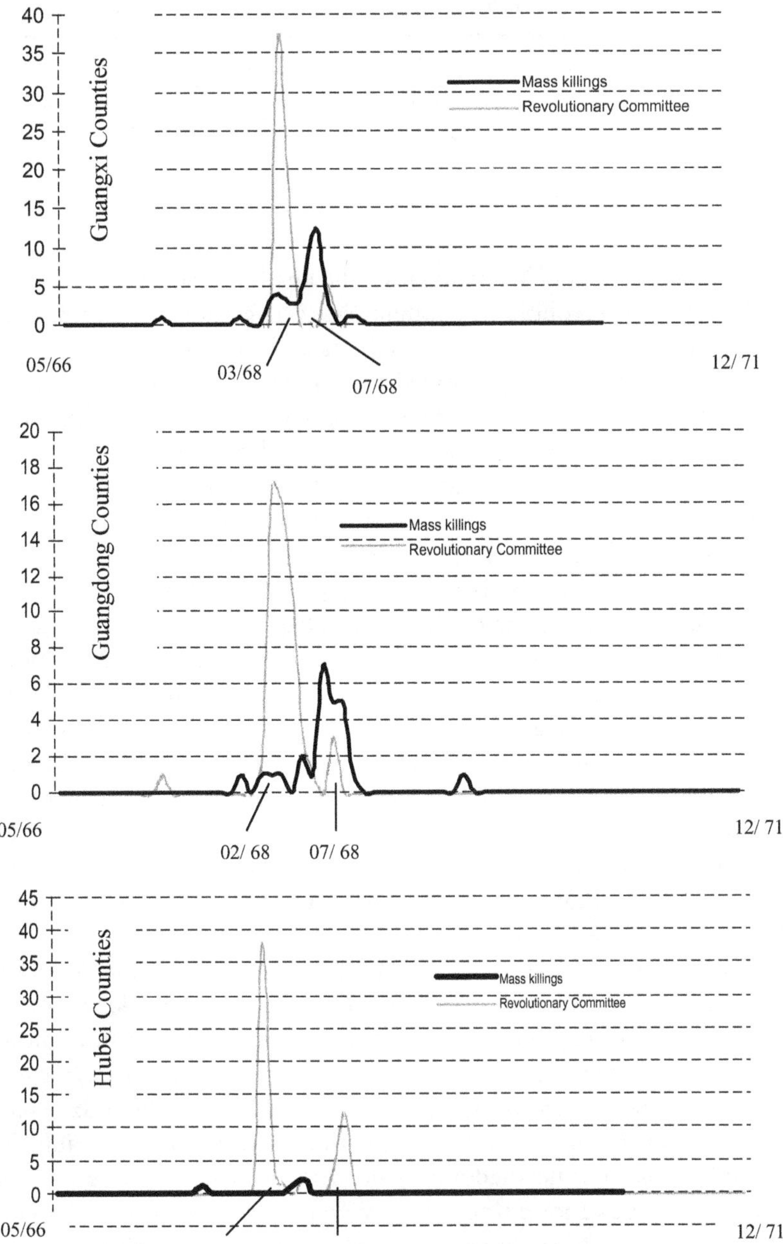

FIGURE 2.1. Comparing timing of mass killings and founding of revolutionary committees.

TABLE 2.3. *Victimization in Three Periods of the Cultural Revolution*

Time Period	Deaths	Injuries	Persecuted
Period 1	5,000	20,000	2.0 million
Period 2	85,000	66,000	540,000
Period 3	257,000	260,000	23.3 million
Overall (1966–1971)	492,000	507,000	27.2 million

The pattern also holds nationally: The death toll peaked in late 1967 and 1968 when revolutionary committees were established; death counts from earlier persecutions and armed battles were comparatively small. In an earlier study, we computed victim statistics – including deaths, injuries, and persecutions – from 1,530 volumes of *xianzhi* from the entire country. We divided the Cultural Revolution of 1966–1971 into three periods: (1) the early campaigns between May 1966 and January 1967; (2) the armed-battle period between the power seizures in January 1967 and the founding of revolutionary committees in late 1967 and early 1968; and (3) the post–revolutionary committee period lasting until 1971. As shown in the first column of Table 2.3, the number of deaths from the first two periods is 90,000; this compares with 257,000 for the third period, which had three times as many deaths. If we consider the fact that many collective killings took place in the months immediately prior to the establishment of revolutionary committees, then the ratio between collective-killing deaths and deaths from earlier campaigns and armed battles must be much larger. As noted previously, the ratio between "other" deaths and deaths resulting from armed battles is 80,000 to 3,000 in Guangxi (i.e., more than 26 times as many) and 1,728,000 to 237,000 in the country (i.e., more than 7 times as many).

Comparing the *xianzhi* with the two *shengzhi* also provides a sense of the baselines that the *xianzhi* provide. From the 65 available volumes in Guangxi, the average number of deaths per county during the Cultural Revolution was 581. Extrapolating this average for 83 counties, the total number of deaths in the province is 49,223. This total is about 62 percent as large as the *shengzhi* estimate, eighty thousand, which is probably also an undercount. For Guangdong counties, the available 57 volumes yield average deaths as 290; extrapolating again for 80 counties yields a total of 23,200, or approximately 55 percent of the *shengzhi* estimate of 42,237 reported previously.

Three points can be made when comparing *xianzhi*-based estimates and the two *shengzhi* totals. First, although deaths reported in the *xianzhi* do not include those in urban centers, the omissions likely do not account for the discrepancy; the majority of Cultural Revolution deaths in Guangxi and Guangdong were rural phenomena, taking place in the lower jurisdictions of townships and villages. Second, the discrepancy may reflect the failure of some county *xianzhi* compilers to report a specific number of deaths rather than merely noting "random killings." Third, although the *shengzhi* estimates likely are undercounts, the fact that they are on the same order as the *xianzhi*-based estimates indicates that the latter have some level of credibility.

Guangdong and Guangxi: The Most Atrocious Provinces

If extensive collective killing is undisputable in Guangdong and Guangxi, was it also common in the other twenty-eight provincial jurisdictions in China? Scattered reports document similar atrocities in Beijing, Yunnan, Inner Mongolia, Qinghai, and Hunan.[44] The best-known case – and perhaps the most tragic – was in Daoxian County in Hunan Province. An article published in a Hong Kong magazine reported that a series of pogroms spread across the county in late 1967; within two months, 4,950 people were killed.[45] However, as reported in 1,530 *xianzhi* volumes, Guangdong and Guangxi appear to be the atrocious outliers, as indicated by analyses of a third province, Hubei, and the nation as a whole.

Using the same criteria as above and from the available *xianzhi*, I identified only four counties in Hubei Province that experienced collective killings (see Table 2.2). These four cases, however, involved large numbers of deaths due to beatings during political witch-hunts. No pogroms or summary executions were reported. If statistics from the county gazetteers reflect the actual historical picture, then Hubei Province stands out as a negative case.[46]

Collective killings were widespread in Guangxi and Guangdong, but counties in Hubei Province were otherwise affected. On the contrary, there was significant persecution of previously and newly designated class enemies. Thirty-eight counties, or 60 percent of the Hubei sample, reported that more than one thousand people were beaten in the persecutions, many of whom suffered permanent injuries. Unlike Guangxi and

44 Song Yongyi 宋永毅 (ed.), *Wen'ge da tusha* 文革大屠杀 [Massacres during the Cultural Revolution] (Hong Kong: Kaifang zazhi she, 2002).

45 Zhang Cheng 章成, "Daoxian da tusha" 道县大屠杀 [The Daoxian Massacre] in four parts. *Open Magazine* 开放杂志 (2001): July, August, September, and December issues.

46 Among the three provinces, Hubei has the shortest average length of accounts of the Cultural Revolution.

Guangdong, however, large-scale beatings in most cases stopped short of collective killings, as described in the following example:

> September 6, [1967]. The county seat witnessed the September 6 "Violent Event." A group of "Rebels" paraded 22 "capitalist roaders" and "stubborn conservatives" during the daytime, and injured 32 individuals (8 permanently) during the night. The practices quickly spread to communes and villages, where 1,015 were severely beaten. Among them 44 suffered permanent disabilities, 1 was killed, and 9 others died of causes related to the beatings.[47]

Most counties that experienced similar large-scale beatings reported fewer than ten total deaths.

The difference in the scale of collective killings between Hubei and the other two provinces in this study is very large. A key question is whether this is due to differences in actual killing or differences in editorial policies in compiling the *xianzhi*. As we have seen, the compilation and publication of county gazetteers were organized by a hierarchy of government agencies, and counties in the same province may have interpreted the policy guidelines differently.[48] It is possible that the compilers in Hubei Province were more conservative and omitted more information than their counterparts in the other two provinces.

The evidence of the reports is, as always, uncertain, but it suggests strongly that there is some reality behind the differences in reporting. On the one hand, the average length of accounts of the Cultural Revolution in the Hubei gazetteers – 2,361 words – is barely half the number of words devoted to the subject in the gazetteers for Guangdong and Guangxi (i.e., 5,198 and 5,117, respectively). As indicated in a previous study, death and injury counts are positively associated with the length devoted to the Cultural Revolution in the *xianzhi*.[49] On the other hand, the Hubei

47 Xianfeng xianzhi bianzuan weiyuanhui 咸丰县志编纂委员会, *Xianfeng xianzhi* 咸丰县志 [Xianfeng County Gazetteer] (Wuchang: Wuhan daxue chubanshe, 1990), pp. 24–25. Among the sixty-five counties of Hubei Province, I decided that four had experienced collective killings due to the number of deaths from the epidemic beatings at the time: Yichang 宜昌 (10 killed, 105 driven to suicide, 60 permanently injured); Enshi 恩施 (2,350 beaten, 51 killed, 314 permanently injured); Zigui 秭归 (2,500 beaten, 40 killed, 440 severely injured, 35 permanently); and Yunxi 郧西 (32 killed in Hejiaqu Commune, the other 512 beaten and 276 "killed or disabled" in the county).

48 Thogersen and Clausen, "New Reflections in the Mirror: Local Chinese Gazatteers (*Difangzhi*) in the 1980s," *Australian Journal of Chinese Affairs* 27 (1992), pp. 161–184; Eduard B. Vermeer, "New County Histories: A Research Note on Their Compilation and Value," *Modern China* 18 (October 1992), 438–467.

49 See Walder and Su, "The Cultural Revolution in the Countryside," especially Table 1 on p. 81.

TABLE 2.4. *Cultural Revolution Violence in Three Provinces Compared to National Figures*

	Deaths per County	Injuries per County	Persecution Targets per County
Guangxi	574.0	266.4	12,616.0
Guangdong	311.6	28.1	6,788.6
Hubei	10.8	44.5	2,317.5
All provinces of China	80.0	68.0	5,397.0

gazetteers do not hesitate to report significant numbers of people who were beaten and injured. In fact, they report many more injuries than the gazetteers of Guangdong (see Table 2.5). Therefore, there is reason to suspect that the differences in the reported numbers of deaths may indicate actual differences in the course of political events across provinces.

What do these findings tell us about the scale of collective killings in China's other provinces? Based on the collection of 1,530 county gazetteers, I calculate that the average number of deaths per county to be eighty. The Guangxi and Guangdong averages are significantly higher than the national average (574 and 311, respectively), whereas Hubei Province (10.8) is significantly lower. The numbers of those injured and targeted for persecution show a similar pattern (Table 2.4), and the county averages for all provincial jurisdictions indicate that Guangxi and Guangdong stand out (Table 2.5): They rank first and second, whereas Hubei Province ranks twenty-third of the thirty provinces. The dubious distinction of Guangxi and Guangdong is clear when listing the counties that report most killings in the *xianzhi*. Of the twenty-four counties that reported one thousand or more deaths, Guangxi had fifteen counties, followed by Guangdong with six. Only three counties outside these provinces reported one thousand or more killings (Table 2.6).

More Damning Official Evidence Leaks Out

In addition to the *xianzhi* and other publicly available materials, never-published internal documents further attest to high numbers of collective killings. These documents also are based on the 1983–1984 wave of local investigations, but they are more candid than the *xianzhi*. I obtained two reports from their author, a work-team leader during the investigations in Cangwu County, Guangxi. He kept a copy of the

TABLE 2.5. *Reported Deaths per County and Average Length of Accounts in the County Gazetteers by Province*

Province	Reported Deaths per County	Average Length (words)
Guangxi	581	5,117
Shanghai	334	7,204
Guangdong	290	5,198
Liaoning	145	3,243
Inner Mongolia	144	3,263
Beijing	101	6,440
Jilin	94	3,680
Shaanxi	90	10,689
Yunnan	81	4,111
Hunan	80	4,266
Hubei	64	5,229
Gansu	58	4,022
Sichuan	44	4,282
Jiangxi	48	2,557
Shanxi	40	2,744
Xinjiang	38	3,881
Fujian	24	3,499
Heilongjiang	24	3,531
Jiangsu	28	3,715
Shandong	18	2,653
Zhe jiang	17	2,089
Guizhou	14	4,423
Hubei	11	2,361
Ningxja	11	3,225
Anhui	11	2,521
Henan	4	4,652
Qinghai	4	2,187
Tianjin	2	3,872
Average	84	4,092

reports – neatly transcribed in longhand – before he submitted them for censorship and rewriting by the county gazetteers.[50] Dated in 1987 and signed by "Cangwu County Party Rectification Office," one report records three "attacking class enemies" meetings organized by the

[50] To pass or obtain this type of government documents carried some level of risk, as a high-profile case in 1998 attests. Song Yongyi 宋永毅, a U.S. librarian, was detained and jailed for four months in 1998. Also, a friend of mine, an anthropology Ph.D. candidate from Chicago, was detained in 2006, months before my trip to China, for taking pictures of Cultural Revolution materials in a public library in Changsha, Hunan.

TABLE 2.6. *Counties Reporting 1,000 or More Deaths by Province, Deaths, and Length of Account*

Province	County	Deaths	Length (words)
Guangdong	Yangchun xian	2,600	6,480
Guanggxi	Wuming xian	2,463	6,114
Guangxi	Gui xian*	2,219	6,280
Guangxi	Quanzhou xinn	2,216	7,560
Guangdong	Wuhua xian	2,136	2,540
Guangxi	Linggui xian	2,051	5,240
Guangdong	Lianjiang xian	1,851	4,320
Guangxi	Du' an yaozu zizhixian	1,714	9,320
Guangxi	Tiandeng xian	1,651	960
Guangxi	Luchuan xian	1,557	4,760
Guangxi	Luocheng mulaozu zizhixian	1,425	3,680
Guangxi	Rong'an xian	1,416	5,520
Guangdong	Mei xian	1,403	5,440
Guangxi	Mashan xian	1,329	9,080
Guangxi	Lingchuan xian	1,321	5,588
Guangxi	Yishan xian	1,250	9,840
Guangdong	Guangning xian	1,218	3,560
Guangxi	Liujiang xian	1,183	4,600
Hunan	Ningyuan xian	1,093	2,916
Inner Mongolia	Keerqin youyi qian qi	1,070	8,640
Guangxi	Chongzuo xian	1,029	6,000
Guangdong	Lian xian	1,019	9,440
Guangxi	Luzhai xian	1,002	3,920
Shandong	Haiyang xian	1,000	2,394

Note: *Renamed Guigang shi in 1988.

revolutionary committee in the early summer of 1968. It also reports actions taken by local townships and villages following those meetings, providing detailed statistics of deaths, injuries, and persecutions that – not surprisingly – are unavailable in the Cangwu County *xianzhi*. The other report, from the same Party office, is an anatomy of a case in which a "landlord" family of seven was killed. It lists the specific timeline of events, justification for the killings, actors involved, and process of killing.

The Cangwu *xianzhi* tersely notes that "580 mass members, 59 cadres, and 23 workers were killed" in the Cultural Revolution[51]; however, the

[51] Cangwu xianzhi bianzuan weiyuanhui 苍梧县志编纂委员会 *Cangwu xianzhi* 苍梧县志 [Cangwu County Gazetteer] (Nanning: Guangxi remin chubanshe, 1997), p. 483.

two internal reports describe what happened. According to one, between May 24 and June 30, 1968, the Cangwu revolutionary committee held three meetings with local cadres. Led by top county leaders, each meeting escalated in jingoistic rhetoric. Township and village cadres competed to share their findings of "conspiracy groups" and their achievements in cracking down on them. The menacing class enemies became a self-fulfilling prophecy through the ever-growing number of persecutions and killings. In total, six conspiracy groups with a membership of 183 were uncovered, 752 individuals were persecuted, and 1,085 people were reeducated from "blindness to deception." After the first meeting alone, 188 were killed in local communes or villages.[52]

According to another report, Zhong Zhaoyang, a landlord's son, tried to resist. Expecting to be killed as his family's "representative," Zhong snatched a gun from his captors and escaped. The militia detained his mother and five brothers as hostages. When Zhong later killed a cadre who happened upon his hideout, he was immediately killed and his three adult brothers were executed. His widowed mother and two underage brothers were then delivered to a lynch mob from the cadre's family, who tortured them to death on a stage during a rally.[53]

As mentioned previously, the post–Cultural Revolution investigations in Cangwu County were conducted by more than one thousand cadres as work-team members. Hundreds of similar reports were no doubt produced from their investigative work. A few retired cadres told me that their reports must be housed in the County Archive. Unfortunately, I failed to get access to these reports, or even the catalog., in my visit to the archival bureau. I was told that both prefecture (i.e., a level of government between province and county) and provincial agencies had collected summary reports from local counties and published internal reports with details at that level. "Chronology of the Cultural Revolution in Guangxi" (*Guangxi Wenge Dashi Nianbiao* [GWGDSNB]) is one such document. It was published by the top official publishing house (i.e., Guangxi People's Publishing House) in 1990 but was quickly suppressed and soon disappeared from bookstores and libraries. I obtained a copy credited to a research service center based in Los Angeles.[54]

52 Zaocheng yanzhong houguo de sange huiyi 造成严重后果的"三个会议 "Three Meetings That Caused Severe Consequences," Cangwu Party Ratification Office, August 1987.

53 Zhulian yijia qikou de mingan 株连一家七口的命案 "The Causes for the Case that Killed Seven Family Members," Cangwu Party Ratification Office, July 31, 1987.

54 *Guangxi wen'ge dashi nianbiao (GXWGDSNB)* 广西文革大事年表 [Chronology of the Cultural Revolution in Guangxi] (Nanning: Guangxi renmin chubanshe, 1990). Reprinted by Chinese Publications Services Center, Los Angeles, CA, 1995.

Three other internal documents came from "Xiao Pingtou," the pen name of a self-proclaimed democracy-movement activist, who has published a series of online reports since 2006. He smuggled the documents to Denmark after outwitting undercover agents sent abroad by Beijing. The three documents include one at the provincial level entitled "Major Events of the Cultural Revolution in Guangxi, 1968" (GWGDSNB, 1968), compiled by the Guangxi Party Rectification Office and printed in 1987. The other two documents are its counterparts compiled by the Party Center offices at the prefecture level: "Major Events of the Cultural Revolution in Nanning Prefecture 1966–1976" (*Nanning diqu wenhua dageming dashiji* 1966–1976) and "Major Events of the Cultural Revolution in Qingzhou Prefecture" (*Qingzhou diqu wenge dashiji*). Xiao Pingtou's reports are painstakingly footnoted with specific page numbers from the original documents.[55] His citations appear to be credible because similar statistics and events appear in reports by at least two other authors.[56] Where they overlap, Xiao Pingtou's reports are consistent with my copy of the "Chronology of the Cultural Revolution in Guangxi."

The reason for secrecy is instantly apparent when one reads about the extreme scale of the atrocities reported in the government documents. The most dramatic revelation is that they confirm the rumor of cannibalism, first reported by Zheng Yi in his controversial book, *The Scarlet Monuments*.[57] At least seventy-three incidents with specific details are

[55] See Xiao Pingtou's five reports on the secret files of the Cultural Revolution. His background and maneuvers with undercover Chinese agents are reported in a series of articles. See Guangxi "fangong jiuguotuan" yuanan shimo – wen'ge jimi dangan jiemi zhi yi 广西"反共救国团"冤案始末 – 文革机密档案揭密之一, available at https://67.15.34.207/news/gb/kanshihai/shishi/2006/1101/172175.html, accessed August 24, 2008; Guangxi Rongan da tusha – wen'ge jimi dangan jiemi zhi er 广西融安大屠杀 – 文革机密档案揭密之二, available at http://www.xianqiao.net:8080/gb/7/1/6/n1581000.htm, accessed August 24, 2008; Guangxi "shangshi nong zong" yuanan shimo – wen'ge jimi dangan jiemi zhi san 广西"上石农总"冤案始末 – 文革机密档案揭密之三, http://news.epochtimes.com/gb/7/3/8/n1639613.htm, accessed August 24, 2008; Guangxi junqu weijiao Fengshan "zaofan dajun" zhenxiang – wen'ge jimi dangan jiemi zhi si 广西军区围剿凤山"造反大军"真相 – 文革机密档案揭密之四, available at http://boxun.com/hero/2007/xiaopingtouyehua/63_1.shtml and http://boxun.com/hero/2007/xiaopingtouyehua/63_2.shtml; Guangxi wen'ge ren chi ren shijian jiemi – wen'ge jimi dangan jiemi zhi wu 广西文革人吃人事件揭密 – 文革秘档揭密之五, available at http://www.64tianwang.com/Article_Show.asp?ArticleID=2319, accessed August 24, 2008.

[56] Xiao Ming 晓明, *Guangxi wen'ge liezhuan* 广西文革列传 [Chronology of Guangxi Cultural Revolution], available at http://www.fireofliberty.org/oldsite/level4/issue3/4-wengeliezhuan-cover.htm, accessed August 24, 2008; and Wu Ruoyu 吴若愚, *Zhonggong jimi wenjian jilu de wen'ge Guangxi da tusha* 中共机密文件记录的文革广西大屠杀, available at http://www.boxun.com/hero/wenge/88_1.shtml, accessed August 24, 2008.

[57] Zheng Yi 郑义, *Hongse jinianbei* 红色纪念碑 [The Scarlet Memorial] (Taipei, Taiwan: Huashi wenhua gongsi, 1993).

described in two of the three classified documents.[58] That the perpetrators would eat the flesh of their victims speaks volumes about the depth of the dehumanization of the so-called class enemies. More important for my purposes, however, these reports detail incidents that further establish the case of collective killings, which are omitted by other publicly available materials.

Working from the self-censored *xianzhi* data, I listed above the fifteen Guangxi counties with a death toll exceeding one thousand. Those counties were the most extreme cases, but the internal documents indicate that some of these counties appear to have grossly under-reported the number of deaths. According to the reports, at least eight other counties belong to this category.[59] Deaths also are tallied at the prefecture level: Yulin Prefecture had 10,156 deaths; Qingzhou Prefecture had 10,359; and Nanning Prefecture (between July and September 1968) had 9,933. According to the provincial report, in the two months of July and August 1968 alone, collective killings in Guangxi Province numbered as many as eighty-four thousand,[60] which is greater than the *shengzhi* estimate for the entire Cultural Revolution era (as reported at the beginning of this chapter[61]).

The reports are also candid about how the massive numbers of deaths were inflicted. The first wave of terror started in early 1968. From February 25 to February 28, 1968, Daxin County held a meeting with public security heads (i.e., People's Armed Forces Office [PAF]) and militia commanders from local communes and enterprises. County leader Zhou Yongshan declared that a so-called "mass dictatorship campaign" against the Four Types was needed to celebrate the establishment of the county's revolutionary committee. During the 17 days between the meeting and

[58] Zhonggong Guangxi zhengdang bangongshi 中共广西整党办公室 [Guangxi Party Rectification Office], *Guangxi wenge dashiji, 1968* [Major Events of the Cultural Revolution in Guangxi, 1968] (Guangxi Party Rectification Office unpublished documents, 1987), cited by Xiao Pingtou 小平头. See Note 55. See also Zhonggong Qinzhou diwei zhengdang bangongshi 中共钦州地委整党办公室, *Qinzhou diqu wen'ge dashiji* 钦州地区文革大事记 [Major Events of the Cultural Revolution in Qingzhou Prefecture] (Zhonggong Qinzhou Prefecture Party Rectification Office unpublished documents, 1987), cited by Xiao Pingtou 小平头. See note 55.

[59] They are Binyang 宾阳 (3,951 deaths), Lingshan 灵山 (3,222), Shanglin 上林 (1,906), Fengshan 凤山 (1,300), Yishan 宜山, Bama 巴马, Du'an 都安, Shangsi 上思 (1,701). Ibid.

[60] Zhonggong Guangxi zhengdang bangongshi 中共广西整党办公室 [Guangxi Party Rectification Office], *Guangxi wenge dashiji, 1968* [Major Events of the Cultural Revolution in Guangxi, 1968] (Guangxi Party Rectification Office unpublished documents, 1987), p. 142.

[61] See Note 1.

the founding of the revolutionary committee, 239 people were killed.[62] On March 16, the same day that Tiandeng County's revolutionary committee was founded, the PAF chief called for "the just to prevail over the evil. In order to ensure the newly born red power, every commune must clear up those criminal and much-hated Four Types or 'bad instigators.'" This declaration was followed by 190 collective-killing incidents across the county, resulting in 630 murders. In Xiangyuan Commune, the dead included nine entire families and all male members of sixteen families.[63] Between March 27 and May 22, 1968, Qing Ximing – a local cadre in Songying Village in Guixian County – and his militiamen killed forty innocent "mass members" with clubs and hoes. The victims included a ten-month-old baby, eleven children, and an elderly blind woman. All males from thirteen families were killed.[64]

On April 13, 1968, an FTT group carried the corpse of a child who had been killed by the United Headquarters (UHQs) to protest the celebration rally for the new Guixian revolutionary committee. The protest failed; the government and the UHQs established "Poor and Lower Middle Peasants' Supreme Tribunal" and held killing demonstration rallies throughout the local communes, murdering 128.[65] On April 15, the village head of Hantian in Beitong Commune, Bubei County, drew up a list of victims and promised militiamen 50 cents for one day's worth of killing work, with bonuses for increased numbers. The mission was accomplished with the murder of twenty-two members of five Four-Type families. To pay these bloody commissions, the village taxed Zhang Yushi, Bu Guanying, He Qianlan, Lu Xiuzhen, and twenty other widows and daughters from the victims' families. "All was squandered on meals."[66] Between April 5 and May 6, 1968, in the village of Shizhunxue Brigade of Beitong Commune, a series of slaughters claimed ninety-two men, women, and children from fifty-six Four-Type families; fifteen of the families were entirely decimated.[67]

Such killings lingered into the early summer of 1968 and then gained new momentum after the Party Center's July 3rd Bulletin, which called

62 Wu Ruoyu 吴若愚, *Zhonggong jimi wenjian jilu de wen'ge Guangxi da tusha* 中共机密文件记录的文革广西大屠杀, available at http://www.boxun.com/hero/wenge/88_1.shtml, section 4; accessed August 24, 2008.

63 Ibid.

64 Ibid., 5.

65 Ibid., (2) 1

66 Ibid.

67 Ibid.

for treating the mass conflict between factions in class-struggle terms. The provincial government and local jurisdictions rushed to provide evidence that they were implementing the Bulletin. In Huining County, fifty-four people were killed before July; the leaders were criticized for being too "conservative." The county subsequently held a three-day meeting beginning on July 16, followed by assaults on "enemies" waged simultaneously in the nine districts of the county, resulting in the deaths of 947 people in three months.[68] In the three months after July 3, the death toll in Nanning Prefecture was 9,933, or 56 percent of the total for the year.[69] In Guilin Prefecture, 1,859 people were killed before July 1968, but the number reached 10,946 by the end of the year.[70]

Characteristics of the Collective Killings

In addition to the scale and timing of collective killings, written materials also provide information on three other characteristics: location and identities of both victims and perpetrators.

Location

Collective killings tended to occur in jurisdictions below the county level, usually in a commune (i.e., township) or brigade (i.e., village). Recalling the previous quotations, specific names of communes or villages are mentioned relative to collective killings. For example, Sanjiang *Brigade* is specified in the well-known Quanzhou (Guangxi) pogrom in which seventy-six Four-Type family members were pushed into a canyon. In the Lingui County case (i.e., Guangxi), the report specified that only 2 of 161 brigades did not experience collective killings. Among the twenty-eight Guangdong counties in which collective killings were reported, six gazetteers contain detailed information regarding names of the related jurisdictions. For example, the *Qujiang xianzhi* states: "In January [1968] serious incidents of illegal killings occurred in Zhangzhi *Commune*. Thirteen *brigades* of the commune indiscriminately arrested and killed; 149 were killed."[71] Other examples include the following: "Large number of

68 Ibid.

69 Ibid.

70 Ibid.

71 曲江县地方志编纂委员会 Qujiang xian difangzhi bianzuan weiyuanhui, *Qujiang xianzhi* 曲江县志 [Qujiang County Gazetteer] (Beijing: Zhonghua shuju, 1999), p. 36; emphases in italic are mine.

TABLE 2.7. *County Characteristics and Mass Killings in Guangxi and Guangdong Provinces*

	Counties *with* Mass Killings	Counties *without* Mass Killings
Average distance from provincial capital (kilometers)	212	179
Population per square kilometer	139.7	219.1
Government per capita revenue (*yuan*)	15.1	20. 8

beatings and killings occurred in the three *communes* Chitong, Zhenglong, and Beijie, resulting in 29 people being killed"[72]; "Mass dictatorship was carried out by the security office of *various communes*..."[73]; "Litong *Brigade,* Xinan *Commune* buried alive 56 'Four Types' and their family members."[74] The contrast between the lack of collective killings in urban settings and their abundance in rural villages may reflect a disconnect between lower-level jurisdictions and upper-level authorities, indicating the weakness of state control at the lower level.

The observation that collective killings were more likely to occur where state control was weakest is supported by another consideration regarding geography: the variation in incidence across counties. In Table 2.7, I compare counties with and without collective killings.[75] The average distance of counties with collective killings from the provincial capital is 212 km, whereas for counties without collective killings, it is 179 km. Counties with collective killings also were more sparsely populated and had lower per capita government revenue.

Victim Identities

It is obvious that the county gazetteers provide few details about identities of the victims, but information regarding locations of the killings helps to identify their composition. As noted previously, collective killings

72 Xinyi xian difangzhi bianzuan weiyuanhui 信宜县地方志编纂委员 *Xinyi xianzhi* 信宜县志 [Xinyi County Gazetteer] (Guangzhou: Guangdong renmin chubanshe, 1993), p. 52.

73 Zhang Xiuqing 张秀清, *Chenghai xianzhi* 澄海县志 [Chenghai County Gazetteer] (Guangzhou: Guangdong renmin chubanshe, 1992), p. 57.

74 Huazhou xian difangzhi bianzuan weiyuanhui 化州县地方志编纂委员会, *Huazhou xianzhi* 化州县志 [Huazhou County Gazetteer] (Guangzhou: Guangdong renmin chubanshe, 1996), p. 65.

75 The table does not include Hubei counties because there were few mass killings in that province.

TABLE 2.8. *Profiles of Victims of Collective Killings, Selected Jurisdictions*

Jurisdiction	Identity of Victims	Number	Percent
Lingui County	Four-Types and their children	918	46.1
	Peasants	547	27.5
	Cadres	326	16.4
	Urban residents	68	3.4
	Workers	79	4.0
	Students	53	2.7
	TOTAL	1,991	100
Binyang County	Rural residents	3,441	88.7
	Cadres	51	1.4
	Teachers	87	2.5
	Workers	102	3.0
	TOTAL	3,681	100
Lingling Special District	Four-Types	3,576	39.3
	Children of Four-Types	4,057	44.6
	Poor and middle peasants	1,049	11.5
	Other backgrounds	411	4.5
	TOTAL	9,093	100

Sources: Lingui xianzhi, 492; *Guangxi wenge dashi nianbiao*, 111; and Zhang Cheng, "*Daoxian da tusha.*"

tended to occur in jurisdictions below the county level, usually in the commune or brigade, with specific names of townships or villages listed. For example, Sanjiang *Brigade* is specified in the well-known Quanzhou (Guangxi) pogrom in which seventy-six members of Four-Type families were pushed into a canyon. In Lingui County (Guangxi), the report specified that only 2 of 161 brigades did not have collective killings. Among the twenty-eight Guangdong counties in which collective killings were reported, six gazetteers contain detailed information regarding names of the related jurisdictions. Where information on victim identities is available, the most frequently mentioned category of the population is the Four Types – that is, those people previously classified as class enemies. A detailed breakdown of victims is available in some counties, such as is cited previously for Lingui County, Guangxi, – as shown in Table 2.8, among the 1,991 victims, almost half (i.e., 918) were Four Types or their children. The table shows clearly that collective killings targeted the weak rather than those who constituted a real threat to the authorities (alleged conspiracy notwithstanding). Also, the majority of the victims were rural residents; that is, collective killings occurred primarily outside the county seat. In addition, in some places, a significant number of non–Four Types and nonrural individuals were killed, which may reflect political witch-hunts or the summary execution of captives. When collective killings were used to eliminate rival faction members, a significant proportion of the victims were other than those of the Four Types. For example, in the Fengshan County case described previously, among the 1,331 victims killed in the wake of a siege, 246 were cadres or workers (i.e., urban residents).[76]

A remarkable fact about the victims was the large number of children in Four-Type households. Some report that the perpetrators' rationale for killing them was preventative, to keep them from seeking revenge as adults.[77] In many cases, however, this seemed to be an afterthought. In Daoxian, after killing the Four-Type adults, the perpetrators returned, dragged the children from their homes and killed them, and then looted the victims' houses.[78] In other cases, however, the children were deemed guilty by association and killed along with their parents.[79]

The Perpetrators

Collective killings were not typically committed by misguided and spontaneous crowds in the manner of a lynching. Available information indicates that the perpetrators invariably were organized by local authorities, usually militia members, members of mass organizations or new volunteers. Without exception, detailed accounts (i.e., for Daxin, Quanzhou, Daoxian, and Fengshan) reported painstaking organizational meetings before the killings. In Zhang Cheng's account about Daoxian, meeting participants voted to decide who would be killed; one by one, potential victims' names were read and votes were tallied. The process lasted for hours.[80] In another district in the county, Zhang reports:

> From district to communes, mobilization took place through every level, involving the district party secretary, deputy secretary, commander of the "Hongliang" [a mass factional organization], public security head and district chief accountants.[81]

76 GXWGDANB.

77 See, e.g., Zhang Cheng 章成, "Daoxian da tusha" 道县大屠杀 [The Daoxian Massacre], *Open Magazine* 开放杂志 (July 2001), p. 71; ibid. (August 2001), p. 77; ibid. (September 2001), p. 61. See also Zheng Yi 郑义, *Hongse jinianbei* 红色纪念碑 [The Scarlet Memorial] (Taipei, Taiwan: Huashi wenhua gongsi, 1993), p. 48.

78 Zhang Cheng 章成, "Daoxian da tusha" 道县大屠杀 (July 2001), p. 71.

79 GXEGDSNB.

80 Zhang Cheng 章成, "Daoxian da tusha" 道县大屠杀 (August 2001), p. 82.

81 Zhang Cheng 章成, "Daoxian da tusha" 道县大屠杀 (July 2001), p. 75.

The victims usually were rounded up and killed in a location away from public view. There also were cases in which a mass rally was held and a large number of people were killed in public, the so-called execution meetings.[82] Indeed, interviews with perpetrators many years later indicate that most of them carried out the killing as a political duty.[83] There is also evidence that such acts were politically rewarded. In late 1968 and early 1969, provinces and counties began a campaign to "rectify" and rebuild the party organization and many activists were recruited. Official statistics reveal a chilling connection between violent zeal and political reward. According to a document published by the provincial government in Guangxi, during the Cultural Revolution, more than nine thousand people who had killed were recruited as new party members; another twenty thousand who had joined the party earlier in the Cultural Revolution through "fast-track" recruitment later committed murders. Another seventeen thousand party members were responsible for killings in one way or another.[84]

Conclusion

Although available records do not allow a full-scale estimate of the collective killings during the Cultural Revolution, their occurrence is beyond any doubt, as indicated by publicly available *xianzhi* and internal documents. Using circumspect official documents that doubtless underestimated the bloodshed, I found that at least 1.5 million were likely victims of collective killings. Using a conservative standard, I found that more than half of the counties in Guangdong and Guangxi – two of the bloodiest provinces – experienced this type of extreme violence. The internal documents suggest that the reality was worse than what the *xianzhi* data portray; these written records are based on massive government-initiated investigations after the Cultural Revolution and are beyond reproach. In the following chapters, I provide further evidence regarding the collective killings by presenting personal stories from survivors and witnesses. The fact that Guangdong and Guangxi appear to be the most severe cases speaks to the importance of examining subnational variations of

82 Ibid., p. 73.

83 Zhang Cheng 章成, "Daoxian da tusha" 道县大屠杀 (August 2001), pp. 81–83; Zheng Yi 郑义, *Hongse jinianbei* 红色纪念碑 [The Scarlet Memorial] (Taipei, Taiwan: Huashi wenhua gongsi, 1993), pp. 23–27.

84 GXWGDANB.

collective killing, a theoretical point I make in the final chapter. Likewise, it is clear that there are great variations across counties and within provinces. These are puzzles that require explanation, to which I will return.

In this chapter, I also document other characteristics of the collective killings, which set the stage for later discussion. First, collective killings occurred in the months surrounding the establishment of revolutionary committees in 1967 and 1968. This timing provides a basis for discussion about the social and political contexts in which collective killing occurred. Second, written records show that killings took place in villages and township – that is, in the lowest levels of the state apparatus with the most tenuous connections to the Party Center. Combined with the fact that the majority of victims were Four Types in rural communities, this provides historical support for my community model.

Finally, I show that the perpetrators of collective killings were individuals closely associated with the party–state as local cadres, party members, or militiamen. Although this seems inconsistent with my argument that the killings were committed in the absence of uniformed state actors, the perpetrators' association with the state does not fully explain their action because the majority of state-related actors in other communities did not commit the same reprehensible crimes. It was on their own initiative that the perpetrators took the most extreme course of action to respond to the political climate of the time.

3

Community and Culture

This chapter describes traditional social divisions in the rural communities – traditional because they were shaped by a history of human interactions long before the 1949 communist revolution. As in communities elsewhere, repeated patterns of human conflict generated primary-group boundaries that underpinned the conception of "us versus them," or in-group and out-group identities. The human imagination must take a "quantum leap" to perceive other people as killable; antagonism toward out-groups is the starting point. These divisions were not sufficient to cause collective killings, but they provided a local impetus for embracing violence when other conditions were in place.

The main unit of organization in the villages of South China was surname lineage. Despite the fact that the 1967–1968 victims were killed under the label "class enemies," clan identities seemed to be at work. In his report on the 1967 Daoxian massacre, Zhang Cheng describes a scene that implicates clan affiliation in collective killings. Before a killing event, village leaders held a meeting to compile a list of targets. Without exception, villagers nominated and then voted for landlords or rich peasants from their rival clans.[1] My own interviews encountered a similar pattern. In one event, militia members from three main surname lineages called one another's clan members to the stage, where hardwood hoe handles were ready in hand for killing.[2]

1 Zhang Cheng 章成. "Daoxian da tusha" 道县大屠杀 [The Daoxian Massacre]. *Open Magazine* 开放杂志, July, August, September and December 2001 issues.

2 Personal interviews with residents of Jinkeng Village, Guangdong. The particular killing event was aborted halfway into it.

Scholars have long pointed out the importance of preexisting social relations in the development of conflict. For example, in his study on the Paris Commune insurgency, Gould details workers' group affiliations and daily interaction routines and argues that they provided the demarcation basis for the formation of insurgent identities.[3] Varshney shows that daily interaction between Muslims and Hindus had a mitigating effect on communal riots.[4] Preexisting ethnic-group boundaries in Rwanda in 1994, according to Straus, were used by genocide organizers to mobilize the perpetrators, although ethnic antagonism had not prevented the two groups from coexisting as neighbors.[5]

After a brief account of my fieldwork experiences, I trace the migration history of the two especially murderous provinces, Guangdong and Guangxi. This long history created major subethnic groups among the Han Chinese as well as a "frontier mentality." I argue that ethnic conflict among these groups perpetuated this mentality and intensified the need for group survival. The result, however, was not a panethnic identity across family clans within each subethnic group. Instead, there was a consolidation within extended families, clans, and surname lineages. These social configurations provide the major sources for group divisions and conflict.

I then discuss how the clan identities encountered and survived class categorization brought by the 1949 revolution and subsequent campaigns. The state-building project after 1949 fundamentally altered the boundaries and nature of rural communities. The Land Reform movement in the 1950s was the beginning of the political demarcation between the formerly poor (i.e., "the people") and the former landowners (i.e., "class enemies"). It also added layers of bureaucracy from the top down and a new way for villagers to move up social and political ladders. However, this new organizational form also preserved key traditional

[3] Roger V. Gould, "Multiple Networks and Mobilization in the Paris Commune, 1871," *American Sociological Review* 56, no. 6 (1991), pp. 716–729; Roger V. Gould, "Collective Action and Network Structure," *American Sociological Review* 58, no. 2 (1993), pp. 182–196; Roger V. Gould, "Trade Cohesion, Class Unity, and Urban Insurrection: Artisanal Activism in the Paris Commune," *American Journal of Sociology* 98, no. 4 (1993), pp. 721–754; Roger V. Gould, *Insurgent Identities: Class, Community, and Protest in Paris from 1848 to the Commune* (Chicago: University of Chicago Press, 1995); Roger V. Gould, "Patron–Client Ties, State Centralization, and the Whiskey Rebellion," *American Journal of Sociology* 102, no. 2 (1996), pp. 400–429.

[4] Ashutosh Varshney, *Ethnic Conflict and Civic Life: Hindus and Muslims in India* (New Haven, CT: Yale University Press, 2002).

[5] Straus, *The Order of Genocide*, pp. 8–10.

features. Notably, it employed the clan as the smallest unit of administration, thereby strengthening this social formation – despite the fact that the ideology of the new state was to transform society. Traditional group identities played a hidden but important role in the new ideological battles, in political conflict among the elite, and in the class struggles among the masses.

One particular subethnic group was immersed in clan culture more deeply than others. Using the *xianzhi* data to compare the severity of the killings, I find that the counties resided by Hakkas experienced more severe killings than other counties during the Cultural Revolution.

But first let me introduce these communities through a brief report on my fieldwork. In this discussion, I address a methodological issue – that is, how my interview data were obtained. I profile a few key informants, people who witnessed collective killings firsthand. Their first-person accounts complement the written records in my claims about collective killings.

The Fieldwork

In 2006 and 2007, I visited four counties in Guangxi and Guangdong. I made attempts to interview people who knew about the history of their community and events during the Cultural Revolution. Ultimately, I was able to meet some thirty witnesses. In one case, I recorded nineteen hours of conversation with a retired county leader who also once served as the head compiler of his county's *xianzhi*. In another case, I met two brothers from a landlord family who took extraordinary measures to escape the collective killings in 1968.

The flow of human contact was punctuated by my encounters with many rivers and community squares. Wherever I went, they emerged to welcome me to a new destination – a city, a township, or a village. Aware of their significance in history – not the least about their role in the mass movements during the Mao era – I often lingered at their sight, as though they were trustworthy, knowledgeable, and welcoming informants. The rivers signify the livelihood of the community and the squares represent political campaigns brought by the communist state to rice cultivators in the region.

Looking down at the landscape from a plane, the dominating view is an unbroken terrain of green mountains. Only at lower altitudes does one see a network of shining lines – some larger and brighter than others – not unlike a system of highways when one looks down from the American sky. For centuries, the river has been closely associated to livelihood in this region of Southern China. Because rice is the subsistence crop, rivers in the landscape are like veins in the human body. Villages are settled throughout irrigable valleys with a river running through them. Cities are located at the waterway intersections where, more often than not, a small plain or basin forms an urban landscape – a pause in the mountainous terrain. But before the revolution, cities did not matter to villagers. If they set foot outside the confines of their village, it was to go to a nearby township on market day to trade their grain, chicken, pork, and handcrafts for tools, salt, and lighting oil.[6]

After the revolution in 1949, however, economic gatherings gave way to political gatherings. As a result of an accelerated political-campaign calendar, the center moved from spot markets to town squares. In the first years of the Cultural Revolution, the two forms of gatherings often were mixed: Red Guards and militias would bring the struggle targets from the square to parade them in the market. With drums and gongs, according to one *xianzhi* record, former landlords and their children were carted through the crowd in a bamboo cage, as an exhibition of "class-struggle education."[7] Eventually, market trading was banned and the town square became the only place that people were allowed to meet in large groups.[8]

[6] The political integration was tried by the Guomindang (GMD; a.k.a. KMT) regime before the revolution. By all accounts, the effort was a clear-cut failure. Within the village, authorities mostly still came from the family clan hierarchy; across villages, the local life was subjected to harassment by bandits and the devastation of wars. See Chen Yiyuan 陈益元, *Geming yu xiangcun: Jianguo chuqi nongcun jiceng zhengquan jianshe yanjiu: 1949–1957, yi hunansheng lilingxian wei ge'an* 革命与乡村: 建国初期农村基层政权建设研究: 1949–1957, 以湖南醴陵县为个案 (Shanghai: Shanghai shehui kexueyuan chubanshe, 2006). A true integrating force may be the market system, as theorized by G. William Skinner in a series of studies that showed that peasants' life reached outside their village to townships and cities – and even to the national and international market – through a hierarchy of levels of trading mechanisms beginning at the spot market in their nearby township. See G. William Skinner, "Vegetable Supply and Marketing in Chinese Cities," *The China Quarterly* 76 (1978), pp. 733–793; G. William Skinner, "Rural Marketing in China: Repression and Revival," *The China Quarterly* 103 (1985), pp. 393–413; G. William Skinner, *Marketing and Social Structure in Rural China* (Ann Arbor, MI: Association for Asian Studies, 2001).

[7] See Chapter 7.

[8] G. William Skinner, "Vegetable Supply and Marketing in Chinese Cities," *The China Quarterly* 76 (1978), pp. 733–793; G. William Skinner, "Rural Marketing in China: Repression and Revival," *The China Quarterly* 103 (1985), pp. 393–413; G. William

My first official identity was as a member of a research team from Beijing for a UN development project. Upon arriving in Nanning, the provincial capital of Guangxi, two colleagues from the Social Science Academy of China and I were treated to a banquet. The next day, we were chauffeured to Cangwu County. The local county officials warmly welcomed us, partly because they were eager to continue their relationship with the UN, partly because we had two provincial officials in tow. Our arrival was even reported in the local newspapers.[9]

In recent years, local governments have competed with one another in building so-called image projects within their jurisdictions. The Cangwu County Square is one of the most extravagant I have encountered. As night falls, the square is brightly lit, and it soon becomes a boisterous scene. Men and women, elderly people and children swarm in, rubbing elbows with one another. There are at a least five different groups, mainly older and middle-aged women, dancing in formation to the music playing from their respective box recorders. Two or three groups are singing, often directed by a self-appointed leader, with a song sheet displayed in enormous characters in front of each group.

I do not know whether the square that held the deadly struggle rallies was located in the same place as the new one. In any event, the crowds in the square look happy and seem to have put the events of the Cultural Revolution behind them. Unlike the Cultural Revolution crowds, the state plays no part in organizing the ones today. These urban residents, many of whom have recently moved to the city from a village, come to the square for fun every morning and evening. It is remarkable to see them blissfully use Cultural Revolution signifiers in their recreational activities. Their dances resemble the loyalty dance that was taught to almost every adult and student during the Cultural Revolution, and their songs betray that they are still ruled by the same party regime:

> We are trailblazers
> We are flower growers
> We are on the socialist path
> We build the mansion of Four Modernizations
> ... ...

Skinner, *Marketing and Social Structure in Rural China* (Ann Arbor, MI: Association for Asian Studies, 2001).

[9] *Xijiang Ribao* 西江日报, September 4, 2006.

Between meetings and site visits for the UN evaluation project, I had the chance to meet a few county officials. I expressed my interest in learning more about local history and my desire to visit the *xianzhi* (i.e., county gazetteers) compiling office and the County Archives, both located within the government compound. The typical reaction was, "Oh, what do you need? I can send someone there to get it for you." I explained that I wanted to talk to the *xianzhi* compilers and to learn how a *xianzhi* is compiled.

The Cultural Revolution has become a taboo topic since the late 1980s, especially after the 1989 Tiananmen Square Movement. Since then, valuable information has been locked up and kept away from the public and academic institutions. In 1994, the Chinese government sent a chill through China scholars throughout the world when a U.S.–based librarian was accused of smuggling state secrets; in fact, he was only buying Red Guard tabloids in a free market. He was detained for four months until more than one hundred China scholars in the United States signed a petition letter to President Jiang Zemin. Although the librarian, Song Yongyi, was freed unharmed and returned to the United States, the incident underscored the perils of doing sensitive fieldwork in China.[10] Just weeks before my China trip, at a conference in Montreal, Canada in the summer of 2006, I had lunch with "W," an advanced Ph.D. student, who warned me that he was kidnapped in his hotel lobby in Changsha by agents of the State Security Bureau and interrogated for three days and nights before his release.

I was hoping on my research trip to meet people who were directly involved in the collective killing – those who gave the orders, those who committed the crimes, or those whose family members were victims. I was not sure if Cangwu County had extensive collective killings, but I knew Mengshan, an adjacent county, was notorious for them. In Zheng Yi's gruesome account of Guangxi pogroms and cannibalism, Mengshan is among the counties with the worst atrocities. He reports that in one village in Mengshan County, not only adult "ghost and demons" were killed but also young children. Toddlers, not knowing the gravity of the situation, would address the killer as "uncle" and plead with him to stop "joking" with a length of rope. Zheng claimed to have read confessions by the killers: "We just put the noose around the neck [of the child], turned around and ran." Among the reports that Zheng read, he wrote

[10] Personal communication with Song Yongyi 宋永毅.

that killing practices were sometimes based on gender: boys were killed and girls were spared; the killer first touched the child's crotch to decide.[11] An entry in the Mengshan *xianzhi* reads as follows:

> March 20, [1968]. Militias in Huangqiao Brigade, Xinlian Commune killed in large numbers on the account that the victims were members of Ping-min Party [an alleged conspiracy group]. That event triggered the countywide killings, particularly severe in Wenping and other places.[12]

Mengshan and Cangwu Counties belong to the same municipal jurisdiction, Wuzhou City. My plan was to meet officials of Wuzhou City, whom I hoped would introduce me to their subordinates in Mengshan.

Mr. Wang was a young man in his thirties. With a college degree in history, he joined the *Cangwu xianzhi* compiling office in 1987, two years after it opened. He is now the vice chief editor, ranked second in the six-member office, which also is responsible for compiling Cangwu County's local history of the Communist Party. The office is a government agency, its members are full-time cadres of the county government, and their work relies on other agencies in local jurisdictions to submit materials. The county's top leaders are the nominal heads of the office; they give speeches and issue directives to ensure local cooperation. The office published the most recent volume of the *Cangwu xianzhi* in 1997. When I visited the cluttered office, Mr. Wang and his staff were busy gathering materials from other agencies and townships in preparation for a new edition.

They were not very cooperative. I learned that investigative materials regarding the Cultural Revolution were housed in the County Archives (located in the next building) but that they were classified. Before I left, I requested one more meeting with Mr. Wang to hear his personal views on Cangwu County history. He recommended Mr. Zhao, a retired county leader who had served as the first editor-in-chief and who was currently a consultant, living in Wuzhou City. Mr. Wang said he would contact him for me. Similarly, I made little headway when I visited the County Archives. The head of the Archives became very animated when he learned that I was a scholar from the United States; he pointed to the "security rules" posted on the office wall and demanded a signed letter from the

[11] Zheng Yi 郑义, "*Guangxi chiren kuangchao zhenxiang: liuwang zhong ge qizi de di ba feng xin*" 广西吃人狂潮真相：流亡中给妻子的第八封信 [The Truth about the Maddening Waves of Cannibalism in Guangxi: The 8th Letter from Exile to My Wife], *Huaxia wenzhai* 华夏文摘 [*Chinese News Digest*], 15 (Supplement Issue, 1993).

[12] Mengshan xianzhi bianzuan weiyuanhui 蒙山县志编纂委员会, *Mengshan xianzhi* 蒙山县志 [*Mengshan County Gazetteer*] (Nanning: Guangxi renmin chubanshe, 1993), p. 27.

local government before I was allowed to read anything. After I telephoned my host agency, the county's Science and Technology Bureau, he relented and permitted me to read only the catalog. It listed a variety of materials related to the Cultural Revolution, but I could not identify exactly what was in the documents. When a county policeman later showed up in my hotel lobby, I knew there was no hope of making any progress through official channels. I gave up trying to gain access to the County Archives and instead decided to interview older people in the areas where written records had documented collective-killing events.

In my three days in Mengshan County, I visited many squares and rivers by taking commercial motorcycle rides. Then I got a welcomed call from Mr. Wang of the *Cangwu xianzhi* office, who informed me that Mr. Zhao was willing to talk to me. After many hours interviewing Mr. Zhao and another retired cadre to whom he introduced me, I wrapped up my first trip to Guangxi and took a long-distance bus to Guangzhou, the provincial capital of Guangdong. Once there, I brought three retired cadres that I had known previously to the two counties I decided to visit: Xingning and Wuhua. This time, I decided to work entirely outside official channels. Mr. Zeng was the former mayor of Xingning and the father of a close friend; Mr. Ping and his wife Ms. Lian were relatives of mine. Mr. Ping worked in Wuhua first as a teacher and then as a county cadre for more than three decades. My new plan was to find appropriate informants through their networks.

The Witnesses

Mr. Zhao is the type of informant of which every researcher dreams. He had witnessed much in his life. His landlord family suffered a great deal while he himself was a young cadre during the Land Reform movement. He was labeled a member of the so-called ghosts and demons (another term for *class enemies*) during the Cultural Revolution; he was county head of the People's Congress after the Cultural Revolution; and he was a leading cadre in a committee that investigated Cultural Revolution cases in 1983. Above all he was articulate and had a habit of keeping written records. I recorded nineteen hours of our conversations.

Mr. Zhao first became a cadre at age nineteen in 1950, Guangxi's first year of the Land Reform. He was drafted from high school despite his landlord-family background. He soon witnessed political atrocities in the so-called Land Reform Rectification campaign in 1952. Many landlords were tortured to yield confessions regarding supposed "hidden treasures" not relinquished during the Land Reform the previous year. At home, his mother was tortured but later spared, thanks to a large sum of money raised by her sons and relatives. At work, he witnessed struggling against the landlords and rich peasants during the day; at night, he saw the struggling against the cadres, who were accused of being soft on landlords and rich peasants. He became indispensable due to his excellent report-writing skills and rose steadily in the cultural sector until the Cultural Revolution. Then he was deemed a member of the ghosts and demons due to his father's status as a former landlord. He was stripped of work until 1973, when he became a high school teacher and then a principal.

The seventy-five-year-old Mr. Zhao beamed when he talked about his moral judgment and foresight thirty-eight years ago. In 1968, in a struggle session that was degenerating into collective killings, Mr. Zhao, who was thirty-seven at the time, rushed to stop the militiamen and his fellow cadres; his action diverted the course of events. "Had the killings occurred that day, I would be the most responsible because I was the highest ranking cadre on site. My fate could have totally been changed by that." When China turned a new political page, he was deemed clean of any "Cultural Revolution problem" and rose steadily to the top in Cangwu County. He was reinstated to the cadre rank, first heading the Party Center history office, then the County Archives, and finally ascending to head of the county government, the People's Congress. He retired and became editor-in-chief for compiling the *xianzhi*. In that capacity and in his earlier role as a work-team leader during the 1983 investigations, he penned many reports about the Cultural Revolution. His work-team was responsible for post–Cultural Revolution investigation and rehabilitation. He kept journals and had a habit of making copies of his official reports. After a few days of interviews, and as our friendship grew, he gave me his copies of two important reports. One detailed the meetings convened by the county's new revolutionary committee to set up key points of class struggle. He insisted that these meetings were directly responsible for the ensuing wave of collective killings in the county. The other report described one such event.

Another informant provided a different type of eyewitness account. Jin Zhilong was only four years old in 1949 when his father, the Guomindang (GMD) (i.e., the Nationalist Party) mayor of Luogang District in Xingning County, fled to Taiwan, leaving his family behind. Jin recounted to me in detail his ordeal of growing up as a landlord's child. His mother died from being tortured during the Land Reform. To avoid discrimination, his brother and two sisters were given up for adoption. After he grew up, Jin left for Jiangxi to work in an anonymous setting, but his coworkers discovered his family background and blackmailed him. Nevertheless, he returned to his hometown during the Cultural Revolution and "represented" his family. When he was nineteen, he was lined up with other victims on the riverbank in Jinkeng Village in Xingning County – awaiting execution in an event that was escalating into collective killings – only to be saved by outside intervention.

On administrative matters, I was helped by Zeng Hongzhong, a guerilla fighter in the 1949 revolution and a rising star who was appointed vice mayor of Xingning County at the age of twenty-two. In 1958, however, due in part to his colleagues' envy, he was labeled a Rightist and sent to the countryside to be "reeducated" for twenty years; he resumed his post during the Deng Xiaoping era in 1978.

For information on mass factionalism during the Cultural Revolution, I interviewed Mr. Wei. As a high school teacher, he became the head of one of two warring factions in the county seat, partly because of his friendship with people in the Security Bureau. In the latter half of the Cultural Revolution, Mr. Wei was a vice chief in the county's education bureau.

If Mr. Zhao was my first breakthrough interview; the finale came when I met the Du brothers in Wuhua County, Guangdong Province. During the waves of mass killings that swept his county, Du Zhengyi hid in the mountains for two months to avoid the fate of his brothers. He was the lone survivor among the male adults from the landlord families in Dukeng Village, where sixty-three people were killed in 1968. When he recounted his ordeal to me, the seventy-eight-year-old man was surprisingly calm at first. However, when his tale came to the point when he briefly reunited with his mother, he suddenly burst into tears and shivered violently. Du's father had been killed during the Land Reform and his mother had lost two sons in mass executions during the Cultural Revolution; she did not know the fate of her fourth son, a teacher in another commune.

Du Jianqiang, the fourth son, had heard about his brothers' executions in his home village and knew that the Dukeng Village militiamen would come to his school to arrest him. To save his own life, he devised an ingenious plan to buy time. He scribbled a few anti-Mao leaflets, bade farewell to his wife and four children, and surrendered at the public security office in the county seat. Du Jianqiang demanded to be arrested because he was a counter-revolutionary, the leaflets being his evidence. He was detained and ultimately sentenced to a labor camp for ten years.

In addition to Mr. Zhao and the Du brothers, I interviewed thirty people in four counties in Guangdong and Guangxi Provinces. They were mostly retirees in their sixties and seventies who had formerly worked as *xianzhi* compilers or as cadres at various levels; some had been active – indeed, leaders – in the factional politics during the Cultural Revolution. I also met and interviewed a number of survivors and relatives of the Four-Type families. I usually settled in a county seat, worked down to townships, villages, and hamlets by taxi, motorcycle, bike, or foot. The interviews confirmed the collective killings recorded in the *xianzhi*, but each county – according to my informants – experienced many more than were recorded. These interviews enabled me to put human faces on the victimization statistics, to construct details of events, and to understand the personal relationships surrounding the history. I did not restrict my inquiries to events during the Cultural Revolution; I also inquired about the period from the Land Reform to the Cultural Revolution. I was interested in how the class enemy was initially labeled, maintained, and deployed as a "killable" category in 1967 and 1968. I was also interested in cadre recruitment and career mobility because the collective killings seemed to be committed by the local cadres and militia activists.

For local traditions and customs, I drew on my knowledge as a native son. I grew up in a Hakka village in Guangdong Province. Born two years before the Cultural Revolution, I did not leave the region until college. My father was a teacher and then a high school principal. In the campaigns leading up the Cultural Revolution, he was drafted as a work-team member. In the heat of the mass conflict during the Cultural Revolution, he was mildly denounced by student organizations and then managed to escape and return to our home village. He remained unemployed for about a year and a half. After the new governments were established, he went back to his school and was quickly recruited as a county cadre. In the latter years of the Cultural Revolution, my father was as a member of a special committee that investigated the denounced cadres.

I lived with my mother and siblings in a village in another county. As a peasant, my mother joined thousands of others in the village who participated in daily rallies and parades and witnessed violence against struggle targets. I was too young to remember the first days of the Cultural Revolution, but I became aware of the movement in its waning years. I recall overhearing adults' discussion of the events of the day and witnessing rallies and violence firsthand. At the height of Mao's personality cult in 1968, at the age of four, I was my family's representative at daily rituals in the morning and evening. Villagers – young and old who represented each family in the production team – lined up in the former ancestor hall in the lineage house. In lieu of ancestor tablets, Mao's portrait was hung. Holding the Little Red Book, we paid homage to our leader twice a day.

Clan Institutions in a Frontier Culture

The Chinese civilization and state originated in the northern part of the country. The first inhabitants were concentrated in regions along the Yellow River. As early as the Qin Dynasty (221–206 BC), the government set up outposts in the south and waves of migration followed. Over the centuries, small numbers of military personnel and government officials were joined by millions of northerners to resettle in a new land previously occupied by aboriginals. The fertile plains along the other two major rivers, the Yangtze and the Pearl, were the first and most coveted destinations. Latecomers found homes in the peripheral highlands and valleys, pushing the aboriginals farther into the high-altitude mountains.[13] By the time of the Yuan Dynasty (1206–1368), the country's population concentration had shifted from the north to the south. The initial 4:1 ratio had been reversed, with the south becoming the dominant region.[14] The influx remained strong after the Yuan Dynasty,[15] and Guangdong and Guangxi Provinces – jointly known as Lingnan – were two emigrant destinations. Early settlers in the fertile Pearl Delta found a relatively stable living for generations, but for the latecomers, the limited land in a mountain valley could sustain only one or two generations. Therefore, clans were forced to migrate again into other frontiers.[16]

As has been extensively documented by historians and anthropologists on both North and South China, the most important and enduring of social institutions is the family clan, which is characterized by ancestor-worship rites and has been shared by all Han Chinese.[17] Scholars of recent

[13] Ge Jianxiong 葛剑雄, Wu Songdi 吴松弟, Cao Shuji 曹树基, *Zhongguo yiminshi: Diyijuan* 中国移民史：第一卷 [*China's Immigration History: Volume 1*] (Fuzhou, Fujian: Fujian renmin chubanshe, 1997), p. 88.

[14] Ge Jianxiong 葛剑雄, Zhongguo renkou fazhan shi 中国人口发展史 (*Historic Changes of Chinese Population*). (Fuzhou, Fujian: Fujian renmin chubanshe, 1991), Chapter 13.

[15] Ge Jianxiong 葛剑雄, Wu Songdi 吴松弟, Cao Shuji 曹树基, *Zhongguo yiminshi: Diyijuan* 中国移民史：第一卷 [*China's Immigration History: Volume 1*] (Fuzhou, Fujian: Fujian renmin chubanshe, 1997).

[16] Ibid.

[17] James L.Watson, *Emigration and the Chinese Lineage: The Mans in Hong Kong and London* (Berkeley: University of California Press, 1975); Maurice Freedman, *Chinese Lineage and Society: Fukien and Kwangtung* (New York: Humanities Press, 1966);

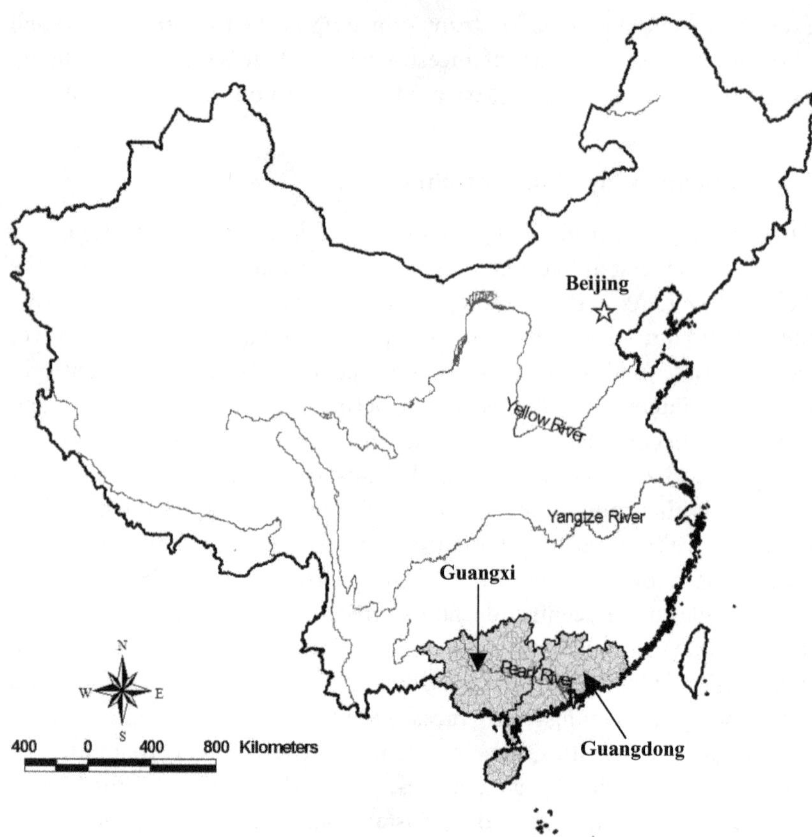

FIGURE 3.1. Guangdong and Guangxi Provinces in China.

history also vouch for the clan's impact on Chinese life and conflict since the 1949 revolution.[18] It is rooted in Confucian philosophy and reinforced

Maurice Freedman, *Lineage Organization in Southeastern China* (New York: Humanities Press, 1965); Qian Mu 钱穆, *Zhongguo wenhua shi daolun* 中国文化史导论 (Taipei, Taiwan: Shangwu yinshuguan, 1994); Jun Jing, *The Temple of Memories: History, Power, and Morality in a Chinese Village* (Stanford, CA: Stanford University Press, 1996); Su Yang 苏阳, "*Jingzu jizu huodong zhong de cunmin yu zuzhi – 1992 nian dui zhongguo xibei kongxing shancun de shidi diaocha*" 敬祖祭祖活动中的村民与组织 – 1992年对中国西北孔姓山村的实地调查 ("Villagers and Organizations in Ancestor Worship Rites: A Field Study on A Kong Village in Northwestern China, 1992"), *Shehuixue yu shehui diaocha* (February 1992): 58–72.

[18] Anita Chan, Richard Madsen, and Jonathan Unger, *Chen Village: The Recent History of A Peasant Community in Mao's China* (Berkeley: University of California Press, 1984); Helen F. Siu, *Agents and Victims in South China: Accomplices in Rural Revolution* (New Haven, CT: Yale University Press, 1989); Isabel Crook and David Crook, *Ten Mile Inn: Mass Movement in a Chinese Village* (New York: Pantheon Books, 1979);

by centuries of imperial rule. Some scholars argue that perpetuating blood lineage through clan organization and worship rites has a transcendent purpose for immortality, thereby providing a type of religion for Han Chinese who otherwise are known to be atheists.[19]

The fieldwork I conducted in 1992 for another project illustrates the institution that is typically practiced among Northern Chinese villagers. The Kong family clan in Dachuan in Gansu Province organizes its ancestor worship at three levels. Four or five generations of families join in prayers and offerings at major festivals, form a mutual-aid funeral group, and share a common cemetery site. The village of about one hundred families built a temple featuring common ancestors of Kongs and ancient forebears including Confucius (i.e., the Kongs are Confucius' descendants). Finally, a genealogy chart has been compiled that links Kongs across the country, including those living in Confucius' birthplace of Shandong.[20]

If the clan institution defines "Chineseness," the southern migrants not only retained it but also practiced it with an intensity unmatched by their northern compatriots. This is largely due to the need to survive as a group in the context of frontier conflict. It was a collective undertaking central to driving away the aboriginals and subsequent fighting with other Han groups. Disputes within a subethnic Han group also were settled primarily on the basis of clan strength.

Ethnic Minorities and Subethnic Han Groups

Backed by military and political might, migrants from the north prevailed over the aboriginals. The Han culture took root in Lingnan and flourished. Some aboriginals were killed, some adopted Chinese names and were converted to become Han Chinese, and others retreated to the mountains. Under communist rule, the fifty-six surviving ethnic groups were officially labeled "minorities". Such ethnic minorities make up 38 percent of the

Isabel Crook and David Crook, *Revolution in a Chinese Village: Ten Mile Inn* (London: Routledge and Kegan Paul, 1959); Edward Friedman, Paul Pickowicz, and Mark Selden, *Chinese Village, Socialist State* (New Haven, CT: Yale University Press, 1991); Zhao Litao 赵力涛, "*Jiazu yu cunzhuang zhengzhi (1950–1970): Hebei mo cun jiazu xianxiang yanjiu*" 家族与村庄政治 (1950–1970): 河北某村家族现象研究 ("A Study on Clans in a Village in Hebei"). *Ershiyi shiji* 55 (October 1999), pp. 1–25; William Hinton, *Fanshen: A Documentary of Revolution in a Chinese Village* (Berkeley: University of California Press, 1997).

19 Qian Mu 钱穆, *Zhongguo wenhua shi daolun* 中国文化史导论 [History of the Chinese Culture] (Taipei, Taiwan: Shangwu yinshuguan, 1994); Jun Jing, *The Temple of Memories: History, Power, and Morality in a Chinese Village* (Stanford, CA: Stanford University Press, 1996); Su Yang, "Villagers and Organizations."

20 Su Yang, "Villagers and Organizations"; see also Jun Jing, 1996.

TABLE 3.1. *Size of Subethnic Han Groups in Guangdong and Guangxi Provinces*

Dialect Group	Guangdong[1]	Guangxi[2]
Cantonese	38,000,000	15,000,000
Xi'nan Guanhua	–	7,600,000
Chaozhou	12,000,000	–
Hakka	14,000,000	5,000,000

Notes:

[1] big5.gd.gov.cn/gate/big5/www.gd.gov.cn/gdgk/sqgm/rkyy/0200606120027.htm.

[2] www.hudong.com/wiki/广西方言.

Guangxi population (the province's population was 20.8 million according to the 1964 Census). In Guangdong, most aboriginal groups fled to Hainan Island and Taiwan; ethnic minorities therefore comprise less than 1 percent of the province's population (the province's population was 42.8 million according to the 1964 census). Ethnic minorities were segregated geographically from the Hans, often by a great distance. In a research trip to Mengshan County, I attempted to visit an ethnic Yao community. After a two-hour motorcycle ride from the county seat, I reached the township government site without seeing a single Yao. Officials informed me that the nearest Yao village was a five-hour journey on foot.

Among the Han Chinese, major subethnic groups formed along linguistic lines. Although remaining proudly Chinese, these groups developed distinctive customs. The ancient Chinese language migrated to Lingnan and evolved into four major dialects: Cantonese, Xi'nan Guanhua, Chaozhou (a Guangdong variant of Minnan), and Hakka. Except for Xi'nan Guanhua, which means Southwestern Official Language, these dialects are no longer consonant with contemporary Mandarin or with one another. They were based on the ancient Chinese at the time when a northern influx of migrants was large enough to prevail culturally and mixed with elements from local aboriginal languages. Cantonese can be dated as far back as the Qin Dynasty (221–206 BC), Xi'nan Guanhua to the Tang Dynasty (618–907), Chaozhou (Minnan) to the Han Dynasty (202–220 BC), and Hakka to the turn between the Song and Yuan Dynasties (circa 1206).[21] These groups of languages differed in size; Cantonese is the largest. The numbers in Table 3.1 are from government statistics

[21] Wu Songdi 吴松弟, *Zhongguo yiminshi: Disijuan* 中国移民史: 第四卷 [*China's Immigration History: Volume* 4] (Fuzhou, Fujian: Fujian renmin chubanshe, 1997), pp. 350–368.

around 2006. Historical population data by language groups are not available; however, the table reflects the relative proportion of the groups and their distribution in the two provinces.

In the hierarchy of ethnic stratification, the Cantonese and Xi'nan Guanhua groups were at the top, due primarily to their early arrival. They inhabited the fertile areas of delta plains and large basins, populating major cities such as Guangzhou and Nanning and their suburbs. Some groups lived along the South Sea, taking up fishing as an alternative occupation to agriculture. Next in the hierarchy after these two groups is the Chaozhou group, which was mainly concentrated in the open lands with coastal access of the Chaoyang and Shantou areas. At the bottom of the hierarchy among the Han groups was the Hakkas, who arrived after all the good land in Lingnan had been settled. They found their niche between the early groups and the aboriginals, mostly in the low-altitude hills such as the border areas of Guangdong, Jiangxi, and Fujian.

The Han–aboriginal conflict quickly receded because of the skewed balance of strength between the sides, but competition and conflict remained fierce among Han subethnic groups for centuries. They cultivated separate niches and lived in geographically segregated communities, but their territories bordered one another and boundaries were constantly being redrawn. Imperial governments and subsequent warlord regimes were both too weak to adjudicate community disputes, so collective disagreements were resolved through shows of force by the disputing parties. Ethnic riots were commonplace, and ethnic identities were sharpened through these antagonistic contacts.

However, the internal consolidation within groups went only so far. There was a peculiar impact from this frontier culture: It strengthened group solidarity in the form of the family clan, thereby reinforcing divisions within the subethnic groups. There are several reasons for this influence. First, language as an ethnic marker was a weak integrating force, unlike others (e.g., religion). Second, the geography in the mountainous regions, particularly for the Hakka people, prevented a large organic community from evolving. Instead, valley dwellers usually formed their own small communities, with an extremely limited reach beyond the mountains. Within a dialect group, competition with other communities was intense, and clan rites were practiced with added fervor.

Clan members encompassing several generations usually shared a housing compound. They collectively built and lived in an enormous building with scores of rooms. An ancestor hall was designated for worship activities. This tradition contrasts with the northern residential patterns. Due in part to the availability of land, northerners built smaller houses and lived with only their immediate family. In the provinces of Guangdong and Guangxi, where clan size was a decisive factor in clan conflict, concern about the number of male descendants became an obsession. Southerners in the area developed a set of local institutions and rites that encouraged childbearing.

Hakka

In 1966, fifteen of the eighty counties in Guangdong Province were entirely Hakka; the other sixty-five had a significant Hakka presence. In Guangxi Province, forty of eighty-three counties were a mixture of Hakka and other groups; the other forty-three counties had no significant Hakka presence.[22] Meixian was a cradle of Hakka culture in the Yuan Dynasty, and five adjacent counties later became purely Hakka.[23] The largest wave of Hakka emigration to Guangxi, which was from Guangdong, took place in the late Qing Dynasty (1616–1911) under an imperial relocation policy.[24]

Historians differ on when the Hakka dialect took shape and whether the population was mainly descendants of northerners or a mixed ancestry of Hans and aboriginals. One theory traces the Hakka population to six waves of migration from the north, beginning in the Xijin Dynasty (265–317) and continuing through the Qing Dynasty (1644–1911).[25] Another view suggests that the Hakka dialect did not take shape until late in the Yuan Dynasty (1206–1368).[26] However, there is agreement on three key points. First, the Hakka dialect is a variant of Chinese with a vocabulary and pronunciations that are traceable to

[22] Hu Xizhang 胡希张, Mo Rifen 莫日芬, Dong Li 董励, and Zhang Weigeng 张维耿, *Kejia fenghua* 客家风华 [*Traditions of Hakka*] (Guangzhou, Guangdong: Guangdong remin chubanshe, 1997), pp. 712–714.

[23] Wu Songdi 吴松弟, *Zhongguo yiminshi: Disanjuan, Disijuan* 中国移民史：第四卷, [*China's Immigration History: Volume* 4] (Fuzhou, Fujian: Fujian renmin chubanshe, 1997), pp. 350–368; Luo Xianglin 罗香林, *Zhongguo zupu yanjiu* 中国族谱研究 [*A Study of Chinese Genealogy*] (Hong Kong: Zhongguo xueshe, 1971).

[24] Zhong Wendian 钟文典, *Guangxi kejia* 广西客家 [Guangxi Hakka] (Guilin, Guangxi: Guangxi shifan daxue chubanshe, 2005a); Zhong Wendian 钟文典, *Fujian kejia* 福建客家 [*Fujian Hakka*] (Guilin: Guangxi shifan daxue chubanshe, 2005b).

[25] Luo Xianglin 罗香林, *Zhongguo zupu yanjiu* 中国族谱研究 [*A Study of Chinese Genealogy*] (Hong Kong: Zhongguo xueshe, 1971).

[26] Wu Songdi 吴松弟, *Zhongguo yiminshi: Disanjuan, Disijuan* 中国移民史：第四卷, [*China's Immigration History: Volume* 4] (Fuzhou, Fujian: Fujian renmin chubanshe, 1997), pp. 350–368.

ancient Chinese. Second, the Hakka culture is mainly Chinese; even if a significant portion of the population were descended from aboriginals, they were quickly assimilated into the dominant Chinese culture. Third, the Hakka first settled in the hilly border territories of Guangdong, Jiangxi, and Fujian and then spread to other similarly harsh areas.[27]

Many features of the Hakka minority discussed herein are also characteristic of other subethnic Han groups in the region, all of which existed in similar cultural, economic, and ecological situations. But because of their precarious position, the Hakka strengthened their ethnic identity and internal clan solidarity to levels unseen elsewhere in the region. The word *Hakka*, or *Kejiaren* in Chinese, means "guest people," a label given them by earlier settlers. Seeking to cultivate a niche between early settlers and aboriginals, the Hakka often fought battles on two fronts. Moreover, even after they prevailed over the aboriginals, the limited available land could sustain only one or two generations; a branch of the clan was always on the move again. Competition among Hakka clans was no less fierce. Typically a village was shared by more than one surname lineage. Land, irrigation water, and mountainous commons were sources of constant dispute and conflict.

The Hakka comprised a subethnic group with customs unknown to other Chinese people, but – paradoxically – they also were the "most Chinese." Indeed, intellectuals often fought polemic battles with other groups to prove that their ancestors were Chinese mandarins from the north. The Hakka took clan solidarity to an extreme. They built *weilongwu*, or a "circled dragon house," an enclosed structure that doubled as a fort-like military structure.[28] The obsession for male descendants among the Chinese and other southerners was outdone by the traditional Hakka annual festival to showcase newborn sons. Elsewhere in China, rich men might have concubines, but it was not unusual for a poor Hakka man to be the husband and father of two families.[29] Clan disputes and conflict were frequent in the south, but in Hakka communities, violent riots often were institutionalized. In my village, the term *jiao* referred to a violent festival

[27] Luo Xianglin 罗香林, *Kejia yanjiu daolun* 客家研究导论 [Preliminary Research on Hakka] (Shanghai: Shanghai wenyi chubanshe, 1992); Ge Jianxiong 葛剑雄, Wu Songdi 吴松弟, Cao Shuji 曹树基, *Zhongguo yiminshi: Diyijuan* 中国移民史: 第一卷 [*China's Immigration History: Volume 1*] (Fuzhou, Fujian: Fujian renmin chubanshe, 1997).

[28] In less intense communities, it mutated as a half circle plus a few rows.

[29] Hakka women are industrious laborers, so they can help support the families.

at which competing clans staged violent showdowns periodically. Until my father's generation, all males in the community trained in the martial arts for the purpose of fighting rival clans.

Violence as Tradition

Imperial governments in the dynasties were too weak to referee local violent disputes. Additionally, they often encouraged local elites to raise their own militias or private armies to keep order or to assist in suppressing rebellion. In the Taiping Uprising in the mid-nineteenth century, the imperial court could not match the Taiping army's strength until large contingents of private armies came to its aid.[30] In the confrontation between the Qing court and Western powers, the Empress Dowager secretly assisted the Boxer movement, which led to the Boxer Uprising against foreign missionaries in 1900.[31] Warlord regimes after the 1911 revolution fared no better in controlling violent means in the hands of the state.[32]

Ethnic riots were not only unchecked by the state apparatus; the corrupt imperial army also was often the cause. The Qing army triggered a series of riots in 1854–1867 that involved multiple counties and claimed thousands of lives. After suppressing a rebellion in Heshan County in Guangdong Province, an army commander led his men to seek payment from a nearby Hakka landowner. The latter refused to oblige, relying on his private militia to repel the army. Chastened by his failure, the commander sought help from the rebellious bandits (who were also locals) that he had just defeated. After the army left, the dispute between the Hakka and the locals intensified. As casualties increased, the battle was joined by Hakka and locals (*bendi*) from eight other counties. Only after years of fighting and an emperor's edict did the riots subside.[33]

This vigilante culture also plagued disputes among village clans. As discussed previously, in a Hakka community, all adult males trained in

[30] Jonathan D. Spence, *God's Chinese Son: The Taiping Heavenly Kingdom of Hong Xiuquan* (New York: W. W. Norton, 1996).

[31] Joseph Esherick, *The Origins of the Boxer Uprising* (Berkeley: University of California Press, 1987).

[32] Chen Yiyuan 陈益元, *Geming yu xiangcun.*

[33] Liu Ping 刘平, *Bei yiwan de zhanzheng: Xianfeng Tongzhi nianjian Guangdong tuke daxiedou yanjiu* 被遗忘的战争 – 咸丰同治年间广东土客大械斗研究 [*The Hakka-Punti War in Guangdong 1854–1867*] (Beijing: Shangwu yinshuguan, 2003).

the martial arts to prepare for clan disputes that could erupt at any time. Jinkeng Village had five surname clans. Among them the major three, the Sus, Zengs, and Lis were known for their fierce competition and conflict since the time of dynasties. Before the 1949 revolution, communal riots broke out frequently. Older people remembered at least two incidents when the Sus and the Zengs fought with firearms.[34]

The Village Meets the New State

A typical rural community in South China is a village. Several lineages build their communal houses at the base of a mountain, scattered in a valley.[35] A small river running through the village supplies water for rice cultivation. A lineage house accommodates about ten households; larger lineages build more than one house. Until 1949, a community like this was a self-contained unit insulated from the outside world. Authority originated from the bottom up. Winners of the lineage competition dominated village politics, and well-off individuals were respected as the lineage leadership. The imperial government reached only to the county level, leaving local communities to self-administration.[36] The GMD government, and the warlord regimes before it, tried to extend into villages with little success.[37]

The 1949 revolution changed this scenario. The Land Reform eliminated property ownership and decimated the status of local elites. Authority now came from the top down. Village leaders – although local peasants themselves – were party members appointed by township leaders who, in turn, were selected by county leaders and so on. Thus, the character of a community could no longer be explained only through social intercourse among villagers; rather, it had to be explained in conjunction with a network of state governments located outside the village: townships, counties, provinces, and, ultimately, Beijing. With authority vested in urban dwellers on the state payroll, the meaning of community changed fundamentally. In referring to a community of collective

34 Personal interview with Mr. Jin, 2006.

35 There are rare cases in which there is only one lineage in a village. See, e.g., Anita Chan, Richard Madsen, and Jonathan Unger, *Chen Village: The Recent History of a Peasant Community in Mao's China* (Berkeley: University of California Press, 1984). In that case, village politics takes a form of competition among clans within the lineage, with a pattern similar to lineage competition.

36 Chen Yiyuan, 2006.

37 Ibid.

TABLE 3.2. *Administrative Units in Selected Counties*

County	Xingning	Wuhua	Cangwu	Mengshan
Number of communes	27	26	30	14
Number of brigades	819	697	225	145

Note: Xingning and Wuhua are in Guangdong Province; Cangwu and Mengshan are in Guangxi Province.
Sources: Xingning, Wuhua, Mengshan, and Cangwu *xianzhi*.

killing in this book, I do not mean only local organizers, executioners, and bystanders; I also include those urbanites who exercised power over the villagers. They all contributed to the social construction of a village.

In 1961, after various reforms and experiments, the Chinese government put in place a rural administration system that consisted of four levels: county, commune, production brigade, and production team. This system remained in place throughout the Cultural Revolution. A brigade corresponded to a village and a team corresponded to a lineage house with about ten households.[38] Table 3.2 lists the administration units in four representative counties. Xingning and Wuhua were two of the eighty counties in Guangdong Province, and Cangwu and Mengshan were two of the eighty-three counties in Guangxi Province.

The party–state ruled the rural population through a cadre of bureaucrats and personnel on the state payroll who resided in urban centers in the townships, county seats, and provincial capitals. The bureaucrats oversaw the politics, taxation, and production of villagers who earned a living from harvests. A caste-like registration system (*hukou*) erected a social wall that was rarely penetrated.[39] The urbanites engineered one social transformation after another by dispatching work-teams into villages to mobilize mass movements. They cultivated new local elites as state surrogates, rewarding them with local power and the coveted prize of ascending to the state payroll. This urban–rural relationship is key to understanding how urban conflict translated into village killings in 1967 and 1968.

38 There are exceptions: Some brigades may consist of more than one small natural village. A family who lived alone in a single house would join a team in a lineage house.

39 See Dorothy J. Solinger, *Contesting Citizenship in Urban China: Peasant Migrants, the State, and the Logic of the Market* (Berkeley: University of California Press, 1999).

State-building after 1949 impacted local communities in three other fundamental ways. First, the changed source of political power transformed the system of social stratification and career mobility. In the bottom-up authority structure in the past, to be prosperous was defined by building a dominant family clan through the accumulation of wealth (typically measured by land ownership), succeeding in imperial exams, or prevailing over other lineages or clans in local struggles. Under communism, conversely, to succeed was defined by being closely associated with the new state.

Second, class identities were imposed on villagers, whose group consciousness was centered on lineage, clan, and family. A landlord in one's own clan was a friend, a patron, and a protector. Class identities had to be imposed because after the Land Reform, property differentiation no longer existed. By the time of the Cultural Revolution, every family was a "commune member" tilling the public land. Despite its lack of economic basis, class identity was one framework by which local affairs were conducted, affecting each individual's fortune and fate.

Third, traditional identities of ethnicity, lineage, and clan were deemed feudal relics to be discarded. Temples were destroyed, ancestor halls were disserted, and rituals were banned; however, evidence shows that such identities were difficult to change. In Chapters 4 and 5, I discuss the first two impacts; here, I elaborate on the third.

Even after the revolutionary transformation, one central community feature remained intact: Members of the same lineage or clan lived together. Thus, the new state inadvertently retained a social basis for traditional identities. Indeed, in 1961, the administration system formed production teams based on geographical convenience, converting lineage houses into economic units. A team was a corporate unit that collectively owned land and distributed food shares; it also constituted the lowest political unit. These economic and political arrangements replaced the ancestor-worship organization as the integrating social force.

The new state showed its strength by preempting unsanctioned collective violence. Communal riots and clan fighting all but disappeared. Violence, however, was still commonplace and was channeled into class-struggle campaigns. Here, competition among the lineages played a hidden role. According to my informants, during the Land Reform, state work-teams balanced the number of targets from each lineage or clan. There also was a division of labor in punishment: Poor family members from the same lineage could give only verbal denunciations, whereas villagers from rival clans did the beating or, sometimes, the killing.

At the elite level, village leadership continued to be dominated by representatives from strong lineages. Ethnographic accounts suggest that this is common in North China.[40] Zhao Litao documents that in "S" village in Hebei, power rotated between the two largest lineages.[41] Similar patterns are reported in research on villages in Guangdong Province.[42] In Jinkeng, a Hakka village where I conducted in-depth interviews, the party secretary was a Li at the outset of the Cultural Revolution. He was overthrown by a Zeng during the power-seizure campaign. Later, when forming the village revolutionary committee, Lis and Zengs fought to a deadlock. As a compromise, commune authorities then chose a Su, but his administration was heavily controlled by Zeng and Li representatives. Su elders told me that Secretary Su did not accomplish much for the Sus during his tenure. In the latter years of the Cultural Revolution, the village was allowed to recommend two youths to attend college – the most coveted prize in many years. Both young men chosen were from the Zeng lineage.[43]

Culture and Collective Killings

The Chinese public, as well as some scholars, tends to invoke a cultural explanation for the atrocities in Guangxi and Guangdong Provinces. They view this region as a "land of Southern aboriginals" (*nanman zhidi*), who are peculiarly prone to violence. After all, it was home to the Taiping Rebellions in the mid-nineteenth century that claimed as many as seventy million lives,[44] not to mention the frequent ethnic riots before the

40 Edward Friedman, Paul Pickowicz, and Mark Selden, *Chinese Village, Socialist State* (New Haven, CT: Yale University Press, 1991); Zhao Litao, 1999.

41 Zhao Litao, 1999.

42 Anita Chan, Richard Madsen, and Jonathan Unger, *Chen Village: The Recent History of a Peasant Community in Mao's China* (Berkeley: University of California Press, 1984); Helen F. Siu, *Agents and Victims in South China: Accomplices in Rural Revolution* (New Haven, CT: Yale University Press, 1989).

43 Personal interviews with Jinkeng villagers.

44 Ge Jianxiong 葛剑雄, Wu Songdi 吴松弟, Cao Shuji 曹树基, *Zhongguo yiminshi: Diyijuan* 中国移民史: 第_卷 [*China's Immigration History: Volume 1*] (Fuzhou, Fujian: Fujian renmin chubanshe, 1997), p. 46.

TABLE 3.3. *Average Number of Deaths in Guangxi Province: Comparison between Minority and Han Counties*

	Counties with None or Less Than 50% Minorities Population	Counties with 50% or More Minorities Population
Deaths per county	835.8	564.1
Number of counties	32	32

revolution.[45] It was also a region, particularly in Guangxi, with a high concentration of ethnic minorities. This cultural argument may have some truth to it, but close examination reveals that the impact of culture is not straightforward.

Previously, I presented anecdotal evidence for clan identities being a cultural factor in the 1967–1968 collective killings. We therefore can expect that the more salient such identities are among a group, the more likely is the occurrence of collective killings. In my review of the migration history of the two provinces, I also established that the frontier mentality had rendered clan identities especially salient in South China. In the long history of inter- and intra-subethnic conflict among the Han Chinese, the Hakka group was the most deeply immersed in the clan culture described above. Therefore, we expect collective killing to be more severe among the Han population than among ethnic minorities; among the Han Chinese, we expect collective killing to be more severe among the Hakka than among other dialect groups.

Indeed, as shown in Table 3.3, counties with minority populations had a lower rate of deaths during the Cultural Revolution than those counties inhabited mainly by Han Chinese. The Guangxi counties are divided by those with 50 percent or more and those with none or less than 50 percent ethnic minorities. The first group of counties with a majority of ethnic minorities had an average of 564.1 deaths during the Cultural Revolution, whereas the counties with mostly Han Chinese had an average of 835.8 deaths. This is a sizable difference and it is statistically significant in a multivariate context (see Chapter 8). This finding suggests that if culture in this sense was a factor in collective killings, then we must examine its forms and effects among the Han Chinese.

45 Liu Ping 刘平, *Bei yiwan de zhanzheng: Xianfeng Tongzhi nianjian Guangdong tuke daxiedou yanjiu* 被遗忘的战争 – 咸丰同治年间广东土客大械斗研究 [*The Hakka–Punti War in Guangdong 1854–1867*] (Beijing: Shangwu yinshuguan, 2003).

TABLE 3.4. *Average Number of Deaths in Guangdong Province: Comparison between Hakka and Mixed Counties*

	Hakka Counties	Counties with Hakka and Non-Hakka
Deaths per county	441.1	274.6
Number of counties	12	42

My data also show that the presence of the subethnic Han group known as the Hakka is positively associated with collective killing. The population composition in the two provinces enables two types of comparison to be made. For Guangdong Province, I contrasted counties with a pure Hakka population to counties populated by both Hakka and other Han subethnic groups. As shown in Table 3.4, the pure Hakka counties have a higher death rate than those with a mixed population: 441.1 versus 274.6 deaths – a 38 percent difference. For Guangxi Province, I contrasted counties with a significant Hakka presence to those without a Hakka population. Again, this comparison demonstrates a Hakka effect: Counties with a Hakka population averaged 873.6 deaths, whereas those without averaged 631.9 deaths (Table 3.5).

These descriptive data suggest that a factor within the Hakka group may have determined the rate of collective killings. The lineage divisions among the Han Chinese may be a cultural factor that contributed to eliminationist killing. Among the different groups, ethnic minorities score the lowest in terms of killings, whereas the Hakka score the highest; other subethnic Han groups including Cantonese, Chaozhou, and Xi'nan Guanhua fall between the two scores. Although collective killing is found to be the most severe among the Hakka populations, the atrocities of the Cultural Revolution were not exclusive to the Hakka. Tables 3.3 through 3.5 show that death counts in non-Hakka counties are also significant. The main point of this comparison is shown by the differential effects of the cultural tradition of Han clan identities. The Hakka

TABLE 3.5. *Average Number of Deaths in Guangxi Province: Comparison between Counties with and without a Significant Hakka Population*

	Counties with Hakka	Counties without Hakka
Deaths per county	873.6	631.9
Number of counties	18	46

group was the most deeply immersed and the ethnic minority groups the least; other dialect groups fell somewhere in between. The extent of collective killings in the Cultural Revolution seems to correspond to this order.

Conclusion

During the Cultural Revolution, collective killings in the countryside were committed in the name of class struggle. However, class identities were imposed on villagers from the outside. Existing reports and my research suggest that victims and perpetrators typically were from different lineage groups. This can be explained by the facts that lineage division was the most salient social cleavage and a village was often composed of multiple lineages. These facts deserve our attention when we try to understand the process of identity formation in collective killing.

However, I do not consider lineage division a sufficient condition for eliminationist killing. Lineage divisions are common in rural China, but only in very few villages and townships did the collective killings take place during the Cultural Revolution. Neither do I consider such divisions to be a necessary condition; in any given community, several other potential divisions may have contributed to the atrocities.

Nonetheless, lineage identity was an important local impetus. The deep-seated in-group/out-group custom eased the process of treating others as outside one's own moral universe. Indeed, local actors adopted the new class identities not as a replacement but rather as an addition: Lineage identity persisted in new struggles and animated actions against the victims chosen from rival clans. The traditional identity was also behind village politics among the new elite, and surname lineage often marked political fault lines. This matters because village cadres were the key individuals who interpreted the war rhetoric promoted from outside and who made decisions about local responses in 1967 and 1968.

Furthermore, my discussion provides a cultural perspective for understanding why Guangdong and Guangxi Provinces are two exceptionally atrocious cases. In South China, the common institution of lineage found an intensified expression in a frontier culture of emigrants. Ethnic competition and conflict sharpened the need for group survival beyond the extended family. The Hakka stood out as a group that fiercely practiced the lineage tradition. If southerners "out-Chinesed" northerners in this regard, then the Hakka group was extreme. Indeed, as the data demonstrate, Hakka counties are associated with collective killings within the bloody provinces of Guangxi and Guangdong.

However, perceiving others as members of an out-group in daily life is many logical steps from eliminationist killing. Another key step is the class label imposed by the revolution, a subject discussed in Chapter 4.

4

Class Enemies

In recounting a violent scene, a *xianzhi* compiler in Xingning County, Guangdong Province, focused on an encounter between a victim of the Cultural Revolution and a group of middle-school students. This moment combined innocence, hatred, and brutality and it raises questions about the concept of class enemies in Mao's China and the impetus behind ordinary people's contempt, hatred, and disregard of them.[1] It was the summer of 1968; the place was *dabali*, or the Great Beach, an open space adjacent to a bank of the Ningjiang River, which runs through the county seat. A struggle rally had been attended by more than ten thousand people, including not only residents from the town but also peasants from nearby communes. Each commune had brought its own Four Types as struggle targets.[2] A joint session like this one was rare; in less fanatical times, each commune would have its own rally. However, the Party Center had recently issued two new directives. The rally ended, the crowds receded, and militiamen began escorting struggle targets back to their respective townships. In at least four instances, however, the formations quickly degenerated into beatings and killings of the captives.[3]

[1] Personal interview with Mr. Liu, 2006.

[2] In this instance, a fifth category, "rightists," was added to the usual Four Types in Xingning County's lexicon, "landlords," "rich peasants," "counter-revolutionaries," and "bad elements."

[3] According to Liu, the *xianzhi* 县志 compiler, he witnessed at least seven killings as he took a walk that afternoon. Based on his reading of an internal document that he could not share with me, the death toll that day was more than two hundred. The county's *xianzhi* 县志 recorded six hundred "unnatural deaths" in those two months of "wild beatings and wild killings." *Xingning xian difang zhi bianxiu weiyuanhui* 兴宁县地方志编修委员会

Among the dead and injured lay Mr. Lan, a man in his early forties.[4] The road was deserted and daylight was waning when a group of middle-school students passed and noticed the bloody and broken body. Mr. Lan moved his lips, possibly asking for a sip of water or pleading for help. The teenagers did not know him, but from the mere fact that he was beaten in this particular setting – they either had attended the rally or were aware of it – they knew that he was a dying class enemy. Instead of extending a helping hand, the teenagers pelted Mr. Lan with rocks. They landed thirty or more; no one knows whether he died before their target practice ended.[5]

This disregard for human life is astonishing when observed from afar. At that time and place, however, the teenagers simply acted in accordance with the situation as defined by society and their parents. The key element of the situation was the concept of class enemy and, with it, the appropriate ways of treating one. Years of education and propaganda had immersed them in this definition. From the teenagers' reaction, we can infer a collective definition of *class enemies*, or individuals who could be killed justifiably. Where did this definition come from? Moreover, the term *class enemies* is a misnomer. Targeted individuals were not only those who had benefited from land ownership but also family members who were born after the Land Reform movement. Therefore, the victims were not defined primarily in economic terms – as the word *class* may suggest – but rather by a set of social and political rules and processes. Historians may characterize Mao's China after 1949 as a time of peace, given the absence of conventional wars; however, that was not what the state's subjects – either the designated "class enemies" or "the masses" – experienced. To understand the tragedy of Mr. Lan and many others like

Xingning xianzhi 兴宁县志 [Xingning County Gazetteer] (Guangzhou: Guangdong renmin chubanshe, 1998).

4 Liu cannot recall the full name but knows that he was a nephew of Lan Shengqing and a son of Lan Daihan, two high-ranking officials in Xingning.

5 Personal interviews with Liu, 2006. Such teenager brutality was by no means uncommon, as attested to by rampant Red Guard violence in urban centers. See Wang Youqin 王友琴, *Wen'ge shounan zhe: guanyu pohai, jianjin yu shalu de xunfang shilu* 文革受难者–关于迫害，监禁与杀戮的寻访实录, available at http://www.xindoor.com/zhuanyeziliao/ShowSoft.asp?SoftID=669, accessed August 26, 2008. In another rural setting, He Jiangsui reported that those local toughs who beat the landlord Ma Zhongtai to death were too young to know Ma or his past deeds. "At that time, Zhongtai, in the view of the radical youths, was not an old man of blood and flesh, but a representative of the 'evil' landlord class, as they learned in school." See Jiangsui He, "The Death of a Landlord: Moral Predicament in Rural China, 1968–1969," in Esherick, Pickowicz, and Walder (eds.), *China's Cultural Revolution as History*, p. 146.

him – some of whom were murdered along with their young children and elderly parents – we must understand the concept of class enemy in Mao's China.

A Constructionist View of Victim Identity

In the history of collective killings, we are familiar with clear demarcations of victim identities such as Jews, Armenians, and Tutsis. It is no coincidence that the early scholars of eliminationist killing used the concept of genocide, noting that destruction is usually aimed at an easily identifiable and self-conscious ethnic or national group. However, scholars quickly ran into complexity as a result of two related findings. First, preexisting social divisions are not good indicators of genocide and mass killing; prior ethnic divisions, for instance, cannot predict genocide.[6] Second, victims of mass killings in communist countries (e.g., China, the Soviet Union, and Cambodia) were newly defined by the states, and victims and perpetrators were often drawn from the same ethnic groups.[7] Indeed, the process of constructing the victim identity by the state is common even in paradigmatic cases such as the Holocaust and the Armenian and Rwandan genocides.[8] In other words, it is the state's interpretation of group boundaries, instead of the existing boundaries that matters. This constructionist insight guides the most recent scholarship on genocide

[6] Valentino provides a concise review and a forceful critique of what he called theories related to preexisting social cleavages, including the theories of plural society. See Valentino, *Final Solutions*, pp. 17–22. See also Harrf's 2003 regression analysis that includes fifty-three cases of genocide, which finds that the variable of prior ethnic division is not significant to predict the occurrence of genocide. Barbara Harff, "No Lessons Learned from the Holocaust? Accessing Risks of Genocide and Political Mass Murder since 1955," *American Political Science Review* 97, no. 1 (2003), pp. 57–73.

[7] Valentino, *Final Solutions*, pp. 18–22; ibid., chap. 4, pp. 91–151. See also Michael Mann, *The Dark Side of Democracy: Explaining Ethnic Cleansing* (New York: Cambridge University Press, 2005), chap. 11, pp. 318–427.

[8] Hilberg (1985) argued that although the discrimination against Jews was age-old, the escalation of mistreatment was based on new waves of state propaganda of Jews as a threat and subhuman. See Hilberg, *The Destruction of the European Jews*. And, according to Gourevitch (1998), the ethnic concepts of Hutus and Tutsis did not become salient until the Belgian colonists chose the lighter skin Tutsis to rule the Hutus. See Gourevitch, *We Wish to Inform You that Tomorrow We Will Be Killed with our Families*. See also Straus, *The Order of Genocide*. For the state propaganda against Armenians before and during the 1915 genocide, see Robert Melson, *Revolution and Genocide: On the Origins of the Armenian Genocide and the Holocaust* (Chicago: The University of Chicago Press, 1992); Florence Mazian, *Why Genocide?: The Armenian and Jewish Experiences in Perspective* (Ames: Iowa State University Press, 1990), chap. 1, pp. 3–19.

and mass killing.[9] In defining *genocide*, some scholars state "that group [victims] and membership in it are defined by the perpetrator."[10]

To appreciate that the victim group is newly constructed has two theoretical implications. First, it enables us to in turn appreciate the contemporaneous forces that contribute to defining victimhood. Second, it enables us to understand why eliminationist killings take place at a particular moment, despite the fact that stigmatization and discrimination have long existed. With regard to the Chinese case at hand, this insight is the foundation of my community model. This and the next few chapters explore the contemporaneous forces that led existing group divisions to take on a genocidal dimension. The so-called class enemy as a category of the rural population had been in place for about two decades after 1949, but not until the Cultural Revolution did it become a victim group for eliminationist killing. This development cannot be explained by the communist doctrine of a classless society because the doctrine as previously practiced in China, for the most part, was not to create this society by physical elimination. Neither can it be explained by the notion that previously propertied classes posed an objective threat, hence that their elimination was imperative. This review of the origin of *class enemy* demonstrates that its creation, maintenance, and treatment all served the politics of the times. Mass-killing scholars who draw on political violence in communist societies for comparison, however, often take a realist view of the concept of class enemy (or "people's enemy," in the case of the Soviet Union). That is, they write as though the opposition to the new communist system was real, with *class enemy* identifying a broad category of individuals who represent plausible or incipient opposition or resistance to the state. In the 1960s, Dallin and Breslauer wrote that "Anticipating such hostility, the authorities, in line with their preconceptions and images of class or group loyalties and grievances, may identify certain strata as requiring preemptive, or prophylactic, suppression, intimidations or removal."[11] The gist of the argument remains unchanged in Mann's (2006) book:

> The vanguard party was faced with an obdurate society and enemies at home and abroad. Capitalists, landlords, petty bourgeois, monarchs, and churches were marked for elimination. But they resisted, aided from

[9] See studies cited previously in notes 6, 7, and 8.
[10] Chalk and Jonassohn *The History and Sociology of Genocide*.
[11] Dallin and Breslauer, *Political Terror in Communist Systems*, p. 6.

> abroad.... The people were the proletariat, and classes opposed to the proletariat were enemies of the people. Communists might be tempted to eliminate classes through murder. I term this *classicide.*[12]

Three components in this realist view are separate from historical evidence, however – at least in the case of communist China. First, the definition of class enemy is supposed to have a real economic base or occupy standard economic positions. In China, one expects former landlords, rich peasants, and capitalists to comprise the category of class enemies. However, if that were true in part in the three years after 1949, those individuals were quickly and completely dispossessed. Their descendents – who bore the brunt of the discrimination and class-struggle campaigns and abuses – certainly were not landlords or large landowners. Even during the Land Reform movement of 1951–1952, many were classified as landlords or rich peasants not based on previous ownership of large tracts of land but rather because of an implicit quota dictated by a political campaign to produce sufficient numbers of class enemies.

Second, those individuals are posited to represent an actual opposition, resistance, or challenge to the communist state. Again, this may have been true two or three years after the 1949 revolution, when the Nationalist Party (or GMD) army still remained in remote pockets of the country (e.g., the regions of Guangxi and Western Hunan). However, in most areas, the Land Reform movement occurred without incident or recrimination. By the mid-1950s, moreover, those who were designated class enemies, whatever their prior economic circumstances, were organizationally deprived and kept under tight surveillance. They dared not utter any criticism of the regime, even in private settings – let alone pose any meaningful collective resistance. Those individuals were repeatedly subjected to discrimination, violence, and sometimes death – not for their deeds but instead for political labels attached to them and then passed down to their descendants patrilineally. It was a type of primogeniture in which no land was bequeathed – only an unfortunate and unwanted political status that severely limited a recipient's life chances.

Third, according to Mann's realist view, the communist regime was "tempted to eliminate classes through murder."[13] However, the exact opposite was true. After the Land Reform movement, China was

[12] Mann, *The Dark Side of Democracy*, chap. 11, pp. 319–320.
[13] Ibid.

transformed into a classless society, if defined only in terms of property.[14] From this classless society, the state created an artificial divide between "the people" and the "class enemy." The toothless enemy class was never designed to be eliminated, either by murder or other means. In the first place, the numbers of class enemies were inflated. Quotas were established and sanctions were applied to local leadership if localities did not have a certain percentage of landlords and rich peasants; the numbers were always greater than their initial landed status would warrant. To underscore the artificiality and arbitrariness of this designation, a few years after Mao's death, class enemies were eliminated as a political class – not by murder but rather by declaration – once the new leadership decided that the categories and campaigns had become counterproductive.

Therefore, the class divides were imposed and maintained by the state and perpetuated through state-sponsored mass campaigns. What purpose, then, did the existence of a constructed enemy class serve? The answer links this artificial class divide to two main political tasks: mobilizing mass compliance and resolving elite conflict. These linkages are the key to understanding why the system deepened the politically constructed divides in times of political crisis. Its elastic nature, then, is the key to understanding why the class categorization could take on a genocidal dimension under extraordinary circumstances.

A Landlord Family in the Land Reform

In 1949, Jin Zhilong was four years old when his father abandoned his family – including his wife and four children, their ages ranging from four to eleven – and fled to Taiwan. They were left to suffer the fate of a landlord family in Jinkeng Village in Xingning County, Guangdong Province. By the time of the Cultural Revolution, Jin – then in his early twenties – was the only member of his family left and on his shoulders was placed the burden of his father's former class status. He was a punching-bag fixture at struggle rallies and parades, and he only narrowly survived the Cultural Revolution. He was sixty-two when I visited him in 2006. During our conversation, he repeated several times a famous quote from Mao: "*Chusheng* may not be up to you, but a life path is within your choice." In Chinese, *Chusheng* means "family background." During the

14 One may argue that the society is not classless in a different sense. That is, the cadres became a de facto bureaucratic class. See Hung Yong Lee, *Politics of the Cultural Revolution*. This being true, the class picture in the propaganda did not exist.

interview, at times Jin seemed genuinely perplexed by the contradiction between his ordeal and the quote; at other times, he seemed to use it ruefully to express his frustration and indignation. His life path could have been very different: if either of his parents or his brother, six years his senior, had remained in the village, Jin would not have been the struggle target. However, his father had fled, his mother had died, and his older brother had been adopted by relatives in another village.

Class enemies in Mao's China were defined and used for their symbolic functions. Prior behavior or even family background mattered less than the needs of mass campaigns for enemies, always called "class enemies." For example, if there were no landlord in a village, a rich peasant would be used. If the family's male householder were absent, his wife or eldest son would serve just as well. The scope of the targeting depended on the rigor of the class-struggle campaign. Such a relationship between a flexible definition and campaign demand is the key to understanding the various fates and harshness of the treatment that befell many.

After the Cultural Revolution, Jin married and moved to his wife's village of Ganzhuan, about 15 *li* from Jinkeng Village. They had two children. In 1979, he was reunited with his father in Hong Kong for the first time in thirty years. When I visited him in 2006, Jin was living a prosperous life in the county seat. He and his family had left behind village life, like many others who had succeeded in China's economic boom in the 1990s. I met with him in the storefront of his family's pharmacy.

In the early 1930s, Jin's father graduated from a spin-off institute of the famous Huangpu [Whampoa] Military Academy in Guangzhou. He was wounded and slightly paralyzed in a battle during the Anti-Japanese War. After the war, he stayed in his hometown and worked first as district police chief and then as district magistrate. Wachitang, a community of a surname clan in Jinkeng, was home. Wachitang consisted of three traditional Hakka *weilongwu*, or circled dragon houses, built in a row adjacent to the mountain. Each house was inhabited by ten Jin families. In this and many other surname communities in the Hakka region of Guangdong Province, the rich and the poor lived together in the *weilongwu* inherited from common ancestors. A family's living space ebbed and flowed depending on its fortunes, as did their land. However, the community banded together in their traditional rituals (e.g., ancestor worship) and in solidarity against other surname communities in the village. When a person addressed anyone who was his or her senior, a title was required that indicated blood relationship (e.g., "sister," "brother," "uncle," or "grandpa"). Jinkeng had five surname clans. The three primary clans – the Jins, the Zengs, and the Lis – were known for their fierce competitiveness since the time of the dynasties. Before the revolution, communal battles broke out frequently. Older people remembered at least two incidents in which Jins and Zengs fought with firearms; a Zeng was killed each time.[15]

In such an environment, anyone ascending to the position of government official brought power and prestige to the surname group. Compared to clan lines, class lines were unimportant – an alien concept.[16] Therefore, Jin's father was something of a local hero – until the Liberation. He had had to leave Xingning for Taiwan so hastily, Jin insisted, that it was impossible to arrange a family exodus, and the situation was so tense and precarious that he did not dare to bring his Huangpu Military Academy diploma with him. He left instructions to have it sent to him, but to no avail. Once he was in Taiwan, Jin's father could not prove who he was and was forced to make a living outside of government service – an undesirable life compared to other GMD ranking officials. Needless to say, he was more fortunate than his wife and children whom he left behind in the mainland.

When the Land Reform movement started in late 1950, Xingning was one of three counties chosen to initiate the reforms in Guangdong Province. Initially, Jin's family was doubly classified as "counterrevolutionary" for his father's service to the deposed Nationalist government and "rich peasant" for the land they owned. With his father absent, his mother answered to the new government as the householder, although family members suffered no physical abuse.

Then, in mid-1951, the Land Reform campaign was relaunched as the Land Reform Rectification. The family's status was upgraded from rich peasant to landlord. Jin's mother was rounded up with other householders of landlord and rich peasant families and repeatedly tortured in the struggle sessions or afterwards. When I visited Jinkeng, older villagers vividly described the torture scenes. That Jin's mother was repeatedly hung by

[15] Personal interview with Mr. Ping, 2006.

[16] As Vogel (1969) stated when he comments on the potential resistances to the class struggle in the Land Reform in Guangdong Province: "The essential fabric of Chinese society was based not on social class but on personal relationships between people in the same village, same surname, same lineage, same school, and same place of work.... The critical cleavages in pre-1949 rural China were not those between middle peasants and rich peasants but between one lineage and another, between one village and another." Vogel, *Canton under Communism*, p. 102.

one of her hands appeared to be common knowledge. The declared goal of the torture was to extract information regarding her family's supposed "hidden treasure." According to one of her neighbors, "Every time she was hung up, she would give out a location for hidden gold, silver, jewelries or even guns. There followed a lot of digging with nothing found. Then she would be hung up again, and a new location. The process went on and on."

Jin was then six years old. With nothing to eat at home, he and his brother, who was thirteen, sought support from an aunt who lived in another village. They were fed and given some sweet-potato chips for the trip home; which they packed and intended to share with their two sisters at home, ages eight and ten. However, on the village road, they met a distant relative, who was the head of the village women's association; they addressed her respectfully as "sister-in-law," as required by local tradition. When she discovered their sweet-potato chips, she confiscated them. They did not resist, but Jin's brother made an empty threat that would cause trouble later: "I will find a knife and stab you!" He was quickly detained by militiamen, which unnerved and unhinged his mother, who had been detained in another room. She attempted suicide by jumping from the rooftop; she died in the detention room a few days later. Three of her four orphans were adopted by relatives in other villages, thus removing their status and label as secondary class enemies. However, Jin Zhilong, her youngest son – who was never a landowner or ever benefited from the land – remained in the village and inherited the negative status, as a primary class enemy, of a father he barely knew. He would later face the terror that was the Cultural Revolution.

The torture and suicide of Jin's mother during the Land Reform Rectification campaign was not unusual. Through a personal connection, I was able to visit the Xingning County Archives that housed the government's internal documents. Under the category of "Xingning County Party Committee," I found three documents that recorded deaths and suicides in this period. In a document dated November 22, 1952, there is a report entitled "Statistics of Suicides in 31 *xiang* [Townships] of 3 Districts of Xingning" (Volume 013, p. 14). Another report, entitled "Surveys of Suicides in No. 6 District" and dated 1952, listed more than twenty tables (Volume 013, p. 25). A third document, dated August 2, 1952, is entitled "Death Statistics during the Second Settling-Scores Struggle Campaigns" (Volume 013, p. 33). Unfortunately, I was only allowed to read the titles; no note-taking was allowed.

TABLE 4.1. *Class Composition and Land Ownership before and after the Land Reform, Xingning County, Guangdong Province, 1950–1953*[17]

Class	Household	Percent Household	Population	Percent Population	Land before (mu per person)	Land after (mu per person)
Landlord	1,108	0.95	9,948	2.04	12.40	0.60
Rich Peasant	2,009	1.72	16,979	3.48	1.26	1.00
Middle Peasant	34,585	29.62	159,491	32.71	0.74	0.87
Poor Peasant	72,386	61.99	287,492	58.99	0.28	0.64
Other		5.72		2.78		
TOTALS	116,775	100	487,624	100	0.74	0.74

Note: Rich Peasants = 富农+半地主式富农; Poor Peasants = 贫农+雇农.
Source: Xingning *xianzhi* (Xingning Gazetteers).

The Land Reform: The Creation of Class Labels by Economic Distinctions

Jin's family was one of the 1,108 households in Xingning County in Guangdong Province that were classified as landlords. Another 2,009 families were classified as rich peasants. Indeed, before the Land Reform, the landlords and rich peasants owned more land than middle and poor peasants. Land ownership per person was 12.40, 1.26, 0.74, and 0.28 mu, respectively (Table 4.1). In this rice-planting region, the land–population ratio was pitifully small, with less than 1 mu per capita (there are 15 *mu* in 1 acre; 1 mu yields approximately 300 kilograms of rice). Before the Land Reform, although landlords owned substantially more land than other groups (i.e., 12.40 *mu* per capita, or more than fourteen times the average), the term *rich peasants* was something of a misnomer because they owned only 1.26 mu per capita, or less than one-tenth of an acre. Landlords leased a significant portion of their land to tenants; rich peasants typically had far less land, worked at least part of it themselves.[18]

The Land Reform underwent two stages, which were repeated in many communities. The first stage was more or less an economic project that was met with virtually no resistance. Some struggle rallies were held but, overall, it was a peaceful exercise of tallying land and redistributing

[17] The People's Republic of China Land Reform Law, 1950.

[18] *Xingning xian difang zhi bianxiu weiyuanhui* 兴宁县地方志编修委员会 *Xingning xianzhi* 兴宁县志 [Xingning County Gazetteer] (Guangzhou: Guangdong renmin chubanshe, 1998), p. 174.

it among community members. This peaceful process is exemplified in the story of Li Maoxiu, whose family was classified as one of the three landlords in Wugong Village in Hebei Province. Li's father had died a few months earlier and his older brother was serving in the communist army. So, although Li was only a teenager, he was treated as a householder in receiving the following news:

> Maoxiu waited in the household courtyard for the delegation, which included two farmhands hired by the Lis. Treating teenager Maoxiu as household head, the delegates declared that compensation was required to settle accounts for past "exploitation" He listened to the demands and accepted them. There was no violence. The festive delegates left accompanied by clanging gongs and booming drums.... A few days after family labels were decided on in Wugong, a confiscation committee completed the transfer. The Lis were left 21 mu of land for the seven household members, an amount equal to per capita holdings of middle peasant households in 1946. They continued to live in one corner of the ample Li courtyard, now shared with seven poorer households. At the meeting following the confiscation, Li Maoxiu was praised for his cooperative attitude.[19]

The land redistribution stage of the Land Reform progressed relatively smoothly, in part because "class" was a new concept for ordinary people. Although the people were aware of who among them was better off, who was a power broker, and so on, relationships in the countryside were primarily defined by clan and lineage. A rich family in one's own clan was an asset in a community in which competition among clans was often fierce. Although the poorer people were happy to have more land, they usually did not see any need to punish those who lost their land because they were frequently other clan members. Aware of this fact, the local leadership carefully balanced the numbers of landlords and rich peasants for each lineage group; officials feared that class and clan cleavages might coincide too greatly. In other words, a class line could not take root in the local community merely by designating the rich and redistributing the land.

The rationale of the Land Reform was to end "exploitation." However, the claim that the "rich" – that is, those classified as landlords and rich peasants – lived by dint of exploitation in the Marxist sense was far from accurate. In fact, the majority of "rich peasants" were primarily laborers themselves who supplemented their income with land

[19] Friedman, Edward, Paul G. Pickowicz, and Mark Selden, *Chinese Village, Socialist State* (New Haven, CT: Yale University Press, 1991), p. 87.

they could not entirely work themselves. This reality was quickly lost in the implementation of the Land Reform because there was a commonly understood quota behind the designation of the new enemy class. Landlords and rich peasants, "less than 10 percent of the rural population," the directive asserted, "held approximately 70 to 80 percent of the land, cruelly exploiting the peasantry."[20]

In one of the early policy pronouncements on Land Reform, the Party Center announced this percentage before groups were designated to guide the creation of class enemies. Although there was no set rule regarding how much land a family must own to qualify as a class enemy, each community was expected to designate between 5 and 10 percent of its population. As shown in Table 4.1, in Jin's Xingning County, the Land Reform produced an enemy class (i.e., landlords and rich peasants) with 2.7 percent of households, or 5.5 percent of the county's population; in Wuhua County in Guangdong Province, it was 6.6 percent or 10.9 percent, respectively[21]; in Cangwu County, it was 9.3 and 12.5 percent, respectively[22]; and in Mengshan County, it was 5.5 percent of the population in one village.[23]

However, the land concentration varied across different regions and communities. Among the cited counties, Mengshan was the closest to the directive; its *xianzhi* records that 732 landlord households, or 3.5 percent of the county's total, owned 65.7 percent of the county's land. In Wuhua County, however, the landlords and rich peasants – 6.6 percent of households or 10.9 percent of the county population – owned only 27.9 percent of the county's land. In Xingning and Cangwu Counties, land owned by landlords and rich peasants was 44.4 and 41.7 percent, respectively. The unit of consideration was the household: Prosperous households had larger families than poor households; therefore, about 5 percent of households and about 10 percent of the population were typically designated as enemy families.

The Land Reform movement in the first stage was mainly an economic task – that is, the redistribution of land. The result was not only the

20 "Agrarian Reform Law," discussed by Selden and Eggleston. See Mark Selden and Patti Eggleston, *The People's Republic of China: A Documentary History of Revolutionary Change* (New York: Monthly Review Press, 1979), pp. 214–217.

21 *Wuhua xian difang zhi bianzuan weiyuanhui* 五华县地方志编纂委员会 *Wuhua xianzhi* 五华县志 [Wuhua County Gazetteer] (Guangzhou: Guangdong renmin chubanshe, 1998), pp. 104–105.

22 *Cangwu xianzhi bianzuan weiyuanhui* 苍梧县志编纂委员会 *Cangwu xianzhi* 苍梧县志 [Cangwu County Gazetteer] (Nanning: Guangxi remin chubanshe, 1997), p. 148.

23 *Mengshan xianzhi bianzuan weiyuanhui* 蒙山县志编纂委员会, *Mengshan xianzhi* 蒙山县志 [Mengshan County Gazetteer] (Nanning: Guangxi renmin chubanshe, 1993), p. 249.

redistribution of land but also the creation of new classes based in part on previous land ownership. The householder was given the title of landlord or rich-peasant element (*fenzi*), whereas the rest of the family was landlord or rich-peasant "family members" (*jiashu*). The *fenzi* was made to answer for the family's sins, whereas it was extremely rare for *jiashu* to be subjected to struggle or violence. However, the political labeling did not die with the initial titleholder; instead, it was passed down through the family patrilineally.

Land Reform Rectification: Solidifying Class Labels by Violence

After the redistribution of land, the second stage of Land Reform began, which was known as the Land Reform Rectification. Although this stage had economic aspects, it served almost entirely political purposes. Designated landlords and rich peasants were rounded up for confessions regarding their supposed hidden treasures; torture was not uncommon. It was during the rectification stage that hatred and antagonism evolved between the new enemy classes and everyone else, sowing seeds of a new social divide based on political labels. It started with criticism of local cadres such as those noted previously for being "soft" on enemies. This stage paralleled a cadre rectification in which many were accused of committing a line mistake and removed from leadership positions. In Guangdong Province, for example, "peaceful land reform" became a negative label from which local cadres wanted to disassociate.[24]

After new leaders replaced the former who had committed the errors of "peaceful land reform," terror and violence reigned. Activists were recruited from among the poorest people – particularly those who held a grudge against a struggle target – through a ritual called "speaking bitterness." Past hardships or complaints now had a class explanation. People were encouraged in struggle rallies to air any past dispute that involved a landlord or rich peasant, as evidence of a crime. These grievances were accompanied by much violence. For example, one activist attributed his land's low yield to a landlord's pine trees that blocked the sunlight (the landlord eventually compensated the activist 3,000 *jin* – about 1,500 kilograms – of sorghum). Another activist revealed that a landlord had bullied him into an unfair trade of his cow (which was returned for

[24] Ezra F. Vogel, *Canton under Communism: Programs and Politics in a Provincial capital, 1949–1968* (Cambridge, MA: Harvard University Press, 1969).

free to the activist).[25] In Nanban Village in Hunan Province, eleven of twenty-five landlords were hung by one hand to force confessions and then beaten. According to a survey about this village and nine others in October 1951, nineteen landlord household heads committed suicide due to the torture.[26]

In 1951, Mr. Zhao joined a Land Reform work-team at age nineteen. He told me that at first he was confused by the development of events. The directives from the Party Center he read were all about land; one even stipulated the protection of the livelihoods of the landlord and rich peasants. He wondered why "hidden treasure" was a Land Reform issue. His confusion ended when he read an editorial published in *Changjiang Daily*, which solved the puzzle: Land Reform was not only about land; it was a political project. Many of his superiors were accused of being soft on class enemies. A common saying at the time was: "Struggle against landlords in the daytime, and struggle against land reform cadres in the night." He witnessed many tortures. As the son of a landlord, Mr. Zhao saw his mother detained, soon to be tortured, who was spared only when he and his brothers raised funds and offered them as her hidden treasure.

The Land Reform violence sowed violent seeds for future political campaigns, culminating in those of the Cultural Revolution. It is not that the persecuted had a chance to fight back, which they did not, but rather because perpetrators of the violence wanted to forestall that possibility. In my interviews, I asked my local informants again and again how village neighbors could inflict extreme cruelty on their neighbors, so much more than their counterparts in urban areas. A common answer was revealing: In urban settings, they said, people did not know one another very well; if you beat someone in a struggle rally, it was likely that the perpetrator and the victim would never see one another again. However, in a village, if a victim survived, he or she knew exactly who the tormentor was and would potentially seek revenge. As one interviewee told me, "That is why when you beat someone, you better kill him; even if you kill him, his brothers or sons may come at you at another time in a

[25] Wang Youmin 王友民, *Geming yu xiangcun: Jiefangqu tudi gaige yanjiu: 1941–1949, yi shangdong junanxian wei geang* 革命与乡村：解放区土地改革研究：1941–1949，以山东莒南县为个案 [translation here] (Shanghai: Shanghai shehui kexueyuan chubanshe, 2006), pp. 101–102.

[26] Huang Ronghua 黄荣华, *Geming yu xiangcun: Nongcun diquan yanjiu: 1949–1983, yi hubeisheng xinzhouxian wei ge'an* 革命与乡村：农村地权研究：1949–1983，以湖北省新洲县为个案 (Shanghai: Shanghai shehui kexueyuan chubanshe, 2006), p. 31.

different campaign." This reasoning may be behind the many collective killings in the Cultural Revolution that targeted all male members of a victim's family. In another vivid account, Zheng Yi described a pogrom in Wenping Village in Mengshan County, Guangxi Province, in which killers identified infant boys for murder by first touching their crotch.[27] With the males eliminated, an entire family would disappear because female members would eventually remarry out of the village.

The basis of class labels in land ownership was lost quickly. By late 1952, no family would own significantly more land than any other family (see the last column in Table 4.1). In any case, land would soon be owned collectively through the collectivization and commune campaigns of the 1950s. Laborers with good family standing became "commune members" who toiled for "work points." Former landlords and rich peasants – landless like everyone else – were put under community surveillance, to labor partly free for various community projects, partly for minimum living subsistence.

Although the class divide lost its economic base, the treatment of these groups as a class continued as a political project, beginning in the second stage of Land Reform and repeated and reinforced in later campaigns. Ironically, their land deprivation and subsequent suffering became the new basis for their misfortune. The artificial class divide gained local significance in the community through repeated violent struggles. The logic was simple and commonly understood: Because the victims lost land and were tortured, they must be hostile to the system and always dreaming of a day of "changed sky." Their previous status was their permanent crime, regardless of their actions in the new era.

The two-stage approach of Land Reform in 1950s in the south had its origins in the Communist base in the north in the 1940s. It has been reported that as early as 1933, Mao proposed the basic economic and political stages of the Land Reform. Problems with the process and results in the period before the GMD defeat may have spurred the policy that was enforced afterward.[28] During the Anti-Japanese War between 1937 and 1945, the Party required the mobilization of all classes to fight the invaders; in the communist base, the second stage was skipped over. Land was redistributed and, in many cases, landlords and rich peasants

27 Zheng Yi 郑义, *Hongse jinianbei* 红色纪念碑 [The Scarlet Memorial] (Taipei, Taiwan: Huashi wenhua gongsi, 1993).

28 Wang Youmin 王友民, *Geming yu xiangcun: Jiefangqu tudi gaige yanjiu: 1941–1949, yi shangdong junanxian wei ge'an* 革命与乡村：解放区土地改革研究：1941–1949，以山东莒南县为个案 [translation here] (Shanghai: Shanghai shehui kexueyuan chubanshe, 2006), p. 75.

still owned slightly more than the originally landless, but there was no violent effort to drive a wedge in the community.[29] A new round of Land Reform was conducted in the communist bases after the Anti-Japanese War. In 1946, a central directive known as the May-Fourth Instructions was promulgated in local communities.[30] After ten years of communist occupation, land had long since been redistributed, and every householder was now a middle peasant. At first, local cadres were at a loss about what to do. As one county leader recalled:

> The land issue had basically been resolved in Binghai Base area. Poor peasants and hired laborers now owned more land than landlords.... After we studied [the May-Fourth Instructions] and deliberated, we decided that we would end up hurting the interests of poor peasants and hired laborers if we did over the land redistribution. That would not be good for protecting the fruits of the revolutionary victories.[31]

However, inaction in the local community was not tolerated at the top. On August 25, 1946, the Binghai Prefecture, a communist base in Shandong Province, issued "supplementary instructions" to roundly repudiate local leaders who were accused of having committed a line mistake, which was a serious charge in the communist system. The leaders of Lunan County mobilized activists to search for unresolved issues involving landlords and rich peasants. "Whether the land issue was salient, it is imperative to train activists. Search for the root of poverty, and demand more land." If there was no landlord in a village, rich peasants were the targets; if there were no rich peasants, land belonging to middle peasants was reconsidered.[32]

[29] See Mark Selden, *The Yenan Way in Revolutionary China* (Cambridge, MA: Harvard University Press, 1971); Mark Selden, *China in Revolution: The Yenan Way Revisited* (Armonk, NY: M. E. Sharpe, 1995). See also Chen's discussion on the Chinese revolution in Chen Yung-fa 陈永发, *Making Revolution: The Communist Movement in Eastern and Central China, 1937–1945* (Berkeley, CA: University of California Press, 1986). See also Chalmers A. Johnson, *Peasant Nationalism and Communist Power: The Emergence of Revolutionary China 1937–1945* (Stanford, CA: Stanford University Press, 1962); Friedman, Edward, Paul G. Pickowicz, and Mark Selden, *Chinese Village, Socialist State* (New Haven, CT: Yale University Press, 1991).

[30] Edward Friedman, Paul Pickowicz, and Mark Selden, *Revolution, Resistance, and Reform in Village China* (New Haven, CT: Yale University Press, 2005), pp. 80–110.

[31] Wang Youmin 王友民, *Geming yu xiangcun: Jiefangqu tudi gaige yanjiu: 1941–1949, yi shangdong junanxian wei geang* 革命与乡村: 解放区土地改革研究: 1941–1949, 以山东莒南县为个案 [translation here] (Shanghai: Shanghai shehui kexueyuan chubanshe, 2006), p. 70.

[32] Ibid., pp. 70–74.

In another communist base in Hebei, leaders of Wugong Village who were fearful of being charged with line mistakes, found a different way out of their predicament. They decided to conduct the new Land Reform and create new enemy-class statuses not based on existing ownership but rather on land ownership ten years earlier, before the communist occupation. In Wugong Village, land was more or less evenly distributed; every household was considered a middle-peasant household. In the previous ten years, those who had lost land to the poorer peasants had been equally active in supporting the war effort; many had sent their sons to fight at the frontlines. This was not considered; after village leaders convened activists to recall the amount of land owned by each family ten years before, two landlords and three rich peasants were classified. As described previously, teenager Li Maoxiu, whose brother was a communist fighter at the frontlines, was retroactively declared such a landlord.[33]

However, these new class declarations usually were not enough to establish and consolidate a class divide in local communities; that would be accomplished by the rectification that immediately followed. Leaders in Lunan County were accused of taking a "rich peasant line," and the rectification was billed as a campaign to identify "spies" from cadres and peasants. Li Yu and other top leaders were publicly repudiated and removed from their posts. The new county leadership issued a Rectification Work Plan, which demanded "thoroughly destroying landlords both in economic and political terms" through a "worker and peasant dictatorship." The directive specified the "concrete methods" in unambiguous terms of violent action: "Start violent insurgencies, that is, arrest, detention, surveillance and expulsion; focus on feudal evil tyrants in the villages and districts, tally, ransack, and dig out all of their properties; beat to death or execute main feudal landlords." Local villagers then set out to take action: they evicted landlords and their families from their homes; they looted the visible treasures and searched for the hidden. In many villages, the excesses went so far as to "redistribute" the landlords' women – converting them into concubines or daughters.[34]

In the rectification campaign in Hebei's communist-base area, internal reports claimed that landlords and rich peasants controlled 248 of 636 Party branches in Wuqiang and Shenxian Counties. Only 24 percent of the Party branches in those two counties were characterized as "good or basically good." A work-team was sent into Wugong Village in Raoyang

[33] See note 27.

[34] See note 28, pp. 75–79.

County. The entire Party branch was set aside, passing village leadership to the peasants' association, which was headed by two poor and disreputable local men. To the five households already classified as landlord or rich peasant, the new campaign added sixty-six. "With 387 village households watching, 71 rich peasant doors were sealed.... Some unfortunates camped out in the dirt lanes during the month-long ordeal. Some set up temporary living quarters in fifteen rooms and two courtyards of the now empty home of landlord Li Huaqi, who had fled Wugong. Others had their doors sealed but were permitted to live in their courtyards. The land, livestock, and implements of targeted households were recorded in preparation for final settlement. Moveable property in the homes of the 71 households was carted off to the Poor Peasant Association headquarters for cataloging." Another village in Raoyang in Hebei Province, which was too poor to have any landlords or rich peasants, was nonetheless labeled as having five landlords and ten rich peasants, who were dragged to public meetings to confess where they had "hidden" their gold and money. Ropes tied to their arms and legs were pulled until they "confessed."[35]

In their ethnographic account, Friedman, Pickowicz, and Selden (1991) also noted the local cadres' thinking behind these campaigns:

> [T]he party's reform measures of the preceding decade had so reduced the power of already declining landlords that the political economy of the base areas had become a party-led society of small tillers. Yet the operative categories imposed by the party insisted that the source of political economic problems was the exploitation of the many poor by the few rich. The party, with its single truth and single career ladder, forced such local officials as Zhang Yunkun [the work-team leader] to run roughshod over local notions of justice in the name of class struggle. To do otherwise might arouse the fury of higher levels and raise questions about one's loyalty to the party and its leadership. To act on local reality could ruin a career by exposing one to charge of rightism, the principal target of attack of the campaign. Under heavy pressure from their superiors to produce results, few officials were prepared to take risks.[36]

In the late 1940s, the Land Reform movement in the communist bases was waged as a new war, but the civil war with the GMD was looming on

35 In a similar practice in another village, two landlords were pulled to their death. See Friedman, Edward, Paul G. Pickowicz, and Mark Selden, *Chinese Village, Socialist State* (New Haven, CT: Yale University Press, 1991), p. 96.

36 Friedman et al., *Chinese Village, Socialist State*, pp. 96–97.

the horizon. To aid the new war efforts, class struggle was deemphasized yet again. The excesses in the rectification process quickly ceased and, in some cases, reversed. For example, the original Party branch was reinstalled in Wugong Village, and the number of those classified as landlords and rich peasants was reduced to five in the winter of 1947–1948.[37] However, the violent Land Reform movement after 1949 in later-liberated southern provinces such as Guangdong and Guangxi was only the first chapter of a long era of terror that peaked in the Cultural Revolution.

Why Perpetuate the Artificial Class Divide?

By a party directive in 1979, two years after the Cultural Revolution ended, the political labels of "landlord" and "rich peasant" were permanently removed. In the years since then, two events have been notable, one that happened and one that did not. After their quarter-century ordeal, former landlords and rich peasants attempted no revenge on their tormentors, the possibility of which was a reason for their repression during the Mao years. If anything, they were grateful for the new policy. In the new economic environment, most of those families prospered, perhaps because of the enterprising acumen inherited from their well-off forebears. What did happen, however, was a fundamental change in the Chinese economic system. By the end of the twentieth century, China had evolved into a de facto capitalist society in terms of property ownership, and the country became a large global market. This "restoration to capitalism," of course, had been another "danger" that the Maoist class-struggle doctrine was designed to avoid. It did not materialize in the form of landlord families regaining lost property, however; instead, the middle class and capitalists in cities filled the ranks of the new propertied classes.

Because the character of the system began to change after Mao's rule, it is tempting to advance an ideological explanation for the class-struggle doctrine and practice in the Mao era. The humiliation rituals and violence against the former propertied classes, this argument goes, reinforced the Party's determination to thwart any wealth concentration in individuals, and the misery of former property owners served as a ringing reminder. This argument has its merits, but it is insufficient to explain the changing pace and intensity of the repression over time. For that, we must discuss two specific challenges that the party–state bureaucracy faced in daily governing in Mao's China.

[37] Ibid., pp. 99–104.

One challenge was to create incentives for mobilizing the mass of peasantry to participate in radical government programs. Mao's class-struggle doctrine created and maintained a hierarchy of political-status groups, with class enemies at the bottom. This structure included sanctions to compel participation. Passivity or noncompliance was interpreted and punished in class terms, and the miserable fate of those at the bottom served as a yardstick and a mirror. In their essay discussing communist terror, Dallin and Breslauer employed Etzoni's conceptual scheme of organizational control. They distinguished three incentive-generating approaches – material, ideological, and coercive means – which exist in all organizational control, but their salience varies across types of organization and over time.[38] Mao's regime is known for its ideological work, but this work is expected to be effective only when combined with the other two incentives – that is, material benefits and coercion. Many scholars – particularly those who studied wartime communist-base areas – have forcefully credited Chinese peasants' enthusiasm to policies that generated material incentives such as rent deduction and land redistribution.[39] After the land redistribution, however, the regime had minimal material resources to reward compliance. As important, most of the subsequent political campaigns – notably, the Land Reform Rectification, the collectivization program, the Great Leap Forward, and the Cultural Revolution – did not result in economic benefits to the peasantry; in fact, the peasants fared worse economically due to the campaigns. Hence, coercion became the most viable choice – that is, the threat of sharing the ill fortune of the enemy class.

The story of "Four-Happiness Li" (a pseudonym created by a local Party newspaper) illustrates the dilemma of the Party in mobilizing peasants to participate in later campaigns after the land redistribution. As a young man, Zhu Zhongli worked as a hired laborer for ten years. After the 1951 Land Reform in Changsha County in Hunan Province, he obtained a piece of land, got married, had a child, and was elected a vice chief

[38] Alexander Dallin and George W. Breslauer, *Political Terror in Communist Systems* (Stanford, CA: Stanford University Press, 1970); Amitai Etzioni, *A Comparative Analysis of Complex Organizations: On Power, Involvement, and Their Correlates* (New York: Free Press of Glencoe, 1961).

[39] See, e.g., Mark Selden, *The Yenan Way in Revolutionary China* (Cambridge, MA: Harvard University Press, 1971); Mark Selden, *China in Revolution: The Yenan Way Revisited* (Armonk, NY: M. E. Sharpe, 1995). See also Johnson (1962) for rejoinder. Chalmers A. Johnson, *Peasant Nationalism and Communist Power: The Emergence of Revolutionary China 1937–1945* (Stanford, CA: Stanford University Press, 1962).

of his township. Neighbors offered congratulations for the "four happinesses" showered on him all at once. He resigned from his government post and decided to return to the village to "plant the field." "I have not had any land and have been poor all my life," he said. "Now that I am given my share of land, I am more than satisfied. Why should I continue to join making revolution?" The local Party newspaper published this story, which was summarized as the "Four Happiness Li" phenomenon for debate.[40]

The Land Reform in the communist-base areas in North China in the 1940s had been conducted shortly before the outset of civil war. Contrary to some studies that maintain that land redistribution was an effective motivation factor to mobilize for the war effort,[41] ethnographic accounts record problems with army recruitment among peasants who had obtained their share of land.[42] In a township of Wulian County in Shandong Province, no one volunteered when the cadres first held an army-recruitment meeting of militia members. The Party blamed a class enemy, or a "bad element," who was accused of "sabotaging." A struggle rally was held; afterwards, twenty-five young men "volunteered" to join the army. In Juzheng Village in Lunan County, Shandong Province, young men went into hiding for ten days when village cadres conducted the recruitment drive; rumors disseminated by class enemies were deemed to be the cause. A struggle rally, billed as attacking the class enemy's sabotage of recruitment, was staged, with two members of landlord families as the targets.

The second challenge of the party–state was to keep the cadre of local state bureaucrats in line. There were several concurrent bureaucratic problems: passivity, corruption, factionalism, over-staffing, and so on. These problems were viewed through the lens of class struggles, with offenses ranging from bourgeois "tendency" and "thought" to "line mistake" and "representing class enemies." Thus, a political campaign often consisted of two parallel campaigns: (1) purging enemy elements within

40 In a similar practice in another village, two landlords were pulled to their death. Chen Yiyuan, 2006: 162–164.

41 See, e.g., Mark Selden, *The Yenan Way in Revolutionary China* (Cambridge, MA: Harvard University Press, 1971); Mark Selden, *China in Revolution: The Yenan Way Revisited* (Armonk, NY: M. E. Sharpe, 1995).

42 See, e.g., Isabel Crook and David Crook, *Ten Mile Inn: Mass Movement in a Chinese Village* (New York: Pantheon Books, 1979); Friedman, Edward, Paul G. Pickowicz, and Mark Selden, *Chinese Village, Socialist State* (New Haven, CT: Yale University Press, 1991).

the cadre ranks, and (2) persecuting class enemies already designated among the mass bases. To prove that one was a good cadre and to avoid being purged often meant they had to be tough on enemies. The following passage from a directive issued by the Party Center in 1962 illustrates how landlords and peasants were framed as the source of bureaucratic problems existing in cadres:

> In Guizhou and Bijie prefectures, the situations of the masses' life and production are dire. Particularly beyond fathom and imagination are problems existed among the cadres, including corruption, waste, violations of the party constitution, illegal activities, and callous attitude toward the life of the masses. Some of these are obviously the result of counter-revolutionary sabotages, committed as class revenge by those feudal forces who have usurped the power of local administrations. This is the fiercest manifestation of class struggle in the countryside. Please remember this. Among the rural population, 8 percent are landlords and rich peasants and their family members. It is 10 percent of the national population if we also include the urban capitalists, bourgeois intellectuals, petty bourgeois elements and their families. Those among them who have not been well reformed are the hidden but daring counter-revolutionaries. They harbored extreme hatred toward socialism, and prepared to "return as a ghost from grave" in their efforts to seize power and to restore [the old system].[43]

In solving all types of problems in the rank of cadres, a common move was to incite the rhetoric of class struggle and accuse the purged cadres of committing the crime of abetting class enemies. In his classic study, *Canton under Communism*, Vogel showed how the Party Center replaced local Guangdong leaders with a more loyal contingent of northerners. The alleged crime of local leaders was to have carried out a "peaceful land reform." By accusing the local guerrilla leaders of committing line error, the Party Center successfully replaced them with an army of southbound cadres led by Tao Zhu and Zhao Ziyang. The "new blood" in the cadre ranks was to be more responsive and compliant to the Party Center. In rejecting the so-called peaceful land reform, Tao and his cadres implemented the Land Reform Rectification with a vengeance that cost Jin Zhilong's mother her life.

In 1952, in the second stage of the Land Reform and after the Party Center removed Guangdong's leaders and replaced them with Tao as

[43] *Guanyu Shandong, Henan, Gansu he Guizhou mouxie diqu suo fasheng de yanzhong qingkuang* 关于山东、河南、甘肃和贵州某些地区所发生的严重情况, cited in *Guo Dehong* 郭德宏 *and Lin Xiaobo* 林小波, *Siqing yundong shilu* 四清运动实录 (*Chronicalizing the Four-Clean Movement*) (Hangzhou: Hangzhou remin chubanshe, 2005), pp. 16–17.

the new "point man," his first political task was to establish a class line in rural society. Having recently entered the Korean War, the Chinese government was reminded that an enemy class was preparing a comeback. Therefore, struggle rallies and violence were required against the suspected members of the enemy class: the newly labeled landlords and rich peasants. Tao's second political task was to implant outside cadres at the provincial level in order to exert central control. This latter task was all the more urgent in light of the reluctance of native leaders to deal violent blows against the local gentry.[44] Tao pushed two parallel lines of the campaigns – one society-wide against landlords and rich peasants, the other within the cadre rank against those who allegedly committed mistakes or crimes during the Land Reform.[45] To unseat the province's No. 1 leader, Fang Fang, Tao and his protégé, Zhao, first convened regional cadre meetings, at which Fang's lieutenants were attacked for undesirable family backgrounds and their prerevolution history. After many of Fang's associates had been "rectified," Fang himself was put on stage to confess his crimes; he subsequently disappeared from public view.[46]

Tao was joined by thousands of cadres descending from the north to Guangdong Province. They accused local cadres of committing line mistakes. In what was a strong political indictment in China, Zhao – a northern leader and one of Tao's top lieutenants – accused Guangdong officials of "being unstable in their class positions" and asserted that bad elements were infiltrating the Party itself.[47] Violence became rampant, with "random killings and random beatings" often reported. At the same time, a large-scale cadre rectification was in full swing. According to the memoir of the secretary of a top provincial leader, in May 1962 alone, 6,515 cadres were demoted or persecuted.[48] As Vogel documented, as many as 80 percent of local cadres at the county-level rank or higher

44 Zhu Zheng 朱正, *Fan youpai douzheng shimo*, vols. 1 and 2. 反右派斗争始末(上, 下) (*The History of Anti-Rightist Movemetn*) (Hong Kong: Minbao chubanshe, 2004). Yang Li 杨立, editor, *Dai ci de hong meigui: Gudacun chenyuan lu* 带刺的红玫瑰：古大存沉冤录 (*Thorny Rose: The Tragedy of Gu Dacun*) (Guangzhou, Guangdong: Zhongong Guangdong shengwei dangshi yanjiushi, 1997); Ezra F. Vogel, *Canton under Communism: Programs and Politics in a Provincial Capital, 1949–1968* (Cambridge, MA: Harvard University Press, 1969).

45 Personal interviews with Zeng Hongzhong of Xingning, Guangdong, and Li Zhao of Cangwu, Guangxi.

46 Vogel, *Canton under Communism*, pp. 110–120.

47 Ibid., p. 115; Yang Li 杨立 (note 40):113.

48 Ibid.

lost their positions in the campaign. Tao and Zhao emerged as the No. 1 and No. 2 leaders in Guangdong Province.[49] The southbound contingent also occupied key positions in the local levels of prefecture, county, and township.[50]

In one of the most extensive national campaigns after the Land Reform movement, the Four-Clean movement first appeared to be an anti-corruption drive to rectify local cadres. First stipulated in 1963, the tasks of auditing – or cleaning-up "workpoints, warehouse, accounting and materials" – seemed to be confined to the economic domain. However, the movement quickly turned political and the persecution of former landlords and rich peasants became a major component. A central directive issued in November 1964 asserted that "the leadership of some places has been controlled by rotten elements; in some places it has been controlled by landlords, rich peasants, counter-revolutionaries and bad element as well as newly emerged bourgeois class elements."[51] A speech by Zhou Enlai stated that the movement was to regain control from these class enemies.[52] By this time, a new Party document redefined the Four-Clean movement as cleaning up "thoughts, politics, organization, and economy."[53]

Local leaders quickly gave specific numbers – with little basis in reality – to validate the Center's diagnosis. The Guangxi Provincial Party Committee reported that at least one third of local administrations were no longer in the control of those who followed the socialist line. In Nanning Prefecture, 73 percent of cadres were believed to be "unclean." Two of sixteen county governments were believed to be totally "rotten"; in one commune, twelve of thirty-seven brigade leadership groups were believed to be rotten.[54] In Guangdong Province, Party Chief Tao suggested that 40 percent of local governments at the county or lower levels had lost their power to class enemies.[55] Violent struggles were staged against both the accused cadres and the rural Four Types. In Chang'an County in Shanxi Province, 2,616 cadres were deemed to have serious problems. The county Party secretary was accused of condoning bad people and removed.

[49] Vogel, *Canton under Communism*, p. 121.

[50] Personal interviews with Zeng Hongzhong, Li Biguang, 2006.

[51] Guo Dehong 郭德宏, and Lin Xiaobo 林小波, *Siqing yundong shilu* 四清运动实录 (*Chronicalizing the Four-Clean Movement*) (Hangzhou, Zhejiang: Zhejiang remin chubanshe, 2005), p. 243.

[52] Ibid.

[53] Ibid., p. 146.

[54] Ibid., p. 241.

[55] Ibid.

A vice secretary labeled as an "active counter-revolutionary" was sentenced to eight years in prison; 182 individuals committed suicide. At the same time, 2,707 more families were reclassified as landlords and rich peasants.[56]

Life as a Class Enemy

In addition to landlords and rich peasants, there were two other categories of class enemies: counter-revolutionaries and bad elements.[57] After 1949, most counter-revolutionaries were classified for their association with the GMD government, including GMD Party members, Youth League members, officers and soldiers in the GMD army, and GMD officials. Some of these individuals owned land in their home community, so they were classified as both a counter-revolutionary and a landlord or a rich peasant. In the countryside, however, the counter-revolutionaries were small in number compared to the number of landlords and rich peasants. For example, based on a 1956 tally in Cangwu County, there were 4,188 landlords and 3,985 rich peasants, whereas there were only 239 counter-revolutionaries.[58] The fourth category, bad elements, referred to those who committed petty crimes such as theft and sexual indiscretions. A complete record of their numbers does not exist, but evidence indicates that this group was even smaller than the third category of counter-revolutionaries.

Although class background was defined by blood relations, there was a distinction between *fenzi* (element) and family members. *Fenzi* was the householder or a representative of the family if the householder had died. In political campaigns before and after the Cultural Revolution, mental and physical abuses applied only to the *fenzi* of Four-Type families. In the 1967 and 1968 collective killings, the types of victims varied across local communities. In some villages, victims were limited to *fenzi*; in others, victims included other male family members; and in the most severe cases, victims included women, children, and the elderly.

56 Ibid., p. 244.

57 In some rural communities during the Cultural Revolution, the class enemies were referred to as Five Types, including Rightists, rather than Four Types. In the Anti-Rightist Campaign in 1957, 600,000 individuals were classified as "Rightists" in China. They were mostly city residents; some were sent to the countryside. Because the number was small in comparison to the other four categories in rural communities, most counties did not include Rightists in the rhetoric of class struggle.

58 *Cangwu xianzhi bianzuan weiyuanhui* 苍梧县志编纂委员会, *Cangwu xianzhi* 苍梧县志 [Cangwu County Gazetteer] (Nanning: Guangxi renmin chubanshe, 1997), p. 555.

Because family status was designated along patrimonial lines, marriage and adoption were two common vehicles to change one's fortune. After the Land Reform, many wives divorced their landlord or rich-peasant husbands, and their children were dispersed to relatives for adoption. In the case of the Du brothers, their father was killed in the Land Reform movement; his widow and eldest son, Du Zhengyi – whose own wife had left him – became *fenzi*. Du Jianqiang, the younger son, married out to his wife's village, a move that in local custom was considered an uncommon and undignified life event for a man. In Jin Zhilong's case, his father fled to Taiwan, his mother committed suicide, and his two sisters and one brother were adopted by relatives. Jin was the sole remaining member of the landlord family and therefore became a landlord *fenzi* at a young age. After surviving the Cultural Revolution, he also married out.[59]

In the late 1950s, a period that was less politically charged, the government "removed the hat" for some landlord and rich-peasant *fenzi*. After a group evaluation of their attitude and performance by the mass members with good family standings, they became "commune members." For example, in 1956 in Cangwu County, 1,630 of 8,374 Four-Type *fenzi* were granted such leniency. However, my informants told me that in the heat of the Cultural Revolution, they and their families were treated no differently than other Four Types.[60]

Four-Type *fenzi* were put under community surveillance. At the village level – or brigade, in the Peoples' Commune system – local governments set up Security and Defense Committees for this purpose. During the day, in conspicuous uniforms, they joined other *fenzi* in Reform Teams to labor for community projects, including cleaning up public areas. After hours, one or two militia members were assigned to watch each of them. In the height of the political campaigns, the *fenzi* were required to report their daily progress in the process of thought reform. In the 1950s, Wuhua County organized 8,893 Four-Type *fenzi* into 696 Reform Teams.[61] In Cangwu County, three to five militia members were responsible for the daily surveillance of one *fenzi*.[62]

During the Cultural Revolution, Jinkeng Village militias conducted an additional nightly inspection at 10 p.m. of Four-Type residences. The

[59] Personal interviews with Du Zhengyi, Du Jianqiang, and Jin Zhilong.

[60] *Cangwu xianzhi bianzuan weiyuanhui* 苍梧县志编纂委员会, *Cangwu xianzhi* 苍梧县志 [Cangwu County Gazetteer] (Nanning: Guangxi renmin chubanshe, 1997), p. 555.

[61] *Wuhua xian difang zhi bianzuan weiyuanhui* 五华县地方志编纂委员会 *Wuhua xianzhi* 五华县志 [Wuhua County Gazetteer] (Guangzhou: Guangdong renmin chubanshe, 1998), p. 422.

[62] *Cangwu xianzhi bianzuan weiyuanhui* 苍梧县志编纂委员会, *Cangwu xianzhi* 苍梧县志 [Cangwu County Gazetteer] (Nanning: Guangxi renmin chubanshe, 1997), p. 556.

fenzi and his family members waited to report on their own behavior. After a long day's work and as soon as night fell, Jin Zhilong stayed in a small room, given to him by the government after the Land Reform movement; to wander around after dark would invite suspicion. On one side of the white wall of his room, Jin had painted a large black circle, in which he had written eight characters in chalk: "Obediently Reform, To Be Reborn a New Man." He did this to demonstrate his good attitude to militia inspectors. Every night, two rifle-toting militia members appeared, who were Jin's third and fourth cousins. "Day in, day out, I knew nothing about what was going on in the Cultural Revolution," Jin told me. "The only times I was involved in the movement was when we were dragged to rally stages for struggle. I have developed this constant fear of drums and gongs since then." Typically, in the hour before a rally began, drums and gongs were sounded to convene participants and create a climate of urgency; that repeated practice obviously took a psychological toll on landlord *fenzi* like Jin.

The militia members from Jin's clan usually treated him less harshly. The third cousin in charge of his daily surveillance often gave him tips about what might happen in a struggle rally – for example, to wear thick trousers if extended kneeling was expected. However, there were exceptions. If there had been family conflicts in the past, a close neighbor could be cruel, especially if that neighbor was seeking career advancement by showing ruthlessness against class enemies. One of Jin's relatives – who later became a top leader of the village – once stopped him in public and wrote "Landlord Cub" in black engine oil on his brand-new T-shirt. When placed under pressure by fanatic cadres, close friends from his clan occasionally betrayed him by making unfounded accusations. For example, after listening to a radio with two friends, they accused him falsely in a struggle rally of tuning to shortwave channels from Taiwan – which made him a counter-revolutionary in addition to being a landlord's son.

With such intense control over the Four Types, any supposed organized conspiracy against the system was a fiction. Nonetheless, the government persecuted alleged affronts to the socialist system as counter-revolutionary crimes and created two categories: (1) the "historically counter-revolutionary," which included those with newly revealed past associations with the GMD government; and (2) the "newly counter-revolutionary" – anyone else who was deemed suspicious. During political campaigns, these groups swelled. In 1966, the first year of the Cultural Revolution, historically counter-revolutionary crimes increased to 8,659 from 3,557 in the previous year, and the newly counter-revolutionary

TABLE 4.2. *Counter-Revolutionary Crimes in China, 1956–1965 and 1977–1980*[1]

Year	Historically Counter-Revolutionary 历史反革命	Newly Counter-Revolutionary 现行反革命[2]	Totals
1956	(See Note 2)		143,972
1957			309,483
1958			822,853
1959	135,179	105,837	241,016
1960	44,255	104,632	148,887
1962	6,267	18,163	24,430
1963	4,741	42,177	46,918
1964	2,277	28,360	30,637
1965	3,557	24,627	28,184
1966	8,659	64,184	72,843
1977	447	19,078	19,525
1978	281	10,114	10,395
1979	107	4,892	4,999
1980	0	517	517

Notes:

1. Newly Counter-Revolutionary 现行反革命=背叛祖国+叛变、策动叛变+反革命集团+反动会道门，+特务、间谍 +叛乱+反革命宣传煽动+杀人+破坏+偷越国境+报复、倒算.
2. The breakdown of the two types is not available for 1956–1958.

Sources: 全国人民法院司法统计历史资料汇编, 1949–1998] [Collected Statistics and Historic Materials of People's Courts of the Country, 1949–1998], 最高人民法院研究室编 [compiled by Research Office of the Supreme People's Court]; Remin Fayuan chubanshe, 2000.

crimes increased to 64,184 from 24,627 (Table 4.2). After central policy abandoned class struggle in 1979–1980, both numbers approached zero. In other words, most of the alleged antigovernment activities were witch-hunts manufactured by the campaigns. It was a long-held doctrine that if the repressive grip over the Four Types were loosened, they would stage a massive counterattack on the system and the "people." After the 1979 Party Center directive that permanently removed class labels, however, the number of newly counter-revolutionary crimes was a minuscule 517 in the entire country.

Conclusion

The tragic fate of the class enemies had its origins in the first years of state-building and in the institutional features of the new regime.

The initial qualification for a new political group was economic status; however, that quickly lost any significance after the land redistribution and especially after the collectivization campaign. To force a class wedge into communities previously dominated by lineage and clan relations, the early campaigns used violence to create a divide between the poor and the formerly rich. The continuing struggle rituals rendered the class line political in the absence of any economic basis.

In other cases of mass killings, particularly those of ethnic groups, potential victims share some level of collective identity and group solidarity. They represent a collective force in political or economic competition with other groups in the majority population. In Nazi Germany, Jews were envied for their economic and cultural successes. At the turn of the twentieth century in Turkey, Christian Armenians belonged to a distinct ethnic and religious group; some rebellious activities were carried out in their name. In Rwanda, a guerrilla force formed in the name of the Tutsi minority and waged occasional sniper attacks from across the border. However, this was not the case with the village class enemies in rural China. There was no group solidarity worthy of a name; the class enemies eked out a desperate existence under tight surveillance. They posed no threat of organized defiance – in word or deed – to the new regime. In heated political campaigns, they served only as targets of mass struggle rallies and parades.

Therefore, the designation of such an enemy group was not based on economic status or the capacity for political resistance; it was rooted in the institutional logic of Mao's regime. The reasons for the class-struggle doctrine remain to be explored, but the historical fact of its practice is beyond dispute. The doctrine remained a pillar of the political system and a reality of daily life from 1949 to 1976 under Mao's rule. Two major functions of this practice were to coerce the masses into compliance and to resolve elite conflict, both of which used the tool of class struggle. The existence of this enemy class was the foundation for the "reality" of class conflict. For this reason, I contend that the enemy class was created for permanence rather than for elimination, as some mass-killing scholars claim.

Scholars including Valentino and Mann attribute communist mass killings to resistance of the former property classes to the radical social transformation.[63] At least in the case in China as described herein, this view is separate from historical facts. Moreover, this view cannot explain

[63] Valentino, *Final Solutions*; Mann, *The Dark Side of Democracy.*

why eliminationist killings were extremely rare in the long history of these regimes. Despite the rampant violence, including execution, the wholesale physical elimination of designated enemies was simply not national policy. To understand those rare moments during the Cultural Revolution in 1967 and 1968, we have to pay attention to the linkage between the class label and the institutional habit of solving political problems in a given period. The tragic events of collective killings took place in a time of political crisis. To restore order, the time-honored approach of exaggerating the existence of and threat from the class enemies was used. The general policy was to emphasize their existence, not eliminate the individuals who embodied the class enemy. However, this dramatizing invoked radical reactions in some rural communities, especially those that were farthest from the reach of central state control. The realist view of victim-identity construction cannot explain this aspect of the Chinese collective killings. The victim identity was politically constructed and its saliency waxed and waned, shaping the misfortunes and fates of many people.

5

Mao's Ordinary Men

Official materials such as *xianzhi* offer little information regarding who committed the collective killings during China's Cultural Revolution; however, there is no similar dearth in the unpublished documents I have obtained. Published reports written by exiled dissidents including Zhang Cheng and Zheng Yi contain vivid accounts of the killings and, in some cases, confessions.[1] In my interviews, I also probed into the question of who was immediately responsible. The survivors, victims' family members, and retired cadres consistently provided the same answer: local cadres and militia members. When the decision to kill and the scope of killings was agreed on, local leaders and militias rounded up members of Four-Type families, with the killings typically following a mass rally attended by the entire village.

I previously recounted an event in Sanjiang Commune, Quanzhou County in Guangxi Province, in which seventy-six Four-Type family members were killed by being pushed off a cliff. Both the *xianzhi* of the county and a provincial-level document recorded this event, identifying the organizer as Huang Tianhui, the commune's militia commander.[2] Based on a county-level internal document, Zheng Yi detailed how the killings were deliberated and planned and who were involved:

> In the morning and the evening of October 2 [1967], Sanjiang Commune's militia commander Huang Tianhui held two meetings to plan

[1] Zhang Cheng 章成 (2001). "Daoxian da tusha" 道县大屠杀 ["The Daoxian Massacre"]. *Open Magazine* 开放杂志, July, August, September, and December issues; see Zheng Yi 郑义, *Hongse jinianbei* 红色纪念碑 [*The Scarlet Memorial*] (Taipei, Taiwan: Huashi wenhua gongsi, 1993).

[2] Tang Chuying 唐楚英 (ed.), *Quanzhou xianzhi* 全州县志 [Quanzhou County Gazetteer] (Nanning: Guangxi renmin chubanshe, 1998); and GXWGDSNB.

> killings. The evening meeting was attended by mass organization activists and militia leaders above the rank of team or platoon. "The masses in Daoxian County, Hunnan [a bordering county] have killed some Four Types because the Four Types in Honghua, Daoxian, conspired to stage armed insurgencies," said Huang. "Xiashui Commune in our district has begun taking similar actions [against the Four Types]. So we must also take action. We must preempt the action of Four Types. We must wipe out their entire family because keeping their children alive will amount to preserving the root of evil."[3]

Huang's radical view did not go uncontested. The commune's public security chief suggested that the action must have a policy justification. Even if the action were taken, he said, it must be "strategic," meaning a limit to the number of victims. His caution was seconded by others in the meeting and a heated debate ensued. On the side of restraint, the commune accountant reminded those at the meeting that some Four-Type families were mixed, including poor or middle peasants by marriage or adoption. In the end, however, Huang prevailed on most of the issues. As for a policy justification, he claimed that he knew the policy well because he had just returned from a meeting held at the district level (i.e., a level of government in Guangxi Province between commune and county), although he did not share specific details. On the issue of scope, those at the meeting agreed that adopted children should be spared as well as female family members who had married into a Four-Type family. Whether radical or cautious in deciding on the scope, all at the meeting apparently agreed to act.[4]

The meeting ended at 2 a.m. and immediately afterward, "Huang Tianhui led militia members to raid landlord and rich-peasant houses, waking up everyone in the household. They [victims] were bound with ropes and escorted to the deep canyon of Huangguachong Mountain."[5] Some of the victims, knowing their own death was inevitable, pleaded to save their children. At least two parents cited the fact that their spouse was of poor-peasant origins and argued that half of their under-aged children should be spared; they failed. The only protest regarding the killings came from a landlord's daughter named Jiang Yingying, a village teacher with a high school education. She asked Huang Tianhui, "Do

[3] See Zheng Yi 郑义, *Hongse jinianbei* 红色纪念碑 [*The Scarlet Memorial*] (Taipei, Taiwan: Huashi wenhua gongsi, 1993), pp. 334–335, in which he cites an internal document with page numbers, 全州文革大事记 [Chronology of the Cultural Revolution in Quanzhou].

[4] Ibid.

[5] Ibid.

you have a policy for this thing you are doing?" She was quickly silenced with clubs and then killed.[6]

Throughout this book, I argue that these collective killings were not solely the actions of the perpetrators. In this chapter, however, my focus is on the perpetrators – the organizers, the killers, and – to some extent – the enablers. I consider the degree to which the organizers and the killers were "ordinary men" in terms of their background and psychological profile. I address whether the perpetrators were following orders or acting on their own. I also consider the subtler and relatively constant career pressures that potential perpetrators faced in the countryside during the Cultural Revolution, as well as situational pressures due to the history of political campaigns under Mao. The motivations were different for the killers, the organizers, and the enablers. Most of the organizers and killers were either state officials or acting as members of local militias; they were ideologically committed to Maoism but were not acting under specific orders to kill. The organizers were mainly local officials motivated to ritualistically show their power after the formation of a new government and who were pushed to extremes by the increasing radicalization of Mao's political campaigns. They also knew that the many new entrants to the state payroll came at the expense of incumbents; therefore, they were constantly seeking innovative ways to prove their adherence to principles of a given campaign to their superiors. Many of the killers were apparently psychologically disturbed, but they also acted in an attempt to improve their community standing.

From their profiles and actions in 1967 and 1968, it is evident that the killers and the organizers had organizational affiliations and ideological identifications with the state. They no doubt were state actors, like perpetrators elsewhere portrayed by the state-policy model. However, they committed the killings not as part of their typical duties prescribed by the state bureaucracy; they proactively innovated or willingly embraced collective killings. Perpetrators did not follow, they *acted*; collective killings were not implemented, they were *made*. Organizers and participants assumed what collective-action scholars call "newly constituted identities" in action events outside the bounds of "contained politics."[7] The evidence of newly self-constituted identities is an empirical base with which to treat collective killings as a special form of collective action

6 Ibid.

7 Doug McAdam, Sidney G. Tarrow, and Charles Tilly, *Dynamics of Contention* (New York: Cambridge University Press, 2001), pp. 7–8.

rather than routine bureaucratic operations. That the state actors took on emergent identities in their participation by no means discounts the significance of their state affiliation. Not only their action was taken in the name of the state but their capacity to stage the community event of collective killings also was derived from such affiliations. More to the point of this chapter, however, their incentives and identities in the emergent event were precisely shaped largely by their previous routine institutional life. Combined with the state indoctrination of class-struggle attitudes, this routine life defined their career path and provided them with an action repertoire and a deadly spirit of innovation.

Ordinary Men and Extraordinary Deeds

One of the most influential academic debates on the issue of perpetrators centers on Browning's "ordinary men" thesis. In his 1992 book, he examined members of Reserve Police Battalion 101, who rounded up Jews for deportation to death camps in Poland, shooting them if there was not enough room on the trains. Browning found that these men were neither demons nor Nazi fanatics but rather ordinary middle-aged men of working-class background. They killed from basic obedience to authority and peer pressure, not blood lust or primal hatred.[8] Browning's thesis – that ordinary people are capable of the most unspeakable crimes under certain circumstances – echoes a long line of research by social psychologists, most notably the Milgram experiment and the Stanford prison experiment by Zimbardo and associates.[9] Goldhagen and Mann joined the debate but demonstrated that the Nazi killers were not as ordinary as Browning portrayed them. For Goldhagen, the killings were committed from a deeply held hatred – which he claimed was prevalent among the German population of that era – compounded by "eliminationist anti-Semitism" ideology.[10] For Mann, executioners tended to be party

[8] Christopher Browning, *Ordinary Men: Reserve Police Battalion 101 and the Final Solution in Poland* (New York: HarperCollins, 1992).

[9] See Stanley Milgram, *Obedience to Authority: An Experimental View* (New York: Harper and Row, 1974); and Stanley Milgram, "Behavioral Study of Obedience," *Journal of Abnormal and Social Psychology* 67 (1963), pp. 371–378. See also Phil G. Zimbardo, *Quiet Rage: The Stanford Prison Experiment* (Video recording) (Stanford, CA: Psychology Department, Stanford University, 1991).

[10] Daniel Jonah Goldhagen, *Hitler's Willing Executioners: Ordinary Germans and the Holocaust* (London: Little, Brown and Co., 1996).

members and elite soldiers or were otherwise more immersed in the Nazi party's genocidal ideology.[11]

For all their disagreement regarding motives, both sides of the "ordinary men" debate agree that the killers were not recruited from criminal elements or psychopaths but instead from the very heart of society. They were either family men with a working-class background (i.e., Browning) or elite members of society and their community (i.e., Goldhagen and Mann). In this sense, they *were* ordinary men. Both sides also agree, in different ways, that the perpetrators acted on their own initiative. Browning pointed out that the commander of Battalion 101 gave his men the choice of opting out but that most chose not to do so.[12] In the accounts of Goldhagen and Mann, the perpetrators internalized the genocidal ideology and acted on it, often going beyond the call of their prescribed official duties.

In an attempt to transcend the debate on Browning's ordinary-man thesis, Valentino proposed a strategic model. For him, the most critical factor that predicts mass killing is the decision of one or a few top leaders. These leaders run out of other options and opt for the "final solution" when confronting wartime challenges, domestic crises, or – in the case of communist countries – implementing radical social-change policies. Regarding the issue of perpetrators, his analysis emphasizes the key role of top leaders in mass killings. According to Valentino, mass killing is a strategic and therefore rational choice of the few top leaders, and killers on the ground are selectively recruited from those with sadistic impulses. A mass-killing event occurs when bad elements in the community are organized, unleashed, and rewarded by the leaders.[13]

[11] See Michael Mann, "Were the Perpetrators of Genocide 'Ordinary Men' or 'Real Nazis'? Results from Fifteen Hundred Biographies." *Holocaust and Genocide Studies* 14(3), pp. 331–366. See also Michael Mann, *The Dark Side of Democracy: Explaining Ethnic Cleansing* (New York: Cambridge University Press, 2005).

[12] See also Christopher Browning, *The Final Solution and the German Foreign Office: A Study of Referat D III of Abteilung Deutschland, 1940–43* (New York: Holmes & Meier, 1978); and Christopher Browning, *The Origins of the Final Solution: The Evolution of Nazi Jewish Policy, September 1939–March 1942* (Lincoln: University of Nebraska Press, 2004). If Browning remains in the school of institutional model of genocide for his insistence on obedience to authorities, he has aligned himself with the factionalist camp with his analysis of local improvisation and radicalization. His other work also questions the wisdom of attributing the killings to Hitler's Final Solution and neglecting other factors.

[13] Benjamin A. Valentino, *Final Solutions: Mass Killing and Genocide in the Twentieth Century* (Ithaca, NY: Cornell University Press, 2004), pp. 30–65.

Three questions raised in this debate motivate my discussion of the Chinese perpetrators. First is whether killers were rational in the sense that they were able to weigh benefits and costs in taking action. Stated differently, did they have a psychological mindset that is different from that of normal human beings? For Browning, Goldhagen, and Mann, perpetrators are ordinary men in psychological terms; they kill due to the organizational environment (i.e., Browning) or from ideological convictions (i.e., Goldhagen and Mann). For Valentino, the top leaders are rational but the killers on the ground are not. In my discussion, I treat all the actors as rational, which is used as a starting point to explore their motives. This treatment works well with most organizers of killings, such as those attending the meeting and the subsequent roundup of the seventy-six doomed villagers of Sanjiang Commune. However, consistent with Valentino's view, I also find that the most cold-blooded killers were disproportionately represented by misfits and outcasts of the community and that some of their behavior is difficult to understand from a rational-choice perspective. The homicidal glee recurs often in accounts of those who carried out the killings.

A second question concerns how different the perpetrators are from the population at large. Browning's ordinary-men thesis suggests there is no real difference, whereas Goldhagen and Mann stress a higher degree of ideological conviction. For Valentino, perpetrators can be highly distinctive in their psychology – those with sadistic impulses are selectively recruited; however, he also suggests (echoing Browning) that situational pressure can turn normal people into killers. Were the Chinese killers different in ideological terms? Their own explanations for their actions implicate deep convictions, but it is unclear whether they were different in this respect from the community at large. Were the killers also psychologically different? The extraordinary cruelties seem to suggest a clear affirmative answer, but a fuller explanation must include the forces that unleashed and channeled their dark impulses.

The third question concerns the content of the "situation," which seems to be a factor agreed on by most scholars. For Browning, it was the bureaucratic structure that turned ordinary men into killers, and he cites peer pressure and the definition of social reality in killing organizations as key factors. Chinese perpetrators, however, were peacetime community leaders and militia members. Their prescribed typical duties did not include killing; they engaged in killing only as a one-time event. Their situation consisted of multiple dimensions, unlike that of the Nazi killers. In Chapters 6 and 7, I discuss the removal of the moral and legal constraints on killing. I focus here on the killers' motive for power in local communities. This discussion begins with the institutional environment ushered in by the fanatic mass political campaigns in the early stage of the Cultural Revolution. This environment called for ever-escalating rhetoric and tactics against "class enemies." I also examine the reward and punishment system in which the bureaucrats and activists found themselves. I discuss the institutional logic of the radicalization of public rituals, as well as the career imperatives to survive in Mao's cadre system.

I expand the concept of perpetrators to include not only those who bludgeoned or shot victims and those who directly ordered the killings but also those who aided and abetted in the atrocities and without whom they could not have happened. These perpetrators included the militia members who rounded up targets and the local leaders who joined the planning meetings, as well as the upper-level leaders. After discussing the historic and institutional background, I examine the group I call the "enablers" – those upper-level leaders who potentially could have stopped the killings but instead chose to look the other way. Then I discuss those most directly responsible for the killings in the local communities. They include two groups of individuals: the organizers and the killers. The former were officials on the ground who decided that killings would occur, typically chose the victims, and then orchestrated the killing events. The organizers were mainly village or township leaders; in some cases, county-level leaders also were involved. The killers are those few who did the "dirty work." They were almost always elite militia members.

Loss and Gain in the Career Equation: Enablers

There were several ways that those not making the decision or carrying out the killings were implicated and could have avoided involvement, prevented, or minimized them. Militia members could potentially opt out by not reporting for duty. More important, local leaders could interpret the directives in a way that fell short of planning to kill or they could more aggressively contest the voices calling for violence. County or provincial leaders could have minimized the most gruesome events by giving instructions to stop the killing once they had caught wind of it. Indeed, in 1967 and 1968, cadres in the two provinces did opt out. For the large number who failed to take this seemingly obvious way out, however, we must ask why. We also must ask about the militia members who agreed to participate once the organizers mobilized to kill. After all, almost all adult males were technically members of their local militias but only some participated in rounding up victims and only a select few killed. I use the stories of a few individuals to illustrate how career considerations may have contributed to the decision to kill.[14]

To Become a Non-Villager

In Mao's China, a resident registration system known as *hukuo* divided the population into two segments. The urban population, which included industrial workers, teachers, army soldiers, and government cadres, earned steady monetary incomes and enjoyed stable food rations. Rural residents, or peasants, received almost no money and their food share was allocated from the harvest of their production team. During the Cultural Revolution, the urban population comprised about 18 percent in China. In rural counties, the urban population was between only 5 and 8 percent and accounted for township and county government cadres, staff, and their families. More than 90 percent of the population lived and toiled in villages.[15]

Life in the countryside was harsh. Rice growers had to constantly work the fields, hoping for a good yield from the limited arable land. Electricity had yet to arrive in most communities; all the tilling and harvesting were done manually. Transportation was also a manual endeavor but pushing a cart was mostly futile in the mountains and ragged valleys. Most adults grew up with "circle legs" – that is, slightly crooked and bowed legs caused by insufficient calcium in their diet and excessive weight placed on their shoulders. Food was scarce after the harvest was taxed to fill the government granary, which ensured the urban population's stable food supply. April and August of the lunar calendar were usually the two starving months, when the rice was still green. The *hukou* was a type of political indentured servitude, with children of a rural family bound to the rural registration. The harshness of peasant life motivated young people in the village to move away to try and become an urban resident.

For these aspiring young people, the main way out of the village was to pass college and professional school exams. However, that opportunity was available to only the brightest few – around 1 percent – and this

[14] It should be noted that these individuals were not involved in collective killings, but their stories are helpful in understanding the situation of those who were.

[15] See Table 5.2.

route was soon closed off.[16] After the "three-year disaster" of 1960–1962, most schools closed; in 1966, when the Cultural Revolution began, college admission simply ceased. The second route out of the village was to join the army; however, this was not very promising and only temporary because few could change their rural status in the army and almost all would return to their village after service. In any case, the proportion of young rural men selected for army service (with virtually no army recruitment among rural females) was very small. The third and increasingly most promising way out was becoming an activist in the village political scene. Occasionally, positions were granted from Party leaders calling for village leaders to reward young activists.

Ms. Lian graduated from middle school in 1961, No. 2 in her class of about 160 in a township in Guangdong Province. However, that was during the three-year disaster, when the government greatly reduced high school and professional school admissions; therefore, her education ended there. She married a teacher and moved to Jinkeng Village in Guangdong Province. With her talent and good looks, she soon became active in the village's propaganda team, starring in the village production of revolutionary operas. Fortune smiled on her when a female work-team member was assigned to live in her household and they became fast friends. Through this new patron, she was recruited to a work-team with the possibility of eventually becoming a cadre on the state payroll. In February 1966, she was selected to attend a "Conference of Studying Mao's Works" at the county seat. She stayed overnight with her husband, who worked as a teacher in an adjacent county and whom she now rarely saw. She became pregnant with their second child, which prevented her from actively participating in the Cultural Revolution – her dream of becoming an urban resident dashed.

About the same time in the same village, Jin Huofeng graduated from middle school with undistinguished grades. He also had a connection with a work-team member. With his ruthless character and the patronage of an admiring cadre, he became a rising star in village politics. By the second year of the Cultural Revolution, when landlord descendants were staged regularly in struggle sessions, Jin had become the head of his village's public security office. He presided over many struggle rallies, including one that almost degenerated into collective killings. In Jinkeng Village, at

16 When I was admitted to college in 1981 from my village, the admission rate in the entire country was 4 percent. The rate for rural students was obviously much lower.

least five young men and women in Lian and Jin's cohort elevated their status as a result of their activism. Jin Huofeng remained a village leader until many years after the Cultural Revolution. When I interviewed him, he was a township cadre on the state payroll.

The Mass Campaign as a Means of Demotion

When the Party Center took over state power in 1949, it hastily began building a vast bureaucracy to rule China's immense population. In the process, the new state was able to reward loyal citizens with upward mobility. During the Land Reform movement and Collectivization these new bureaucrats became the managers of state resources. However, bureaucratic expansion started to stagnate, and career opportunities began to dry up after about seventeen years into the new state-building process. This was due in part to the completion of staffing the new bureaucracy and in part to the series of setbacks in the overly ambitious industrialization attempts and ensuing famine in the early 1960s.[17] The state gave and the state took away. Mobility worked in two directions, and the villages became the dumping grounds to where most purged cadres were dispatched, as well as labor camps. The primary punishment of such a cadre was the loss of urban status, although some unfortunate people also were designated a member of the village Four Types.

The pattern was of fast growth that quickly leveled off and was followed by decline; this pattern holds for the total number of cadres, the number of Party members, and the urban population. The changes in total number of cadres are shown in Table 5.1. The years between 1949 and 1956 witnessed steady growth; China's total of almost ten million cadres in 1956 was more than ten times the 1949 total. However, this growth stagnated until 1965, with only twelve million cadres nine years later. Such stagnation is dramatic because during the same period, the

[17] Roderick MacFarquhar, *The Origins of the Cultural Revolution / 1, Contradictions among the People 1956–1957* (New York: Columbia University Press for the Royal Institute of International Affairs, 1974); Roderick MacFarquhar, *The Origins of the Cultural Revolution / 2, the Great Leap Forward, 1958–1960* (Oxford: published for the Royal Institute of International Affairs, 1983); and Roderick MacFarquhar, *The Origins of the Cultural Revolution / 3, The Coming of the Cataclysm, 1961–1966* (Oxford, NY: Oxford University Press and Columbia University Press, 1997). See also Dali L. Yang, *Calamity and Reform in China: State, Rural Society, and Institutional Change since the Great Leap Famine* (Stanford, CA: Stanford University Press, 1996); and Shiping Zheng, *Party Vs. State in Post-1949 China: The Institutional Dilemma* (Cambridge: Cambridge University Press, 1997).

TABLE 5.1. *Stagnation of State-Building prior to the Cultural Revolution: Cadres in China, 1949–1971, by Status (in thousands)*

Year	Cadres 干部总数	Ji-Guan Cadres 机关干部
1949	908	
1950	2,680	
1951	3,593	
1952	5,503	
1953	6,285	
1954	6,632	2,092
1955	7,170	2,126
1956	9,768	2,815
1957	9,536	2,582
1958	9,551	2,460
1959	10,471	2,578
1960	11,326	2,735
1961	11,551	2,748
1962	10,607	2,126
1963	11,031	2,288
1964	11,513	2,378
1965	11,923	2,411
1971	12,928	2,471

Note: Cadres in Chinese official statistics include all individuals who work on the state payroll in the government sector (excluding industrial workers and soldiers); *Ji-Guan Cadres* refer to leaders and staff in local government and governmental agencies.
Source: Zhongguo ganbu tongji wushi nian (China Cadre Statistics in 50 Years) (Dang shi dang jian chubanshe, 1999).

Chinese population increased 16 percent, from 628 million to 725 million. Table 5.2 shows the overall population and the percentage of urban residents in a county in Guangdong Province. The urban population grew steadily in both raw and percentage terms until about 1960, when it began to decline. As shown in the last column of Table 5.2, the yearly increase in the urban population was as high as more than 20 percent in the first few years after 1949. That increase declined to almost zero in 1966, with three negative years already registered in 1960, 1962, and 1964. These changes occurred in the context of steady growth in the overall population in the entire period.

TABLE 5.2. *Changes in Total Population and Nonagricultural Population in Xin-feng County, 1949–1966*[a]

Year	Total Population	Nonagricultural Population (NAP)	Percent NAP	Yearly Increase of NAP
1949	95,130	1,967	2.1	
1950	97,302	2,535	2.6	28.9
1951	99,272	3,084	3.1	21.7
1952	101,794	4,000	3.9	29.7
1953	104,617	3,711	3.5	−14.5
1954	106,159	4,250	4.0	14.5
1955	107,710	4,760	4.4	12.0
1956	109,022	5,246	4.8	10.2
1957	110,193	5,569	5.1	6.2
1958	111,602	6,701	6.0	20.3
1959	113,198	8,394	7.4	25.3
1960	113,710	7,854	6.9	−6.4
1961	115,884	8,738	7.5	11.3
1962	121,819	8,573	7.0	−1.9
1963	126,602	9,757	7.7	13.8
1964	130,545	9,044	6.9	−7.3
1965	135,067	9,642	7.1	6.6
1966	138,793	9,657	7.0	0.2

Source: Xin-feng *xianzhi* (Xin-feng County Annals), 1998.

At least forty-six major political campaigns occurred in the seventeen years prior to the Cultural Revolution.[18] Political campaigns functioned as an occasion for career demotion, with incumbents removed to make room for new recruits. Because of the lack of new positions, career advancement increasingly became a "zero-sum game" in which one person's advancement meant another's demotion. Tables 5.3 and 5.4 document the recruitment and demotion of cadre ranks in two provinces. Except for the first few years after 1949, the numbers of people entering the cadre ranks are similar to the numbers of those leaving. During the Anti-Rightist Campaign in 1957–1958, many more people were stripped of their cadre rank than were appointed to the same, reflecting the extensive purges of the era. The years immediately before the Cultural Revolution also were ominous: Cadre dismissals far exceeded the recruitment totals in 1961 and 1962 for both provinces.

[18] Shiping Zheng, *Party Vs. State in Post-1949 China: The Institutional Dilemma* (Cambridge: Cambridge University Press, 1997).

TABLE 5.3. *Promotions to and Demotions from Cadre Rank in Guangdong Province, 1949–1971 (in thousands)*

Year	Entering Rank	Leaving Rank
1954	17.6	8.4
1955	11.7	3.3
1956	31.8	2.6
1957	6.2	11.4
1958	17.2	28.9
1959	23.3	4.5
1960	27.9	17.6
1961	29.9	26.5
1962	15.3	39.8
1963	23.9	18.1
1964	17.9	7.3
1965	15.1	9.7
1971	65.1	

Source: Zhongguo ganbu tongji wushi nian (China Cadre Statistics in 50 Years) (Dang shi dang jian chubanshe, 1999).

TABLE 5.4. *Promotions to and Demotions from Cadre Rank in Guangxi Province, 1949–1971 (in thousands)*

Year	Entering Rank	Leaving Rank
1954	15.4	1.5
1955	11.2	1.1
1956	27.3	2.4
1957	2.9	5.2
1958	6.8	9.6
1959	10.1	2.5
1960	21.1	5.8
1961	12.3	16.9
1962	13.4	27.7
1963	14.6	13.7
1964	12.8	2.8
1965	10.3	3.6
1971	33.1	

Source: Zhongguo ganbu tongji wushi nian (China Cadre Statistics in 50 Years) (Dang shi dang jian chubanshe, 1999).

The following summary of statistical accounting from one county indicates that the cadre turnover rate was high during political campaigns, especially near the end of the 1950s. In 1953, Dapu County in Guangdong Province had a population of 250,000, with about 3,000 cadres.

- 1952, Three-Anti and Five-Anti Campaigns: 18 cadres detained, 15 dismissed, and 26 cases submitted to higher authorities.
- 1956–1958, Cadre Rectification and Suppress Antirevolutionary Campaigns: 2,560 cadres placed under investigation, 679 designated as "targets" of investigation, 595 found to have "historical problems."
- 1958, Anti-Rightist Campaign: 472 cadres labeled as rightists, sent to labor camps.
- 1958–1961 [various political campaigns]: 2,236 cases reported, 792 party members named as "targets."[19]

Political campaigns and the real possibility for demotion in mass campaigns had important behavioral implications for all cadres. The tendency to favor "redness" over expertise, as in the cases of Ms. Lian and Jin, signaled the increasing importance in political campaigns for cadres to burnish their "red" credentials. With career promotion and demotion becoming a zero-sum game, avoiding demotion was of overriding importance to state bureaucrats. Paradoxically, as Walder pointed out, risk-aversion incentives pushed collective action in radical directions.[20]

A Victimizer Victimized: The Tale of Tao Zhu

At the outbreak of the Cultural Revolution, Tao Zhu was called on by Mao to serve as the Party's propaganda department chief, a position vacated by Lu Dingyi, one of the first victims of the new mass campaign. Tao reported to Beijing on June 4, 1966, the same day that the *People's Daily* published its infamous editorial, "Sweep Away All Demons and Ghosts." Like many other leaders of the time, he probably did not imagine that he would be one of the swept-away demons or ghosts. However, he soon found himself accused of being the "No. 1 Loyalist" because he allegedly sided with the two highest-ranking "power-holders-who-take-the-capitalist-road." After seven months in power, Tao was detained, placed under house arrest, and subsequently served

19 Dapu xian difangzhi bianzuan weiyuanhui 大埔县地方志编纂委员会, *Dapu xianzhi* 大埔县志 [Dapu County Gazetter] (Guangzhou: Guangdong renmin chubanshe, 1992).

20 Andrew Walder, "Implications of Loss Avoidance for the Analysis of Political Movements," *Hong Kong Journal of Sociology*, no. 1 (2000), pp. 83–102.

occasionally as a target in struggle rallies until his death on November 30, 1969.[21]

Tao was no stranger to the lofty rhetoric or grim reality represented by the mass movement and was rumored to enjoy deep connections with Mao and Marshall Lin Biao. His ruthlessness was legendary. After 1949, he garnered fame for his leadership in pacifying the bandits in Guangxi Province. He reportedly wired the following words to Mao: "Guangxi: 450,000 bandits pacified; 40,000 killed; one third [among the killed] may or may not deserve death."[22] In 1952, he was sent to oversee the Land Reform movement in Guangdong Province, which had started under local leadership the previous year. He demonstrated political cunning by pushing two parallel lines of the campaign: one directed against landlords and rich peasants, the other against cadres who allegedly committed "mistakes" or "crimes" during the Land Reform.[23] To unseat the No. 1 leader of the province, Fang Fang, Tao convened regional cadre meetings at which Fang's lieutenants were attacked for undesirable family backgrounds and prerevolution histories. After many of Fang's associates had been "rectified," Fang was forced to confess three crimes, none of which was related to the main "mistake" of the provincial party leadership: "peaceful land reform." Fang then disappeared from public view in Guangdong Province.[24]

Like many others, Tao Zhu was a cadre who had descended from the north to Guangdong Province. "Peaceful land reform" became a catchphrase signifying an "incorrect" form of Land Reform. The entire Guangdong Province leadership was accused of embracing this erroneous practice, thus committing "line mistakes." Zhao Ziyang, another northerner and Tao's top lieutenant, accused Guangdong officials of "wavering in their class positions." He asserted that bad elements were located in the Party.[25] A Land Reform Rectification program was instituted in

21 Zheng Xiaofeng 郑笑枫 and Shu Ling 舒玲, *Tao Zhu zhuan* 陶铸传 [*The Biography of Tao Zhu*] (Beijing: Zhongguo Qingnian Chubanshe, 1992).

22 Yang Li 杨立 (ed.), *Dai ci de hong meigui: Gudacun chenyuan lu* 带刺的红玫瑰：古大存沉冤录 (*Thorny Rose: The Tragedy of Gu Dacun*) (Zhongong Guangdong shengwei dangshi yanjiushi, 1997), p. 111.

23 Interviews with Zeng Fanzhong of Xingning County, Guangdong Province, and Li Zhao of Cangwu County, Guangxi Province (姓名).

24 Ezra F. Vogel, *Canton under Communism: Programs and Politics in a Provincial Capital, 1949–1968* (Cambridge, MA: Harvard University Press, 1969), pp. 110–120.

25 Ibid., p. 115; and Yang Li 杨立, 1997 (ed.), *Dai ci de hong meigui: Gudacun cenyuan lu* 带刺的红玫瑰：古大存沉冤录 (*Thorny Rose: The Tragedy of Gu Dacun*) (Zhongong Guangdong shengwei dangshi yanjiushi, 1997), p. 113.

villages across the province, with rampant "wild killings and wild beatings" reported. At the same time, a large-scale cadre purge was in full force. According to the memoir of a secretary of a top provincial leader, 6,515 cadres were demoted or persecuted in May 1952 alone.[26] As many as 80 percent of the local cadres at the county-level or higher rank lost their positions in the campaign.[27] Tao and Zhao emerged as the No. 1 and No. 2 leaders in Guangdong Province, respectively. Tao so impressed Mao that he was summoned to Beijing to help with the Cultural Revolution. The rise and fall of Tao Zhu as a communist bureaucrat reveal his tragic trajectory as a victimizer turned victim. Other leaders, including Liu Shaoqi and Deng Xiaoping, fell into the same category. The No. 1 victim of the Cultural Revolution, Liu was the mastermind and executioner of the 1942 Yan'an Rectification Movement. Deng, the No. 2 victim, was the architect of the Anti-Rightist Campaign of 1957–1958.

Tao's story also offers a glimpse of a key aspect of the political campaigns in China: the relationship between mass campaigns and cadre positions. As Gao Hua wrote regarding the Yan'an Rectification Movement in 1942: "The high-level struggle inside the party and the leadership reorganization had always been of the central importance."[28] In the Land Reform Rectification in Guangdong Province, the majority of local cadres were purged for not being forceful and ruthless enough in waging mass campaigns. However, the "errors" they committed were simply a pretext for the need to vacate positions for northern cadres deemed more loyal to the regime.

Some cadres, including Tao Zhu, took up the task of mass mobilization with ideological certitude backed by career motives. More often, though, cadres found themselves in situations in which their choice of action was confined to participating in active mobilization, regardless of their intentions. They were aware that some among them would be purged in the campaign, and inaction invited accusations of resisting the campaign – an accusation that would surely brand them as a target. The aim of a Maoist campaign was to search for hidden class enemies. Under the

26 Yang Li 杨立 (ed.), *Dai ci de hong meigui: Gudacun chenyuan lu* 带刺的红玫瑰：古大存沉冤录 (*Thorny Rose: The Tragedy of Gu Dacun*) (Zhongong Guangdong shengwei dangshi yanjiushi, 1997), p. 113.

27 Ezra F. Vogel, *Canton under Communism.*

28 Gao Hua 高华, *Hongtaiyang shi zenyang shengqide* 红太阳是怎样升起的：延安整风运动的来龙去脉 [*How Did the Red Sun Rise over Yan'an?: A History of the Rectification Movement*] (Hong Kong: The Chinese University of Hong Kong Press, 2000), p. xi.

circumstances, a safe bet for local leaders was always to round up those already confirmed from previous campaigns as "demons and ghosts."[29]

The Logic of Radicalization

Political campaigns before the Cultural Revolution were a form of public ritual with the function of clarifying and consolidating power relations. From peaceful meeting to struggle rally, from verbal attack to physical abuse, there was a wide variety of tactical choices in the existing repertoire of ritual, all of which demonstrated the power hierarchy. For example, many elements of a political rally – before resorting to violence – helped differentiate power and status. These elements included the seating and order of speakers on the stage, as well as the designated seating areas for the "people" and those with a questionable political background. Beatings on stage and humiliating parades also demonstrated power and a person's position without resorting to killing. However, the atrocious innovation that was collective killing requires additional explanation: To conduct public executions was a new level of radicalization.

Tactical Innovation at Wit's End

Social-movement scholars have long been aware of the need for innovative collective action. A new tactic can jolt public attention and create a new wave of participation. After a period, however, the tactic wears out and excitement diminishes. In McAdam's words, a "lull of mobilization" follows. Only a new format of action rejuvenates potential participants and renews the process. In his analysis of the civil rights movement in the United States in the 1950s and 1960s, McAdam documented six waves of "tactical innovation," each producing a peak of mobilization activity. He also noted a trend of radicalization: Each form of action tended to be more disruptive and violence-prone than its predecessor.[30]

[29] This has been amply documented by regional conflict in Beijing, Guangzhou, Wuhan, and Shanghai. See Hong Yung Lee, *The Politics of the Chinese Cultural Revolution: A Case Study* (Berkeley and London: University of California Press, 1978); Andrew G. Walder, *Chang Ch'un-ch'iao and Shanghai's January Revolution* (Ann Arbor, MI: Center for Chinese Studies of the University of Michigan, 1978); Shaoguang Wang, *Failure of Charisma: The Cultural Revolution in Wuhan* (Hong Kong and Oxford: Oxford University Press, 1995); see also Elizabeth J. Perry and Xun Li, *Proletarian Power: Shanghai in the Cultural Revolution* (Boulder, CO: Westview Press, 1997).

[30] Doug McAdam, "Tactical Innovation and the Pace of Insurgency," *American Sociological Review* 48, no. 6 (1983), pp. 735–754.

In 1967, one year into the Cultural Revolution, the typical local community had experienced much. Struggle rallies and humiliating parades had been a daily staple of collective activities. Methods of mistreating targets were constantly devised. Many new theatrical elements in public humiliation and torture had been deployed. One of my informants told me of a special dunce cap made of bamboo, about 1 meter high and weighing 50 *jin* (i.e., 25 kg).[31] Also common in South China was putting targets in an animal bamboo cage, and parading them through town as a "class-struggle exhibition."[32] Also in this period, news of armed battles abounded, coming from urban centers including county seats and larger towns close to villages. Violent death was losing its shock value.[33] The origin of collective killings as a new tactic of public ritual must be understood in this context. In most of the communities that engaged in this form of public action, it was not an indigenous creation. One of the earliest killing events in Guangxi Province took place in December 1967 in Quanzhou, a county bordering Daoxian in Hunan Province – the home of the Daoxian Massacre that occurred in the summer of the same year.[34] The tactics diffused across communities, giving local leaders elsewhere who were eager for new rigor and intensity in mass mobilization and engaging in struggle.

Competition among Units

In social protest by a challenging group, organizers seek tactical innovation for another reason: to catch their movement opponents off-guard. The impact is neutralized only after the opponents learn to contain the movement's disruptive effect.[35] In China, in addition to the public and local rivals in their own community, local leaders conducting mass campaigns had another audience in mind: their superiors in the upper levels of government. Scholars of China's mass campaigns identified a pattern that they call "*danwei* mobilization." *Danwei*, or working unit, refers to an administrative unit defined by the perspective of superiors. In a rural county, districts, communes, and villages are *danwei*; similarly, a county is a *danwei* for provincial leaders. The process of a campaign can be summarized as follows: First, when the Party Center announces

31 Personal interview with Su Qinglong, 2006.

32 See Chapter 7 on class-struggle exhibitions.

33 See Chapter 6.

34 See Chapter 1, p. 3.

35 Doug McAdam, "Tactical Innovation and the Pace of Insurgency," *American Sociological Review* 48, no. 6 (1983), pp. 735–754.

general campaign tasks and purposes, it selects a few experimental *danwei*; second, the Center extensively propagates them as model *danwei*, using newspapers, study meetings, wall posters, and work-teams; and finally, every related *danwei* tries to emulate the model with great enthusiasm. This approach was honed in the wartime guerrilla base in Yan'an and used as a standard campaign method after 1949.[36]

In the campaign, superiors not only demand compliance, they also encourage innovation. The reason for compliance is straightforward, rooted in the Leninist party discipline.[37] Any sign of noncompliance meets severe sanctions that range from dismissal to political persecution. However, campaign directives are often general rather than specific; how the goal is achieved locally must be tried "on the ground." Any innovative unit may stand out as a model, and leading one's unit to model status can be a ticket to higher offices. Hence, the creative implementation of a general policy is a skill that local leaders strive to attain.

Another influence on local implementation is the difficulty for superiors to gather information on compliance. Always fearful of noncompliance, superiors tend to reward reports that have quantifiable actions. Compliance is evidenced in the numbers of study sessions, meetings, and rallies. When class struggle was called for, the proof provided typically included enumerations of struggle rallies, uncovered conspiracy groups, arrests, and – ultimately – killings. Based on the reports, local unit leaders were classified in the so-called advanced, middle, and backward groups; the advanced group earned praise and rewards and the backward group accrued criticism or was purged. To gain advanced standing and to avoid being labeled as backward, local cadres often inflated their statistics and strove to stage extraordinary events.

The Problem of Monitoring

In this context, subordinates do their best to suppress negative information, creating an enormous monitoring problem. According to Walder, when signs of doubts and dissent appear to the superiors, they cannot determine whether they are signs of disloyalty or actual problems in the policy.[38] One way to gather independent information is to send in

36 Shinichi Tanigawa, "The Danwei and the Cultural Revolution: A Review Essay," *Ritsumeikan Journal of International Relations and Area Studies* no. 14 (1999), p. 207.

37 Andrew G. Walder, "Collective Behavior Revisited," *Rationality and Society* 6, no. 3 (1994), pp. 400–421.

38 Ibid.

work-teams; however, these cadres have vested interests in cultivating the lower unit and making it a model, often colluding with local cadres in inflation and radicalization. A more common approach is that superiors "double down" on mobilization of the Party organization, raising demands for conformity. The process feeds on itself and the appetite for quantifiable results becomes insatiable. The cycle ends only when a rectification campaign is waged – but not before enormous excesses have occurred.

This organizational pathology explains the massive Chinese famine of 1959–1961, which was a result of a politicized production campaign known as the Great Leap Forward. Dissidents of the unrealistic economic program were purged or sent to labor camps, production statistics were inflated, and news of food shortages were muffled. Disaster ensued: According to one estimate, thirty million people died.[39] The collective killings of 1967–1968 apparently were driven by similar dynamics. Although the killings started in local communities as early as 1967, most lives were lost following two Party Center directives in July 1968. The two provincial governments interpreted and relayed the directives as instructions to "preemptively attack class enemies," demanding concrete results. The system of collective killings was one local innovation. The logic of radicalization inherent in the relationship between local leaders and the upper authorities explains why collective killings occurred, paradoxically, when local governments were reestablished rather than earlier, when government authorities were in flux.

Mao's Ordinary Men

In the previous sections, I outlined a social-mobilization system with built-in incentives for state bureaucrats and other state-related individuals to pursue the politics of the time with fanatic enthusiasm. This system rendered some of those individuals enablers of collective killings. In this section, I discuss those who were most directly involved in the killings: the organizers and the killers.

The Organizers

"I do not complain that I am now in jail, neither would I even if my head rolled; because the consequence [of the Daoxian Massacre] was grave.

[39] Thomas P. Bernstein, "Stalinism, Famine, and Chinese Peasants: Grain Procurements during the Great Leap Forward," *Theory and Society* 13, no. 3 (1984), pp. 339–377.

But I cannot agree with the part of my verdict that said I orchestrated the killings in the entire county. At that time, I checked in with this [superior], and I checked in with that [superior]; but I never got a response. No one said we should not kill. No one came out to stop. Being just a district PAFD [People's Armed Forces Department] chief, how could I be responsible for such a big consequence [for the entire county]?"[40]

Those words were spoken by Guan Youzhi in an interview with writer Zhang Cheng in a government prison, ten years after the Daoxian Massacre occurred. Guan admitted his organizational role, although he believed he was made a scapegoat in post–Cultural Revolution politics. His account showed that his superiors acquiesced in his decision to kill, doing nothing to stop him. What is also strikingly clear, however, is that no one gave him an explicit order to kill; he made the decision on his own initiative. He also described to Zhang Cheng his thought process in reaching his deadly decision.

First, he pointed to his unwavering loyalty to the Party, due in part to his gratitude and indebtedness. In his words, he would "do whatever the Party asks." He joined the army in 1950, when he was recruited into the Party and then promoted to the cadre ranks. He was discharged eight years later and quickly became a district PAFD chief. In his nine-year tenure before the 1967 killings, he strove to be a model cadre. His honors included attending "Conference of Outstanding Individuals in Studying Mao's Work" at the provincial level, and his district was rewarded with a tractor for his work. "Just think for a minute. How could a big-coarse man like me become a party member and cadre if not for the Chinese Communist Party and Chairman Mao?"[41] Guan's official position and background represents a typical killing organizer. An army veteran with little education, he was the head of the PAFD.[42] It is not clear with whom Guan consulted at the county level when he was making

[40] Ibid, p. 81.

[41] Ibid.

[42] Despite the name, the PAFD at the local levels (i.e., commune and district) was a civilian office in charge of public security and militia training. In normal times, it was just one of many government branches with limited power, such as the transportation and health departments. During the Cultural Revolution – a period plagued by factional street battles and constant reshuffling of local governments – the PAFD emerged as the biggest winner of the power struggles. Indeed, more often than not, PAFD chiefs became the official or de facto head of the entire local government of a county, district, or commune. For example, after the powerseizure campaign, Wen Xueyi of Cangwu County in Guangxi Province and Shi Yishan of Huaxian County in Shannxi Province – both former PAFD heads – took the No. 1 position in their county.

the killing decision, but in his own district, he probably reported to no one.

Guan then described the general political climate as he perceived it: "Day in and day out, what I studied was to Never Forget Class Struggle.... " Finally, he mentioned as the immediate justification the factional conflict in the Cultural Revolution and rumors of rebellion among the Four Types: "In the time of the Cultural Revolution armed battles, the Rebel faction raided the PAFD office and ransacked weapons away. At the same time, it was said that the Four Types wanted to settle the old scores and to change the color of the sky [i.e., to restore Chaing Kai-shek to power], and that they wanted to rebel against the red government [meaning the newly established revolutionary committee]."[43]

Guan Youzhi may have engineered slaughters in his district without orders from his superiors, but self-initiative is even more evident in the case of Yuan Lipu, a district mayor in Daoxian. Yuan organized a three-day killing orgy that claimed 569 lives. He continued the murders even after a military directive to stop the killing was relayed to him personally by telephone. According to Zhang Cheng, during the climax of the Daoxian Massacre, the Lingling Prefecture Military Sub-District (which oversaw counties including Daoxian) issued a directive, which read in part: "The Four Types should not be indiscriminately killed. The children of Four Types should not be treated the same as Four-Type elements; instead, they should be united and educated as required by policies. The boundaries between dictatorship targets and nondictatorship targets should be drawn."[44] To implement this directive, the county authorities convened a meeting, which was attended by district-level cadres, including Jiang Guangde, Yuan Lipu's subordinate. Jiang left the meeting and telephoned Yuan. After relaying the spirit of the directive, Jiang added: "From now on, killings may still be allowed, but they must be approved by the upper level. It looks like they will come to an end soon, so it will be harder in the future. The situation requires us to hurry." Yuan regretted that they had not begun the killings earlier. He then quickly convened a crusading rally, featuring gongs and drums and a banquet. Afterwards, 120 elite militia members were dispatched to kill.

43 Ibid.

44 Zhang Cheng 章成, "Daoxian da tusha" 道县大屠杀 ["The Daoxian Massacre"], *Open Magazine* 开放杂志 (August 2001), pp. 81–82.

Yuan called his campaign, which wiped out 569 lives in three days, "the grand sweep."[45]

When Zhang Cheng met him at the prison, Yuan refused to take responsibility. His excuse was the enabling climate of the time: "The conviction of my crime is divorced with the historical facts. We should respect history; we should respect facts. The fact of the matter was that from the beginning to the end, no one from above came to me and said the killings were wrong. [The slogans of the time were that] rebellion was justified and revolution was no crime. We were told to trust the masses and respect their creative power." By creative power, he probably meant the willingness to raise the level of terror. Like the PAFD chief Guan, he offered no evidence that anyone from a higher level instructed him to organize the killings.[46]

Like Guan and Yuan, most killing organizers that appear in records were leaders in districts, communes, and villages. However, in a few notorious instances, county leaders were directly involved in organizing mass killings, including Wang Jianxun and Wang Guizeng – the revolutionary committee director and vice director, respectively, of Binyang County in Guangxi Province. The county *xianzhi* credited these top two leaders with organizing county-wide killings that claimed 3,883 lives, one of the highest totals for a county in the province.[47] There is also evidence that some county leaders convened cadre meetings to demand that local governments show concrete results of class struggle. Some meetings were accompanied by killings of Four Types to demonstrate compliance with the policy. Du Jianqing, the teacher from Wuhua who found refuge in a labor camp to avoid his brothers' fate, was told by fellow inmates that the killings in his county started with a demonstration rally organized by the county leaders in Mianyang Commune.[48] This sequence of events has credence in light of similar meetings and rallies reported elsewhere. A post–Cultural Revolution report compiled in 1987 by the Party Ratification Office of Cangwu County describes three such meetings, concluding that they greatly contributed to "random repudiations, random struggles,

[45] Ibid.

[46] Ibid.

[47] Binyang xianzhi bianzuan weiyuanhui 宾阳县志编纂委员会 *Binyang xianzhi* 宾阳县志 [Binyang County Gazetteer] (Nanning: Guangxi renmin chubanshe, 1987). For specific details of their role in organizing, see Zheng Yi 郑义, *Hongse jinianbei* 红色纪念碑 [*The Scarlet Memorial*] (Taipei, Taiwan: Huashi wenhua gongsi, 1993), pp. 2–40.

[48] Personal interview with Du Jianqiang, 2006.

random arrests, random imprisonments, random beatings, and random killings" in 1968.[49] The random killings were responsible for most of the 580 "unnatural deaths" in the county during the Cultural Revolution.[50]

On May 24, 1968, the newly established Cangwu County revolutionary committee held a Political Work Meeting in Lihu Commune. Attendees included Li Xuandian, first vice director; Shi Guang, vice director; Zhang Xi'ai, an army representative; a rebel organization leader from the county administration; and directors and PAFD heads from the local commune's revolutionary committees. The meeting site was chosen for the commune's outstanding performance in a campaign two weeks earlier. On May 9, the county had called for local communes to wage the "first wave of ferociously attacking class enemies." Although all communes heeded the call, Lihu stood out for its extensive persecutions. The commune's revolutionary committee and the Defending Red Headquarters dispatched thousands of militiamen, who ransacked 545 households, arrested 11, repudiated more than 100, and killed 5. A "live human exhibition" was staged to display ten struggle targets. The purpose of the May 24 meeting was to promote the Lihu example for other communes to emulate. The widespread abuses and killings were lauded in a second county-level meeting on June 9 and 10, 1968. Again attended by commune leaders from throughout the county, the meeting escalated the rhetoric about the supposedly impending threat from class enemies.[51]

Unlike the direct action of county officials in Binyang County in Guangxi Province, county-level authorities in these cases did not directly organize the killings, but they clearly gave the go-ahead to local cadres to do so. In counties without county-level cadre meetings or deadly demonstration rallies, the cadres likely knew what was happening in lower jurisdictions. The testimonials by district organizers Guan and Yuan confirm this; however, a central point remains true: Organizers received no orders to kill and were not coerced to do so. They killed from their own convictions and their understanding of the situation at the time. Even in counties where county-level meetings were held to

[49] Cangwu Party Ratification Office 苍梧整党办公室, "Zaocheng yanzhong houguo de 'sange huiyi'." 造成严重后果的 "三个会议" ["Three Meetings That Caused Severe Consequences"], unpublished documents (August 1987).

[50] Cangwu xianzhi bianzuan weiyuanhui 苍梧县志编纂委员会, *Cangwu xianzhi* 苍梧县志 [Cangwu County Gazetteer] (Nanning: Guangxi remin chubanshe, 1997), p. 482.

[51] Cangwu Party Ratification Office 苍梧整党办公室, "Zaocheng yanzhong houguo de 'sange huiyi'." 造成严重后果的 "三个会议" ["Three Meetings That Caused Severe Consequences"], unpublished documents (August 1987).

encourage class-struggle activity, county leaders never detailed a specific course of action. They neither defined the scope of targets nor recommended killing.[52] Community leaders at the district, commune, and village levels orchestrated the planning and execution of collective killings themselves. How can we understand the motives of these organizers?

The undercurrent of the political campaigns was elite competition and conflict.[53] Leaders with differing backgrounds found their fortunes waxing and waning, depending on the direction of the movement. If a production drive was billed as the primary political task, those with professional expertise and managerial skills prevailed; if a campaign was about peaceful study sessions to raise public consciousness, those schooled in political work became the new leaders; if the time was described as fraught with immediate and tangible threats from the class enemies, weaponry experts and security personnel took central stage. For this reason, local leaders competed in interpreting campaign policies from their superiors and strove to turn local movements and situations to their advantage. Such "turf wars" – that is, leaders from a branch of government taking over the central leadership as the political winds shifted – had been fought in previous campaigns. A common battle was between the "red" and the "expert," or political personnel and professionals. In time, as Mao accelerated political campaigns and emphasized class-struggle doctrine, the red increasingly dominated all levels of government.[54]

However, leadership replacement took on a new character during the Cultural Revolution. The power-seizure campaign and the turmoil that followed elevated a specific group of individuals,[55] who Tilly called "specialists in violence." They were "people who control means of inflicting damage on persons and objects," including "military personnel,

52 However, in the case of Cangwu County, radical leaders seemed to enjoy praise in subsequent meetings.

53 See Chapter 3.

54 See Andrew G. Walder, "Property Rights and Stratification in Socialist Redistributive Economies," *American Sociological Review* 57, no. 4 (1992), pp. 524–539; and Jonathan Unger, *Education under Mao: Class and Competition in Canton Schools, 1960–1980* (New York: Columbia University Press, 1982), for elaboration on elite selection based on the criteria of "red" and "expert." See also Shaoguang Wang, *Failure of Charisma: The Cultural Revolution in Wuhan* (Hong Kong and Oxford: Oxford University Press, 1995); and Eddy U, *Disorganizing China: Counter Bureaucracy and the Decline of Socialism* (Stanford, CA: Stanford University Press, 2007). Both document such turf wars in various guises – for example, between old regime personnel and new cadres, between political commissioners and production managers, and between party workers and intellectuals.

55 See Chapters 6 and 7 for a description of the typical sequence of events.

police, guards, jailers, executioners, and juridical officers."[56] In the jurisdictions in rural China, they included leaders and staff of the Public Security Department (PSD) and the PAFD. Cadres from the PAFD were particularly important because they had a dual role as civilian liaisons with the military and commanders of civilian militia. The county-level PAFD chiefs typically were also uniformed military officers. The militia consisted of almost every adult male in the population and was organized to the village level. They trained regularly and were armed with at least a few rifles in each village. At each level, the commanders were battle-tested army veterans. That veterans disproportionally filled the cadre ranks was not new: After 1949, southbound army officers and local guerrilla fighters discarded their uniforms and became cadres in counties, districts, and townships. They learned to oversee production and other civilian matters and gradually transformed into civilian leaders. Before the Cultural Revolution, the PSD and PAFD were two significant government branches but no more important than the department of health or transportation, for example.

The power-seizure campaign that began in Shanghai in January 1967 quickly swept the country, down to the village level. All leaders were removed as disgraced "power holders"; most were army veterans turned civilian leaders. In forming the new government, or revolutionary committees, the Party Center designated a "Three Combination" principle: The new leadership was to include equal shares of old leaders, mass-movement activists, and army officers. This policy greatly benefited PAFD cadres, and their leadership of the militia was key. Some joined the new leadership as old leaders, with the militia as mass support; others simply turned the militia into mass organizations and then joined the new leadership as mass-movement activists. Their connection to the military was advantageous because the new government was infiltrated by army officers. The turmoil and ever-growing drumbeat of class struggle primarily underscored the importance of their professional skills and institutional capital as specialists in violence. Once in power, the new community leaders were in full control of the social order. There were no actual potential challenges – definitely not from the Four Types and, in most cases, not even from recalcitrant mass organizations. However, the power and prestige of the new leaders had not been tested and consolidated in their colleagues' view, those who had just lost the power competition. To

[56] Charles Tilly, *The Politics of Collective Violence* (Cambridge: Cambridge University Press, 2003), p. 35.

escalate class struggle – ultimately, with extreme violent displays – was their solution to the problem. The killings clarified the political situation of the time and announced the depth of the new leaders' power.

The Killers

In Chapter 1, I introduced Zheng Mengxu, who killed Sha Kaichu and four other sons of former landlords in Xiaojiang Village, Hunan Province. Before the Land Reform, he was a shiftless drifter from another village, where he had worn out his welcome with a reputation for laziness, larceny, and misogyny. After 1949, he was invited to settle in Xiaojiang Village because he was the "poorest of the poor" and he had a relative there who was a village leader. He also was given part of the house originally owned by the Sha family. He had been a militia member since the Land Reform, always in the forefront of violent actions taken against the village's Four Types in subsequent campaigns. The village leadership relied on people like him to incite enthusiasm for political campaigns. Having little education, however, he never joined the ranks of the village leaders and had little prospect of doing so in the Cultural Revolution. Nonetheless, he enjoyed more power and prestige than ordinary villagers because of his close relationship with the village administrators and because he placed himself in the public eye – although doing so through actions that most villagers found deplorable. My informants speculated that he probably never overcame his inferiority complex, of which he was constantly reminded by his next-door neighbors – the previous owners of his house. The Cultural Revolution killings in Xiaojiang Village gave him the opportunity to finally excise this reminder. The Sha family dissolved after Kaichu's death. His wife remarried out of the village, taking three of the four children. The remaining son, a teenager, was later found guilty of a counter-revolutionary crime and sent to a labor camp.[57]

A similar figure was described by Zhang Cheng in his detailed account on a village pogrom in Daoxian County, Hunan Province, known as the Daoxian Massacre. Hu Maochang was illiterate, lazy, bad-tempered, and respected by few people in the village. In the summer of 1967, when his village set up a "Poor and Middle Peasant Supreme Tribunal" and "sentenced" twenty-four Four-Types to death, Hu volunteered to join the militia killing squad. "When it comes to the matter of killing class enemies, no one has the right to stop me," he said. When other volunteers seemed to hesitate at the execution site, he grabbed a knife from a militia member

[57] Personal interviews with Sha Kaiping and Ms. Li.

and chopped seven victims to death. He was so excited by the killings that afterwards, he returned to the village to search for more targets; he killed two toddlers in a landlord's house. He was rewarded with not only his self-perceived "heroism" but also with 55 *yuan*, a handsome sum that was more than his yearly "dividend" (i.e., the worth of his labor minus the cost of his food share, received from the production team).[58]

In the early 1980s, not long after the large-scale post–Cultural Revolution investigations in Guangxi Province, government officials welcomed writer Zheng Yi to conduct research into the collective killings and cannibalism. According to the book that he later published overseas, Zheng was given extraordinary access to internal documents and witnesses. In one case, he interviewed a former killer, Yi Wansheng, who was leisurely playing cards with two other old men. In a report by the county's public security bureau, Zheng learned that in May 1968, Yi killed a teenager and then mutilated the victim and ate his liver. Asked by Zheng about the killing and cannibalism, Yi was defiant and unrepentant: "Yes, I admit everything! Why should I be afraid of jail? I am eighty-six years old and have lived long enough." His explanation as to why he killed the teenager Deng was not entirely coherent but nevertheless provided a kind of self-justification:

> Why did I kill him? Because they camped in the mountains as bandits, causing trouble for the entire village. [Here, he must be referring to class enemies in general. In the early years after 1949, GMD elements and landlords waged resistance against the new government. The victim Deng was only an infant or toddler at the time, but that fact apparently mattered little to Yi.] I was a militia member at that time, and I had to report to patrol duties every night. For tens of days, my rifle rubbed my clothes until they were torn.... What was his father's crime? In the starving season that year, he was not willing to lend foodstuff to us villagers but to people from other villages.... He also led bandits to raid our village [after 1949].... [Deng] was killed by me. I will admit this to whoever asks. I was not afraid at all, because I had support from so many masses. Ha ha! In making revolution, our hearts are red. Did Chairman Mao not say this: If we do not kill them, they will kill us? Either you die or I die. This is what class struggle is like.[59]

These accounts suggest that the killers were recruited from unsavory elements in rural communities. However, Mao's class-struggle ideology

[58] Zhang Cheng 章成, "Daoxian da tusha" 道县大屠杀 ["The Daoxian Massacre"], *Open Magazine* 开放杂志 (September 2001), p. 61.

[59] See Zheng Yi 郑义, *Hongse jinianbei* 红色纪念碑 [*The Scarlet Memorial*] (Taipei, Taiwan: Huashi wenhua gongsi, 1993), pp. 38–40.

also played a significant role in their perception of the killing tasks. Older men with pre-1949 experience seemed particularly able to relate such ideology to their actions. Although class-struggle ideology did not call for the extermination of enemy families, as I argued in the last chapter, local killers made no distinction between Four-Type elements (i.e., *fenzi,* householders who carried the political label) and their family members, especially males (see Chapter 4).

Although it is unclear in the previous description whether killers selected victims only from rival clans, other accounts reveal that to be the case. My personal interviews with informants from Jinkeng Village in Guangdong Province suggest that in a rally leading up to the collective killings, militia members from Lis, Zengs, and Jins shouted names of Four Types from respective rival clans to go onto the stage and kneel. Zheng Cheng records this meeting in Daoxian, in which participants voted for targets from rival lineages to compile a victim list:

> The [village] party secretary Tang Shaozhi organized elite activists to discuss who should be killed and who should not. He nominated a name, followed by a discussion and a vote.... The Tangs wanted to protect [Four-Type] Tangs, and the Zhous wanted to protect [Four-Type] Zhous. When Tang Shaozhi first nominated Zhou Yuliang, the Tangs in the meeting all raised hands, while there was no hand from the Zhous. Then when someone nominated a Tang, the Zhous shouted "agree" in unison, and they all raised hands.... At the end, the meeting decided on a list of twelve.[60]

From these individual profiles, the influence of party class-struggle ideology on the perpetrators can be detected. Unlike the Nazi ideology, however, the Maoist version of victimization ideology never called for extermination. If the killers and organizers misunderstood, why did the misunderstanding focus on the most reprehensible actions possible? We can also detect – as in the case of Mo Zhengxun of Xiaojiang Village – the harboring of personal animosity against the victims. However, one killer was often responsible for many victims, including those with whom he had no prior disagreements. Zheng Mengxu not only killed his neighbor Sha Kaichu, but also four others from his village. Hu Maochang killed seven people and then sought out and slaughtered two toddlers. For those organizers who often were responsible for tens or hundreds of deaths, personal animosity simply cannot account for their motivation. The perpetrators sometimes cited rumors of the Four Types' supposed collective

[60] Zhang Cheng 章成, "Daoxian da tusha" 道县大屠杀 ["The Daoxian Massacre"], *Open Magazine* 开放杂志 (August 2001), p. 82.

action against the poor and middle peasants as a whole. Needless to say, these excuses are deplorably implausible.

An indication of the real reason lies in the public nature of the collective killings. Always a sensational event, the killings unfolded in front of the entire community. The organizers and killers made no attempt to hide them – to the contrary, rallies were held, gongs and drums played, banquets attended, and rewards announced. Spectators flooded to the riverbanks and roadsides to witness their neighbors' executions. Therefore, these events were foremost a public ritual; that is, the instrumental utility mattered less than the symbolic display.

Killers killed to demonstrate their power to fellow villagers and to clarify and enhance their social standing in the community. Among their motivations to kill, I enumerated ideological conviction, loyalty to leaders, and – in some cases – monetary rewards. To this list I add an intrinsic value of public killing: to announce the ultimate power of deciding another's life and death. The killers were individuals with questionable reputations. They were accustomed to being treated with scorn and contempt by other members of the community. Without education or talent, they had little opportunity to reverse these attitudes with ability. Ruthlessness and cruelty became their human capital to raise their status and join others: the village leaders, activists, and elite militia members. To be associated with the state in a village under Mao's regime was to finally enter the mainstream of the community.

Conclusion

The participants in the collective killings – the killers and organizers, as well as the enablers – were all "ordinary men" in that their actions were motivated primarily by personal gain or the avoidance of personal loss. However, they were distinctly different from the population at large. First, they were all associated with the state – as local cadres, elite militia members, or upper-level officials. Second, their profiles attest to a deeply held ideological belief in Mao's class-struggle doctrine, as evidenced by their lack of sympathy for their victims. Third, although there is no extensive evidence, some of the killers seemed to be psychologically disturbed, as demonstrated by their willingness to kill the extremely weak and their sometimes extraordinary displays of cruelty.

Despite their connections to the state, the perpetrators killed in the absence of any direct orders and without coercion, and they acted on their own initiative. This is demonstrated by the fact that their counterparts in most localities did not go to the same extremes in their interpretation of central directives. For the organizers, the public act of killing was their way of announcing to their intended audience the power that they now possessed. The reconstitution of local governments during the Cultural Revolution advanced former specialists in violence to the central stage of the new administration. Directing the mass movement in such an extreme direction was their way of consolidating power and neutralizing potential rivals. Some individuals with questionable social standing in their community became killers, hoping to improve their community standing and possibly their political standing as well.

The mass campaign degenerated into these atrocities for two reasons. During the Cultural Revolution, there was a need for tactical innovation because violent displays short of killing had become commonplace; earlier campaigns had deprived small-scale violence of its shock value. The upper-level authorities who did not endorse the killings could not contain the escalation due to the organizational pathology in Mao's government. Once immersed in a new campaign, leaders could not directly obtain sufficient information to monitor local cadres' behavior. Remedies came only after the human disaster had occurred.

The harshness of rural life motivated young men and women to join the cadre ranks. Yet, when they did, they found themselves in a tenuous position. New positions became scarce as the population increased and the economy worsened. Political campaigns increasingly became a zero-sum game of survival for both leaders and ordinary cadres. These were the elements of the "situation" in which the potential perpetrators found themselves. Chapters 6 and 7 describe how the legal constraints against violence disappeared and how a domestic war was fabricated in the months leading to the collective killings.

6

Demobilizing Law

To call the Cultural Revolution a time of lawlessness is an understatement. Liu Shaoqi, China's president, died in a solitary prison cell, never having been tried for any crime.[1] Photographs survive showing Peng Dehuai, the defense secretary deposed a few years earlier, on a stage with his hands bound behind him and a large placard hung around his neck, being "tried." In one of the rallies, beatings by the Red Guards broke two of his ribs.[2] Peng Zhen was "arrested" by Red Guards and paraded through the streets of Beijing – a city he had led as the mayor just months earlier – and then jailed for eight years without charge.[3] These denials of due process for the grand and powerful were not nearly as great as for those individuals out of the public eye who were deemed outcasts, such as former landlords and rich peasants in the countryside.

Lawless though it was, China was far from without rules and was not in a state of anarchy. China under Mao was a highly regulated society; behavior and thoughts were strictly channeled and programmed. Society was worthy of the term *tyranny*. In such an environment, taboos and boundaries abounded, including limits on political violence – that is,

[1] Hebei Ribao-Shukan Bao 河北日报-书刊报, "Dang'an jiemi: gongheguozhuxi Liu Shaoqi yuansi shilu 档案解密：共和国主席刘少奇冤死实录" ["Archives Unsealed: How the President of the Republic Died"], January 12, 2005; available at http://news.china.com/zh_cn/history/all/11025807/20050112/12061076.html; accessed September 10, 2008.

[2] Wenzhai Bao 文摘报, "Ai pudou bei daduan lianggen leigu 挨批斗被打断两根肋骨彭德怀生命最后时光" ["The Last Days of Peng Dehuai: Two Ribs Broken as Struggle Target"], August 15, 2008.

[3] Pitman B. Potter, *From Leninist Discipline to Socialist Legalism: Peng Zhen on Law and Political Authority in the PRC* (Stanford, CA: Stanford University Press, 2003), p. 5.

including the prohibition of unsanctioned killings of any civilian groups, the so-called class enemies included. In this chapter, I discuss the depletion of three sources of social control: the legal system, the party-state bureaucracy, and the political mass campaign. Law had a brief renaissance under Mao, but social control quickly turned away from the rule of law. In the Cultural Revolution, the regime displaced bureaucratic control – the main routinized form of authority – with the mass campaign. Not only was law (as it is commonly understood) demobilized; so also were other rules and institutions governing social behavior in a society mostly not under the rule of law.

Collective killings in 1967 and 1968 – with public killings unchecked for months and perpetrators unpunished for years – were in part a result of the two-stage demobilization of "law," understood here not only as laws in the conventional sense but also as rules of discipline maintained by the party–state apparatus. The first stage started in 1957–1958 when the Party reversed its brief course of building a nation with rule of law. A constitution enacted in 1954 proclaimed the protection of citizens' rights; however, all hope was dashed when a national campaign in 1957 resulted in hundreds of thousands being jailed or forced into labor camps as "Rightists."[4] The Party's supremacy was imposed on all levels of government bureaucracy, including the remaining nominal legal agencies.[5] Law as it is known in the West – with penal codes, due process, and the protection of individual rights – was next to nonexistent. In the following decade, a disciplined party–state bureaucracy ruled, combined with tightly controlled mass campaigns. Social and political behavior was regulated by bureaucratic directives and sanctioned by a command structure. The Cultural Revolution, with its signature campaign known as Power Seizure, again transformed the authority structure. Mass organizations ascended to become parallel governments and local governments were reorganized to become campaign machines.

My view is in contrast to two common misconceptions. Within China, the contemporary Chinese discourse usually blamed the "chaos" for past atrocities. "Ten years of turmoil" is a conventional intellectual framework

4 Ding Shu 丁抒, *Yangmou: Fan youpai yundong shimo* 阳谋: 反右派运动始末 [*Open Conspiracy: The Complete Story of Chinese Communist Party's Anti-Rightist Campaign*] (Hong Kong: Kaifang zhazhishe, 2006); Dali L. Yang, *Calamity and Reform in China: State, Rural Society, and Institutional Change Since the Great Leap Famine* (Stanford, CA: Stanford University Press); and Zheng Shiping, *Party vs. State in Post-1949 China: The Institutional Dilemma* (New York: Cambridge University Press, 1997).

5 Zheng, *Party vs. State in Post-1949 China*.

for retrospective examinations of the Cultural Revolution.[6] The other view, held by many Western observers, blames the violent and totalitarian nature of Mao's regime. Political killings are seen mostly as an outcome of intentional policies. Totalitarianism, however, is too simplistic and global a concept to explain why violence was more severe at some times than at other times.[7] Instead, I trace the collective killings in part to the breakdowns in "law" in China under Mao. The forms of organizational control in Mao's China set boundaries on behavior. When they failed in the Cultural Revolution, previously unacceptable actions became "all the rage."

Changing Modes of Social Control

Three ideal-typical modes of control are found in Mao's China: legal, party-bureaucratic, and mass campaign. The evolution of society from 1949 to the eve of the collective killings was a history of the changing emphases among the three modes. The collapse of legal constraints on violence in 1967 and 1968 was a result of two significant steps: the legal mode gave way to the party-bureaucratic mode, and then the party-bureaucratic mode gave way to the mass campaign.

My analysis draws from works by scholars of organizational control. Ouchi distinguishes three ideal types of organizational control – market, bureaucracy, and clan – and he suggests that the real-life control is often a combination of the three. "Market" is an efficient mode of control but is subject to the condition of sufficient information flow to form a meaningful "price." It monitors only the output of behavior. "Bureaucracy" builds on established authority structures and monitors both behavior and its output. It takes enormous personnel and it is often plagued by pathologies long recognized by theorists since Weber. "Clan" is a mode of control that invokes common values and beliefs. It aims at the human

6 CCP Central Committee 1981, "Resolution on Certain Questions in the History of Our Party since the Founding of the People's Republic of China," in Michael Schoenhals (ed.), *China's Cultural Revolution, 1966–1969: Not a Dinner Party* (Armonk, NY: Sharpe, 1996), pp. 296–303.

7 In her study on capital punishment under Mao, Zhang Ning notes: "This system is often represented as a form of totalitarianism where law was reduced to a simple instrument of control and repression, a point of view which is not mistaken but which does not illustrate the specific characteristics of Maoism." See Zhang Ning, "Political Origins of Death Penalty Exceptionalism: Mao Zedong and the Practice of Capital Punishment in Contemporary China," *Punishment & Society* 10 (2008), pp. 117–118.

mind to achieve desired behaviors and behavior outputs.[8] Ouchi's conceptual scheme echoes Etzioni's three types of incentives for compliance: remunerative, coercive, and normative. Dallin and Breslauer employed Etzioni's incentive types in their analysis of political terror in communist systems.[9]

Scholars often attribute Maoist practices in China to communist ideological doctrine, as though they came from a preexisting playbook.[10] After all, the new regime was built in the wake of revolutionary mobilizations that promised an egalitarian "heaven." However, this view does not recognize the fact that Mao, like most political leaders, was first and foremost a pragmatist in consolidating his rule. The dilemmas facing the Chinese rulers are not hard to recognize. Their control could not rely on an independent legal system. Under the rule of law, by definition, citizens are free to act as they see fit as long as they do not violate the law. That is, the law can monitor only the outcome of behavior, not behavior itself; therefore, the state has no way to mobilize citizens into collective action. Neither could control rely on the bureaucracy alone. Using rules and a disciplinary hierarchy, bureaucratic control can monitor behavior as well as the outcome of behavior, but this requires a large army of manpower and an effective way for monitoring the bureaucrats themselves. The Chinese state in the decades after 1949 simply was unable to support a sufficient number of bureaucrats. Moreover, a bureaucracy, by definition, is at risk of stagnation and corruption.[11] The control system needs an external entity to control itself.

Here is where the concept of the mass campaign comes in. Through rituals, this mode of control mobilizes values and beliefs aiming at a moral community. It works not only on behavior and behavioral outcomes but also on values and beliefs – it engineers a new spirit in hope of voluntary

[8] William G. Ouchi, "A Conceptual Framework for the Design of Organizational Control Mechanisms," *Management Science* 25 (1979), pp. 833–848.

[9] Amitai Etzioni, *A Comparative Analysis of Complex Organizations: On Power, Involvement, and Their Correlates* (New York: Free Press of Glencoe, 1961); and Alexander Dallin and George W. Breslauer, *Political Terror in Communist Systems* (Stanford, CA: Stanford University Press, 1970).

[10] See, e.g., Michael Mann, *The Dark Side of Democracy: Explaining Ethnic Cleansing* (New York: Cambridge University Press, 2005); and Benjamin A. Valentino, *Final Solutions: Mass Killing and Genocide in the Twentieth Century* (Ithaca, NY: Cornell University Press, 2004).

[11] For rampant bureaucratic pathologies in the Chinese system, see Harry Harding, *Organizing China: The Problem of Bureaucracy, 1949–1976* (Stanford, CA: Stanford University Press, 1981); and Ezra F. Vogel, *Canton under Communism: Programs and Politics in a Provincial Capital, 1949–1968* (Cambridge, MA: Harvard University Press, 1969).

compliance. Moreover, mass campaigns generate a large amount of information, often at the expense of local cadres who allegedly deviate from the Party line. When the "loudspeaker" directly communicates with the crowd, the marshals are checked. These three modes were interrelated. A case in point: Ushering in mass campaign as the major mode of control in the Cultural Revolution inevitably undermined the legal system and the bureaucracy. As the legal system and the party–state bureaucracy were dismantled, previously unacceptable behavior openly emerged without the necessary checks. The history of Mao's China leading up to the Cultural Revolution was of changing combinations of these three control modes. This is the subject to which I now turn.

Party versus Law: Before the Cultural Revolution

The first decade of the new regime witnessed the Communist Party's initial efforts in establishing a new legal system and then a fundamental reversal by the decade's end. The construction of a new legal system began with the destruction of the system that preceded it. A Party Center directive issued in February 1949 ordered the Six Legal Codes of the Nationalist (GMD) government to be repealed, including the constitution, civil, criminal, and commercial laws and civil and criminal procedures. A mass political struggle was launched to destroy the institutions of the GMD's legal order.[12] A State Council instruction signed by Zhou Enlai in October 1950 included an explicit statement of the Marxist principle: "Law is a tool for the oppression of one class by another." It blamed government workers who were still using legal concepts from the GMD era. In the first few years, executions were carried out in the court-martial style of mass justice.[13]

The most exemplary application was the so-called people's tribunal, a practice that would later be commonly used in collective killings during the Cultural Revolution. "This was a special court separate from, and independent of, the regular court of criminal and civil justice. Presided over by leaders of a work unit and consisting of political activists as judges, the people's tribunals had enormous judicial powers, ranging from summons for interrogation, arrest and detainment, to passing sentence and awarding the death penalty."[14]

[12] Ibid., p. 53.

[13] Laszlo Ladany, Marie-Luise Näth, and Jürgen Domes, *Law and Legality in China: The Testament of a China-Watcher* (London: Hurst, 1992), pp. 61–62.

[14] Zheng, *Party Vs. State in Post-1949 China*, p. 57.

Peng Zhen, the mayor of Beijing who would suffer from the mass version of justice during the Cultural Revolution, reportedly presided at one such tribunal. He spoke before a struggle rally in March 1951:

> Comrades, what should we do with all the criminals, bandits, secret agents, evil landlords, and heads of reactionary Taoist sects?" The crowd unanimously roared: "Shoot them." The mayor agreed and commented: "Truly it is not cruelty. It is mercy. We are protecting the lives of the people whom they harm.... This act we perform according to law. Those who have to be killed, we kill.[15]

Those executed in this type of tribunal included Sha Kaichu's father in Xiaojiang Village, Hunan Province, and Du Zhengyi's father in Dukeng Village, Guangdong Province.[16]

1954: A Year of Hope

The first three years after 1949 saw the passage of three major laws on marriage, land, and unions.[17] However, it was 1954 that seemed to herald a new path of state-building. A truce was signed in June 1953 to end the Korean War and military operations ended in late 1953 in suppressing resistance activities. The first National People's Congress (NPC) convened on September 15, 1954, in Beijing and approved the first state constitution. It granted "a galaxy of freedoms," as Ladany stated, including freedom of speech, publication, association, demonstration, and religious beliefs. It also proclaimed that no citizens were to be subject to arrest without warrants and that individuals from the former propertied classes were to be granted a means of livelihood.[18] In all seriousness, Mao himself commented on the new constitution: "Once it is approved, the whole nation, one and all, should observe it."[19]

The NPC also passed several organic laws for reconstructing the major branches of the government, including the judiciary (i.e., the People's Court and the People's Procuratorate). These laws declared the independence of the legal system and proclaimed equality under law for all citizens. For example, the People's Court Organization Law prescribed

[15] Ladnay et al., *Law and Legality in China*, pp. 62–63.

[16] See Chapters 1 and 3.

[17] They were the Marriage Law (April 1950), the Land Reform Law (June 1950), and the Trade Union Law (June 1950). See Ladnay et al., *Law and Legality in China*; and Zheng, *Party Vs. State in Post-1949 China*.

[18] The People's Republic of China Constitution, 1954; and Ladnay et. al., *Law and Legality in China*, p. 66.

[19] Cf. Zheng, *Party Vs. State in Post-1949 China*, p. 59.

the blueprint of an elaborate system of legal organizations. It declared that "the people's courts are independent, only subject to law." It stated that within the law, all citizens are equal with regard to trial proceedings regardless of race, ethnicity, gender, occupation, social origins, religion, education, property, or length of residence. The law designated standard legal procedures including a two-staged trial (i.e., preliminary and conclusive trials) and appeals processes. Another law was enacted for the People's Procuratorate system with similar provisions in terms of legal independence and equal rights.[20]

A complete judicial system was to be established. The constitution and the two organic laws defined the structures, functions, jurisdiction, and legal methods of the court and procuratorate. Under the Supreme People's Court, a three-level court system was set up. If these laws were to be honored, people's tribunals would lose their legitimate judicial powers. By July 1957, a total of 4,108 laws, legal codes, regulations, and rules were approved. Chinese legal scholars optimistically predicted a "new historical stage."[21] Liu Shaoqi, the No. 2 man in the Party Center, reinforced this impression in a speech in 1956: "The period of revolutionary storm and stress is past; new relations of production have been set up, and the aim of our struggle is changed.... A complete legal system becomes an absolute necessity."[22] Mao confirmed this observation in 1957: "The law must be observed and the revolutionary legal system must not be undermined."[23]

1957–1958: A Reversal

However, the new legal system was stillborn. Khrushchev's 1956 speech on Stalinist crimes shocked many in the West; in China, however, it alerted Mao of the danger of "revisionist restoration."[24] In the summer of 1957, hundreds of thousands were labeled "Rightists" – a new category of class enemies – and purged from state payrolls. Central among the contradictions in the experiments of legal reform was the relationship between

[20] The People's Republic of China People's Court Organization Law, 1954, Articles 4, 5, and 11; The People's Republic of China People's Procuratorate Organization Law, 1954, Articles 5, 6, 15, and 16.

[21] Zheng, *Party Vs. State in Post-1949 China*, pp. 58–60.

[22] Cf. Zheng, *Party Vs. State in Post-1949 China*, p. 61.

[23] Zheng, *Party Vs. State in Post-1949 China*.

[24] Xiao Donglian 肖东连, Xie Chuntao 谢春涛, Zhu Di 朱地, and Qiao Jining 乔继宁, *Qiusuo zhongguo: wen'ge qianshinian*, vol. 1 求索中国: 文革前十年 (上) [*Exploring the Chinese Way: 10 Years before the Cultural Revolution*] (Beijing, China: Hongqi chubanshe, 1999), pp. 37–52.

the revolutionary party and the new state. "The courts were responsible to the corresponding governments on county and provincial levels. The prosecutor's offices were to act on their own. However, all worked under the all powerful Communist Party headed by Mao [Zedong] – who, up till 1959, also held the post of head of state."[25] One critic pointed out that "the National People's Congress merely carries out the formality of raising hands and passing resolutions."[26] That opinion was seconded by another: "On many occasions when major matters were under discussion, often only the democratic personages spoke, whereas the party members declined to utter a word. Does this indicate that the party has already discussed and made its decisions on the matters concerned?"[27] Was the party above the law? A third critic pointed out: "Although the constitution has come into force, yet there are still a section of the leaders who take a nihilist standpoint toward law, maintaining that it is only natural for the party to take the place of the government, that the party's orders are above the law, and [that] words of party members are regarded, by themselves, as 'golden rules and jade laws.'"[28]

These criticisms came to the public domain in the notorious months of early 1957, known as "One Hundred Flowers Bloom." Mao encouraged intellectuals, noncommunists, and government workers to speak out to help rectify the Party. Thirteen forums were organized in Beijing, and they were copied at local levels. By May, university students had begun to put up posters on campus to proclaim their views and criticism.[29] However, the volume and ferocity of criticism alarmed Mao and the Party, which then decided to reverse course. The first new order of business was to persecute the critics. The "anti-Rightist" campaign commenced in the summer of 1957. An informant in Cangwu County told me that even after the national policy had reversed and the persecutions began, cadres and intellectuals were lured into criticism forums, and their words would be used against them immediately afterwards.[30]

By Mao's estimate, as many as 10 percent of noncommunists and intellectuals were "Bourgeois Rightists."[31] Quotas were sent to the cultural and educational sectors and local government agencies. According

[25] Ladnay et al., *Law and Legality in China*, p. 66.
[26] Zheng, *Party Vs. State in Post-1949 China*, p. 65.
[27] Ibid.
[28] Ibid.
[29] Ibid.
[30] Personal interviews with Mr. Zhao, 2006.
[31] Zheng, *Party Vs. State in Post-1949 China*.

to official figures published twenty years later, 552,877 people nationwide were designated as Rightists in 1957–1958,[32] although Ding Shu suggests that a more accurate number is 800,000.[33] They were subsequently subjected to denunciations and dismissals from offices and jobs; many were exiled from the cities to labor camps in remote rural areas. According to the *xianzhi*, the numbers of Rightists in Mengshan, Cangwu, and Xingning Counties were 148, 310, and 732, respectively. Among the 310 Cangwu Rightists, 13 were sentenced to jail, 43 were exiled to labor camps, 89 were expelled from their offices to home villages, and 149 were forced into labor under surveillance.[34]

The campaign marked the end of the new legal system. Once designated as a Rightist, a victim immediately lost every right granted by the 1954 constitution. Guilt was established in struggle sessions in which individuals attacked one another, with no semblance of due process. This pattern would be repeated in subsequent political campaigns. Although by June 1957 the draft criminal law had gone through dozens of revisions, the onset of the new political campaign ended the process. A Party committee on legal affairs reported the following to the Politburo: "According to the actual conditions in our country, it is no longer necessary to formulate criminal code, civil code, and procedural laws."[35] The Party exercised complete organizational control after the campaign. In a Party conference in 1957, Mao clarified the new policy as follows: "The politics and law, as well as cultural and educational departments of local governments, must receive instructions from provincial, municipal, or autonomous regional party committees, and provincial, municipal, or autonomous regional people's governments, provided there is no violation of the polices and

[32] Ibid.

[33] For detailed accounts of the campaign and its victimization, see Ding Shu 丁抒, *Yangmou: Fan youpai yundong shimo* 阳谋: 反右派运动始末 [*Open Conspiracy: The Complete Story of Chinese Communist Party's Anti-Rightist Campaign*]; Zhu Zheng 朱正, *Fan youpai douzheng shimo*, vols. 1 and 2. 反右派斗争始末(上, 下) [*The Chronology of the Anti-Rightist Campaign*] (Hong Kong: Mingbao chubanshe, 2004). For detailed biographical stories of the high-profile Rightists, including Shi Liang, who was in charge of the legal system, see Zhang Yihe 章怡和,zuihou de guizu [最后的贵族] (*The Last Aristocrats*) (Hong Kong: Oxford University Press, 2006).

[34] Mengshan xianzhi bianzuan weiyuanhui 蒙山县志编纂委员会, *Mengshan xianzhi* 蒙山县志 [*Mengshan County Gazetteer*] (Nanning: Guangxi renmin chubanshe, 1993); Cangwu xianzhi bianzuan weiyuanhui 苍梧县志编纂委员会, *Cangwu xianzhi* 苍梧县志 [*Cangwu County Gazetteer*] (Nanning: Guangxi remin chubanshe, 1997); and Xingning xian difang zhi bianxiu weiyuanhui 兴宁县地方志编修委员会, *Xingning xianzhi* 兴宁县志 [*Xingning County Gazetteer*] (Guangzhou: Guangdong renmin chubanshe, 1998).

[35] Zheng, *Party Vs. State in Post-1949 China*, p. 74.

regulations of the Center."[36] After the 1957–1958 Anti-Rightist Movement, the mass campaign returned as the predominant institution of authority – a practice honed in wartime and elevated in the Land Reform. Class struggle was the dominant framework for resolving social and political conflicts. In one of the most forceful statements on this matter in the intervening years before the Cultural Revolution, Mao stated in a Party Congress in 1962: "In a socialist country, we have to recognize the existence of class and class struggle.... From now on, the issue of class struggle must be talked about every year, every month, every day."[37]

Legal Institutions at the Grassroots

According to the county gazetteers, or *xianzhi*, procuratorates and courts were established at the county level following the 1954 series of national legislation, in addition to the security bureaus established earlier. Despite the 1957–1958 campaign, these three remained in place as government branches and functioned in their limited ways until the Cultural Revolution. A typical account reads as follows: "Panyu People's Prosecution Yuan was founded on June 4, 1955. Toward the end of 1957, the county was engaged in the Anti-Rightist campaign, which denounced the oversight function of the Prosecution Yuan. The prosecution work was paralyzed.... The Yuan resumed work on June 10 [1959].... As the Cultural Revolution started, the county's security bureau, prosecution Yuan, and court were put under military leadership; the prosecution function was default, and the Yuan ceased to function. After the founding of the Panyu Revolutionary Committee on March 1, 1968, the functions of the three branches (security, prosecution, and court) were delegated to a security committee. The Prosecution Yuan was disbanded."[38] Similar descriptions are found under the headings of "Security Bureau" and "the People's Court."[39]

The legal statistics available in some *xianzhi* indicate that these institutions continued to function after 1957. For example, Wuhua *xianzhi*

36 Ibid., pp. 74–75.

37 Xiao Donglian 肖东连, Xie Chuntao 谢春涛, Zhu Di 朱地, and Qiao Jining 乔继宁, *Qiusuo zhongguo: wen'ge qianshinian*, vol. 2 求索中国: 文革前十年 (ト) [*Exploring the Chinese Way: 10 Years before the Cultural Revolution*] (Beijing, China: Hongqi chubanshe, 1999), p. 952.

38 Panyu shi difangzhi bianzuan weiyuanhui 番禺市地方志编纂委员会, *Panyu xianzhi* 番禺县志 [*Panyu County Gazetteer*] (Guangzhou: Guangdong renmin chubanshe, 1995), p. 642.

39 Ibid., pp. 634–653.

TABLE 6.1. *Civil and Criminal Cases in China, 1950–1965*

Year	Total	Criminal	Civil
1950	1,154,081	475,849	678,232
1951	1,866,279	959,398	906,881
1952	2,202,403	723,725	1,478,678
1953	2,202,815	344,909	1,857,906
1954	2,186,826	896,666	1,290,160
1955	2,098,655	1,077,716	1,020,939
1956	1,523,344	722,557	800,787
1957	1,796,391	868,886	927,505
1958	2,372,808	1,899,691	473,117
1959	960,838	560,157	400,681
1960	864,686	543,868	320,818
1961	1,074,249	437,750	636,499
1962	1,187,850	317,769	870,081
1963	1,238,816	415,648	823,168
1964	929,030	262,199	666,831
1965	818,520	237,660	580,860
Cumulative total, 1950–1965	24,477,591	10,744,448	13,733,143

Source: David Bachman (2006), "Aspects of an Institutionalizing Political System: China, 1958–1965."

records that, on average, there were 511 criminal cases between 1955 and 1957, 294 between 1960 and 1962, and 146 between 1963 and 1965.[40] These institutions, however, were far from independent of the local Party committee and government, working in conjunction with political campaigns. For example, the Xingning County *xianzhi* records that in 1955, counter-revolutionary crimes comprised 60 percent of criminal cases. Also, most political prosecutions took place in struggle sessions and campaign rallies, bypassing these institutions.

The rule of law gave way after 1954 but, before 1967, legal agencies (e.g., the police and courts), as part of the party–state bureaucracy, continued to exert control in certain situations. They were particularly significant for sanctions of individual crimes outside the bounds of political campaigns. Execution, for example, belonged to a certain level of approval.[41] Table 6.1 lists criminal and civil cases in China between 1950

[40] Wuhua xian difang zhi bianzuan weiyuanhui 五华县地方志编纂委员会, *Wuhua xianzhi* 五华县志 [*Wuhua County Gazetteer*] (Guangzhou: Guangdong renmin chubanshe, 1998), p. 432.

[41] See my discussion on the death penalty later in this chapter. Yang Su, "Tumult from Within: State Bureaucrats and Chinese Mass Movement, 1966–71" (Ph.D. dissertation, Stanford University, Stanford, CA, 2003).

TABLE 6.2. *Types of Criminal Cases in China, 1950–1965*

Year	Criminal	Of Which Property-Related Crimes	Of Which Crimes against People	Of Which Murder	Percent Murder Violent Crime	Rare	Percent Rape Violent Crime
1950	475,849	51,553	109,228	11,260	10.31	4,358	3.99
1951	959,398	70,539	92,427	16,887	18.27	19,060	20.62
1952	723,725	64,872	159,384	13,193	8.28	41,118	25.80
1953	344,909	70,900	211,101	17,606	8.34	44,349	21.01
1954	896,666	5,350	25,718	–	–	16,559	64.39
1955	1,077,716	34,763	24,034	–	–	17,815	74.12
1956	722,557	75,834	126,948	8,066	6.35	21,094	16.62
1957	868,886	133,467	166,760	8,315	4.99	24,938	14.95
1958	1,899,691	360,547	114,833	17,621	15.34	48,641	42.36
1959	560,157	108,891	46,288	7,931	17.13	16,499	35.64
1960	543,868	161,687	29,170	10,727	36.77	11,050	37.88
1961	437,750	153,045	30,878	9,096	29.46	6,472	20.96
1962	317,769	26,412	40,518	5,457	13.47	6,974	17.21
1963	415,648	105,584	192,702	5,393	2.80	13,822	7.17
1964	262,199	39,531	65,067	4,960	7.62	11,988	18.42
1965	237,660	33,929	61,473	4,599	7.48	12,639	20.56

Source: David Bachman (2006), "Aspects of an Institutionalizing Political System: China, 1958–1965."

and 1965. The categories range from political crimes such as "counter-revolutionary" to personal crimes such as murder, rape, theft, and forgery.[42] Crime categories varied slightly over the years, but by and large remained the same. Table 6.2 reproduces the prosecution statistics of murder cases from 1950 to 1965. It is clear from the two tables that the legal system played a significant role in social control.

Professional legal proceedings appear to be only a minor part of the daily operation of the legal agencies. They were woefully understaffed, reflecting the government's limited capacity to support workers on the state payroll. In 1958, there were only 10 cadres and officers in the security bureau of Cangwu County, which had a population of 90,302 that year.[43] More important, they served mainly as guiding agencies for a vast network of mass organizations: that is, the village security committees, staffed by part-time members of the people's militia. In 1951, Cangwu

[42] Zuigao renmin fayuan yanjiushi 最高人民法院研究室, *Quanguo renmin fayuan sifa tongji lishi ziliao huibian: 1949–1998 (Xingshi bufeng)* 全国人民法院司法统计历史资料汇编: 1949–1998 (刑事部分) (Beijing: Renmin fayuan chubanshe, 2000).

[43] Cangwu xianzhi bianzuan weiyuanhui 苍梧县志编纂委员会, *Cangwu xianzhi* 苍梧县志 [*Cangwu County Gazetteer*] (Nanning: Guangxi remin chubanshe, 1997), p. 419.

County established Security and Defense Committees in its 69 townships and 814 villages with a part-time staff of 1,482,[44] not including many other militia members not on the committees. In 1951, each village in Cangwu County had forty to fifty militia and fifteen to twenty rifles. After the 1953 national policy to develop militias, militiamen constituted 20 percent of the population; every male between sixteen and forty-five years old was expected to join.[45]

Mao repeatedly warned the population of possible wars imposed by "imperialist" countries such as the United States and, later, the Soviet Union. Two of his slogans were featured on village walls everywhere: "Let the entire population become soldiers" and "Greatly develop militia brigades."[46] Every volume of the *xianzhi* featured a section entitled "Military Matters," in which "Militia" was a prominent chapter. Xingning County is typical example, which claimed to have 321,819 militia members in 1958, or 47.3 percent of the population (apparently, membership was not limited to males) and 240,000 during the Cultural Revolution. Whereas other legal institutions shrank in the Cultural Revolution, the militia organizations expanded.[47] In the recurrent mass campaigns, the militia was the most critical linkage between the population and the state violence machine. It performed duties of the police, prosecutor, and court and constituted the backbone of the people's tribunals that murdered Four Types and their family members in 1967–1968.

Bureaucracy versus Campaign: The Cultural Revolution

The Party also used mass campaigns to attack and reform its bureaucracy. The local authority in transition created new patterns of interaction between the bureaucracy and the mass campaign. In some ways, bureaucratic control was weakened; in other ways, it was strengthened. The contradictory process helped usher in collective killings, an extreme form of collective violence that had not existed in the past.

Mao's China had a history of political campaigns – not a year went by without a new major campaign, as shown in Table 6.3. A political

[44] Ibid., p. 553.

[45] Ibid., p. 606.

[46] Personal interviews with informants in Xingning, Cangwu, and Wuhua Counties, 2006. (姓名).

[47] Xingning xian difang zhi bianxiu weiyuanhui 兴宁县地方志编修委员会, *Xingning xianzhi* 兴宁县志 [*Xingning County Gazetteer*] (Guangzhou: Guangdong renmin chubanshe, 1998), pp. 604–605.

TABLE 6.3. *Campaigns in China: 1950–1969*

Year	Campaign	Scope
1950	Party/Army Rectification	Party organization
1950–52	Agrarian Reform	Newly liberated areas
	Suppression of Counter-revolutionaries	Nationwide
1950–53	Resist U.S. and Aid Korea	Nationwide
1951	Party Rectification and Building	Party organization
	Criticizing Wu Xun	Cultural and ideological areas
1951–54	Mutual Aid Teams	Countryside
1951–52	Democratic Reform	Industrial enterprises
	Thought Reform	Intellectuals, teachers
	Three-Antis	Nationwide
1952	Five-Antis	Urban industrialists
1952–54	Party Member Registration	Party organization
1953	New Three-Antis	Party and government officials
	Organizing Primitive APCs	Countryside
	Study of Marxism–Leninism	Rural cadres
	Study of the Party's General Line	Nationwide
	Criticizing Yu Pingbo and Hu Shi	Areas of literature
1953–54	Opposing Gao-Rao Anti-Party Alliance	High-ranking Party officials
1955	Agricultural Collectivization	Countryside
1955–56	Anti-Hu Feng	Nationwide
	Anti-Idealism	Academic and cultural areas
	Socialist Reform of Private Business	Private entrepreneurs
1955–57	Exposing "Hidden Counter-revolutionaries"	Party, government, and army
1957	"Hundred Flowers"	Intellectuals
1957	Party Rectification	Party organization
1958	Criticizing Ma Yinchu	Colleges/universities
1957–58	Anti-Rightists	Nationwide
1958–59	Great Leap Forward	Nationwide
	Socialist and Communist Education	Countryside
1959	Criticizing Bourgeois Literature and Art	Literature and art areas
1958–60	People's Commune	Countryside
1959–60	Anti-Rightist Deviation	Party organization
1960	Setting Up Communal Mess Halls	Countryside
	Learn from Anshan Steel Company	Enterprises and large cities
	Strengthening Ideological Work	Army & government institutions
1961	Rectification of People's Communes	Countryside
	Reeducation of Party Members	Party organization
1963	Learn from Lei Feng	Nationwide
	Criticizing Art and Academic Authorities	Art and academic areas

(*continued*)

TABLE 6.3 *(continued)*

Year	Campaign	Scope
1963–64	Five-Antis Campaign	Party and government agencies
	Art and Literature Rectification	Professional associations
1964	Learn from Daqing	Industry and transportation sectors
	Learn from Dazhai	Countryside
	Party Rectification	Party organization
1964–66	Socialist Education	Rural cadres
1965	Preparing for War	Nationwide
1966–69	Cultural Revolution	Nationwide
1969	Party Rectification	Party organization

Sources: Zhongguo gongchandang lishi dashiji ("A Chronology of the Chinese Communist Party History"), Party History Research Office of the CCP Central Committee (Beijing: Renmin chubanshe, 1989); *Dangshi yanjiu, yu jiaoxue* ("Research and Teaching of Party History"), published by the Party History Teaching and Research Office of the Central Party School.

campaign served two purposes: one related to the elite, the other related to the masses. Leaders had few ways of monitoring their lower-level subordinates, and the mass campaigns compensated for the information deficit. Moreover, the campaigns served to vacate bureaucratic positions in order to reward young activists. Purges became the main source of new positions because the size of bureaucracy was stagnant because of dismal economic performance.[48] To justify purges, elite conflict was framed in class-struggle terms. Therefore, campaigns also served to renew the artificial class divide between the masses, which was a cornerstone of the "reality" of class struggle.

Campaigns endangered the preexisting authority; however, before the Cultural Revolution, they were conducted by the party–state bureaucracy, often assisted by work-teams sent from the above. This pattern was altered during the Cultural Revolution – an unprecedented campaign that dismantled and reorganized local bureaucratic units. Consider the analogy of a crowded village square controlled by two mechanisms: a loudspeaker and a group of marshals on the ground. The loudspeaker grants authority to the marshals, and the marshals enforce instructions

[48] Andrew G. Walder and Yang Su, "The Cultural Revolution in the Countryside: Scope, Timing, and Human Impact," *The China Quarterly* 173 (2003), pp. 74–99; Yang Su, *Tumult from Within: State Bureaucrats and Chinese Mass Movements, 1966–1971* (Ph.D. dissertation, Stanford University, Stanford, CA, 2003, Chapter 3); and Yang Su, "State Sponsorship or State Failure? Mass Killings in Rural China, 1967–68." (Irvine, CA: Center for the Study of Democracy, University of California, Irvine, 2003).

by the loudspeaker. Then, the loudspeaker calls for the crowd to replace the marshals; chaos ensues.

The Movement Comes to the Countryside

As implied by its name, the Cultural Revolution was first meant to be a movement within cultural and educational sectors. However, a series of policies ended up extending the movement to the general population. The first major document about the movement – the May 16 Notice in 1966 – was distributed to county-level governments.[49] Rural county leaders studied it and strove to find local relevancy by organizing campaigns in their small cultural and educational sectors (i.e., teachers, artists, doctors, and students). Two months later, on August 8, another major document appeared that still stressed that "the current focus of the Cultural Revolution movement should be drawn on cultural and educational units, and the party's and governmental agencies in the *major or middle cities*."[50] At the end of 1966, the Party Center issued on December 15 yet another document addressing campaign policies for rural counties. By this time, however, mass organizations in the countryside had "mushroomed" beyond government agencies and cultural and educational units.[51]

As the Main Events section in the *xianzhi* show, the movement in the countryside was under bureaucratic control until September 1966. In the first stage, typical practices of a county movement included setting up a Cultural Revolution Committee and issuing a countywide notice – time-honored tactics to respond to calls for a new political campaign. In Guangdong and Guangxi Provinces, two thirds of the counties reported the formation of a committee and one third reported the issuance of a notice.[52] Authorities then often sent work-teams to "key-point units," such as high schools, hospitals, and theaters; about one third of counties reportedly did so. Their inspiration may have come from newspaper reports about the practice in urban centers. However, if work-teams in urban centers were a response to the disorder caused by student rebellions,

49 CRRM. *Zhongguo renmin jiefanjun guofang daxue dangshi dangjian zhenggong jiaoyanshi* 国防大学党史党建政工教研室, *Wenhua da geming yanjiu ziliao* 文化大革命研究资料 (上) [*The Cultural Revolution Research Materials*], vol. 1 (Beijing: Zhongguo renmin jiefanjun guofang daxue dangshi chubanshe, 1988), pp. 1–4.

50 Ibid., p. 76, emphasis added by the author.

51 Ibid., p. 189.

52 For these and other statistics of county reactions, see Su, *Tumult from Within*, Chapter 3.

it is unclear whether the practice in rural counties was just a mimicking gesture. Some *xianzhi* explicitly addressed the purpose of the work-team: It was not tasked to quell disorder or rebellion but rather to coordinate organized mass actions. Moreover, about two thirds of the counties in each province reported organizing the masses during denunciation sessions to repudiate the "Three-Family Village" – that is, the three fallen Beijing leaders. Some county *xianzhi* reported another action, "dragging out black gangs," which refers to local individuals who conducted deeds similar to the Three-Family Village, or those who simply had "historical problems" (e.g., former landlords). A fourth response included study sessions in which teachers were asked to criticize one another. Similar study and struggle sessions were conducted among the staff and cadres from hospitals, theaters, and writers' guilds. As a result, school principals, educational and cultural bureau chiefs, and county secretaries and mayors in charge of cultural, educational, and health sectors comprised the first group of leaders to be purged.

As a new political phenomenon, the Red Guards first reached local counties through reports of Mao's inspections in Tiananmen Square.[53] On August 18, 1966, Mao inspected one million Red Guards, an event that was prominently publicized in newspapers throughout China. Four days later, led by the *People's Daily*, newspapers celebrated the fact that Red Guards in Beijing and other major cities took to the streets, beginning the "Smash Four Olds" campaign, which was designed to destroy all physical embodiments of "old thoughts, old cultures, old customs, and old habits."[54] In the days that followed, students in local counties followed suit, burning books, raiding homes, and tormenting individuals who were allegedly associated with the "four olds." The students were typically organized by the school youth-league leadership. Armbands and other paraphernalia were bought and distributed by local governments. Empowered by this campaign, students gradually gained autonomy – many eventually disavowing their governmental sponsors and turning against them. In the beginning, they mainly targeted authority figures in their immediate circle, mostly teachers and principals who had been

53 In the nation's capital, Beijing, the first Red Guard group was formed by a group of students in Qinghua University Attached High School. They named their group "Red Guards" as early as May 1966. In early August, a letter and three of their posters reached Mao through Jiang Qing. Mao not only publicly praised them but also counted himself as a member of the Red Guards in the first of his series of inspections of the "Little Generals of Revolution" on Tiananmen Square.

54 CRRM, Vol. 1, pp. 86–89.

labeled as legitimate targets by the government in the study and struggle sessions.

On September 5, 1966, the Party Center and the State Council jointly issued a call to organize Red Guards to learn "revolutionary experiences" in Beijing.[55] Although the notice seemed applicable only at the provincial level, most local counties reportedly selected Red Guard representatives among students and teachers to join the incursion. Typically, a few hundred students and teachers were selected by the government to join the crowd in Tiananmen Square for Mao's inspection. At the same time, wave after wave of urban Red Guards from major cities entered local counties for the "Great Link-Up" (*chuanlian*). Local governments were asked to provide support, usually by setting up reception stations to provide room and board as well as supplies for creating banners and posters. County governments sponsored the Red Guards *chuanlian* not only organizationally but also financially, hoping to cultivate loyal mass organizations.[56]

Instead, the incoming and returning Red Guards shook up the local bureaucracy. In Huaxian County in Shanxi Province, the county authorities dutifully organized a rally at the bus station to receive a group of returning Red Guards. However, "the very next day, there emerged a new slogan, 'Smash the two committees [i.e., the county's party committee and the county government named the People's Committee at the time]; thoroughly make revolution!' Overnight, the streets of the county seat were swaddled with new big-character-posters."[57] County leaders gingerly weathered the political storm in the first months of the Cultural Revolution; however, by the end of year, disorder could no longer be averted because Mao called for attacks on the so-called bourgeois reactionary line in the entire Chinese bureaucracy. At the same time, a new state policy extended the right to organize from students to the population at large.

55 Ibid., p. 412.

56 Pingnan xianzhi bianzuan weiyuanhui 平南县志编纂委员会, *Pingnan Xianzhi* 平南县志 [*Pingnan County Gazetteer*] (Nanning: Guangxi renmin chubanshe, 1993), p. 38; Gongcheng Yaozu zizhixian xianzhi bianzuan weiyuanhui 恭城瑶族自治县县志编纂委员会, *Gongcheng Xianzhi* 恭城县志 [*Gongcheng County Gazetteer*] (Nanning: Guangxi renmin chubanshe, 1992), p. 305; Tiandong xianzhi bianzuan weiyuanhui 田东县志编纂委员会, *Tiandong Xianzhi* 田东县志 [*Tiandong County Gazetteer*] (Nanning: Guangxi renmin chubanshe, 1998), p. 482; and Luchuan xianzhi bianzuan weiyuanhui 陆川县志编纂委员会, *Luchuan Xianzhi* 陆川县志 [*Luchuan County Gazetteer*] (Nanning: Guangxi renmin chubanshe, 1993), p. 26.

57 Huaxian difangzhi bianzuan weiyuanhui 华县地方志编纂委员会, *Hua Xianzhi* 华县志 [*Huaxian County Gazetteer*] Uncensored and unpublished version, p. 11.

The first wave of nonstudent mass organizations emerged from staff and low-ranking cadres in governmental agencies – the Party county committee, county government, and various functionary bureaus. Earlier county administrations had established nonstudent organizations, often called Scarlet Guards (*chi wei dui*), whose main mission was to maintain order in government compounds and fend off rebellious Red Guards; they often were backed by local law enforcement agencies. But, like their Red Guard counterparts, Scarlet Guards gained increasingly more autonomy, and both provided a mass base for the new wave of organizing. About half of the counties in Hubei and Guangdong Provinces and 70 percent of the counties in Guangxi Province reported when their first nonstudent mass organization was formed, most of which occurred in October and November of 1966.

At the end of the year, it became imperative for the local movement to single out at least a few top county leaders as new targets. By this time, anyone in a leadership position in the state bureaucracy was dubbed a "power-holder," making each a legitimate target. Daily struggle rallies were held, with leaders "staged" for denunciation. Tens of thousands of ordinary citizens attended the rallies in squares or paraded in the streets. Not surprisingly, mass organizations could not agree about whom to struggle against and whom to protect. The debate on the fate of different leaders often prompted the formation of two organizational alliances, each accusing the other of being "conservative." When the Power Seizure of January 1967 reached local counties, one faction announced the seizure of power over the local government, the other challenged the legitimacy of the seizure. Mass factional struggle became the major form of the movement in the next year and a half. Historians call the two organizational alliances "mass factions."

In many places, such factional conflict escalated into barricaded street battles, often with firearms, causing many deaths and injuries. In some cases, the mass factionalism and violence lasted for months after the new government was established. The severity of mass conflict was reflected in the number of street battles that the *xianzhi* called "armed battles" and in the related deaths and injuries. The scope and human impact of armed battles in the counties in Guangdong and Guangxi Provinces are shown in Table 6.4. In Guangxi Province, forty-six counties of sixty-four (71.9 percent) had armed battles; in Guangdong Province, thirty of fifty-four counties (55.6 percent). In terms of human loss in the battles, there were 24.8 deaths per county in Guangxi Province and 3.0 deaths in Guangdong Province.

TABLE 6.4. *Reported Armed Battles and Related Deaths in Guangdong and Guangxi Provinces*

	Guangdong	Guangxi
Number of Counties	54	64
Number of Counties That Have Armed Battle	30	46
Armed-Battle–Related Deaths per County	2.91	24.83

Source: Xianzhi.

Authority in Transition[58]

In the first week of 1967, mass organizations in Shanghai – China's largest city – announced to the nation that they had seized power over the municipal Party committee and the municipal government. The move reportedly had been approved by Beijing beforehand, and the news ran in major Party newspapers across the country. An editorial in the *People's Daily* called for "seizing power from the capitalist roaders" everywhere.[59] In the following month, a power-seizure campaign swept the country, reaching as far as village administrations.[60] At the county level, 83 percent of county gazetteers in Guangxi Province and 70 percent in Guangdong

58 In the environment absent of law, bureaucratic form of control had been the major mechanism to mark behavior boundaries. Disputes raised by the mass campaign were to be settled bureaucratically. This was so even in the time of ferocious mass campaigns. Liu Shaoqi, the No. 2 man in the Party hierarchy and the president of the state, was denounced from very early on. In 1968, mass organizations from all over Beijing besieged Zhongnanhai, the central-government compound, to demand his detention by the masses. Although Mao and Zhou Enlai did not send him out, the masses inside were allowed to struggle and parade him. However, his case did not end with mass justice. The bureaucratic procedure was also at work at the same time. A special case committee gave an ultimate verdict on September 18, 1968. One of my informants worked in Wuhua County government for many years after 1968. He and his fellow committee members investigated thousands of cases generated by the mass campaigns. This type of bureaucratic verdict, if anticipated by the actors during the campaign, should have deterred excesses. But the transformation of bureaucratic structures and authorities during the Cultural Revolution slowed down the operations. As for the case of collective killings, the investigations only took place after 1978, ten years too late.

59 CRRM, vol. 1, pp. 231–256. For the January Power Seizure campaign in Shanghai, see Andrew G. Walder, *Chang Ch'un-ch'iao and Shanghai's January Revolution* (Ann Arbor, MI: Center for Chinese Studies of the University of Michigan, 1978). See also Elizabeth J. Perry and Xun Li, *Proletarian Power: Shanghai in the Cultural Revolution* (Boulder, CO: Westview Press, 1997).

60 For a vivid account of "power seizure" at the village level, see Anita Chan, Richard Madsen, and Jonathan Unger, *Chen Village under Mao and Deng* (Berkeley: University of California Press, 1992). My interviews also encountered similar cases. For example, in Jinkeng Village in Guangdong Province, the power changed hands from the Li lineage to the Zeng lineage.

Province reported the power-seizure events, although it is most likely that each county followed the policy. The sweep was thorough: top leaders in every jurisdiction or work-unit administration became "power-holders" by definition and experienced their downfall.[61]

Despite its portentous name, the Power Seizure was more a reform than a revolution. A revolution is typically against a political system but the Power Seizure was against individuals deemed power-holders, who were accused of deviating from the correct line. Because the old system that they were accused of representing – that is, the bourgeois reactionary line – was a fiction, to remove them served only to reinforce the Maoist system, which was characterized by class struggle, mass campaigns, and a top-down authority structure. New mass organizations mushroomed. However, the vertical control of the party–state remained intact. Indeed, when the Party's Central Committee issued a directive on March 11, 1967, local governments dutifully followed, installing a Grasp Revolution, Promote Production (GRPP) headquarters as the new administrative organ to fill the power vacuum.[62] Mengshan County *xianzhi*, for example, recorded the following: "March 20 [1967], the county's People's Armed Forces Department established the 'Grasp Revolution, Promote Production' headquarters, exercising power [that] previously belonged to the party committee and the government. Local districts also formed GRPP headquarters accordingly."[63] Most county *xianzhi* reported similar events taking place some time in March, following the central directive.

Yet, the Power Seizure exerted a profound impact on the bureaucracy as well as state–society relations. The mass campaign as a social-control mechanism advanced at the expense of bureaucracy. This was accomplished through two related processes. First, two parallel local authorities emerged: the government agencies and mass organizations. Mass organizations increasingly acted like governments: issuing directives, organizing militias, possessing arms, and persecuting selected targets. Second, government organs were not only reduced in size, positions also were vacated for those who were supported by mass organizations and movement activists. Among the leaders who remained at their posts were those whose previous duties included security and military work; Mao and

61 See Su, *Tumult from Within*, Chapter 3.

62 CRRM, vol. 1, p. 344.

63 Mengshan xianzhi bianzuan weiyuanhui 蒙山县志编纂委员会, *Mengshan xianzhi* 蒙山县志 [*Mengshan County Gazetteer*] (Nanning: Guangxi renmin chubanshe, 1993), p. 26.

the Party Center had sent officers and soldiers to localities to ensure order after the Power Seizure campaign. Leaders from the Public Security Bureau – that is, the PAFD – were in an advantageous position, given their control of armed personnel and, as important, their authority over the vast army of citizen militias. For example, the PAFD head in Cangwu County, Wen Xueyi, declared his support for a group of rebellious high school students and took over the county government authority. He then became head of the county's GRPP headquarters and subsequently the director of the revolutionary committee.[64] An uncensored *xianzhi* from Huaxian County in Shannxi Province detailed a similar path to power of another PAFD head.[65] Mass organizations functioned as a parallel government, and the government itself became a mass-movement organization.

Bureaucratic control had been weakened. The composition of the leadership was constantly changing and its authority was continually contested by mass organizations. The functional agencies (e.g., security and legal organs) ceased to operate and mass organizations exercised powers that previously belonged only to the government. Equally important, however, the new local government developed additional capacities by becoming a campaign machine and took advantage of the removal of previous legal and bureaucratic constraints. Dominated by leaders from security- and military-related agencies, the government became militarized and exercised power accordingly, commanding a large mass base consisting mainly of citizen militias. This combination of weakening and strengthening created the space in which social control failed to prevent collective killings.

Legal Channels Abolished

The 1957–1958 reversal had greatly diminished legal institutions. Their functions were weakened after the Cultural Revolution began, and they were entirely abolished after the Power Seizure campaign. Prosecutions, including executions, took place through mass justice in the extralegal domain. To incite mass crowds, the Party Center issued a series of directives to restrain public-security forces from intervening. As early as August 22, 1966, the Center relayed a notice via the Public Security Ministry to

64 Cangwu xianzhi bianzuan weiyuanhui 苍梧县志编纂委员会, *Cangwu xianzhi* 苍梧县志 [*Cangwu County Gazetteer*] (Nanning: Guangxi remin chubanshe, 1997); see also personal interviews with Li Zhao, 2006.

65 Huaxian difangzhi bianzuan weiyuanhui 华县地方志编纂委员会, *Hua Xianzhi* 华县志 [*Huaxian County Gazetteer*] (Shanxi renmin chubanshe, 1992) (the Song copy).

"earnestly forbid using police to crack down on revolutionary student movements." It even demanded that "the police should not respond in kind even if revolutionary students assault them."[66] In the height of the mass factional conflict, mass organizations rushed to obtain weapons, often from local military bases. These actions were interpreted as tolerable by another directive from the Central Military Commission on April 6, 1967: "The masses, whether from the Left, the Middle, or the Right, who had joined in raiding the military should be held accountable.... Those actions should be used as the basis to judge their [political] orientation as the Left, the Middle, or the Right."[67]

Mao's diagnosis of a bourgeois reactionary line was felt most in the legal branch of the government. Luo Ruiqing, the head of the Public Security Ministry, experienced a rapid downfall; his replacement, Xie Fuzhi, called for the dismantling of the security and legal systems. In a public speech on August 7, 1967, Xie said: "From the very beginning of the Cultural Revolution until the January Storm, the majority of agencies of security, prosecution, and court had been diehard protectors of the power-holders taking the capitalist road and suppressors of the revolutionary masses." His solution was draconian: "This cannot be changed unless the old machine is thoroughly smashed. The problem will remain the same if you just remove a layer or take care of a certain logistic group."[68] In local counties, the courts and procuratorates were put under military control after the Power Seizure and ceased to function. When the revolutionary committees were established, the two branches were displaced by "defense committees" that combined security, prosecution, and courts.[69] These legal agencies would not be reestablished until 1978.[70] Most criminal offenses were handled through mass movements. In 1967, 1968, and 1969, the recorded criminal cases in China were about one third of that in 1966.[71]

66 CRRM, vol. 1, p. 91.
67 Ibid., p. 390.
68 Ibid., p. 530.
69 For example, see Panyu shi difangzhi bianzuan weiyuanhui 番禺市地方志编纂委员会, *Panyu xianzhi* 番禺县志 *[Panyu County Gazetteer]* (Guangzhou: Guangdong renmin chubanshe, 1995), p. 642.
70 For example, see Cangwu xianzhi bianzuan weiyuanhui 苍梧县志编纂委员会, *Cangwu xianzhi* 苍梧县志 [*Cangwu County Gazetteer*] (Nanning: Guangxi remin chubanshe, 1997), pp. 549–569.
71 The People's Supreme Court 2000: 1.

Death Penalty: Policy and Practice

The mode of social control changed; accordingly, behavioral boundaries contracted and expanded. In this section, I address the death penalty, which was governed by various principles, frameworks, and scopes of targets. One principle was that the Party placed great value on violence in its post-revolution state-building and governing. As early as 1927, in his famous report on peasant movements in Hunan Province, Mao unequivocally recommended killings as an "effective method for repressing reactionaries: In each district, there must be executions of at least some people found guilty of the most odious crimes" because "this kind of execution of an abusive nobleman or a local bully makes the whole district shake with fears; it is very effective for eliminating the vestiges of the feudal regime."[72] The same rhetoric was continuously repeated in campaigns after 1949.[73] After military campaigns against resistance activities, Mao contended that killings continued to be necessary because "the counter-revolutionaries are still present," even if they are "greatly diminished in numbers."[74] In the same year, he stated: "From now on, we should make fewer arrests and kill fewer people. But we cannot announce that we will no longer kill or that we will abolish capital punishment."[75]

A second principle governing the use of the death penalty was a lack of respect for law and legal procedures. For Mao and his Party, the previous law was only a superstructure, an integral part of the bourgeois state; as such, it constituted an essential target for the proletarian revolution. Following Marx and Lenin, Mao and the Party considered the state machine a tool for one class to oppress another. The new state was billed as "the proletarian dictatorship,"[76] under which "politics and law are no longer the sole property of officials dressed in mandarin robes, but of workers

[72] Mao 1967, vol. 1: 26, cf. Zhang Ning, "Political Origins of Death Penalty Exceptionalism: Mao Zedong and the Practice of Capital Punishment in Contemporary China," *Punishment & Society* 10 (2008), pp. 117–136.

[73] See, e.g., Mao 1984: 403; cf. Zhang Ning, "Political Origins of Death Penalty Exceptionalism," pp. 117–136.

[74] Mao 1977: 378, cf. Zhang Ning, "Political Origins of Death Penalty Exceptionalism," pp. 117–136.

[75] Mao 1977: 281–282; cf. Zhang Ning, "Political Origins of Death Penalty Exceptionalism," pp. 117–136.

[76] Mao 1984: 4; cf. Zhang Ning, "Political Origins of Death Penalty Exceptionalism," pp. 117–136.

and peasants.... They will make laws according to their convictions."[77] Yet, under Mao, little effort was expended in creating new laws and those that were promulgated were soon superseded by other political needs.

A third and related principle was that the guilt of those receiving the death sentence need not be established by the deeds of the accused but instead could be based on political reasons. Mao and the central authority often gave out quotas and numerical guidelines to determine the number of counter-revolutionaries. In one of the early campaigns before the Cultural Revolution, a central directive – written according to Mao's instructions – announced that "the number of counter-revolutionaries in each province must be limited to a certain proportion: As a general rule, in the countryside, it should not exceed one thousandth of the population; in cities, it is appropriate to aim for one half of one thousandth.... As a rule, one or two out of ten should be executed."[78] Officials throughout the country strove to meet their quotas. Official statistics show that the numbers of executed victims exceeded this expected proportion: During that campaign, 2,630,000 were arrested; of those,712,000 were executed.[79]

Zhang Ning distinguishes the following four periods and types of executions or killings of noncombatant civilians under Mao's leadership: (1) killings in the mode of traditional banditry in the mid-1920s during the peasant uprisings in Hunan Province; (2) Stalinist-type "purges" within the Communist Party and in the Red Zones in Jiangxi Province (1930–1931) and in Yan'an (1942); (3) military sentences pronounced during the war and the agrarian reforms in the communist bases in the 1940s; and (4) the Maoist institution of capital punishment in peacetime, beginning with the repression of the so-called counter-revolutionaries in the 1950s.[80] Three institutional frameworks were involved. The first framework was military: In Types 1 and 3, although the targets were civilians, the justification was to win a war. The second framework was political: In the purges of the second type, guilt was established politically and punishment was carried out through bureaucratic procedures. The third

[77] Mao 1920, cf. Zhang Ning, "Political Origins of Death Penalty Exceptionalism," pp. 117–136.

[78] Pang Xianzhi 逄先知 and Jin Chongji金冲及 (eds.), *Mao Zedong Zhuan (1949–1976)* 毛泽东传 (1949–1976) [translation here] (Beijing: Zhonggong zhongyang wenxian yanjiushi, 2006); cf. Zhang Ning, "Political Origins of Death Penalty Exceptionalism," pp. 117–136.

[79] Yang Kuisong 杨奎松, "Zhongguo 'zhenya fangeming' yundong yanjiu" 中国 镇压" 反革命运动研究. *Shixue yuekan* 1 (2006).

[80] Zhang Ning, "Political Origins of Death Penalty Exceptionalism."

framework was legal: Many executions of the fourth type went through law-like proceedings.

This discussion mainly concerns peacetime killings in the period after 1949, but I contend that the three frameworks were simultaneously at work. Which was the more salient depended on political conditions – that is, which mode of social control was most salient – and the radical scale of a campaign can be measured by whether a legal, bureaucratic, or military framework predominated. The diminishing role of law and bureaucracy during the Cultural Revolution helped to radicalize the killings. As discussed in Chapter 7, a domestic equivalent of war was framed in the countryside, and the Four Types were killed as if they were enemy combatants.

The radical scale also can be measured by the scope of the targets. In a less radical campaign, officials made an effort to connect those chosen for capital punishment to specific deeds they committed. Indeed, official campaign directives often designated punishment for acts and called for proof before the punishment. For example, seventeen crimes were specified in the Regulations Concerning the Repression of Counter-Revolutionaries issued in 1951: high treason, inciting defection, armed rebellion, espionage, spreading counter-revolutionary ideas, illegal border crossing, and so on.[81] In reality, however, large campaigns selected targets based on identity; particularly vulnerable were those people previously classified as the enemy class or deemed to have "historical problems." Once targets were selected, the deeds could be fabricated through "mass revelations" in struggle sessions. Relatives of potential targets also were vulnerable; however, before the Cultural Revolution, killing typically did not extend to them. The need to connect victims to specific deeds – even if they often were fabricated – served to limit capital punishment.

The most radical scope of choosing targets for execution was based on association, mainly blood relations. Imperial China had a long tradition of addressing crime by punishing an entire family or clan.[82] The communists continued this practice – to label the whole family as landlords or rich peasants on the theory that family members of those executed would harbor antisystem sentiments. To extend killing to family members was the newest level of the political-campaign radicalization. Maoist campaigns had a tendency to radicalize – that is, to move from the legal to the

[81] Yang Kuisong 杨奎松, "Zhongguo 'zhenya fangeming' yundong yanjiu" 中国 镇压"反革命运动研究. *Shixue yuekan* 1 (2006).

[82] Ladnay et al., *Law and Legality in China*, p. 37.

military mode of killings and to extend the scope from deeds to identity and association. This occurred because violence and fear served as an effective tool to mobilize a new campaign. To incite a community was a political task that local leaders had to perform to demonstrate compliance. Moreover, evaluation of the performance required quantification, with numbers of the persecuted and killed being the most credible statistics. Nonetheless, until the Cultural Revolution, the execution of targets based on association was rare.

In part, that was because there were three contravening forces against escalations. First, after a campaign, there was often an accounting that addressed extremism. Zealots and fanatics often were promoted, but local leaders were also criticized as being "ultra-leftist" – that is, too radical or extreme. Second, because of the importance of the death sentence, moreover, the Party Center often sent directives clarifying and identifying who had the authority to execute civilians. For example: "In order to guard against 'leftist' deviations that are developing with the movement of repression, we have decided that, starting on June 1st, nationwide . . . the power to kill will be restored to the exclusive authority of the provincial government."[83] Another example is as follows: "All cases punishable by the death penalty or long-term imprisonment must be instructed and judged by the court before execution of the sentence is approved by the provincial governor."[84] Finally, in 1951, Mao proposed a kind of "cooling-off" period, "the death sentence with two-year reprieve." These contravening factors infrequently decreased the killings in mass campaigns, which depended greatly on local conditions. For example, the two-year reprieve proposal obviously was not heeded in most cases of collective killings, which often happened quickly; in any case, it did not become an official law until many years after the Cultural Revolution ended.[85]

State Reaction to Collective Killings in 1967 and 1968

No record exists to show that the Party Center sanctioned the extreme version of violence: the killing of children, women, and the elderly from

[83] Mao 1977: 40; cf. Zhang Ning, "Political Origins of Death Penalty Exceptionalism," pp. 117–136.

[84] Mao 1999: 198, cf. Zhang Ning, "Political Origins of Death Penalty Exceptionalism," pp. 117–136.

[85] David Johnson and Franklin Zimring, "The Death Penalty in China," in Johnson and Zimring (eds.), *New Frontier: National Development, Political Change, and Death Penalty in Asia* (New York: Oxford University Press, forthcoming).

a Four-Type family.[86] Indeed, in the months of terror, the provincial authorities repeatedly issued warnings against such practices. When severe cases were revealed, the Center and provincial authorities sent the army to stop them. As early as November 20, 1966, the Party Central Committee distributed a Beijing municipal policy directive to all local governments nationwide, prohibiting "unauthorized detention stations, unauthorized trial courts, and unauthorized arrests and beatings." The directive warned that those behaviors were a "violation of state law and party discipline."[87] Thereafter, the spirit of "struggle through reason, not violence" was reiterated by the center through a series of major policy pronouncements.[88]

Although it is debatable whether a provincial government such as in Guangxi Province was genuine when it warned against excessive violence, it did explicitly make those pronouncements. In December 1967, about one month after a new wave of collective killings spread across the province, provincial authorities issued a ten-point order that included this statement: "Mass organizations should not randomly arrest, beat, or kill. All the current detainees should be released immediately." From this point on, a new term was coined – "indiscriminate beatings and killings (*luanda luansha*)"[89] – to label the widespread violence as a violation of social and political order. For example, on December 18, 1967, provincial authorities issued a report on *luanda luansha* in Li Village in Rongxian County; on May 3, 1968, they issued an order to stop *luanda luansha* after an investigation in nine counties; on June 24, 1968, they issued the document "Instructions about Prohibiting *luanda luansha*"; on September 19, 1968, they confiscated firearms from the mass

86 That the Center did not endorse eliminationist killing is supported by the fact that there was almost no such killing in Hubei Province. In this regard, Hubei seems more typical among the country's thirty provinces. In Hubei and most other provinces, the Center had earlier sided with the rebel faction that challenged the provincial authorities. This created a different political environment from that in Guangdong and Guangxi Provinces. See more discussion in Chapters 2 and 8.

87 "Zhonggong zhongyang pizhuan Beijing shiwei zhongyao tongzhi" ["CCP Central Committee Transmits Important Notice of the Beijing Municipal Party Committee"], November 20, 1966, in CRRM, vol. 1, p. 163.

88 See, e.g., December 15, 1966; January 28, 1967; April 6, 1967; June 6, 1967; May 15, 1968; July 3, 24, and 28, 1968; and December 26, 1968, in CRRM, vols. 1–2 (Beijing: Zhongguo renmin jiefangjun guofang daxue dangshi chubanshe, 1988).

89 The Chinese character *luan* has multiple meanings: random, indiscriminate, and chaotic. It also describes actions that violate law and order, particularly against or lacking proper authority.

organizations; and, finally, on September 23, 1968, they issued "Notice about Stopping *luanda luansha*."[90]

The most compelling evidence of official opposition to excessive violence is that in many locations, once the information about killings was passed to higher levels, the authorities dispatched leaders or the army to intervene. For example, in the earliest incident of collective killings in a suburb of Beijing, a county leader went to Macun Village five times to stop them. His effort involved high-ranking leaders of the Beijing city government.[91] In the case of the most severe collective killings in Daoxian County, Hunan Province, an army division was sent in to end the slaughter.[92] Although no detailed information is available in the *xianzhi* about how the collective killings came to an end, the data show that they were usually concentrated in a certain period. In most counties, the upsurge in killings occurred only once, indicating that external constraints were imposed from higher levels.

Such policy directives from central and provincial authorities no doubt prevented mass violence from further escalation, but these efforts were relatively ineffective. One reason was that the official policy did not provide for any real punishment. The stated admonitions were usually meant to serve only as a guide for the future. The following quote from a speech by the Minister of Public Security, Xie Fuzhi, on May 15, 1968, is a telling example of the leniency toward perpetrators of violence. In the same speech that was supposed to admonish against violence, he seemed to suggest that no violence would be punished: "Even counter-revolutionaries should not be killed, as long as they are willing to accept re-education. It is doubly wrong to beat people to death. *Nonetheless, these things [killings] happened because of lack of experience; so there is no need to investigate the responsibility.* What is important is to gain experience so as to carry out in earnest Chairman Mao's instructions to struggle not with violence but with reason."[93] The prosecution of perpetrators did

90 *Guangxi wen'ge dashi nianbiao* 广西文革大事年表 [*Chronology of the Cultural Revolution in Guangxi*] (Nanning: Guangxi renmin chubanshe, 1990), pp. 58–127. Reprinted by Chinese Publications Services Center, Los Angeles, CA, 1995.

91 Zhang Lianhe 张连和, "Wu jin Machun quan ting sha" 五进马村劝停杀 ["Five Visits to Ma Village to Dissuade Killings"], in Zhe Yongping 者永平 (ed.), *Nage niandai zhong de women* 那个年代中的我们 [*We as in That Era*] (Huhehot, Inner Mongolia: Yuanfang chubanshe, 1998), pp. 398–404.

92 Zhang Cheng 章成, "Daoxian da tusha" 道县大屠杀 ["The Daoxian Massacre"], *Open Magazine* 开放杂志 (December 2001), p. 71.

93 CRRM, vol. 2 (Beijing: Zhongguo renmin jiefanjun guofang daxue dangshi chubanshe, 1988), pp. 119–120, emphasis mine.

not happen until the late 1970s, ten years after the fact. In any case, the warnings against extreme violence were undermined by countervailing directives. For example, the list of Guangxi Province directives warning against collective killings coincided with another long list of policies persecuting class enemies. Although the province may have perceived the *luanda luansha* in communes and villages as unwarranted, its incentive to encourage violence against oppositional mass organizations in the cities undercut its role as the guardian of social order.

Another reason for the ineffectiveness of the policy was that the very nature of the Cultural Revolution – that is, dismantling and rebuilding local governments – had damaged the bureaucratic hierarchy, breaking the chain of command. By August 1967, the attack on public security and legal systems had been called for by Minister of Public Security Xie.[94] According to county gazetteers, the agencies in these systems ceased to function in local counties, communes, and villages in 1967. Detentions and prosecutions were carried out not according to any sense of law but rather by the political standards of the moment. Although the policies of the central and provincial authorities were genuine, there were no regular administrative authorities to implement them.

A key result of the Cultural Revolution was clogged channels of information. In particular, when bad things happened at the lower reaches of the state, the upper-level authorities typically did not learn of them until it was too late. When local leaders publicized their "achievements" in the movement, violence was covered up. For example, in January 1967, the Beijing municipal government submitted a report about how the new administration of Tsinghua University faithfully carried out the Center's policy, painstakingly describing how people who had committed "bad deeds" were well treated and given opportunities to reform. The report drew Mao's attention and he instructed it to be distributed across the nation as a model for emulation.[95] Not until 1978 would another report – issued in an entirely different political

[94] Xie Fuzhi, August 7, 1967, in CRRM, vol. 1, p. 530.

[95] "*Zhonggong zhongyang, zhongyang wenge zhuanfa Beijing shi geming weiyuanhui zhuanlai zhu Qinghua daxue de gongren, jiefangjun xuanchuandui guanyu 'jianjue guanche zhixing dui zhishi fenzi zai jiaoyu gei chulu de zhengce' de baogao*" ["CCP Central Committee and Central Cultural Revolution Group Transmit the Report of the Qinghua University Worker-PLA Propaganda Team Submitted to the Beijing Municipal Revolutionary Committee on 'Resolutely and Thoroughly Implementing the Policy Towards Intellectuals of Reeducation and Providing a Way Out'"], January 29, 1969, in CRRM, vol. 2, pp. 275–281.

climate – rebut the initial account, detailing the true fate of struggle targets at the university. Within two months of the class-cleansing campaign, more than ten people were killed.[96] Similarly, in local counties, the failure of information flowing from the bottom up resulted in upper-level authorities intervening only after massive numbers of people had been killed.

Conclusion

By definition, the state regulates violence within its territory,[97] and Communist China under Mao was no exception. In this chapter, I discuss the legal framework – that is, state rules governing violence – in which collective killings came into being in 1967 and 1968. Despite the fact that the revolutionary party never shied away from using violence to govern after 1949, collective killing – that is, to single out individuals to kill because of their blood relations – were an extraordinary development even by Maoist standards. This type of extreme violence had its roots in the process of state-building history before the Cultural Revolution and the unprecedented mass campaigns during its first few years.

The state-building years witnessed two major shifts in rules that governed social life: (1) from an inspiration of rule of law to bureaucratic control monopolized by the Party; and (2) from bureaucratic control to using mass campaigns to reorganize the bureaucracy. Accordingly, the means of violence first evolved into the Party's ideological tool, and was later exercised in the form of citizen tribunals during the Cultural Revolution, even when local government authorities were involved. Collective killings were the extreme form, as legal due process evolved from tenuous to none.

The collapse of legal constraints on violence echoes the concept of "openness" in the political-opportunity models in social-movement research. If the state was able to enforce its intended control, collective killings would not be tolerated. After one year of mass campaigns that resulted in a thorough overhaul of local governments, not only legal institutions were set aside but also the bureaucratic chain of command was broken. Mass movements in the lower-level jurisdictions, particularly

[96] CRRM, vol. 2, pp. 281–283.

[97] Max Weber, *Economy and Society: An Outline of Interpretive Sociology* (Berkeley: University of California Press); and John A. Hall and G. John Ikenberry, *The State* (Minneapolis: University of Minnesota Press, 1989).

in communities remotely located from political centers, were granted free rein in tactical innovations, including eliminationist killings unprecedented in China's communist history.

Hence, the Chinese collective killings were not a result of the enforcement of state laws but rather the failure of state control. This dynamic is in stark contrast to the process of genocide as portrayed by the state-policy model. The Stalinist regime of the Soviet Union, for example, maintained penal codes and certain legal proceedings. All political victims, according to Solzhenitsyn, were judged according to Article 58 of the penal code published in 1926.[98] Similarly, beginning in 1937, Nazi Germany enacted a series of laws that meticulously defined Jews and other victims as targets for discrimination and eventual extermination.[99] Although eliminationist pogroms were common in local settings (i.e., incidentally, killings that require explanations unavailable in the state-policy model), the systematic extermination policy – the so-called Final Solution – came down from the Nazi Party Center. It was the gas chambers and execution squads prevailing in the early 1940s that defined the Holocaust.[100]

That local actors would organize and participate in collective killings requires more than the failure of legal and bureaucratic control. In Chapter 7, I discuss the removal of moral constraints in a community.

98 Ladnay et al., *Law and Legality in China*, p. 56; Aleksandr Solzhenitsyn, *The Gulag Archipelago, 1918–1956: An Experiment in Literary Investigation*, I-VII (New York: Harper & Row, 1974–1978).

99 Saul Friedlander, *Nazi Germany and the Jews, Volume I: The Years of Persecution, 1933–1939* (New York: Harper Perennial, 1997), pp. 177–210.

100 Saul Friedlander, *Nazi Germany and the Jews 1939–1945: The Years of Extermination* (New York: Harper Perennial, 2006).

7

Framing War

At 1 a.m. on July 25, 1968, Zhou Enlai, Kang Sheng, and six other prominent central leaders held a meeting with representatives of Guangxi Province's mass-organization leaders in the People's Meeting Hall in Beijing. Speeches by the leaders heavily favored the United Headquarters (UHQ), one of two mass alliances in Guangxi, at the expense of April 22 (or Four Twenty Two [FTT]), the rival faction. Zhou and Kang also announced the existence of a vast counter-revolutionary conspiracy organization, which they called the Anti-Communist Party Patriotic Army (ACPPA). They did not cite any concrete evidence for, indeed, there was none to cite, but this supposedly anti-communist force was portrayed as widespread, extending far beyond Guangxi Province.[1] The meeting

[1] "The July 25 Speeches"; cf. Xiao Pingtou's five reports on the secret files of the Cultural Revolution: *Guangxi "fangong jiuguotuan" yuanan shimo – wen'ge jimi dangan jiemi zhi yi* 广西"反共救国团"冤案始末 – 文革机密档案揭密之一, available at https://67.15.34.207/news/gb/kanshihai/shishi/2006/1101/172175.html, accessed August 24, 2008; *Guangxi Rongan da tusha – wen'ge jimi dangan jiemi zhi er* 广西融安大屠杀 – 文革机密档案揭密之二, available at http://www.xianqiao.net:8080/gb/7/1/6/n1581000.htm, accessed August 24, 2008; *Guangxi "shangshi nong zong" yuanan shimo – wen'ge jimi dangan jiemi zhi san* 广西"上石农总"冤案始末 – 文革机密档案揭密之三, available at http://news.epochtimes.com/gb/7/3/8/n1639613.htm, accessed August 24, 2008; *Guangxi junqu weijiao Fengshan "zaofan dajun" zhenxiang – wen'ge jimi dangan jiemi zhi si* 广西军区围剿凤山"造反大军"真相 – 文革机密档案揭密之四, available at http://boxun.com/hero/2007/xiaopingtouyehua/63_1.shtml and http://boxun.com/hero/2007/xiaopingtouyehua/63_2.shtml; and *Guangxi wen'ge ren chi ren shijian jiemi – wen'ge jimi dangan jiemi zhi wu* 广西文革人吃人事件揭密 – 文革机密档案揭密之五, available at http://www.64tianwang.com/Article_Show.asp?ArticleID=2319, accessed August 24, 2008. See also Wen Yuqiao, 闻于樵, "Wen'ge 'qierwu jianghua': bujinjin shi Guangxi zaofan zuzhi de zhongjie"

effectively endorsed the war rhetoric used by the provincial government, now dominated by the UHQ, which had first claimed that its political opponents in the FTT were members of this anti-communist army. Collective killings had begun in Guangxi counties and soon spread to Guangdong Province.

Since 1949, the new regime had maintained a politically constructed class divide and governed using the doctrine of class struggle (see Chapter 4). The doctrine was not merely a theoretical principle; in a self-fulfilling-prophecy fashion, it also turned into "reality" by the constant campaigns against class enemies. "Sabotage acts" against the state were identified – although they were either exaggerated or fabricated – and discriminations, persecutions, and abuses were publicly featured to reconfirm the "truth" of class struggle. Thus, those targeted by this rhetoric of class struggle were framed, in that they were persecuted on a flimsy factual basis. Following social-movement scholars Snow and Gamson, class struggle also was framed in another sense: a discursive framework that identifies problems, responsible parties, and actions to be taken to address the problems.[2] From this perspective, class struggle is a frame that catalogs social and political problems in class-struggle terms, identifies class enemies as responsible, and advocates mass-movement actions against them. To use the term coined by Snow and Benford, it also is a *master frame* – that is, an overarching framework to interpret every problem, whether for analysis or action.[3]

This master frame underwent a "frame transformation" in the environment of the political problems confronting the Chinese government

文革七二五讲话：不仅仅是造反组织的终结 ["July 25 Speech: Not Merely the Termination of Guangxi Rebel Organization"], *Hua Xia Wen Zhai* [华夏文摘], vol. 287 (supplemental issue, 2002), available at www.cnd.org, accessed August 11, 2008.

2 David A. Snow, E. Burke Rochford, Jr., Steven K. Worden, and Robert D. Benford, "Frame Alignment Processes, Micromobilization, and Movement Participation," *American Sociological Review* 51, no. 4 (1986), pp. 464–481; William A. Gamson, *The Strategy of Social Protest* (Homewood, IL: Dorsey Press, 1975); William A. Gamson, *Talking Politics* (New York: Cambridge University Press, 1992); William A. Gamson, "Construction Social Protest," in Hank Johnston and Bert Klandermans (eds.), *Social Movements and Culture* (Minneapolis: University of Minnesota Press, 1995), pp. 85–106; David A. Snow and Robert D. Benford, "Master Frames and Cycles of Protest," in Aldon D. Morris and Carol McClurg Mueller (eds.), *Frontiers in Social Movement Theory* (New Haven, CT: Yale University Press, 1992), pp. 133–155; and Robert D. Benford and David A. Snow, "Framing Processes and Social Movements: An Overview and Assessment," *Annual Review of Sociology* 26 (2000), pp. 611–639.

3 Snow and Benford, "Master Frames and Cycles of Protest."

during the Cultural Revolution.[4] If the class-struggle frame maintained that the threat was insidious and widespread, the policy pronouncement at the midnight meeting in Beijing insisted that the threat was now organized, ferocious, and imminent. "War" became the new master frame. An upgraded level of action was prescribed, although the specifics were unclear. The context here is important: In the course of establishing the new type of government – that is, revolutionary committees – provinces such as Guangdong and Guangxi were unable to disband mass organizations and disarm warring factions in urban centers. Street battles continued into late 1968, providing the "factual basis" for a war diagnosis of the political problems.

Yet, this new master frame had two implications that were not necessarily intended by policy makers in the Party Center. The first concerns the scope of its application. Their immediate concern was mass factions in the cities – armed and frequently engaged with one another. However, the master frame was quickly relayed by bureaucrats – ever eager to show compliance – to rural communities where class enemies were the easiest to identify, although violent conflict was much less (if any) of a problem there. The second implication concerns the master frame's lack of specification. Although the new master frame called for an escalated level of action based on a grim diagnosis, it allowed bureaucrats at various levels of government to take specific action as they saw fit. In framing-analysis terms, the policy makers provided only a problem frame and a diagnosis frame without an action frame. Innovations by local actors proliferated, such as the "class-struggle exhibitions" I describe in this chapter. Collective killing as a new prescription to address class conflict emerged in this context.

There was no actual war, especially in rural communities where the newly reorganized administrations seemed to be in full control of social order (see Chapter 5), but once war was successfully framed, it created a new moral standard in the community with regard to violence. In the past, physical abuse and occasional executions seemed to be the upper limit of violence. In "wartime," however, speedy slaughters of "enemies" became less than extraordinary in the eyes of communities possessed by a political fever. Moral constraints against collective killings were

[4] See discussion on frame transformation in David A. Snow, E. Burke Rochford, Jr., Steven K. Worden, and Robert D. Benford, "Frame Alignment Processes, Micromobilization, and Movement Participation," *American Sociological Review* 51, no. 4 (1986), pp. 464–481.

dissolved. In this chapter, my account begins at the most tumultuous time in the Cultural Revolution. I first chronicle mass factional battles in the cities, a political problem for which the Party Center demanded an immediate resolution and, accordingly, constructed the war frame to solve it. I then describe how the Center and local governments established the newfound "threat," developing a "factual" basis to transform class struggle into "war." Approaches included pronouncing the widespread existence of conspiracy groups and staging public exhibitions of class struggle. Next, I discuss how the war frame found deep resonance in rural communities where class enemies could be readily identified despite the absence of mass conflict similar to that in urban areas. Last, I explore how the war frame removed moral constraints against extreme violence. First, however, I glean insight from existing literature on the relationship between war and mass killings.

War and Eliminationist Killing

To kill unarmed civilians in large numbers, often including women and children, is an act that invokes norms of battlefield combat. It is insufficient simply to designate as subhuman a category of individuals who are subject to surveillance and discrimination, as in China with its "class enemies" after the Land Reform movement of the 1950s. It also requires that a community believe in an imminent threat. This perception is related to two conditions: (1) there is an ongoing war, and (2) potential victims provide critical support for the enemy, so that to combat the enemy requires killing the supporters. In 1967 and 1968, the ongoing armed street battles between mass factions had signaled a wartime situation, and the government's assertion about conspiracy groups endorsed treating political conflict as a sign of impending insurgency.

Historical cases of mass killings are mostly associated with war in some manner. The Armenian genocide was in the context of World War I and victims were considered to have provided sanctuary, intelligence, and other support to the neighboring enemy countries. Some Armenian groups even established armed insurgencies. In Nazi Germany, Jews were designated as the enemy of national security. When war escalated and when the Germans faced the possibility of defeat after 1939, the Final Solution emerged as an explicit policy. In the 1994 Rwanda genocide, Tutsis waged guerilla warfare from a neighboring country, occasionally raiding the border regions. In mass killings in the Soviet Union and

Cambodia, although no actual war was fought, a perpetual war between the state and certain segments of the population was framed.[5]

Mass killing is particularly common in counter-guerrilla warfare. In most cases, guerrillas rely directly on local civilian populations for logistical support including food, shelter, supplies, and intelligence. No one would appreciate this fact more than the Chinese communists, who not long ago had waged one after another successful guerrilla insurgency against the GMD government and the Japanese invaders before 1949. Mao Zedong famously wrote: "Because guerrilla warfare basically derives from the masses and is supported by them, it can neither exist nor flourish if it separates itself from their sympathies and cooperation.... Many people think it is impossible for guerrillas to exist for long in the enemy's rear. Such a belief reveals lack of comprehension of the relationship that should exist between the people and the troops. The former may be likened to water and the latter to the fish who inhabit it."[6]

When such a linkage is established – likening guerrillas to fish and civilians to water – it is often a strategic choice for counter-guerrilla war planners to kill large numbers of civilians – that is, to drain the "water." In his discussion on mass killing in connection with guerrilla warfare, Valentino noted the following: "Counter-guerrilla forces often sought to defeat insurgencies by terrorizing and intimidating the guerrillas' supporters among the civilian population. By killing individuals suspected of collaborating with the insurgents, often in the public and sometimes in an especially gruesome manner, leaders seek to intimidate the rest of the population into shunning the guerrillas or revealing information about guerrilla activities."[7] One such case familiar to the Chinese concerned

[5] Samantha Power, *A Problem from Hell: America and The Age of Genocide* (New York: Basic Books, 2002); Michael Mann, *The Dark Side of Democracy: Explaining Ethnic Cleansing* (New York: Cambridge University Press, 2005); Hannah Ardent, *Eichmann in Jerusalem: A Report on the Banality of Evil* (New York: Penguin Classics, 1994); Saul Friedlander, *Nazi Germany and the Jews, Volume I: The Years of Persecution, 1933–1939* (New York: Harper Perennial, 1997); Saul Friedlander, *Nazi Germany and the Jews 1939–1945: The Years of Extermination* (New York: Harper Perennial, 2006); Robert Conquest, *The Harvest of Sorrow: Soviet Collectivization and the Terror-Famine* (New York: Oxford University Press, 1987); Ben Kiernan, *How Pol Pot Came to Power: Colonialism, Nationalism, and Communism in Cambodia, 1930–1975* (Second Edition) (New Haven, CT: Yale University Press, 1985); and Benjamin A. Valentino, *Final Solutions: Mass Killing and Genocide in the Twentieth Century* (Ithaca, NY: Cornell University Press, 2004).

[6] Mao Zedong, *On Guerrilla Warfare* (New York: Prager, 1961), pp. 44, 92–93. Cf. Valentino, *Final Solutions*, p. 198.

[7] Valentino, *Final Solutions*, p. 200.

the Japanese atrocities in the late 1930s and early 1940s. The Japanese army adopted a "Three-All Policy" – that is, "kill all, burn all, loot all" – toward civilians in the areas suspected of association with the communist insurgents. One source estimates that more than eight million civilians perished during the Japanese occupation.[8]

Although the historical connection between counter-guerrilla tactics and mass killing is difficult to dispute, the situation in China in the late 1960s was unusual. First, there was no real ongoing war. Some mass groups in urban areas were armed and engaged in occasional skirmishes, and some military personnel were split into competing camps, possibly supporting those activities. However, there was no open defiance against the Maoist system as a whole, with both sides vowing to be the genuine defenders of Mao and the communist state. Second, even if there had been armed resistance, the Four Types in the countryside were in no position to provide support for it. In fact, they were used as scapegoats by both sides of the fighting factions. Therefore, both the war and the alleged association between the victims and the "enemies" were framed from fiction.

Writers such as Zheng Yi, Song Yongyi, Xiao Ming, and Xiao Pingtou argued that the extreme violence in Guangxi Province was an organized campaign by a conservative faction against its rival, using government as a tool.[9] Therefore, the context of extreme violence was more of an actual war situation than I suggest here. This conventional wisdom is built on two premises that I have found to be untenable. First, it assumes a vertical factional divide reaching from urban areas to communes and villages, where most collective killings were perpetrated. However, whereas the conflict between a government-backed faction and its "rebel" rivals existed in major cities, there is no evidence that such a divide reached into local communities. To be "conservative" or "rebellious" could have entirely different meanings for factions in major cities and in county-level or lower jurisdictions. For example, in Cangwu County in Guangxi

8 John W. Dower, *War without Mercy: Race and Power in the Pacific War* (London: Faber, 1986), pp. 295–296; cf. Valentino, *Final Solutions*, p. 204.

9 Zheng Yi 郑义,1993, *Hongse jinianbei* 红色纪念碑 [*The Scarlet Memorial*]. Taipei, Taiwan: Huashi wenhua gongsi. Song Yongyi 宋永毅, "Zhonggong de guojia jiqi xingwei" 中共的国家机器行为 ["The Behavior of CCP's State Machine"] pp. 15–26 in Song Yongyi 宋永毅 (ed.), *Wen'ge datusha* 文革大屠杀 [*Massacres during the Cultural Revolution*] (Hong Kong: Kaifang zazhishe, 2002). For a series of reports by Xiao Pingtou 小平头 published online, see "List of Chinese Articles That Cite Unpublished Documents with Page Numbers" at the end of this book. Xiao Ming 晓明: 广西文革列传, available at http://www.fireofliberty.org/oldsite/level4/issue3/4-wengeliezhuan-cover.htm.

Province and Xingning County in Guangdong Province, the local factions had different names from those at the provincial level and the "rebel" faction controlled the county administration in both counties. Moreover, many communes and villages experienced no factional conflict before initiating collective killings of the Four Types.

Second, the "real war" argument assumes that the victims of slaughter provided or had the potential to provide some type of meaningful support for the antigovernment faction. This assumption also is untenable. As I describe in Chapter 4, the Four Types were under tight surveillance and devoid of political rights before and during the Cultural Revolution. Their participation in campaigns was limited to being scapegoats. At the outset, the Party Center specifically issued directives stating that these class enemies were excluded from participation. Despite the rumors, there was no evidence that the victims supplied any meaningful support to any of the mass factions. Guangxi and Guangdong Provinces were among the latecomers to establish new revolutionary committees, causing anxiety in and inviting numerous interventions from the Party Center. The Center's resolve culminated in two harshly worded notices in the summer of 1968 (dated July 3 and July 24), which targeted the situation in Guangxi and Shannxi but were distributed nationwide with great fanfare. The two notices, along with central leaders' speeches in the earlier months, validated the local governments' counter-guerilla tactics as if there were an ongoing war and ushered in a new level of terror and atrocity.

Given the class-struggle logic in Mao's China, the fact that the Four Types had no connection to urban groups did not matter. According to class-struggle doctrine, any contemporary enemies were individuals that represented the interest of the former propertied classes (e.g., landlords and rich peasants). When evidence was absent, organized rallies and collective killings manufactured a sense of "war." Terror served as a self-fulfilling prophecy. Four Types in villages were targeted not because of any role in factional struggles but rather because, as known "enemies," they were weak and in the open.

Eliminationist executions took place mostly in rural villages, whereas mass factionalism and armed street battles were mainly urban phenomena.[10] This echoes what Kalyvas described as "disjunction between center and periphery" in his studies on violence in the context of civil war.

[10] Yang Su, "State Sponsorship or State Failure? Mass Killings in Rural China, 1967–68" (Irvine: Center for the Study of Democracy, University of California, Irvine, 2003); and

"Actions on 'the ground' often seem more related to local or private issues than to the war's driving (or 'master') cleavage." He further asserted that "[I]ndividual and local actors take advantage of the war to settle local or private conflicts bearing little or no relation to the causes of the war or the goals of the belligerents."[11]

Street Battles in Cities

In the summer of 1968, urban areas in both provinces were plagued by a new wave of street battles. In Guangzhou, the provincial capital of Guangdong, armed conflicts persisted between two warring factions: (1) the General Faction backed by the provincial authorities and the army; and (2) the Red Flag. Six incidents were the most severe and influential in this wave of violence, which was known as the Great Armed Battles.[12] On May 3, a battle at the Guangzhou Paper Mill resulted in more than 150 injuries, 50 of them severe.[13] On May 20, a violent engagement at the Guangzhou Electricity Plant resulted in the burning of a building, which killed five people (including a child) and injured forty-three; among the wounded were eleven soldiers who had been sent to intervene. The battle was triggered by a verbal dispute using so-called big-character posters. The dispute escalated into a brawl, in which Yang Ziqing of the General Faction used a knife to kill one person and wound another.[14] On June 1, an attack on a Red Flag stronghold in the Twenty-Second Middle School involved machine guns, grenades, and military-style charge ladders. Sixty-nine Red Flag fighters were captured and subsequently tortured. Afterward, the General Faction claimed that it attacked because the school's Red Flag organization had previously raided a military base to take weapons, wounding many soldiers in the process.[15] On June 3, fighters from a Red Flag organization at Zhongshan University besieged the Physics Department building, burning it almost to the ground. Forty

Andrew G. Walder and Su Yang, "The Cultural Revolution in the Countryside: Scope, Timing, and Human Impact," *The China Quarterly* 173, (2003), pp. 74–99.

[11] Stathis N. Kalyvas, "The Ontology of 'Political Violence': Action and Identity in Civil Wars," *Perspectives on Politics*, vol. 1, no. 3 (September 2003), pp. 475–494.

[12] Hai Feng 海枫, *Guangzhou diqu wen'ge licheng shulue* 广州地区文革历程述略 [*Mapping the Cultural Revolution Trajectory in Guangzhou Area*] (Hong Kong: Youlian yanjiu chubanshe, 1972), p. 368.

[13] Ibid., pp. 370–375.

[14] Ibid.

[15] Ibid.

General Faction fighters were captured and later tortured.[16] On June 6, when a Red Flag member was captured by a General Faction organization, students from the Twenty-Ninth High School staged a rescue mission, resulting in ten injuries and the death of Chen Zhiyi, a high school student, who was posthumously recognized by his colleagues as an Exemplar Red Guard.[17] On June 8, two hundred fighters from four General Faction organizations charged into the Guangya high school, burned down the science building, and set fire to a dormitory, from which nine victims jumped to their death.[18]

Nationally, Mao and the Party Center had called for a "great revolutionary unity" in September 1967, which was intended to end the ever-escalating mass mobilization that had lasted for more than a year and to pave the way to unity governments in local jurisdictions.[19] The response to heed the call to unite, however, differed greatly throughout the thirty Chinese provinces. By the end of 1967, six provincial jurisdictions had celebrated their achievement of great unity and established their revolutionary committees; ten others joined the list in the winter of 1968.[20] However, most jurisdictions fell behind schedule. Dismayed by a divided and militant population, Mao stipulated that the laggards must form revolutionary committees by the beginning of the Chinese New Year in February 1968.[21] However, the last provincial revolutionary committee was not set up until September 1968 (i.e., in Xinjiang Province); other lower-level revolutionary committees were not established until September 1969.[22]

On November 14, 1967, in a meeting with mass-organization representatives from Guangdong Province, Zhou Enlai said, "It is hopeful to form the revolutionary committee [in Guangdong] by the end of the

[16] Ibid.

[17] Ibid.

[18] Ibid.

[19] Zhongguo renmin jiefangjun guofang daxue dangshi dangjian zhenggong jiaoyanshi 国防大学党史党建政工教研室, *Wenhua da geming yanjiu ziliao* 文化大革命研究资料 (中) [*The Cultural Revolution Research Materials*], *CRRM*, vol. 2. (Beijing: Zhongguo renmin jiefanjun guofang daxue dangshi chubanshe, 1988), pp. 582–584.

[20] *CRRM*, vols. 1 and 2.

[21] Shaoguang Wang, *Failure of Charisma: The Cultural Revolution in Wuhan* (Hong Kong and Oxford: Oxford University Press, 1995), p. 181.

[22] "*Beijing daxue geming weiyuanhui shengli dansheng*" ["Victorious Birth of the Beijing University Revolutionary Committee"], *Renmin ribao*, October 6, 1969, in *CRRM*, vol. 2, p. 373.

year."[23] Guangdong formed its provincial revolutionary committee on February 20, 1968; Guangzhou also established its municipal counterpart that day. These achievements were on paper only, however, and devoid of any real great unity – which involved disarming and disbanding warring mass factions. The makeup of the new government and the municipal revolutionary committee of Guangzhou heavily favored the General Faction, but the Red Flag refused to give in.

Central policy required revolutionary committees to be constructed according to a "three-combination" principle. This meant that leaders were to be selected from military officers, old cadres, and mass-organization leaders in equal thirds. Initially, in the new provincial government, the two factions were fairly represented, but it quickly underwent reorganization at the expense of the Red Flag; some Red Flag representatives were purged: Wang Shilin was arrested and jailed, Wu Chuanbing was detained for "self-examination," and others were staged for a mass repudiation. Meanwhile, mass-organization leaders from the General Faction were placed in key leadership positions. Among them, Liang Xiuzhen was appointed a vice director and Lin Liming, Ma Fu, and Jiao Linyi were placed in charge of daily operations. The Red Flag fared even worse in subprovincial committees; for example, the Red Flag occupied only five seats in the eighty-member revolutionary committee in Hainan Prefecture and there was no Red Flag representation in the revolutionary committees of Puning, Huaiji, Lingshui, and Yaxian Counties.[24]

Although the provincial authorities and the military had backed the General Faction for more than a year, the Red Flag remained a formidable mass alliance, comparable in strength to its rival for three main reasons. First, the Party Center had treated the two sides in Guangdong Province more or less even-handedly – occasionally even favoring the Red Flag – until July 1968. Zhou Enlai and other central leaders met with representatives of the two factions at least five times between April and November of 1967, affirming that the Center considered both factions legitimate. In the first meeting in Guangzhou on April 14, 1967, Zhou promised the Center's continuing support for Huang Yongsheng, the military commander and de facto head of provincial authorities at the time. Then,

[23] Hai Feng 海枫, *Guangzhou diqu wen'ge licheng shulue* 广州地区文革历程述略 [*Mapping the Cultural Revolution Trajectory in Guangzhou Area*], p. 342.

[24] Ibid., pp. 353–358.

to thunderous applause from the General Faction representatives, he said: "Some said *Di Zong*, *Hong Zong* [General Faction organizations] are conservative organizations. I disagree." He quickly added, however, to the delight of the Red Flag representatives at the meeting: "But they *are* a little bit conservative though." Although the Center maintained its support for the key provincial leaders – and, by extension, the General Faction – it also worked to strengthen the Red Flag by encouraging pronouncements. Zhou also met alone with Red Flag representatives three times.[25]

Second, the Party Center generally supported the more militant factions such as the Red Flag. According to Xu Youyu's summary of provincial-level conflicts nationwide, in twenty-four of twenty-nine provincial jurisdictions, Mao and the Party Center supported the mass factions that had challenged the pre–Cultural Revolution authorities.[26] Prior to the founding of their revolutionary committees, all provincial capitals experienced mass mobilization by factions and numerous reorganizations of the government. Two opposing alliances emerged; typically, one sought to overthrow the pre–Cultural Revolution government, whereas the other made more moderate demands or defended the government. Power often shifted back and forth between the two sides after the January Storm of 1967. However, after the Wuhan Incident on July 20, the balance of power shifted in Hubei Province and twenty-three other provincial jurisdictions. With the tacit support or explicit approval of the Party Center, the more militant faction was designated as the "revolutionary," or officially backed, side. The government was thoroughly reorganized and the moderate alliance discredited. Many members of the more militant alliance were incorporated into the new government.[27]

Guangdong and Guangxi Provinces proved to be two of the five exceptions. According to Xu, the Center's policy was different for border

[25] For example, on August 14 and 16, 1967, he received representatives from eleven Red Flag organizations in Beijing. He praised the achievements reported by them: "Very good. You can establish Revolutionary Committee now." One of the organizations, the "August 1st Combat Brigade," was earlier labeled by the army as counter-revolutionary. Their representatives pitched their case in the meeting, and Zhou promised a reinstatement. As a result, on August 20, 1967, Huang Yongsheng and another military leader sent a self-criticism letter to the Party Center. Ibid., pp. 121, 236–300.

[26] Xu Youyu 徐友渔, *Xingxing sese de zaofan: hongweibing jingshen suzhi de xingcheng ji Yanbian* 形形色色的造 反：红卫兵精神素质的形成及演变 [*Rebels of All Stripes: A Study of Red Guard Mentalities*] (Hong Kong: Xianggang zhongwen daxue chubanshe, 1999), pp. 86–108.

[27] Wang, *Failure of Charisma*, pp. 149–202.

regions due to national-security considerations.[28] In this group of provinces – which also included Inner Mongolia, Xinjiang, and Tibet – the faction that was more supportive of the incumbent government was designated as revolutionary. They then assumed the major role in the formation of the revolutionary committee, which in turn cracked down on the more militant rebel faction. This tilt toward the less militant faction was not made clear to Red Flag leaders until mid-1968, when speeches by Zhou and other Party Central leaders linked them to the counter-revolutionary conspiracies (e.g., ACPPAs). Before that moment, the Red Flag and its rank-and-file members had been as hopeful as their more successful counterparts in most of the other provinces.

The third reason for the persistence of the Red Flag was that rebel factions were able to build strong organizations on a broad mass base. It is debatable whether rebels relied significantly on the networks of disgruntled individuals disadvantaged by the pre–Cultural Revolution system.[29] However, it is clear that in the first year, local governments victimized legions of cadres and masses alike, who would later join rebel organizations by the tens of thousands. In the first months of the Cultural Revolution, the Party and government agencies of Guangdong Province and Guangzhou municipality were embroiled in organized campaigns against individuals accused of being "black elements." As many as 30 percent of the cadres were named and repudiated by August 1966. In one governmental bureau, the number was 80 percent, among which 10 percent was considered politically unredeemable "ox ghosts and snake demons."[30] The early persecutions were so widespread that many victimized former

[28] According to Xu, political events unfolded in a similar fashion in Jiangxi, although that province is not in a border region. See Xu Youyu 徐友渔, *Xingxing sese de zaofan: hongweibing jingshen suzhi de xingcheng ji Yanbian* 形形色色的造反：红卫兵精神素质的形成及演变 [*Rebels of All Stripes: A Study of Red Guard Mentalities*], pp. 100–108.

[29] See the debate on the conservative–radical thesis in Hong Yung Lee, *The Politics of the Chinese Cultural Revolution: A Case Study* (Berkeley and London: University of California Press, 1978); Anita Chan, Stanley Rosen, and Jonathan Unger, "Students and Class Warfare: The Social Roots of the Red Guard Conflict in Guangzhou (Canton)," *The China Quarterly* 83 (1980), pp. 397–446; Andrew G. Walder, "Beijing Red Guard Factionalism: Social Interpretations Reconsidered." *Journal of Asian Studies* 61 (2002), pp. 437–471; Andrew G. Walder, "Ambiguity and Choice in Political Movements: The Origin of Beijing Red Guard Factionalism," *American Journal of Sociology* 112 (2006), pp. 710–750; and Yang Su, "Tumult from Within: State Bureaucrats and Chinese Mass Movement, 1966–71" (Ph.D. dissertation, Stanford University, Stanford, CA, 2003).

[30] Hai Feng 海枫, *Guangzhou diqu wen'ge licheng shulue* 广州地区文革历程述略 [*Mapping the Cultural Revolution Trajectory in Guangzhou Area*], pp. 37–38.

cadres turned to the rebel faction, bringing along their networks and leadership. Moreover, the military was not immune to the political campaigns of the time; for example, students in military academies who were loyal to their disgraced commanders often joined forces with rebel organizations.

In one high-profile incident in August 1967 in Guangzhou Garrison, a big-character poster appeared that targeted Wen Yucheng, a top commander. Two political commissioners seized on this rebellious act as an opportunity to unseat Wen. When the attempt backfired, the commissioners denounced the officers who had marched to present the poster and deemed the event a "counter-revolutionary incident." More than two hundred people were implicated and commanded to self-repudiate, thereby creating a segment of military personnel sympathetic to the rebel factions.[31] When the movement escalated to the staging of street battles between mass organizations, both sides armed themselves by raiding the military's weapons depository – which would have been impossible if the military had truly resisted. An informant told me that the "raiding" in most cases was fake. Army units tipped off mass leaders about the location of weapons; when the "raid" took place, soldiers remained idle or quickly retreated.[32]

By the early summer of 1968, the Red Flag's favor had run out and the Party Center had thrown its support behind the government-backed faction in Guangdong and Guangxi Provinces. In July, the Center issued the high-profile July 3rd Notice to the nation, demanding to "immediately stop armed battles, dismantle forts and strongholds." Although the purpose of the notice was to solve the "Guangxi Problem," it was distributed nationwide and required specific actions throughout the country.[33] On the surface, the notice seemed to target mass organizations of all hues, but it accompanied the Center's stated support of existing provincial authorities in both provinces.[34] By denouncing the Red Flag and the FTT, the government-backed factions – that is, the General Faction and the UHQ – were named "winners" of the political battle. Their assault

[31] Ibid., pp. 40–42.

[32] Personal interview with Mr. Zhao.

[33] *CRRM*, vol. 1, pp. 138–139.

[34] Huang Yongsheng, the military commander in Guangdong Province and a long-time target of the Red Flag, was in fact promoted to joint chief of staff of the PLA and a new member of the Politburo. See Hai Feng 海枫, *Guangzhou diqu wen'ge licheng shulue* 广州地区文革历程述略 [*Mapping the Cultural Revolution Trajectory in Guangzhou Area*], p. 355.

on factional opponents had now been officially declared the equivalent of war.

In Guangxi Province, Wei Guoqing – an accomplished general in the pre-1949 wars – was another military chief entrusted by Mao with a frontier province. This one bordered Vietnam, and the Vietnam War was in full swing in 1967 and 1968. To mobilize mass insurgency, Mao and the Party Center had overseen the downfall of other high-ranking military leaders in other provinces of the Middle Southern region. However, Wei and Huang Yongsheng, whose Guangdong Province bordered Hong Kong – a British colony at the time – retained unwavering backing from the Center because of geopolitical concerns until the end of the Cultural Revolution.[35]

Nevertheless, the rebel faction in the Guangxi provincial capital of Nanning, the FTT, was strong. Indeed, on August 24, 1967, in a meeting in Beijing with representatives from both factions, Zhou Enlai declared the FTT a "rebel organization," whereas the UHQ was deemed only a "mass organization." In the Cultural Revolution lexicon of the time, *rebel* meant revolutionary; thus, the FTT was the favored side at the time.[36] The FTT was one of the most unruly mass alliances in the nation, and its strength was evidenced by widespread and large-scale armed battles with the UHQ in Nanning and other major cities – even after the founding of the Nanning municipal revolutionary committee in April 1968 and the provincial revolutionary committee in July 1968, both of which were led by the UHQ.[37]

35 Xu Youyu 徐友渔, *Xingxing sese de zaofan: hongweibing jingshen suzhi de xingcheng ji Yanbian* 形形色色的造 反：红卫兵精神素质的形成及演变 [*Rebels of All Stripes: A Study of Red Guard Mentalities*], pp. 98–99.

36 Ibid. See also *Guangxi wen'ge dashi nianbiao* 广西文革大事年表 [*Chronology of the Cultural Revolution in Guangxi*] (Nanning: Guangxi renmin chubanshe, 1990), pp. 49–50. Reprinted by Chinese Publications Services Center, Los Angeles, CA, 1995. Hereafter, GXWGDSNB. After the meeting, the No. 5 Garrison stationed in Liuzhou issued an official statement pledging support for the FTT, *CRRM*, vol. 1, p. 50. The FTT also appeared to have secret backing from the Central Cultural Revolution Group (CCRG). On August 22, 1967, a reporter sought out the FTT representatives stationed in Beijing, giving instructions on behalf of the CCRG. The reporter said that the Center would solve the "Guangxi Problem" soon, and asked them to be prepared for possible fates bestowed on Wei Guoqing by the Center. See *CRRM*, vol. 1, p. 49.

37 In one of the early confrontations, on June 11, 1967, a few hundred FTT members blocked a train for more than three days, receding only after Zhou intervened. The first severe violence took place on June 13, 1967, in Nanning First High School, when the FTT and UHQ members engaged in a rock-throwing fight, with two hundred hospitalized with severe injuries. On August 1, 1967, the UHQ organized more than ten thousand fighters to attack the *Guangxi Daily* building occupied by the FTTs. On August 18,

Despite the daily street battles in urban centers, Guangxi earned its name as the most atrocious province in the Cultural Revolution through local UHQ militia's assaults in areas where, in fact, the FTT was weak or nonexistent. Backed by governmental commands and military personnel, the militias used overwhelming force to sweep areas suspected of harboring FTT fighters, often in remote county seats, townships, and villages. A typical incident took place in Licun Village in Rongxian County in November 1967 (described at the beginning of this chapter), in which sixty-nine people were killed, including suspected FTT members, along with Four Types and ordinary peasants.[38]

These campaigns generated terror and excesses in villages where there were no signs of the FTT – where killings took place for reasons completely unconnected to factional battles. The earliest incident of eliminationist killings was on October 2, 1967, in Dongshan Commune in Quanzhou County. For two days, seventy-six family members from Four Types were killed by being pushed off a cliff.[39] The killings apparently were influenced by events in the adjacent Daoxian County in Hunan Province, where more than 4,950 Four-Type family members were killed in July and August of 1967.[40] The Quanzhou killings began with a

1967, in Jinjie Village, three hundred FTT fighters looted a military train heading for Vietnam and seized more than four thousand bombs. The CCRG telegraphed them to return the munitions. Guns and cannons were used by the FTT in a street battle on April 11, 1968, in Wuzhou City. After the battle, UHQ members looted Wuzhou Military District, taking military supplies. Ibid., pp. 36–37, 47–49, 80.

38 See Xiao Pingtou, *Guangxi "fangong jiuguotuan" yuanan shimo – wen'ge jimi dangan jiemi zhi yi* 广西 "反共救国团" 冤案始末 – 文革机密档案揭密之一, available at https://67.15.34.207/news/gb/kanshihai/shishi/2006/1101/172175.html, pp. 12–13, accessed August 24, 2008. See also *CRRM*, vol. 1, p. 58. In another large-scale operation, after a joint meeting of public security officers from several counties on August 18, 1968, "… the People's Armed Forces Department (*renmin wuzhuangbu)* in each county went ahead to carry out the 'order.' About 4,400 (a number that exceeded what had been stipulated in the meeting) armed individuals of the 'United Headquarters' besieged the members of '7.29' [a dissenting mass organization] who had fled to Nanshan and Beishan of Fengshan County. More than 10,000 were detained (the county population was then 103,138). During the siege and the subsequent detentions, 1,016 were shot to death, making up more than 70 percent of the total Cultural Revolution deaths of the county.… After the violence swept across the county, the establishment of the Revolutionary Committee of Fengshan County was finally [announced] on the 25th [of August, 1968]." GXWGDSNB, p. 119.

39 Tang Chuying 唐楚英 (ed.), *Quanzhou Xianzhi* 全州县志 [*Quanzhou County Gazetteer*] (Nanning: Guangxi renmin chubanshe, 1998), pp. Hereafter, *Quanzhou Xianzhi*.

40 Zhang Cheng 章成, "*Daoxian da tusha*" 道县大屠杀 ["The Daoxian Massacre"], *Open Magazine* 开放杂志 July, August, September, and December, 2001.

meeting that relayed the news about the Daoxian events and was attended by local militia leaders and UHQ activists.[41]

By the end of 1967, the UHQ faction clearly had the upper hand in the mass-factional conflict. With General Wei now enjoying the Party Center's full support, provincial authorities pushed ahead the campaign for great unity and demanded the dissolution of the FTT. The boundaries gradually became nonexistent between the traditional militia controlled by the government and military and the UHQ mass organizations. The People's Militia was a vast organization consisting of workers in factories and peasants in villages. It was controlled by the military through the PAFD at every level of government, down to the village. Although the FTT refused to disarm, it was no longer comparable in strength to the UHQ. The collective killings committed by local militias were clearly aimed at intimidating the FTT. In response, on December 26, 1967, the FTT assembled an "anti-massacre committee" in Nanning that was attended by representatives from local counties. They organized a rally of two thousand people in front of the Guangxi military district auditorium, demanding that the provincial authorities and the military stop "massacres" in local counties.[42] Such peaceful protests against mass killings were staged repeatedly throughout 1968.[43] In the first half of 1968, the government, the military, and the UHQ violently cracked down on the FTT in urban centers, and local leaders slaughtered thousands of Four Types and their family members in the countryside.

Alleging Conspiracy Networks and Staging Class-Struggle Exhibitions

By mid-1968, the government, the military, and the UHQ began working together to articulate their incursions against the FTT into a wider theoretical justification. At the center of these claims was the ACPPA. Although an organization with this name had contested the new communist government in the immediate aftermath of the 1949 revolution, the original ACPPA had been routed long ago. This new ACPPA was a fictional organization that allegedly threatened the Chinese government and now had the FTT at its center. Essentially, the UHQ sought to discredit and delegitimize its factional rivals for power by associating

41 *CRRM*, vol. 1, p. 53.

42 Ibid., p. 63.

43 Ibid., pp. 66, 71.

them – however preposterously – with the remnants of the Guomindang, which had been decisively defeated in the civil war.

The existence of such a conspiracy network was first manufactured by the UHQ faction in the wake of the Rongxian County incident. In July 1967, four hundred members of the UHQ attacked an FTT organization in Licun Village in Rongxian County. Twelve were killed and twenty-one injured, with another one thousand fleeing to the border areas near Guangdong Province. The incident prompted an investigation by provincial authorities; however, given their composition, the conclusion was biased in favor of the UHQ faction. To justify the attack and killings, the UHQ newspaper invoked the supposed ACPPA. A report dated February 2, 1968, claimed that ACPPA groups existed throughout Rongxian County, allegedly uncovered in the county seat and in many communes.[44] The witch-hunt spread into other counties in both Guangxi and Guangdong Provinces. On May 20, 1968, the Guangxi provincial authorities and the military district sent a joint report to the Party Center identifying this new "threat." A month later, a UHQ newspaper reiterated the alleged link between the ACPPA and the FTT and issued the following action statement: "ACPPA is deeply rooted in the FTT, whose leaders are in fact ACPPA elements . . . the proletarian revolutionaries must act to uncover ACPPAs. Those who resist arrest should be executed on the spot. We must defeat them into threads and pieces politically, organizationally, and militarily."[45]

The supposed danger was dramatized by a wave of Class-Struggle Education exhibitions throughout the two provinces. One exhibition in Guangdong Province even earned praise from Mao.[46] On May 12, 1968, ten former cadres under UHQ detention were put in a wooden cage for a three-day exhibition in Nanning, Guangxi Province. Thousands streamed in to watch this "Beast and Fowl Exhibit." The captured cadres were all brutally tortured. On August 12, 1968, another exhibition took place in a military headquarters in Nanning; lasted for fifty-two days. The number of viewers was a staggering 489,365. The victims in the cages were tied up and placards were attached naming them as traitors, spies, ACPPA, and war criminals. On August 16, 1968, a third exhibition in a local government headquarters displayed seven former cadres in cages;

44 Xiao Pingtou, *Guangxi "fangong jiuguotuan" yuanan shimo – wen'ge jimi dangan jiemi zhi yi* 广西 "反共救国团" 冤案始末 – 文革机密档案揭密之一, p. 12.

45 Ibid., pp. 90–97.

46 Hai Feng 海枫, *Guangzhou diqu wen'ge licheng shulue* 广州地区文革历程述略 [*Mapping the Cultural Revolution Trajectory in Guangzhou Area*], p. 401.

thousands visited the site. The most spectacular exhibition, at Guangxi University, reportedly was visited by 1,600,000 people from 25 provinces and regions throughout China. The total number of these exhibition victims in Guangxi Province was more than ten thousand.[47]

Guangdong Province staged similar exhibitions displaying weapons, poison, paperwork, torture dungeons, and daily operation facilities. The sites were chosen from buildings previously occupied by rival mass organizations. One building was located in Shahe in Guangzhou, where an exhibition opened in July 1968. In May, organizations from the Red Flag had occupied the building. Organized by provincial and municipal authorities after the building was retaken, the exhibition displayed weapons, bullets, communication devices, medicines, poison, and daily necessities. At another exhibition site, visitors saw a prison and dungeons allegedly used to torture "revolutionary masses." They were told that Red Flag leaders killed the captives and ate their hearts. These exhibitions were hailed as a great success, so much so that Huang Yongsheng, the army chief of the province, sent a congratulatory telegraph and called for more, which were provided.[48]

In a July 25, 1968, meeting, Zhou asserted that network headquarters were based in Guangzhou, the provincial capital of Guangdong. He castigated the FTT as follows: "Is there no ACPPA in your organization? Why are there so many counter-revolutionary crimes in Guangxi? They [ACPPA] are the black hands behind the scene. The headquarters of ACPPA is in Guangzhou, and there are branches in Guangxi. They have infiltrated in [mass organizations] whenever they have a chance. Both sides [UHQ and FTT] must investigate."[49] Kang Sheng accused one of the FTT organizations as being a "hotbed" of the ACPPA: "It is no coincidence that there are ACPPAs in your province. The headquarters is in

47 *Zhonggong Nanning diwei zhengdang bangongshi* 中共南宁地委整党办公室 [Nanning Ratification Office]. *Nanning diqu wenhua da geming dashi ji 1966–1976* 南宁地区文化大革命大事记 1966–1976 (unpublished documents, 1987); see also Xiao Pingtou, *Guangxi "fangong jiuguotuan" yuanan shimo – wen'ge jimi dangan jiemi zhi yi* 广西"反共救国团"冤案始末 – 文革机密档案揭密之一, pp. 35–36.

48 In Sanyangli, a suburban commune, a third exhibition was opened, aiming to educate not only urban residents but also peasants. On August 30, 1968, a fourth exhibition opened. It focused on alleged crimes of underground conspiracy groups, including the ACPPA and the so-called China People's Party. Put on display were action statements, daily documents, and radio devices allegedly used to communicate with Taiwan. See Hai Feng 海枫, *Guangzhou diqu wen'ge licheng shulue* 广州地区文革历程述略 [*Mapping the Cultural Revolution Trajectory in Guangzhou Area*], pp. 401–404.

49 Ibid.

Guangzhou, and there are branches in Guangxi. Have you [FTT] had connections with the Red Flag [one of two faction alliances] in Guangdong? Many leaders of the Red Flag are in fact leaders of ACPPAs. Therefore, there should [be] the same problem in your organization." Zhou joined this allegation, adding, "Have you not meted out two such leaders? There must be more in the FTT."[50] The menace of the ACPPA was also heralded as a sign of a much larger threat.[51]

These assertions from the central leaders definitively endorsed the definition of a warlike political climate as devised by local provincial governments for their own faction-fighting purposes. On May 17, 1968, Guangxi authorities sent a telegram to the Party Center entitled "Report on Uncovering the Case of Jiang Bandits 'Republic of China Anti-Communist Patriotic Army,'" which linked the alleged conspiracy to the pre-1949 enemy government.[52] The report claimed that sixty-three leaders had been arrested, including the Army's commander, deputy commander, and political director. Incriminating evidence included an action statement, an official seal, guns, bullets, and the correspondence addresses of foreign intelligence agencies.[53] One month later, provincial authorities issued the following public advisory: "The key elements of this counterrevolutionary organization have infiltrated into mass organizations. Some of them have become leaders, waving [the] red flag to oppose [the] red flag. They used mass organizations as their cover to engage in their counterrevolutionary activities."[54]

The Guangxi government welcomed this notice and on July 11, massive rallies were organized throughout the province and were attended by as many as three million people. In the counties, the government demanded specific actions in response to the notice; for the Party Center, it outlined the achievements in a sequence of memoranda entitled "Briefings on Implementing the July 3rd Notice." The *Guangxi Daily* published nine

[50] Ibid.

[51] Kang also suggested that the conflict of the time was between the enemy and the people, and that there were elements of Trotskyites and the Nationalist Party (GMD) in the enemy. He said, "In today's Guangxi, there exists a problem of revolution versus counterrevolution. As the July 3 Notice pointed out, there were many contradictions among the people, but the main issue is the antagonistic contradictions. ACPPAs are among you, and there are remaining elements of Trotskyites and GMD." Ibid.

[52] Xiao Pingtou, *Guangxi "fangong jiuguotuan" yuanan shimo – wen'ge jimi dangan jiemi zhi yi* 广西"反共救国团"冤案始末 – 文革机密档案揭密之_, p. 12.

[53] Guangxi shengzhi, volume of "main events," p. 390.

[54] GXWDSNB, p. 98.

editorials calling for action in the spirit of the Notice.[55] By the time the Beijing meeting was held in the People's Meeting Hall on July 25, 1968, Guangxi Province had become a virtual hell of atrocities.

Without questioning the diagnosis or practices associated with it, the Party Center issued the so-called July 3rd Notice demanding a quick end to the factional conflict, including the disarming and disbanding of mass organizations. Instead of tamping down the killings, Zhou Enlai and Kang Sheng's speeches added fuel to the fire. Not only did they signal approval from the Party Center; they also demanded that the July 3rd Notice be implemented in other provinces. In addition, they ratified the Guangxi government's struggle with the FTT. It recognized as real the fictional ACPPA and went even further, identifying the ACPPA headquarters as being in Guangzhou, the capital of Guangdong Province. Zhou and other Party leaders inadvertently but effectively exported the Guangxi massacres of Four-Type scapegoats to Guangdong as well.

Village Four Types as Scapegoat

The impact of the Party Center's endorsement on local communities was swift and violent. Class-struggle exhibitions reached new heights of prominence. More important, county and township militias waged a "tsunami" of attacks on imagined enemies. "By October 1968," the xianzhi compilers of Debao County in Guangxi wrote, "the county had arrested 1,504 ACPPA members, detained in 'concentration camps' in various locations (storage rooms, classrooms, or caves)." The camps were equipped with interrogation chambers and numerous torture instruments. Rallies attended by massive crowds were held in every commune, "where militias mistreated the 'criminals' with fists, kicks, sticks, and rocks. Two hundred eighty-four were killed, 127 maimed, 1,016 injured, and 24 missing."[56] In Du'an County, a mass campaign was mobilized following the province's June 17 report on the ACPPA, for the purpose of "meting out 'evil elements,' cutting off 'black hands,' and uncovering 'assassination squads.'"

The campaign reached the village level. On August 2, Sanbiao Brigade of Lalie Commune was identified as a hotbed of conspiracy, with not only ACPPA presence but also a new variation called the Youth Party and a

55 Ibid., pp. 99–120.

56 *Debao xian difangzhi bianzuan weiyuanhui* 德保县志编纂委员会, *Debao Xianzhi* 德保县志 [*Debao County Gazetteer*] (Nanning: Guangxi renmin chubanshe, 1998), p. 353.

liaison station.[57] One of the most severe cases of collective killings was in Lingui County: "From mid-June to the end of August [1968], 1,991 were killed as members of various conspiracy groups in such names as 'assassination squad,' ACPPA, 'such and such black gangs.'... Among the 161 brigades of the county, only two, Wantian and Dongjiang, did not experience arrests and killings."[58] Quanzhou County, where seventy-six family members of former landlords and rich peasants were pushed off a cliff in October 1967, did not escape the new wave of terror: "On July 4, 1968, a ten-thousand rally was held in Fenghuang Commune, thirty-six landlords, rich peasants, and their children were shot to death.... From July to December, each commune established a 'Poor and Lower-Middle Peasant Court'; 850 landlords, rich peasants, and their children were executed with firearms."[59]

The campaign in Guangdong Province was no less ferocious. On July 27, 1968, the Fengkai County revolutionary committee held a rally of five thousand people to call for implementation of the July 3rd and July 24th Notices from the Party Center. By the end of the year, 5,000 victims had been persecuted, of which 524 were killed. In August 1968 in Heyuan County, 10,200 people were persecuted with accusations including "spies," "capitalist roaders," "GMD elements," and "traitors." Twenty-six were killed.[60] In Heping County, an alleged GMD party branch was uncovered. As many as 38,000 people were struggled against in a rally or a parade; among the victims, 750 were injured and 249 killed.[61] On October 7, 1968, the Huaji County revolutionary committee organized a mass rally in a stadium under the banner of "Action Mobilization Rally to Thoroughly Purge Counter-Revolutionary Groups." At the meeting, it was announced that an ACPPA group was in the county, implicating more than two hundred people; thirteen were later killed.[62]

[57] *Du'an yaozu zizhixian difangzhi bangongshi* 都安瑶族自治县地方志办公室. *Du'an Xianzhi* 都安县志 [*Du'an County Gazetteer*] (Nanning: Guangxi remin chubanshe, 2002), p. 649.

[58] *Linggui xianzhi bianwei* 临桂县志编委, *Lingui xianzhi* 临桂县志 [*Lingui County Gazetteer*] (Beijing: Fangzhi chubanshe, 1996), p. 493.

[59] *Quanzhou xianzhi*, p. 17.

[60] *Heyuan xian difangzhi bianzuan weiyuanhui* 河源县地方志编纂委员会, *Heyuan Xianzhi* 河源县地方志 [*Heyuan County Gazetteer*] (Guangzhou: Guangdong renmin chubanshe, 2000), p. 51.

[61] *Heping xian difangzhi bianzuan weiyuanhui* 和平县地方志编纂委员会, *Heping Xianzhi* 和平县志 [*Heping County Gazetteer*] (Guangzhou: Guangdong renmin chubanshe, 1999), p. 25.

[62] *Huaiji xianzhi bangongshi* 怀集县志办公室, *Huaiji Xianzhi* 怀集县志 [*Huaiji County Gazetteer*] (Guangzhou: Guangdong renmin chubanshe, 2005), p. 29.

There is no evidence that Four Types in the countryside provided any support to warring factions in the cities. They were excluded from participation in the campaigns except to serve as struggle targets. In the first two years of the Cultural Revolution, Jin Zhilong – the sole surviving son of a landlord family from Jinkeng Village in Xingning County, Guangdong Province – had been working as a pine syrup collector in the mountains in Xunwu County, Jiangxi Province. In June 1968, when a directive issued by the Jiangxi authorities expelled all migrant workers from its territory (a common practice at the time), he returned to his village and was immediately placed under daily surveillance. Like his fellow Four Types, Jin did not participate in any political activities and did not talk in public regarding the ongoing campaigns. He knew nothing about political issues, especially in faraway places like Guangzhou. Nevertheless, he was immediately taken to join other Four Types as a target in village rallies and parades.

Jin's main concern was avoiding injury when serving as a struggle target. Fortunately, Jin Tieguang, the militiaman in charge of his daily surveillance, was from the same clan. He would warn Jin beforehand, for example, to wear thick trousers when kneeling would be part of the day's plan (rally organizers deliberately lay pebbles on the ground). In the heated political climate following the July 3rd Notice, all Four Types were rounded up in a village rally for a mass execution, but Jin and other Four Types survived when the killings were diverted.[63] The Du brothers, who survived in Dukeng Village in Wuhua County in Guangdong Province, told me of their similar noninvolvement in any factional conflict.[64]

In reading the 120 *xianzhi* (county gazetteers) of Guangdong and Guangxi Provinces, it is clear that factional armed battles were common in county seats but extremely rare in townships and villages. Was this simply an omission because the *xianzhi* did not record events taking place at levels lower than the county seat? The information I have suggests that factional battles indeed were rare in townships and villages. First, the *xianzhi* were typically explicit about major events such as collective killings. Often, the names of the brigade (i.e., the village-level political jurisdiction) and the small team (i.e., the level below the brigade) were thoroughly specified. Second, during my trips to four counties (two in each province), I found records indicating that only one armed battle between two factions of high school students occurred outside a

63 Personal interview with Su Qinglong, 2006.

64 Personal interviews with Huang Zhanji and Huang Jiajun, 2006.

county seat (i.e., in Luogang Commune in Xingning County, Guangdong Province).This finding from the four counties attests to the accuracy of the *xianzhi* records regarding the infrequency of armed battles in rural villages.

There was no organizational linkage between urban conflict and village Four Types and neither was there a psychological link. An influential line of scholarship on conflict in urban centers suggests the existence of a conservative–radical divide, with rebel factions at war with government-backed factions supposedly supported by those with less desirable family backgrounds, including Four Types. However, a growing body of literature recently has revealed that the so-called conservative–radical thesis is a myth. Factional fault lines were created not by the preexisting class structure but rather by the early campaigns between June and December of 1966, which victimized with equal force those with and without a "good" family background.[65] In a detailed account that lists key players in the rebel faction in Wuhan City, Hubei Province, Wang Shaoguang shows that the leaders, in fact, were party–state cadres who harbored grudges due to mistreatment before the Cultural Revolution or in the first six months of the movement.[66]

Indeed, in the two provinces, the only connection between the Four Types in the villages and the battling factions in the cities and county seats was the implausible fiction propagated by provincial authorities: the ACPPA. The authorities wanted others to believe that their factional opponents – typically insurgents like members of the FTT and the Red Flag – were collaborating with remnants of the completely routed pre-1949 government and army. The Four Types were the only vestiges of this regime, and they were simply symbolic. After all, most Four Types had never owned property and certainly did not during the Cultural Revolution. They simply had the misfortune of being related to former property owners or assigned to such a family to meet a locality's predetermined quota. By the time of the Cultural Revolution, the Four Types had long been devoid of political rights and were not involved in the political struggles of the day. For symbolic reasons, these Four Types were anathema to any faction (e.g., the FTT and Red Flag) seeking legitimate authority in Mao's China.

[65] For the conservative–radical thesis, see Lee, *The Politics of the Chinese Cultural Revolution*; Chan et al., "Students and Class Warfare"; for its debunking, see Walder, "Red Guard Factionalism"; and Walder, "Ambiguity and Choice in Political Movements."

[66] Wang, *Failure of Charisma*.

In any case, the fault lines between the two primary mass alliances at war in the provincial capitals – one favoring the existing authorities (i.e., the UHQ in Nanning and the General Faction in Guangzhou), the other opposed (i.e., the FTT in Nanning and the Red Flag in Guangzhou) – did not reach the county or lower levels. In the four counties where I conducted extensive interviews, three had factional splits that were in opposition with those in the capital. In Cangwu County, the Power Seizure campaign in January 1967 was waged by a group of high school students supported by the county PAFB. The majority of county cadres resisted, forming a faction that was later linked to the provincial UHQ. The PAFB head, Wen Xueyi, and the students formed another faction, calling themselves the FTT. Wen remained the chief county authority, hence making the county's factional divide the opposite of the pattern in Nanning: The county's FTT was supporting the county authorities whereas the UHQ was challenging them.[67] In Wuhua and Xingning Counties, the two factions did not even use the same names as those in Guangzhou. Instead, the factions were called the Red Flag and the Red Alliance, which are the names of two main groups within the Red Flag, the rebel faction in Guangzhou.[68]

Factional conflict was as heated in some county seats as in provincial capitals, even when the national policy of great unity was promulgated in late 1967. In December, Cangwu County in Guangxi Province was embroiled in factional conflict. "Two factions of the mass organizations, self-proclaimed as 'Cangwu UHQ' and 'Cangwu FTT,' were formed in the county. Each side, based in buildings such as the County Committee Building, the Cadre Cafeteria, the county commerce building, and cinema, traded constant verbal attacks through high-wattage speakers."[69] Gunfire was sometimes exchanged. Li Yibiao was making homemade grenades with his FTT colleagues when an explosion injured his right hand. He was rushed to the county hospital and – to his misfortune – the

[67] Personal interview with Li Zhao, 2006. See also *Cangwu xianzhi bianzuan weiyuanhui* 苍梧县志编纂委员会, *Cangwu xianzhi* 苍梧县志 [*Cangwu County Gazetteer*] (Nanning: Guangxi remin chubanshe, 1997), pp. 48, 480–483. Hereafter, *Cangwu xianzhi.*

[68] Personal interviews with Liu Biguang and Wei Rongtao, 2006. See also *Wuhua xian difang zhi bianzuan weiyuanhui* 五华县地方志编纂委员会, *Wuhua Xianzhi* 五华县志 [*Wuhua County Gazetteer*] (Guangzhou: Guangdong renmin chubanshe, 1998); hereafter, *Wuhua Xianzhi*; and *Xingning xian difang zhi bianxiu weiyuanhui* 兴宁县地方志编修委员会, *Xingning Xianzhi* 兴宁县志 [*Xingning County Gazetteer*] (Guangzhou: Guangdong renmin chubanshe, 1998); hereafter, *Xingning Xianzhi*.

[69] *Cangwu xianzhi*, p. 49.

attending doctor was a member of the rival faction, the UHQ. The doctor decided not only to alert his UHQ colleagues to the FTT's "criminal plan," he also amputated Li's hand – possibly unnecessarily, according to my source. The next day, the UHQ organized a massive demonstration to denounce the enemy's conspiracy, using as evidence a glass jar containing Li's amputated hand, which apparently was provided by the doctor.[70]

However, rather than an ideological difference, the conflict mainly revolved around which leaders from the old government were to be purged and which movement activists were to be installed in the new government. Both sides vowed to defend Mao and his revolutionary line. Also common to the dueling factions was their attitude toward class enemies, the Four Types. Lest they be accused by their opponents of being on the wrong side of the class struggle, no organizations allowed Four Types or their family members to join. Moreover, to show revolutionary zeal, both sides routinely harassed and victimized the Four Types in their rituals of class struggle. Although the campaign pronouncements issued from the Party Center accused the Four Types of wishing for continuous chaos, the truth is that the Four Types suffered the most from the chaos.

The connection between urban conflict and Four Types in villages was established not by demonstrating their support for disfavored factions but rather by the logic of class-struggle doctrine in Mao's China. This rhetoric was trumpeted exponentially in 1967 and 1968. A typical policy statement was the following 1968 New Year editorial that appeared simultaneously in the Party's flagship publications: "Chairman Mao says: 'All reactionary forces will fight to the last gasp at their pending doom.' A handful of traitors, spies and capitalist power-holders in the party, the demons and ghosts (i.e., those *landlords, rich peasants, counter-revolutionaries, bad-elements, and rightists* who have not yet been well reformed) in the society, and the running dogs of the American imperialists and Soviet Revisionists are bound to continue their sabotage and instigation with all possible means, including spreading rumors and planting divisions."[71]

A class enemy was whomever the local government deemed to be standing in the way of the new social order. "Whether or not one is willing to overcome factionalism," asserted the same editorial, "is the most

[70] Personal interview with Mr. Zhao, 2006.

[71] "The 1968 New Year Editorial," *People's Daily, Liberation Army Daily,* and *Red Flag,* in *CRRM*, vol. 2, p. 3. Emphasis added by the author.

important sign of whether or not one is willing to be a real revolutionary under the present circumstances."[72] As at other times, party policy was general rather than specific; although it stressed the existence of class enemies and their potential threat, it did not provide any criteria for identifying them. Local governments could define *class enemy* as they saw fit. To compensate for the deficiency in general pronouncements, the Party promoted a series of exemplary local practices. For example, four days after the quoted editorial was published, the Party Center issued a directive praising the work of "deeply digging out traitors" in Heilongjiang Province.[73] At mid-year, a report about a Beijing factory's experience of "fighting enemies" was distributed nationwide with great fanfare.[74] Governments in the countryside emulated these examples to comply with the national policy but applied them to local conditions. To root out the "class foundations" of antigovernment forces, Four Types and their families became the most conspicuous targets.

The Guangxi provincial government produced six subsequent memoranda to report its accomplishments to the Party Center. This demonstrates that the July 3rd Notice policy demanded local governments to produce concrete results in the implementation of central directives. At the county level, authorities convened meetings with grassroots cadres and representatives to discuss specific actions to be taken. Some meetings were accompanied by collective killings of Four Types to demonstrate compliance with the policy. A post–Cultural Revolution report compiled in 1987 by the Party Ratification Office of Cangwu County described the details of three such meetings. The report concluded that the meetings greatly contributed to "random repudiations, random struggles, random arrests, random imprisonments, random beatings, and random killings"

72 Ibid., p. 4.

73 "*Zhonggong zhongyang, guowuyuan, zhongyang junwei, zhongyang wenge zhuanfa Heilongjiang sheng geming weiyuanhui 'guanyu shenwa pantu gongzuo qingkuang de baogao' de pifa*" ["CCP Central Committee, State Council, Central Military Commission, and Central Cultural Revolution Group Authorize the Circulation of the Heilongjiang Province Revolutionary Committee's 'Situation Report on Rooting Out Traitors'"], February 5, 1968, in *CRRM*, vol. 2, p. 16.

74 "*Zhonggong zhongyang, zhongyang wenge zhuanfa Mao zhuxi guanyu 'Beijing xinhua yinshuachang junguanhui fadong qunzhong kaizhan duidi douzheng de jingyan' de pishi de tongzhi*" ["CCP Central Committee and Central Cultural Revolution Group Transmit Chairman Mao's Remarks on 'Experience of the Beijing Xinhua Printing Plant Military Control Committee in Mobilizing the Masses to Struggle Against Enemies,'" in *CRRM*, vol. 2, pp. 126–130.

in 1968.[75] The "random killings" accounted for most of the 580 "unnatural deaths" in the county during the Cultural Revolution.[76]

On May 24, 1968, the newly established Cangwu County revolutionary committee held a Political Work Meeting in Lihu Commune. On May 9, the county government had called for local communes to wage the "first wave of ferociously attacking class enemies." Lihu Commune stood out for its extensive persecutions. The commune's revolutionary committee and the Defending Red Headquarters group dispatched thousands of militiamen, who ransacked 545 households, arrested 11, repudiated more than 100, and killed 5 people. A live-human exhibition was staged displaying ten struggle targets. The purpose of the May 24 meeting was to promote the Lihu Commune experience for emulation by other communes.

Not to be outdone, leaders from other communes reported their own repressive responses. The PAFB head of Shiqiao Commune reported that it had uncovered a counter-revolutionary group in the commune's high school. Led by a physical education teacher, he said, the group had seventy members and possessed thirty-five guns. Leaders from Shatou Commune reported their experiences of killing Four Types in large numbers. In his concluding speech at the three-day meeting, county leader Li Xuandian said: "Class enemies will never rest their mind as long as they live their body.... In the mass dictatorship, don't throw cold water to discourage when a few Four Types are killed." Following the meeting, local communes took immediate action to implement the "meeting spirit." The Sizhou Brigade of Changzhou Commune held a mass rally on May 30 and executed a Four Type named Chen Yanqiu. Ren Commune held a cadre meeting, killing two victims on the spot. One day after a rally at the commune level, five members of the Huang family were killed in Dangwan Brigade in Shatou Commune. Within ten days of the May 24 meeting at Lihu Commune, a total of sixty-three were killed.[77]

The widespread abuses and killings were lauded in a second county-level meeting held on June 9 and 10, 1968. Again attended by commune leaders from throughout the county, the meeting escalated the rhetoric about pending threats from class enemies. Among those who reported

75 Cangwu Party Ratification Office 苍梧整党办公室, "*Zaocheng yanzhong houguo de 'sange huiyi'*," 造成严重后果的 "三个会议" ["Three Meetings That Caused Severe Consequences"] (unpublished documents, August 1987).

76 *Cangwu Xianzhi*, p. 482.

77 Cangwu Party Ratification Office 苍梧整党办公室, "*Zaocheng yanzhong houguo de 'sange huiyi'*." 造成严重后果的 "三个会议" ["Three Meetings That Caused Severe Consequences"].

fabricated conspiracy groups, Wu Chaojie, director of the Xindi Commune revolutionary committee, said the following:

> After the Lihu Meeting, the situation has greatly changed. A few prominent conspiracy groups have been uncovered. The first is a Guangxi ACPPA mainly consisting of landlords and rich peasants. Their thirty members have met for four times. Their plans include occupying Xindi Brigade as base, attacking Xindi Commune, bombing a bridge, looting banks and granaries. Their goal is to eventually take Wuzhou, link with another organization, reach Guangzhou, and return to Guangxi. The second is "Cangwu Brigade of ACPPA" led by landlord Li Fangqing of Xindi Brigade. They held a meeting in Gumao Mine. The third "Anti-Red Flag Army" had thirty-six members. They have stamps and activity funds.

The meeting also tallied the number of Four Types that had been killed to date: 109 victims based on statistics from 10 communes.[78] Ten days later, a third meeting was held by the county revolutionary committee. Six counter-revolutionary groups were uncovered by June 11, implicating 183 individuals; by the end of July, 367 victims had been killed.[79]

The general political climate encouraged rumors of conspiracy and threat in the communes and villages. Allegations about tangible threats abounded – "assassination squads" and "action manifestos" were reportedly uncovered. In the previously cited cliff-killing case in Quanzhou County in Guangxi Province, the commune militia head returned from a meeting in a nearby county and informed his subordinates that the Four Types were poised to act; therefore, the first group of victims would be cadres and Party members, followed by poor peasants.[80] A speech by the county leader recorded in Zhang Cheng's detailed account of Daoxian County (in Hunan Province) illustrates the typical rhetoric that manufactured an imminent threat before the collective killings occurred:

> At this present time the class struggle is complicated. A few days ago, there appeared reactionary posters in the No. 6 district.[81] The class enemies spread rumors that Chiang Kai-shek and his gang will attack mainland China soon and the American imperialists will launch a new World War. Once the war breaks out, they [class enemies] will first kill

[78] Ibid.

[79] Ibid.

[80] GXWGDSNB, p. 53.

[81] *District* as used here is an intermediate level of administration between the county and the commune. It was not very common in China. As discussed previously, a typical county consists of three levels of governments: county, commune (township), and brigade (village).

> party members, then probationary party members. In the No. 1 district, a [former] puppet colonel [serving the puppet army during the Anti-Japanese War] sought out the brigade [party] secretary and the peasant's association chair and demanded reinstatement. [82]

The War Frame Removes Moral Constraints

To local communities, war was not a remote concept in their history and neither was large-scale killing. The pre-1949 wars savaged most counties of Guangdong and Guangxi Provinces. Many sons and daughters of ordinary villagers died for both sides. Local historians recorded a long list of communist martyrs in the county gazetteers. In Cangwu County in Guangxi Province, 175 people died in the pre-1949 civil wars and the pacification campaigns in 1950 and 1951; another 113 died in the Anti-Japanese War.[83] In another Guangxi Province county, Mengshan, the number of martyrs was 46, but as many as 229 locals had joined the GMD army.[84] In Xingning County in Guangdong Province, 686 natives were recognized in the wars, including the civil wars before 1949 and the Korean War in the early 1950s.[85] In Wuhua County in Guangdong Province, the number was 160, counting only those with a rank of or above captain or township head.[86] During the Anti-Japanese War, Mengshan and Cangwu Counties were occupied by the Japanese army, which adopted the notorious "Three All" policy in many communities.[87] During the civil wars, both Wuhua and Xingning Counties were important bases for the communist guerrillas. During a suppression campaign by GMD troops on February 17, 1928, two thousand civilians were killed, including ten family members of the guerrilla leader Gu Dacun.[88]

In the first few years after 1949, an anti-communist conspiracy and insurgency did exist. The remaining GMD troops cooperated with local landlords and rich peasants to organize fighters stationed deep in the mountains. In some cases, the ACPPA was the name in which guerrilla

[82] Zhang Cheng 章成, "*Daoxian da tusha*" 道县大屠杀 ["The Daoxian Massacre"] (2001), p. 68.

[83] *Cangwu xianzhi*, pp. 673–685, 794–807.

[84] *Mengshan xianzhi bianzuan weiyuanhui* 蒙山县志编纂委员会, *Mengshan Xianzhi* 蒙山县志 [*Mengshan County Gazetteer*] (Nanning: Guangxi renmin chubanshe, 1993), pp. 618–629. Hereafter, *Mengshan xianzhi*.

[85] *Xingning Xianzhi*, p. 908.

[86] *Wuhua xianzhi*, p. 673.

[87] *Mengshan Xianzhi* and *Cangwu Xianzhi*.

[88] *Wuhua Xianzhi*, pp. 655–656.

attacks were waged. On July 22, 1949, a landlord led a group of insurgents in attacking Dengfeng Township in Wuhua County and killed a vice chair of the township government and his entire family.[89] On April 29, 1950, one hundred insurgents attacked the People's Government of Shengzhou Township in Cangwu County, killing three members of a work-team and capturing one female member. On June 8, 1950, seventy insurgents attacked Shizhai Village, stealing a great amount of food and valuables and killing two cadres. Four other attacks occurred that year. When Cangwu County was pronounced as pacified in July 1951, the county recorded 542 "bandit-suppression" battles fought, 1,510 "bandits" killed, and 13,086 guns captured. On the side of the new government, eighty-eight were killed.[90] During a mass rally on August 16, 1950, the Xingning People's Court sentenced to death four people who were accused of being the leaders of the South China ACPPA Guangdong Border Area Headquarters. The *xianzhi* reported that by that time, three hundred insurgent bandits had been killed and more than one thousand guns had been captured. In another rally, twenty-two spies and bandits were executed.[91]

During the Cultural Revolution, collective killings took place in public. Typically, a struggle rally on a village square enumerated the Four Types' "evil attempts" and pronounced the decision of the "mass dictatorship." The victims then were taken to an open space, such as a riverbank, for execution. Mandated to attend the rally, ordinary peasants reacted to the terror with silence. Some of the young and curious voluntarily followed the execution contingent – the militiamen and the victims – to the riverbank.

In one of the six mass rallies in July and August of 1968 in Dukeng Village of Wuhua in Guangdong Province, which killed sixty-three male Four Types and their male descendants, Huang Caijiao, the sixteen-year-old son of a former landlord, did not die. The killings were typically carried out using various farm implements, which were not always effective. After the killers and spectators had dispersed, Huang woke up and began to crawl away. He approached a house near the riverbank, where a widow he called "aunt" lived. He asked for food and water. The woman was horrified by his visit and told him, "Caijiao, I am so sorry. I cannot help and you should go. I do not want to invite any trouble for

[89] *Wuhua Xianzhi*, p. 28.
[90] *Cangwu Xianzhi*, pp. 35–37.
[91] *Xingning Xianzhi*, pp. 38–39.

your brothers and sisters [his cousins]." Possibly betrayed by the widow, Huang was quickly recaptured and escorted the next day to the same riverbank. The militia forced his cousin, a son of poor peasants, to finish the job. A witness told me that, using a hoe, the cousin "was trembling for the whole time."[92]

On the morning of June 16, 1968, a landlord's wife and two of her sons were tortured and killed on the rally stage in Niancun Village in Cangwu County in Guangxi Province. "The killings in this rally were so cruel that most of the masses were horrified and left the scene before the end," according to a post–Cultural Revolution report by the Cangwu Party Ratification Office.[93] As a measure of implementing the Lihu Commune meeting's "spirit," days earlier Zhong Yangzhao had been captured and tortured by the militiamen, led by two village leaders who harbored hostility against the Zhong family. Knowing his impending fate, Zhong snatched a gun from his militia escorts and escaped; he later shot a man, Qing Chongwen, who happened on his hideout; shortly after, Zhong was found and killed. The commune and village militias also rounded up Zhong's four brothers and widowed mother. His two adult brothers were killed quickly, whereas his mother and two younger brothers were "saved" for the revenge of Qing's brigade. In a rally on June 16, Qing's brother cut off the ears of Zhong's mother and younger brothers and then stabbed them to death. The atrocities unfolded on stage in front of hundreds of villagers.[94] "Revenge may be OK, but that way of killing was too much," many villagers said, according to a cadre who was in charge of a post–Cultural Revolution investigation.[95] Another cadre who led the investigation told me that the general sentiment among the villagers was "they may deserve death for the crime Zhong Yangzhao [another of the woman's sons] committed, but the way of the killing was too cruel to be acceptable."[96] Even if the majority of villagers opposed the extreme violence at the time, there was no realistic option for them other than silence.

92 Personal interview with Du Jianqing, 2006.

93 Cangwu Party Ratification Office 苍梧整党办公室, "*Zhulian yijia qikou de mingan*" 株连一家七口的命案 ["The Causes for the Case that Killed Seven Family Members"], July 31, 1987.

94 Cangwu Party Ratification Office 苍梧整党办公室, "*Zhulian yijia qikou de mingan*" 株连一家七口的命案 ["The Causes for the Case that Killed Seven Family Members"],Cangwu Party Ratification Office, July 31, 1987.

95 Personal interview with Mr. Yang, 2006.

96 Personal interview with Mr. Zhao, 2006.

The long-standing classification of the Four Types as enemies and the ongoing heralding of a possible insurgency removed moral constraints on excessive killings, which is illustrated by another example. In July 1968, the height of the "proactively attacking class enemies," a group of brigade leaders in He Kou Village in Guangping Commune, Cangwu County in Guangxi Province detained Gan Bingzhao, a young FTT supporter with a poor-peasant background. After a series of tortures, all signs pointed to execution. Mr. Zhao, a county cadre who was sent to the brigade as a work-team member, learned of the situation and persuaded the brigade leader to stop the killing. Zhao, who was a conscientious cadre and had stopped other killings, stated his reasons this way: "Gan Bingzhao cannot be killed. Be careful, because he is from poor-peasant family background. Chairman Mao has told us that poor peasants were allies of the revolution. It will definitely be big trouble if a poor peasant is killed." Implicit in his reasoning was that had the detainee been from a Four-Type family, killing him would have been acceptable.[97]

Conclusion

Although local communities at the county level or lower had generally established the revolutionary committees, cities in Guangdong and Guangxi Provinces were still plagued by armed mass conflict. Following the traditional class-struggle doctrine, the Party Center endorsed the provincial diagnosis of the problem and promoted a new war frame. It was claimed that conspiracy groups were widespread; bureaucrats backed up these claims with class-struggle exhibitions and rigorous persecutions. The war frame resonated in some rural communities, where moral constraints disappeared and collective killings occurred.

As portrayed by the state-policy model, a professional executioner's rationale for his participation in mass killings is muted; the burden for justification rests on his superiors, who give the orders. Responsibility for the consequences reaches the top level. However, when collective killings are perceived as a special form of collective action, people participate from their own initiative. For them, the rationale – that is, recognizing the problem, seeking the culprits, and identifying a form of action – is a most important motivational factor for their actions. The extreme nature of collective killings as a public event demands more commitment than other forms of collective action.

97 Personal interview with Mr. Zhao, 2006.

In the late 1960s, the Party Center in China was directly involved in promoting the master frame of war. This fact, at first glance, seems to support the institutional model that emphasizes a central policy of extermination. However, further analysis reveals flaws in the state-policy account. The war frame promoted by upper-level authorities did not imply any intent to exterminate. It encompassed only two of the three key framing tasks: It defined the problem and attributed the problem to class enemies but fell short of clarifying what action was necessary regarding these class enemies. The third task – framing the action, or devising a prescription for action – was completed by killing.[98] In other words, the framing process for collective killings was accomplished jointly by the Party Center, middle-level leaders, and actors in local communities. Only by this division of labor can we explain why some communities engaged in killings and others did not, despite being governed under the same regime and central policy. This discussion represents another dimension of support for the community model.

This chapter completes the discussion of the five processes that led to collective killings in China: (1) the historical underpinning of social grouping, (2) the designation of killing categories, (3) the preparation of potential perpetrators, (4) the demobilization of the law, and (5) the removal of moral constraints through framing war. In Chapter 8, I document empirical patterns of killings and the numbers of deaths to appraise the merits of the community model.

[98] For discussion on key framing tasks, see Benford and Snow, "Framing Processes and Social Movements."

8

Patterns of Killing

In Chapter 1, I propose two contrasting models of collective killings. The state-policy model traces the source of killings to a state's policy of elimination and expects the policy to be carried out by state organizations and military personnel. My community model, conversely, suggests that collective killings could occur absent a genocidal state policy, and local conditions could turn conflict into atrocities, perpetrated by civilian killers. In Chapter 1, I also present a series of factors based on aspects of state mobilization and state breakdown, which I argued would help promote killings at the local level.

In Chapters 2 through 7, I present extensive evidence supporting the community model and casting doubt on the state-policy model. In 1967 and 1968, there was no central Chinese policy calling for the wholesale destruction of any segment of the population. Neither were the collective killings committed by professional execution squads coordinated by a central command. There are vast variations in the collective killings across provinces, counties, townships, and villages. The state-policy model is generally concerned only with national-level atrocities and conditions, but these patterns of killings call for serious attention to local conditions to explain them. Exploring the implications of these variations is the task I take up in this chapter. I address why some communities had extensive collective killings while similar communities did not – or, to put it differently, which factors account for the cross-unit variations?

In at least one key instance, the community and state-policy models yield differing predictions. The state-policy model suggests that the more integrated in the state's political structures, the more likely a community is involved in collective killings. The great variations thus might be explained as simply the state's lack of reach into rural communities. The community model predicts the opposite outcome: Communities distant from state control are more likely to have experienced the most extreme collective killings, whereas integration with the Party Center had a dampening effect.

I argue that collective killings were a result of both state mobilization and breakdown. *Mobilization* refers to state policies that promoted the creation of political categories – notably class enemies – and provided war framings and rhetoric (i.e., *global mobilization*). It also refers to local interpretations and innovations that led to violent excesses viewed as a means of compliance or to advance careers (i.e., *local mobilization*). *Breakdown* refers to destroying legal institutions (i.e., *global breakdown*) and the inability and the failure of upper-level authorities to monitor and control local actors. In China under Mao, global mobilization reached the remotest corners of society. However, a community's position vis-à-vis the state structure made local mobilization and breakdown different among communities. One of my claims is that the farther away a community was – in terms geography and organization – the more likely it would experience a breakdown in authority, take its own approach to local mobilization, and suffer collective killings. A series of factors related to state mobilization and breakdown may have promoted the collective killings, including conditions that (1) contributed to the breakdown of law and bureaucratic authority, and (2) promoted elite conflict and warlike frames in the countryside. Specifically, where factional fighting was intense late in the Cultural Revolution, war framing would have more influence because factional conflict persisted only in certain provinces and counties. I also argue that where clan affiliations were strong and cross-clan conflict was endemic, particularly among the Hakka people, collective killings were more likely.

I address these issues from three levels. First, I address overall differences between rural and urban areas; that is, there were far more collective killings in rural areas than in urban areas. Second, using case studies of the bloody provinces of Guangdong and Guangxi, I compare all provinces: for example, Hubei province had similar characteristics but experienced few collective killings; whereas an average province experienced somewhat higher numbers. Third, using data collected from the county gazetteers (i.e., the *xianzhi*), I conduct a series of regression analyses to test hypotheses drawn from these models, analyzing data across the counties in Guangdong and Guangxi Provinces. This is possible because the *xianzhi* provide information not only on killings but also on the county's location, population, government revenue, Party organization, and other measures of interest.

Based on 122 volumes of *xianzhi* collected from the two provinces (of the 162 rural counties in 1965),[1] I develop a dataset that measures both the collective killings and the relevant county characteristics. I adopt a strict standard in deciding whether the county had collective killings by examining the relevant text in the *xianzhi*, deriving the conservative measures described and used in Chapter 2. For this categorical measure, I use as a cutoff point ten victims in a specific time and location. This categorical measure is used in much of the following discussion. In the second dependent measure, continuously employed in multiple-regression analyses, I calculate total deaths from collective killings. This is measured by subtracting deaths from "armed battles," as listed in the *xianzhi,* from the total of Cultural Revolution deaths.[2]

Rural–Urban Differences

The contrast between rural and urban communities is striking. All the collective killings reported in this book took place in a township or a village and among rural residents.[3] By contrast, none of the voluminous research on the Cultural Revolution in major cities has ever revealed similar cases. The material includes meticulous chronologies of events in Beijing, Shanghai, Wuhan, Guangzhou, and Hangzhou – accounts that have become contemporary classics.[4] Furthermore, in the unpublished

[1] Ministry of Civil Affairs, The People's Republic of China (ed.), 中华人民共和国民政部编. *Zhonghua renmin gongheguo xingzheng quhua, 1949–1997* 中华人民共和国行政区划 [*Jurisdiction Zoning of The People's Republic of China, 1949–1997*]. Beijing: Zhongguo shehui chubanshe, 1998.

[2] In Chapter 2, I stated that the majority of deaths took place in the period of collective killings. Armed battles were the only other occasion to incur significant numbers of deaths, although much fewer by comparison.

[3] There are reports that in Nanning and other cities, armed-battle fighters were categorically executed after they were captured and disarmed. However, these killings were closely related to battlefield combats, and the victims were determined by their preexisting social identities or blood relations. Therefore, I exclude these killings from my focus of discussion.

[4] For accounts about major cities, see Hong Yung Lee, *The Politics of the Chinese Cultural Revolution: A Case Study* (Berkeley: University of California Press, 1978); Elizabeth J. Perry and Xun Li, *Proletarian Power: Shanghai in the Cultural Revolution* (Boulder, CO:

documents about Guangxi Province that I refer to in this book, no collective killings are recorded for cities such as Nanning and Guangzhou.[5] This absence also applies to smaller urban settings such as county seats. County leaders were sometimes involved in collective killings, but they chose sites at the commune level to hold the killing demonstration rallies. The county seat was also the site of cadre conferences, but commune (i.e., township) and brigade cadres returned to their home community to do the "dirty work"(see Chapters 5 and 7).

The absence of collective killings in the cities cannot be explained by state-policy factors, and it was not because there were no designated class enemies among urban residents. Living among the urban population were former capitalists and historical counter-revolutionaries (i.e., those who served in the GMD government before 1949). The Anti-Rightist Campaign in 1957–1958 added new types of enemies, most of whom were represented in the cities. Among the workers, cadres, teachers, and other professionals, there were also thousands of adult children of former landlords and rich peasants. Neither was the absence of collective killings due to a lack of potential organizers and killers. Cadres and mass-movement activists were equally eager to employ the label "class struggle" for any political task; indeed, beatings and torture abounded. What is more, citizen militias in the cities were equally strong if not stronger than their rural counterparts. Cities such as Beijing and Shanghai were known for their worker militias, which played a key role in campaigns before, during, and after the Cultural Revolution.[6] Moreover, factional conflicts during the Cultural Revolution were ferociously fought in cities in ways unmatched by rural communities. All of the cities mentioned here were plagued by street battles among mass organizations that resulted in many deaths and injuries. In rural areas, if armed battles existed at all, they mainly took place in county seats.

Why the difference, then? I propose three possible reasons, each of which is correlates to my community model. The first is related to

Westview Press, 1997); Wang Shaoguang, *Failure of Charisma*; Hai Feng 海枫, *Guangzhou diqu wenge licheng shulue* 广州地区文革历程述略 [*Mapping the Cultural Revolution Trajectory in Guangzhou Area*] (Hong Kong: Youlian yanjiu chubanshe, 1972).

5 GXWGDSNB, *Nanning wenge dashiji; Qingzhou diqu wenge dashiji*. Hai Feng 海枫, *Guangzhou diqu wenge licheng shulue* 广州地区文革历程述略 [*Mapping the Cultural Revolution Trajectory in Guangzhou Area*] (Hong Kong: Youlian yanjiu chubanshe, 1972).

6 Elizabeth J. Perry, *Patrolling the Revolution: Worker Militias, Citizenship, and the Modern Chinese State* (Lanham, MD: Rowman & Littlefield, 2006).

information flows. The news of urban eliminationist killings was easily verifiable and then quickly relayed to the Party Center. With no central policy endorsing collective killings, such behavior earned scorn rather than political reward. It is true that the news of collective killings in townships and villages reached the provincial capitals, Nanning and Guangzhou, before more atrocities were committed; however, the remoteness of the events made them sound more like rumor than fact. When the atrocities were verified, armies were sent in to stop them and policies regarding executions were clarified. Because there was no central state policy to kill, collective killings were discouraged in urban areas.

Second, and paradoxically, severe mass conflicts in the cities may have had a deterrent effect on collective killings. In urban areas, there were typically two mass factions with comparable strength. The rebel faction that opposed governmental authority constantly documented and broadcasted the "crimes" by the government and its mass surrogates. In Nanning, the FTT factions held numerous rallies to condemn "indiscriminate killings" in the countryside.[7] It is conceivable that these demonstrations disseminated the unspeakable news and prompted the Party Center to intervene. Had such killings occurred in Nanning, their reports would have been perceived as more credible, and deterrent action would have come more swiftly. However, the deterrent effect of mass conflict on urban collective killing does not contradict the argument that such conflict was also, in part, a reason for more severe rural scapegoating. As discussed in this chapter, counties that had experienced armed battles (mostly in county seats) had much higher rates of collective-killing deaths. The reason for this is that the urban conflict created a wartime atmosphere, allowing leaders of rural communities to apply the rhetoric, disingenuously, to their local conditions, where in fact there was no organized resistance.

Last, the difference may be attributed to the diverging patterns of social organization between urban and rural communities and their varied connections to lineage clans. In cities, work units consisted of individuals from various origins. No surname lineage or clan membership was implicated in these arrangements, which mixed members of different lines and led to cross-cutting cleavages in work and family units. In the countryside, however, lineage and clan boundaries coincided with the production teams and production brigades. Clan identities remained intact; indeed,

[7] GXWGDSNB.

they were often reinforced under the new conditions. The tradition of clan competition provides a cultural basis to imagine those outside one's clan as "others" – and killable, as noted in Chapter 3.

Provincial Differences

A key difference is between the bloody provinces of Guangxi and Guangdong and the relatively "quiet" (for collective killings) province of Hubei (see Chapter 2). Despite being similar demographically and in other ways, the difference in the scale of collective killings between Hubei and the other two provinces was very large. In the counties for which I have data from 1,530 county gazetteers, the average number of deaths was 574 in Guangxi Province and 311 in Guangdong Province, with the average in Hubei Province only 11.[8] In addition, no other provinces were as bloody as Guangxi and Guangdong; according to these accounts, Guangxi had significantly more killings than Guangdong. Data from the 1,530 county gazetteers indicate that the national average of deaths per county was 80. The numbers of those injured and targeted for persecution show a similar pattern (Table 8.1), which leads to a few key questions. What accounts for the dramatic difference in killings between Guangxi and Guangdong and the other provinces? Between these two provinces, why did Guangxi stand out? What accounts for the unusually low level of deaths in provinces such as Hubei?[9]

[8] Although the length of accounts was typically higher in the bloody provinces, the differences are so great that they cannot be attributed to this difference. The numbers suggest that the level of violence is a function of both national politics and local conditions.

[9] The baseline hypothesis is that the provincial difference documented here is not a historical fact but rather an artifact of editorial policies in compiling the *xianzhi*. The compilation and publication of county gazetteers was organized by a hierarchy of government agencies. Counties in one province may have followed a set of policy guidelines different in another. Among those guidelines was the principle known as "recording in broad strokes, not in detail" on the history of the Cultural Revolution. It is possible that the compilers in Hubei Province were more conservative and left out more information than their counterparts in the other two provinces. Indeed, the average length of accounts of the Cultural Revolution in the Hubei gazetteers – 2,361 words – is barely half that devoted to the subject in the gazetteers for Guangdong (5,198 words) and Guangxi (5,117) (Walder and Su, *The Cultural Revolution in the Countryside*, p. 81, Table 1.) Conversely, although the Hubei Province gazetteers rarely report collective killings, they do not shy away from reporting large numbers of people who were beaten and injured. In fact, they reported many more injuries than the gazetteers of Guangdong (see Table 5). Therefore, there are reasons to suspect that the differences in the reported number

TABLE 8.1. *Deaths, Injuries, and Numbers Persecuted per County in Three Provinces*

	Deaths per County	Injuries per County	Numbers Persecuted per County
Guangxi	574.0	266.4	12,616
Guangdong	311.6	28.1	6,788
Hubei	10.8	44.5	2,317
All provinces	80	68	5,397

Some of the differences in death tolls can be linked to the divergent paths of prior conflicts leading to the founding of revolutionary committees. According to Xu Youyu's summary of provincial-level conflicts nationwide, Hubei and Guangxi and Guangdong (together) represented two different paths.[10] Prior to the establishment of their revolutionary committees, all provincial capitals experienced numerous government reorganizations and mass mobilization by factions. Everywhere, two opposed alliances emerged; typically, one sought to overthrow the pre–Cultural Revolution government and the other made more moderate demands or sometimes fought to defend the government. After the January Storm of 1967, power often alternated between the two sides. After the Wuhan Incident in July of that year, however, the balance of power shifted in Hubei and in most other provinces. With the tacit support or explicit approval of the Party Center, the more militant faction was designated as the "revolutionary," or favored, side. The government was thoroughly reorganized and the moderate alliance was discredited. Many members of the more militant alliance were incorporated in the new government.[11]

There were exceptions to the scenario in which the more radical faction was chosen, and both Guangdong and Guangxi Provinces were among them. According to Xu, the Center's policy was different for border regions due to national-security considerations, including the provinces

of killings may actually indicate real differences in the course of political events across provinces.

10 Xu Youyu 徐友渔. *Xingxing sese de zaofan: hongweibing jingshen suzhi de xingcheng ji yanbian.* 形形色色的造反：红卫兵精神素质的形成及演变 [*Rebels of All Stripes: A Study of Red Guard Mentalities*] (Hong Kong: Chinese University of Hong Kong Press, 1999), pp. 86–108.

11 Wang Shaoguang, *Failure of Charisma: The Cultural Revolution in Wuhan* (Hong Kong: Oxford University Press, 1995), pp. 149–202.

TABLE 8.2. *Average County Death Tolls in Two Types of Provinces*

	Deaths per County	Number of Counties
Type 1 provinces	45.2	1,271
Type 2 provinces	451.0	259
Type 2 provinces, excluding Guangdong and Guangxi	70.3	135

of Inner Mongolia, Xinjiang, Tibet, Guangdong, and Guangxi.[12] In this group of provinces, the faction that was more supportive of the incumbent government was designated "revolutionary" and assumed the central role in the revolutionary committee or new government. Once installed in power, the revolutionary committee cracked down on the more militant rebel faction. Perhaps more important, the process of establishing the new government was more drawn out in Guangxi, Guangdong, and other provinces. This means that factional fighting continued well into 1968. The Party Center grew impatient with the conflicts and began to promote war framing, including the accusation of fictitious subversive groups being involved in the battles.

In provinces such as Hubei – which I call Type 1 provinces – the government incorporated many who had stridently opposed the pre–Cultural Revolution government. A new fault line developed between opposition rebels who were included in the revolutionary committee and their former allies who were excluded. Conversely, in provinces such as Guangdong and Guangxi – like the others in which the moderate faction was deemed revolutionary, or Type 2, provinces – the revolutionary committee united officials from the former government with leaders of the more moderate faction and then used their combined power to crush the rebel opposition. The classification of provinces in these two types is presented in Table 8.2, which summarizes information from a national sample of 1,530 counties. The table makes clear that the death toll in the 259 counties located in Type 2 provinces far outstripped the Type 1 provinces. The average number of deaths per county in Type 2 provinces was 451; in Type 1 provinces, it was only 45, a tenfold difference. Even if Guangxi and Guangdong Provinces – those with particularly extensive killings – are excluded, the average number of deaths per county in Type 2 provinces is significantly greater.

[12] According to Xu, political events unfolded in a similar fashion in Jiangxi, although that province is not in a border region. See Xu Youyu, *Xingxing sese de zaofan*, pp. 100–108.

Some scholars suggest that the severe violence in Guangdong and Guangxi Provinces can be attributed to retaliation by "conservatives" operating as government-backed militias against the opposition faction.[13] As I have shown, however, the majority of victims were so-called Four Types. There is no evidence that they joined the rebel faction in disproportionate numbers; indeed, they were largely stripped of political rights and under extreme surveillance. In the remote villages and communes where collective killings were most extensive, moreover, factional mobilization prior to collective killings was unlikely.

I propose a different explanation. Some scholars have suggested that a more representative polity deters outright destruction of the targeted population.[14] The government in Hubei and other Type 1 provinces was more representative of the oppositional elements than the Guangdong and Guangxi provincial governments. As discussed previously and documented in Chapters 6 and 7, during the long months of collective killings in Guangxi Province, the oppositional mass faction FTT had noted the incidents early and immediately worked to stop them. They organized street rallies and marches to broadcast the atrocities. Had the provincial government consisted of their allies, as was the case in Type 1 provinces, their voice would have deterred any further escalation.

Therefore, the distinctive political trajectories may have contributed to the higher death tolls in these two provinces. However, also contributing to this difference may be the added intensity of two of the five processes that I argue lead to collective killings in the country as a whole. As documented in Chapter 3, the two provinces were more immersed in the culture of clan identities and clan competition than Chinese elsewhere in the country. This provided a particularly strong beginning of social divisions for later processes. Moreover, as discussed in Chapter 7, because the Party Center was unhappy with their delay in establishing provincial-level revolutionary committees and the persistence of factional fighting in these provinces, China's central leaders introduced the war framing of these conflicts. In the two bloodiest provinces, the leadership

13 In support of this explanation, for example, the mass execution of captives in Guangxi Province was apparently an instance of retaliation. Also, in Guangxi the opposition FTT faction repeatedly organized protests against collective killings in Guangxi. GXWDSNB, pp. 61–63, 71, 75.

14 Barbara Harff, "No Lessons Learned from the Holocaust? Assessing Risks of Genocide and Political Mass Murder since 1955," *The American Political Science Review* 97(2003), pp. 57–73.

explicitly endorsed the assertion of the so-called ACPPA conspiracy networks by the favored faction. The campaign to root out their fictional supporters took on extraordinary ferocity, and war-framing became menacing.

Of Guangxi and Guangdong Provinces, the former experienced far more killings than the latter (see Table 8.1). The reasons become apparent after the predictors of collective-killing deaths are documented by analyzing cross-county variations. On average, Guangxi Province scored a value in all of the significant predicting measures, which is associated with a higher death rate. For example, the regression models show that the death rate is positively related to remoteness and poverty; Guangxi counties were located farther from urban centers, were poorer, and had a lower population density than Guangdong counties (Table 8.6). In addition, the difference may be accounted for by the fact that Guangxi Province was a more recent migration society than Guangdong; therefore, its Han population was more deeply immersed in the local culture of clan identities and clan competition. Whereas the Guangdong settlements by northern migrants dated back more than a thousand years, the majority of the Han population in Guangxi consisted of those who branched out from Guangdong communities only in the last century (see Chapter 3).

Explaining Collective Killings Across Counties

The analyses of this section are based on data from sixty-seven counties in Guangxi and fifty-seven counties in Guangdong where the *xianzhi* were available. I chose these cases for further analysis in part because the two provinces scored high on the five main elements of my community model. Yet, even within these provinces, there are important variations in the cultural and political aspects of my model.

In my analyses, I first tabulate bivariate relationships between the existence of collective killings in counties and key covariates derived from the state-policy and community models. From there, I turn to the results of multiple-regression models that examine the total number of killings in the two provinces. I present the bivariate relationships in some detail for ease of presentation but mainly because almost all of the bivariate relationships discussed here continue to be significant in the multivariate regressions of the numbers of killings.

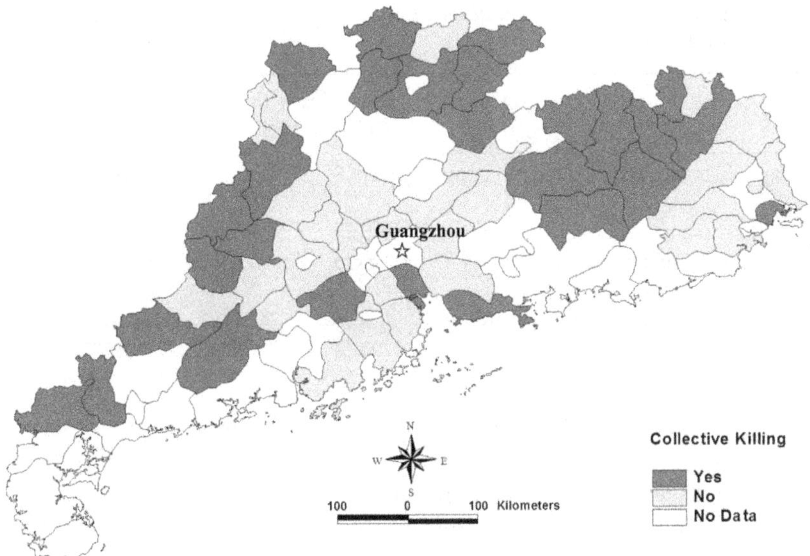

FIGURE 8.1. The geography of collective killings, Guangdong Province, 1967–1968.

Distance from Urban Centers and Socioeconomic Factors

Were the counties with the most collective killings close to the provincial capitals? Figures 8.1 and 8.2 are maps of the two provinces, with the counties that experienced collective killings shown as shaded. The figures indicate that the darkly shaded counties were generally located farther from the urban centers – that is, the provincial capitals of Nanning and Guangzhou. This impression is confirmed by comparing the average distance from the provincial capitals between the two types of counties. As shown in Table 8.3, counties with collective killings were 209.8 kilometers from their provincial capital, whereas the average distance for those counties that did not experience collective killings was 182.3 kilometers, a 27-kilometer difference. That is, a county closer to an urban center was less likely to have collective killings and a remote county was more likely. Although it is not obvious from the maps, the counties with collective killings were more remote in another sense: they were more likely to be in mountainous areas.

Although the greater distance from an urban center is basically in accordance with the community model, these preliminary findings raise the question of how *remoteness* is defined. Does it indicate a lack of information flow, which could cause the misinterpretation of policies

TABLE 8.3. *County Characteristics and Collective Killings (Guangxi and Guangdong Provinces)*

	Counties with Collective Killings[a]	Counties without Collective Killings
Average distance from provincial capital (km)	209.8	182.5
Population density (per square km)	139.9	217.2
County government revenue in 1965 (*yuan* per capita)	15.0	20.8
Party members per thousand population	19.5	19.6

[a] See definition in Chapter 2.

sent from higher levels of government? Does the distance represent weakened organizational control from the Party Center? The distance from urban areas also may be masking other community characteristics. Two other measures reinforce the impression that physical remoteness had socioeconomic components. Counties with collective killings were less populated and poorer. The contrasts are stark: In counties with collective killings, there were only 139.9 residents per square kilometer, whereas in counties without collective killings, there were 217.2 residents per square

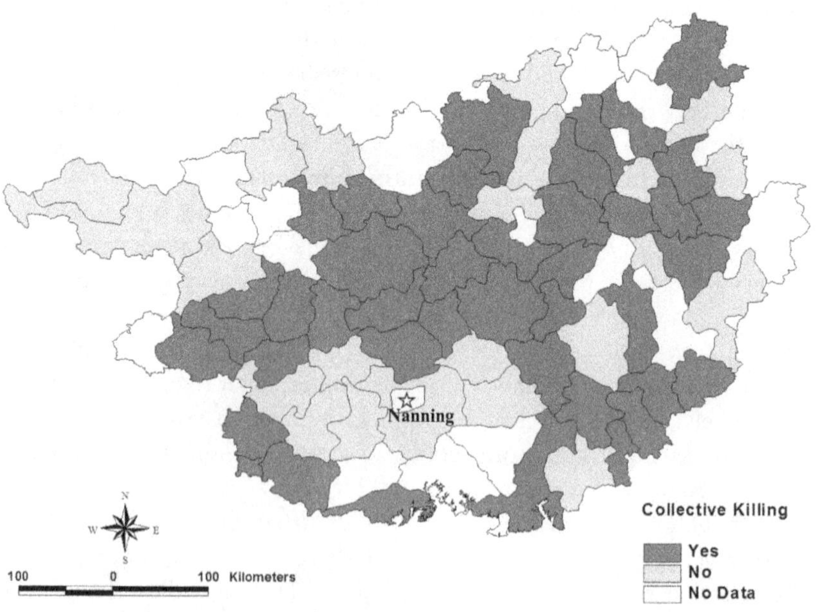

FIGURE 8.2. The geography of collective killings, Guangxi Province, 1967–1968.

kilometer. The counties with collective killings were poorer, having only 75 percent of the revenue of those that did not experience collective killings. The overall picture is that the counties that suffered most from the collective killings were more likely to be located in the harsh environment of the mountainous areas. In the multiple-regression models presented later, the effect of distance is greatly diminished when population density and county revenue are introduced.

Ethnicity

I view collective killings as connected in part to strong clan affiliations and identities, which were more salient among the Han Chinese than the ethnic minorities; among the Han Chinese, the Hakka group stands out. A possible reason that the killing counties are associated with mountainous areas is that the Hakka people were disproportionately located in those areas, compared to other Han Chinese groups in the region. As discussed in Chapter 3, the counties in the two provinces can be classified according to their ethnic and subethnic composition. I found that counties with significant ethnic minorities were the least likely to experience collective killings, followed by counties with no significant presence of the Hakka subethnic group. By contrast, counties that mixed Hakka and non-Hakka groups and counties with a pure Hakka population experienced the most severe collective killings. These findings are reproduced in Table 8.4. I suggest that these differences are due to the differing saliency of clan institutions in rural communities and that class-struggle conflict was exacerbated by the clan identities. This finding holds true in the multiple-regression analyses.

Previous County Leadership Structure

Before the Power-Seizure Campaign, each county had three to six top leaders serving as the Party committee secretary or vice secretaries. In Guangdong and Guangxi Provinces, each county had leaders with origins from outside the county, mostly cadres who came from North China during the Land Reform movement (see Chapter 4). In some counties, the secretary and vice secretaries consisted exclusively of migrants; in other counties, leaders were a combination of outsiders and locals. In a separate study, I show that the heterogeneous makeup of leadership groups had a positive effect on mass factionalism and armed-battle occurrences during the Cultural Revolution, each of which I see as influencing collective

TABLE 8.4. *Comparing Means of Collective Killing Deaths by Selected County Characteristics*

	Means of Collective-Killing Deaths	Number of Counties
County with 50% minorities or more (Guangxi Province)		
Yes	552.7	32
No	792.9	32
County with pure Hakka population (Guangdong Province)		
Hakka Only	439.7	12
Mixed with Hakka and Non-Hakka	271.1	42
County with mix of Hakka and Non-Hakka (Guangxi Province)		
Mixed with Hakka and Non-Hakka	821.7	18
Non-Hakka only	614.6	46
County leadership mixed origin		
Yes	490.1	43
No	368.5	67
County experienced armed battle		
Yes	670.1	78
No	209.5	42

killings at the local level.[15] I expect that heterogeneous leadership also contributed independently to the likelihood of collective killings.

Among the many possible sources of elite division in local Chinese governments, the conflict between the local and outside cadres was the most significant and persistent. There are two reasons for that. Culturally, among the Chinese birthplace has great significance in defining one's identity. This is partly due to the religious aspects of life that involve ancestor worship and partly due to diverse dialects that function as quasi-ethnic markers. Historically, northern cadres were dispatched by the Party Center during the Land Reform movement to take over leadership of the local communities in the south. Because the northern cadres decisively prevailed over local leaders in the Land Reform (see Chapters 4 and 6), the resulting cleavage and factionalism became a perpetual issue in political campaigns ever since. Vogel reported that campaigns against "localism" – that is, alleged activities by the local cadres to resist the leadership of the

[15] Yang Su, *Tumult from Within: State Bureaucrats and Chinese Mass Movements, 1966–1971*, Ph.D. dissertation, Stanford University, Stanford, CA (2003), Chapter 4.

northerners – were repeatedly waged in Guangdong Province; the tension between local and outside cadres, in effect, was the main axis of conflict in the major political campaigns before the Cultural Revolution. Hai Feng reported that the anti-localism theme reemerged during the Cultural Revolution in the provincial capital of Guangdong.[16]

Although power seizures in early 1967 had removed the Party secretaries from leadership, repudiating them as power-holders, it is plausible that the previous leadership cleavage continued to play a role in subsequent elite conflicts. The mass factions drew their fault lines according to their relationship with the previous leaders. Their treatment – that is, how harshly to struggle against them or whom among them to "rehabilitate" into the new government – was the most contentious issue of the time. As discussed previously, new leaders during this period were in constant fear of being accused as soft on enemies. Therefore, differences in elite origins had a tendency to deepen elite conflict, and elite conflict in turn had a tendency to exacerbate scapegoating among the previously labeled class enemies. The data corroborate this reasoning. As shown in Table 8.4, among 43 counties with mixed leadership, the average number of collective killings was 490.1; among 67 counties with only outside secretaries, the average was only 368.5 – a difference of more than 130 deaths per county.

Previous Mass Conflict

Previous mass conflict in county seats may facilitate collective killings for three reasons that are consistent with my argument. First, severe mass conflict was often an indication of severe elite conflict – that is, mass fault lines were mostly drawn along the issue of cadres and leadership – and the resolution of elite conflict often involved scapegoating. Second, like their superiors at the provincial level, county leaders would drum up class struggle and war rhetoric in their effort to disband and disarm mass organizations. Third, armed battles taking place within the county – almost always in the county seat – rendered the war framing more realistic because the fighting was close to home. The conflicts among mass organizations in townships and villages rarely degenerated into street battles; however, in county seats, as in other urban settings, factional

[16] Ezra F. Vogel, *Canton under Communism: Programs and Politics in a Provincial Capital, 1949–1968* (Cambridge, MA: Harvard University Press, 1969); Hai Feng 海枫, *Guangzhou diqu wenge licheng shulue* 广州地区文革历程述略 [*Mapping the Cultural Revolution Trajectory in Guangzhou Area*] (Hong Kong: Youlian yanjiu chubanshe, 1972).

armed battles were not uncommon. Among the 118 counties for which I have information, 76 counties experienced armed battles. According to the data, counties with armed battles had far more collective killings. As shown in Table 8.4, among the counties that experienced armed battles, the average death count was 670.1; those without battles averaged 209.1. Elite conflict meant that mass battles continued longer; thus, not only was war framing more plausible, it also happened in the context of the mass battles.

Party Organizational Strength

A positive influence of Party cadres on collective killings might seem to support the state-policy model, which assumes that the stronger the Party control at local levels, the more likely these localities would carry out a policy of extermination. However, as I have shown, the Party Center was not promoting such a policy; therefore, the stronger Party organizations presumably had a negative effect on collective killings. A positive relationship fits comfortably in the framework of the community model, however. Stronger Party organizations would likely induce local communities to embrace the war rhetoric and framings of the situation, which I argue facilitated the collective killings. As shown in Table 8.3, the Party organizational strength, measured as Party membership per capita, was similar for both groups of counties. However, the effect becomes significantly positive in the multivariate analysis when other measures are considered.

Multiple-Regression Results of County-Level Variations in Killings

To ensure that these relationships are still credible when all the factors are considered and technical factors such as the length of a *xianzhi* account are controlled, I conducted multiple-regression analyses. The details are in the Appendix, but I outline here how they were performed. For the dependent variable, I employed total killings, which was the number of deaths recorded minus those that were battle-related.[17] Almost all recorded deaths not attributed to battles were civilian killings. Given the distribution of this dependent measure, I employed the Poisson regression model.

Despite the control measures, all of the bivariate effects discussed earlier are significant in the regression analyses. In addition, when all the

[17] See Chapter 2 for the justification of this computation.

TABLE 8.5. *Odds Ratio of Selected Measures from Poisson Regression Models Predicting Collective Killing Deaths in Guangdong and Guangxi Provinces*

Distance from provincial capital (100 km)	0.969
Population density (thousands per square km)	0.757
County government revenue per capita (*yuan*)	0.746
Party members per 1,000 population (person)	1.034
Previous armed battle	2.268
County Party secretaries' origins mixed	1.100
Minorities 50 percent or more	0.698
Hakka County	1.218

Source: Model 2 in Appendix A, Table A3.

measures are introduced, there is a positive and significant relationship between Party membership and killings (see Table A3 in the Appendix). Table 8.5 summarizes these effects in the form of "odds ratios" – that is, the rate of increase or decrease in the dependent measure due to a unit change in a specific independent measure. Following are highlights of these results. Distance from urban centers and population density remain significant. The odds ratio for distance is greater than 1, indicating that the farther away a county is, the higher the number of killings it may be subject to; whereas the odds ratio for population density is smaller than 1, indicating that the more densely populated areas were subject to few collective killings. As for socioeconomic factors, a one-*yuan* per capita increase in the county government revenue decreases the number of collective-killing deaths by a rate of 0.746. Stated differently, the poorer counties incurred more deaths by a ratio of 1.340. A county with a one-*yuan* per capita decrease in government revenue suffered 34 percent more collective-killing deaths. These results suggest that remoteness in both senses contributed to the collective killings. I found that the poorer the county, the more extensive the killings – but also, the more remote the county in distance from the urban center, the greater the number of killings. This result gives credence to my claim that – despite there being no central policy of extermination – local actors in the remote areas were taking matters into their own hands and may have missed signals from the Party Center to desist once information was received.

Ethnic factors remain influential in explaining the collective killings. As discussed previously, ethnic minorities are negatively related to the killings, whereas the Hakka presence had a significant and positive effect. In Guangxi Province, counties with a 50 percent or more minority population had a lower rate of collective killings by a factor of 0.698. That is, the death count in counties that were predominantly Han Chinese was 1.43 times that of those with a 50 percent or more minority population. The results uphold my claim that clan divisions among the Hakka people facilitated conflict and promoted collective killings when political conditions changed and a warlike atmosphere was framed. In a Hakka county (defined in Guangdong as a predominantly Hakka county and defined in Guangxi as a mixed population of Hakka and non-Hakka) the death count increased by a factor of 1.218.

Political factors also remain important in explaining the collective killings. A mixed leadership accounts for 10.0 percent of the additional killings. Also, the influence of armed battles remains significant. Collective-killing deaths in counties with armed battles were 2.27 times greater than those without armed battles, a substantial increase. Thus, the warlike atmosphere that may have been absorbed in the more rural areas due to the battles may have made it easier to scapegoat the Four Types. What is more, Party membership becomes significantly positive when other measures are controlled. Every additional Party member increased the collective-killing deaths by a rate of 34, or 3.4 percent. This may not seem like much, but a ten-member increase in Party membership resulted in a 39.7 percent increase in collective killings. The Party membership per thousand of county population ranged from 2.7 to 66.5, so the differences were often substantial. This last result may provide support for the state-policy model, given that Party members are expected to be instrumental in carrying out the Party Center's extermination policy. Given, however, as previously discussed, that the Center tried to stop collective killings once evidence of them was revealed, the result is consistent with my alternative interpretation that Party members were carriers of war rhetoric and promoted a wartime atmosphere in a peacetime setting.

Moreover, when taken together, results at the county level support that collective killings resulted from both state mobilization and state breakdown. The political factors attest to the power of mobilization. The armed factional battles and Party members promoted the killings. Indeed, the mountainous regions, where communication lines from the Center to the hinterlands were tenuous at best, experienced extensive collective killings. Ethnic factors played a role, providing a type

TABLE 8.6. *Differing Average Scores in Key Predictors of Collective Killings in Guangxi and Guangdong Provinces*

	Guangxi	Guangdong	Notes
Average distance from provincial capital (km)	218.7	172.9	**
Population density (per square km)	248.2	111.3	***
County government revenue in 1965 (1,000 *yuan* per thousand population)	1.2	2.4	***
Party members per thousand population	17.8	19.6	***
Percent counties that had prior armed battle	70.7	52.6	**
Percent counties with heterogeneous leadership type	56.1	68.4	

Notes: ** p > .05; *** p > .01, F test with one-way ANOVA.

of underlying conflict that – in the context of the political campaign of the Culture Revolution and the state mobilization and breakdown factors – had an independent influence on collective killings.

Having established the significant predictors of collective killings through the multivariate analysis, we can now revisit the differences between Guangdong and Guangxi Provinces. As shown in Table 8.6, the counties in Guangxi, on average, were located farther from urban centers, had lower population density, were poorer, and had a higher percentage of factional armed battles. All of these factors contributed to the higher death toll in Guangxi Province. The exception is that Guangxi had a lower density in Party-member networks, but it apparently fails to offset the combined contribution of the other factors.

Conclusion

If the collective killings were a result of a state policy as well as the work of professional executioners – or even if professional killers were absent and the state had called on society to accomplish the atrocities – the patterns of occurrence and number of the dead would not necessarily be uniform in the geographical distribution. One would expect that the pockets of severe tragedies were where the state policy had its strongest influence and the most organizational resources to implement the policy. However, that is not what happened in China in 1967 and 1968. Instead, remoteness – measured in several ways – is associated with more severe collective killings, and this is true in terms of both the occurrence and number of lives lost. Massive numbers of killings tended to be committed in lower-level (i.e., village or township) rather than higher-level jurisdictions (i.e., county, prefecture, or province); in rural communities rather than cities; and in communities farther from rather than closer to urban centers. This finding of remoteness is further reinforced by two related findings: (1) Counties with a lower population density tended to have more collective-killing deaths; and (2) counties with less government revenue per capita tended to be more prone to the killing madness, which reflects the effects of poverty and a weak government.

Also in line with the community model are findings on four political measures. First, preexisting elite factional cleavage radicalized the conflict into an extreme expression. Collective killings were more severe in counties with a mixture of leaders from the north and local leaders. This finding recalls my discussion on the relationship between elite conflict and mass conflict in Chapter 3. Leaders were often afraid of being accused as soft on class enemies; a time-honored defensive measure was to scapegoat previously designated targets. Second, counties that had experienced more fierce mass campaigns – as reflected in armed street battles – tended to generate more deaths.[18] Armed conflict in a county rendered the war framings of 1968 more salient than in those counties where the county seats experienced few factional battles.

The diverging trajectories of political development marked two types of provinces in the nation. The special policy from the Party Center created a distinct pattern of mass alignment and related government composition in provinces like Guangdong and Guangxi. The absence of significant representatives from the oppositional mass faction emboldened their repression efforts with measures that resulted in local excesses. This seems to suggest that collective killings were an outcome of the central policy. However, the finding still supports the community model in that the differential policies from the Party Center originated from the security considerations of the border provinces, without any extermination policy against the rural Four Types. The data show that Party organizational strength was associated with a higher rate of collective-killing deaths. The more Party members in a local community, the more susceptible it was to the war framing promoted by upper-level authorities. Because the policy never defined a concrete action plan, local Party members initiated and organized the collective killings (see Chapter 5).

[18] Yang Su, *Tumult from Within: State Bureaucrats and Chinese Mass Movements, 1966–1971*, Ph.D. dissertation, Stanford University, Stanford, CA (2003), Chapter 4.

Although elsewhere collective killings occurred, they were far more extensive in those where the five processes had played out most extensively. Within the bloodiest provinces, the worst counties and localities were those where the processes played out most fully. Theoretically, these patterns urge us to move beyond the analysis of the nature of state policy making; local conditions matter more. In the same state – genocidal or not – not only did killing outcomes differ across local communities, they also were more prevalent where the reach of the state was weaker.

9

Understanding Atrocities in Plain Sight

The twin tasks of this book are to make historical and theoretical cases about collective killings in the countryside during the Cultural Revolution. I want to explain what happened and why. For the historical case, I establish the facts and patterns of collective killings in 1967 and 1968 in two provinces during the Cultural Revolution. I also document key aspects of Maoism between the 1949 revolution and the eve of the extreme atrocities. These aspects – the formation and transformation of a rural culture, the creation and maintenance of a class divide, the social mobility of the rural population, and the demobilization of legal institutions – provide a historical narrative and backdrop for understanding the collective killings. A central theme in this narrative is "actually existing Maoism"[1]: a set of practices that were not only inspired by the communist ideology but also shaped by real-life challenges and contradictions. The leaders, their cadres, and ordinary citizens did not follow a master plan in the revolutionary transformations but rather reacted to reality – in specific times and places – in a pragmatic and often ad hoc fashion, improvising as they went along. In this context, collective killings, like many other actions, were *emergent* actions rather than part of routine politics. The overall nature of the regime and its explicit policies are insufficient to account for these emergent outcomes.

Theoretically, this book does not purport to explain why Mao's China was violent – violent though it was – but rather to explain why the

[1] I borrow this term from Walder, "Actually Existing Maoism." See Andrew G. Walder, "Actually Existing Maoism." *The Australian Journal of Chinese Affairs* 18, July (1987), pp. 155–166.

violence developed into such an extreme and why such extreme violence could be so blatantly public. This cannot be explained only by Mao's ruthless character or the violent nature of the state. Neither, as I have shown, can it be explained by a genocidal policy at the nation-state level; there was no such policy. Between the state's violent nature and the occurrence of collective killings, between a cold-blooded supreme leader and village neighbors, are many specific details. To document them has been the task of this book. In this concluding chapter, I tie these specifics together in a sociological framework that is meaningful in a broader context.

The Chinese case of collective killings poses a challenge to the state-policy model in the existing literature. Whereas the model is useful for explaining genocide and mass killings that stem from a clear eliminationist policy or ideology (e.g., the Holocaust), it is less effective for explaining mass killings that stem from the local actors' self-initiative. The latter is better treated not as part of institutional politics but rather as emergent, situational, and extra-institutional events. That is, mass killings (for the Chinese case, I use the term *collective killings*) are better seen as a special form of collective action. There is no doubt that institutional politics is a major force that gives birth to, facilitates, shapes, or impedes events of collective action, but such events have their own logic of emergence and development. Therefore, my community model to explain collective killings represents a departure from the state-policy models of genocide and mass killings and draws extensively from the insight of scholarship on social movements and collective action.

Yet, the Chinese case presented in this book also questions social-movement scholarship. Guided by the central idea of strategic mobilization, this scholarship has been successful in explaining the emergence of collective-action events but says little about the issue of the character of collective action. Collective killings require organizational resources, political opportunities, and framing ideas and in that way echo typical collective actions. However, it is a special case because of the extraordinary nature of the action: inhuman acts that are usually suppressed by state laws and forbidden by social mores. This unusual aspect of the collective action makes the mobilization theory an insufficient explanation. My alternative explanation relies on both traditions in social-movement research: mobilization models and breakdown theories. In the past, the literature has been presented as two conflicting research paradigms. Finding usefulness in both, my book provides empirical grounds for building a bridge between them.

Atrocities in Plain Sight

To recap the social phenomenon that I seek to explain, I recount two scenarios from previous chapters. Within two days starting on October 2, 1967, village militias rounded up seventy-six people – including women, children, and the elderly – from Dongshang Commune in Quanzhou County in Guangxi Province. They were escorted to a mountain cliff and forced to jump to their death. The killers and victims were neighbors. Official records show that among the victims were Liu Xiangyuan, a thirty-four-year-old son of a former landlord, and his two children, aged one and three.[2] In another community in the summer of 1968, six pogroms killed sixty-three people from Dukeng Village in Wuhua County in Guangdong Province. All but two male members older than sixteen of so-called Four-Type households were murdered. The killings took place on the riverbank in broad daylight as the entire village looked on. Militias from the same village used farm tools to kill and the victims' screams reached all corners. The terror lasted for about a month and a half until upper-level authorities intervened.[3]

Characteristic in these episodes was a self-contained environment in which extraordinary acts of public killings met with no condemnation, intervention, or punishment. For a sustained period, their extraordinariness had been neutralized by new perceptions of law and order and morality; a transformation had taken place in the community. The atrocities ended only when outside intervention restored a different order. Such extraordinary moments in a self-sustained community are by no means unique to the Chinese case of collective killings. I previously cited the Salem witch-hunt in colonial Massachusetts in the late seventeenth century. For more than three months, neighbors in the Salem community accused innocent men, women, and children of being witches or wizards, which was punishable of death. On a summer day in 1941, in Jedwabne, a village in Nazi-occupied Poland, half of the town murdered the other half: 1,600 men, women, and children – all but seven of the town's Jews. The killing community can be constituted temporarily without previous geographical boundaries; the lynching crowd in the American South in the nineteenth century is an example. A killing community can be large in

[2] See Tang Chuying 唐楚英 (ed.), *Quanzhou xianzhi* 全州县志 [*Quanzhou County Gazetteer*] (Nanning: Guangxi renmin chubanshe, 1998); see also GXWGDSNB *Guangxi wen'ge dashi nianbiao* 广西文革大事年表 [*Chronology of the Cultural Revolution in Guangxi*] (Nanning: Guangxi renmin chubanshe, 1990). Reprinted by Chinese Publications Services Centre, Los Angeles, California, 1995.

[3] Personal interviews with Du Jianqiang and Mr. Wei (2006).

scale: In the 1994 Rwanda genocide, for about one hundred days, ordinary Hutus nationwide shared the same definition of acceptable behavioral boundaries in killing hundreds of thousands of Tutsis.[4]

To borrow a term from Danner and Sullivan, these are episodes of "atrocities in plain sight."[5] Seen from within, the community develops a temporary norm so that atrocities not only take place but also persist *in plain sight*. When seen from without, however, atrocities are by definition an aberration in a society. A killing community therefore represents a failure on the part of the outside world. Whether or not the state or organization has a "policy" to kill, the point of failure is evident in high-profile cases of solider misconduct in the U.S. Army in recent history. In the My Lai Massacre during the Vietnam War, a group of U.S. Army forces murdered from 347 to 504 unarmed Vietnamese civilians on March 16, 1968. That some of the perpetrators were court-marshaled afterwards indicates that the collective killings were in no way acceptable to the rules-of-war conduct.[6] A similar case that resulted in military trials took place during the Iraq War. Responding to a roadside bombing in Haditha on the night of November 19, 2005, U.S. soldiers raided nearby civilian houses and murdered twenty-four Iraqi men, women, and children.[7]

There are two ways to approach the puzzle of a community of public atrocities. In a free society like the United States, it can be studied through information on state policies that proliferates and becomes public after the event becomes known to the outside world. In the cited cases of soldiers'

4 See Marion Lena Starkey, *The Devil in Massachusetts: A Modern Enquiry into the Salem Witch Trials* (Garden City, NY: Doubleday & Co., 1969); Paul S. Boyer and Stephen Nissenbaum, *Salem Possessed; The Social Origin of Witchcraft* (Cambridge, MA: Harvard University Press, 1974); Mary Beth Norton, *In the Devil's Snare: The Salem Witchcraft Crisis of 1692* (New York: Alfred A. Knopf, 2002); and Jan T. Gross, *Neighbors: The Destruction of the Jewish Community in Jedwabne, Poland* (Princeton, NJ: Princeton University Press, 2001). The exact number is disputed by later accounts, especially forcefully by a report from a group of Polish historians. See Antony Polonsky and Joanna B. Michlic (eds.), The Neighbors Respond: The Controversy over the Jedwabne Massacre in Poland (Princeton, NJ: Princeton University Press, 2004). See also Philip Gourevitch, *We Wish to Inform You that Tomorrow We Will Be Killed with Our Families: Stories from Rwanda* (New York: Picador, 1998).

5 Mark Danner, "Abu Ghraib: The Hidden Story," *The New York Review of Books*, October 7, 2004; and Andrew Sullivan, "Atrocities in Plain Sight," *The New York Times*, January 13, 2005.

6 Herbert C. Kelman and V. Lee Hamilton, *Crimes of Obedience: Toward a Social Psychology of Authority and Responsibility* (New Haven, CT: Yale University Press, 1989), pp. 1–20.

7 "U.S. Military Mourns 'Tragic' Haditha Deaths." Available at www.cnn.com. Accessed June 1, 2006.

misconduct, voluminous archival data reveal that the killings were not merely due to lapses in the chain of command. Instead, some elements of the war policy were partially responsible. In the case of My Lai, the practice of tallying the "enemy body counts" by the military encouraged unlawful killings of civilians.[8] In the case of Haditha, the propaganda of treating any resistance as "terrorism" by the Bush administration clearly contributed to the mindset of the soldiers. It was a result of a broken chain of command.[9]

The other way to understand the creation of a killing community is to examine local conditions. In the Jedwabne pogrom in Poland, Gross points out that although the Nazi policy of genocide clearly provided a general climate for killings, the village's previous history contributed to why Jedwabne was particularly susceptible. Immediately before the Nazi occupation, the village was occupied by the Soviet army, which relied on Jews to set up the local government. This period exacerbated the long-standing anti-Semitism among the non-Jewish Poles in the village.[10] In the Salem witch-hunt, Boyer and Nissenbaum point to the local factional politics among the villagers as a critical factor. The tenure of the township priest, Samuel Parris, had been challenged by a faction of villagers, a group of relatively well-off families engaged in commercial trades. During the witch-hunt, the priest preached the menace of the alleged evil of witches and encouraged the other faction, the traditional farmers, to come forward as accusers.[11] In a series of studies on the lynchings of blacks in the American South, Tolney, Beck, and associates marshaled systematic data to account for variations across counties and uncovered significant factors such as geographical location, demographic composition, migration, and economy.[12]

[8] Seymour M. Hersh, *Cover-Up: The Army's Secret Investigation of the Massacre at My Lai 4* (New York: Random House, 1972).

[9] See note 5.

[10] Gross, *Neighbors.*

[11] Boyer and Nissenbaum, *Salem Possessed.*

[12] See Stewart E. Tolnay and E. M. Beck, *A Festival of Violence: An Analysis of Southern Lynchings, 1882–1930* (Urbana: University of Illinois Press, 1995); E. M. Beck and Stewart E. Tolnay, "A Season for Violence: The Lynching of Blacks and Labor Demand in the Agricultural Production Cycle in the American South," *International Review of Social History* 37 (1992), pp. 1–24; Stewart E. Tolnay and E. M. Beck, "Black Flight: Lethal Violence and the Great Migration, 1900–1930," *Social Science History* 14 (1990), pp. 347–370; and Stewart E. Tolnay, Glenn Deane, and E. M. Beck, "Vicarious Violence: Spatial Effects on Southern Lynchings, 1890–1919," *The American Journal of Sociology* 102 (November 1996), pp. 788–815.

I have followed these two traditions, but the emphasis is on the latter – that is, to establish local patterns and conditions. Although the role of the state is a central focus, I must approach it through inference based on the patterns of killings and the sequence of events. Before I discuss the role of the state and local conditions in the next two sections, I present a brief review of the collective-killing characteristics in Guangdong and Guangxi Provinces.

First, the collective killings took place in 1967 and 1968 during the Cultural Revolution. There is no evidence that similar eliminationist killings occurred at other times in Mao's more than twenty-seven-year rule. Moreover, the mass killings were concentrated in the months after most counties had established their new revolutionary committees or local governments but at a time when the provincial capitals were still entangled in mass factionalism. The peaks of mass killings coincided with the two July 1968 directives from the Party Center that banned factional armed battles and disbanded mass organizations. These findings help to understand the nature and source of mass killings. The fact that there were no collective killings prior to the Cultural Revolution compels us to move beyond the general ideology of Maoism for the explanation. The fact that most of the collective killings occurred after the new revolutionary committees were established indicates that they were the result of repression by the local state rather than conflicts between independent mass groups. The fact that they coincided with the crackdown of the oppositional mass organizations in the provincial capital indicates that the provincial authorities promoted the rhetoric of violence – although the extreme violence that occurred in local communes and villages may not be what they intended.

Second, collective killings were primarily a rural phenomenon; that is, they occurred not in provincial capitals or county seats but rather in communes and villages. This is in stark contrast to earlier mass movements of the Cultural Revolution, such as the campaigns against intellectuals and government officials and the factional street battles that occurred mostly in urban settings. The imagery of top-down diffusion does not apply to the collective killings, which suggests that the class-struggle rhetoric disseminated from urban centers found expression in extreme violence in rural townships and villages, possibly due to the state's failure to hold the lowest-level bureaucrats accountable for their actions. This explanation is supported by additional evidence: the poorer and more remote counties were more likely to have mass killings.

Third, the collective killings varied greatly across provinces. This pattern indicates that the occurrence of collective killings was more a function of province-specific political conditions than national politics as a whole. I attribute these provincial differences in part to provincial patterns of mass factional alignment vis-à-vis governmental authorities. In the bloody provinces of Guangxi and Guangdong, the opposition was excluded from power and the revolutionary committees were more prone to use violence against insurgents. By contrast, in Hubei – a similar province socio-economically but with few collective killings – the opposition faction, having prevailed in the previous conflict with the central government's support, was incorporated into the new government.

Fourth, even within the bloodiest provinces of Guangxi and Guangdong, collective killings varied greatly across counties. A key finding is that they were more likely to occur in the counties that were remote from political centers, in the poorer and mountainous areas. This suggests that the conditions existed for the community to insulate itself and to develop a local reality and norms that differed from the outside world. These conditions also made it difficult for the Party Center to intervene. The patterns show the limitation of policy analysis for understanding collective killings, calling attention instead to local social and political conditions.

State Sponsorship, State Failure, or Both?

What do these patterns say about the role of the state in the collective killings? To answer this question, I explicate my conception of the Chinese state that has implicitly guided the discussion thus far. I differentiate the state into three levels: the Party Center, the province, and the local governments (i.e., county, commune, and brigade). The central authorities in Beijing deployed class-struggle rhetoric (its time-honored method) to solve the problem of the moment – that is, to establish local governments and demobilize mass movements. In this sense, they had a sponsoring role in the mass killings. However, the policy pronouncements also denounced extreme violence at the local level as an indication of unwarranted disorder. The Party Center had previously used this rhetoric many times, although with less extreme bloody results. In this sense, the fact that mass killings nonetheless occurred represents the state's failure to influence local actors' behavior.

The provincial authorities, particularly in Guangxi and Guangdong, had the incentive to promote class-struggle rhetoric in dealing with mass opposition in the cities. They may have had more tolerance for violence than the Party Center due to the particularly severe challenges they faced. In this sense, the state again was an indirect sponsor of collective killings. In fact, the high point of mass killings came precisely when the provinces used the central directives of July 1968 to crack down on mass opposition. However, it is unlikely that the massive number of collective killings in local communes and villages – mostly of unorganized Four Types – helped in the struggle against opposing factions in the cities. That is, the provincial authorities also perceived the collective killings in villages as unwarranted, an indication of state failure at the provincial level.

By comparison, the local governments at the county, commune, and village levels were clearly the direct sponsor of the mass killings, although the motivation is not clear. They may have misinterpreted the policies disseminated from above and zealously showed their compliance or they may have perceived terror as a convenient way to solidify their power hold on the local community. Whatever the reason, it was the local bureaucrats and their followers who committed the violent acts. Yet, at the same time, the deficiency of state authority is highly implicated in the results. Formal public-security and court systems had ceased to function. In such a context and an era when the justification for violence seemed palpable, local leaders – particularly those at the grassroots level and in remote areas – were unaccountable. In short, when the state is considered a collection of actors at various levels, mass killings were created not by state sponsorship or state failure alone but rather by a combination of both. The tragedy of collective killings during the Cultural Revolution was rooted in this paradox of state sponsorship and state failure.

Four notable lessons are gleaned from the analysis of the state's role in the Chinese case. First, states are not unitary, coherent, and well-oiled machines of repression. Instead, they comprise a set of disparate apparatuses replete with contradictions and conflicts. Expressed differently, states include a vast network of individuals with diverse interests facing different challenges under different pressures. Second, state policy statements are not equivalent to policy outcomes. As scholars of organization studies have long pointed out, *decoupling* – that is, ad hoc practices improvised by local actors that deviate from overall organizational goals – is a fact of life in any bureaucracy. This is especially true for a state machine that has myriad complex levels and that was being dismantled and rebuilt in mass campaigns. Third, control mechanisms at times may contradict one another. In the case of Mao's China during the Cultural Revolution, the mass campaign as a mode of social control disabled legal and bureaucratic controls. Fourth, state actors have multiple, concurrent roles to play, including the newly self-constituted identities not prescribed by the duties of a state actor.

Departing from the conventional model that relies on state policy to explain collective killings, I emphasize the distinction between policy and policy outcomes. A policy is only a starting point for explanation, far from sufficient. That any policy would produce unintended outcomes is a truism for all societies. As discussed in Chapter 1, a genocidal policy may not result in as thorough an extermination as planned, whereas genocidal events nonetheless can occur without such a policy. Another truism is that the operations of any state are fraught with contradictions and conflicts. Hence, I also stress the importance of disaggregating state apparatuses into different levels and parts. With such a disaggregation, I can compare and analyze local conditions that produced divergent outcomes at subnational levels. The result is a sociological model that addresses not only political and institutional variables at the nation-state level but also political, social, and cultural factors at local levels. As important, the model considers local processes of interaction between state and society.

Local Conditions

If state sponsorship and state failure provide the external impetus to advance a community to become a community of killing, then local conditions impede or facilitate this process. My examination of geographical variations revealed a set of predictors for collective killings in the Chinese case. Most are political factors, but an important one is not. First, I find that the killings vary across ethnic and subethnic groups of the population. I interpret this as a cultural factor: The more salient the traditional clan identities, the more severe the collective killings. The underlying reason is that clan identities – formed contentiously in history and persisting under communism – provided a starting point to perceive out-group individuals in antagonistic terms.

Two other factors speak to the political connection of local governments to the Party Center. The degree of a community's integration in the political system has a deterrent effect. This is part of the argument that collective killings were not a product of direct state policy but rather an outcome of control failure. The level of integration is measured by a series of characteristics: whether the community is rural or urban, the level of jurisdiction, the distance from the political center, the economic development, and so on. However, when measured by party organizational strength, the integration seems to be a facilitating factor. Moreover, preexisting factionalism in the local polities exacerbated collective killings. I compared counties whose top leaders were all from outside and those whose top leaders include both outside and local cadres. The mixed leadership is predictive of more collective killings. This finding can be understood relative to the relationship between elite conflict and class struggle among the masses. As discussed in Chapter 3, government officials often competed with one another in whipping up rhetoric and escalating tactics for fear of being accused as "soft on class enemies." Preexisting factionalism exacerbated this process.

Finally, the diverging trajectories of local political processes had differing impacts on collective killings. On the provincial level, two types of mass factional alignment produced a stark contrast in terms of collective killings. The comparison group – that is, the counties in Hubei Province – experienced almost no collective killings, whereas more than half of the counties in Guangdong and Guangxi Provinces experienced them. I attribute the difference to two different types of provincial government that resulted from the varying policies of the Party Center. The Center's policy was different for border regions, including Guangdong and Guangxi Provinces, due to national-security considerations.[13] In this group of provinces, the faction that was more supportive of the incumbent government was designated as "revolutionary" and assumed the central role in the revolutionary committee or new government. Once installed in power, the revolutionary committee cracked down on the more militant rebel faction. Apparently, these two provinces were engaged in extreme terror without being checked by any organized opposition. By comparison, in Hubei and most other provinces, the government was thoroughly reorganized and the moderate alliance discredited. Members of the more militant alliance were incorporated in the new government in large numbers.[14] The Hubei provincial government was more representative of the oppositional elements, which seemed to have a deterrent effect on extreme violence.

13 According to Xu, political events unfolded in a similar fashion in Jiangxi, although that province is not in a border region. See Xu You-yu 徐友渔, *Xingxing sese de zaofan: hongweibing jingshen suzhi de xingcheng ji yanbian* 形形色色的造反：红卫兵精神素质的形成及演变 [*Rebels of All Stripes: A Study of Red Guard Mentalities*]. (Hong Kong: Xianggang zhongwen daxue chubanshe, 1999), pp. 100–108.

14 Shaoguang Wang, *Failure of Charisma: The Cultural Revolution in Wuhan* (Hong Kong and Oxford: Oxford University Press, 1995), pp. 149–202.

At the county level, if a county experienced factional street battles, collective killings were more likely. Armed battles underscored the depth of the political crisis, prompting local leaders to employ terror and violent rituals to demonstrate the power of the newly established governments (see Chapter 5). Moreover, the presence of armed conflict in a county facilitated the war-framing efforts promoted by the Party Center downward and also promoted collective killings (see Chapter 7).

The Mobilization Paradigm Revisited

In the social-scientific endeavor of studying emergent, episodic human events, the most influential is the scholarship of social movements and collective action. The last three decades witnessed a well-developed research paradigm hinging on a simple but powerful idea pioneered by Tilly and Gamson and articulated by McCarthy, Zald, McAdam, Snow, Tarrow, and many others: that is, mobilization. The paradigm focuses squarely on purposive and strategic actors and identifies the available resources, opportunities, ideas, and action repertoires to act collectively. Scholars have found this paradigm to be productive particularly for explaining collective action in Western democracies.[15]

By the turn of the century, statesmen of the paradigm including Tilly, Tarrow, and McAdam began to take stock of their success and critically reevaluate the "classic social-movement agenda."[16] They duly acknowledged the narrow focus on social movements in Western democracies and coined a new term, *contentious politics*, as a call to extend the research scope to include diverse episodes. The effort is another paradigm shift but the articulation of the new paradigm awaits the accumulation of research on diverse episodes, especially those studies that boldly challenge the basic premises of the mobilization paradigm. The call has been heeded

[15] Charles Tilly, *From Mobilization to Revolution* (Reading, MA: Addison-Wesley Publishing Co., 1978); William A. Gamson, *The Strategy of Social Protest* (Homewood, IL: Dorsey Press, 1975); John D. McCarthy and Mayer N. Zald, "Resource Mobilization and Social Movements: A Partial Theory," *American Journal of Sociology* 82 (1977), pp. 1212–1241; Doug McAdam, *Political Process and the Development of Black Insurgency, 1930–1970* (Chicago: University of Chicago Press, 1982); David A. Snow, E. Burke Rochford, Jr., Steven K. Worden, and Robert D. Benford, "Frame Alignment Processes, Micromobilization, and Movement Participation," *American Sociological Review* 51 (1986), pp. 464–481; and Sidney G. Tarrow, *Power in Movement: Social Movements, Collective Action, and Politics* (Cambridge: Cambridge University Press, 1998).

[16] Doug McAdam, Sidney G. Tarrow, and Charles Tilly, *Dynamics of Contention* (New York: Cambridge University Press, 2001).

by a legion of new studies of contentious politics in nondemocratic settings, ranging from communal riots in India, to guerrilla insurgencies in El Salvador, to lootings in Argentina, to the political Islam movement in Egypt, to peasant resistance in communist China.[17] These studies introduce patterns of contention unfamiliar to the classic social-movement agenda, and anomalies that require reconsideration of basic tenets of the old paradigm.

My analysis of the collective killings in China benefits from the mobilization paradigm but also demonstrates some of its deficiencies. It considers classic social-movement theory as a cornerstone. I treat all actors involved as purposive and strategic to the extent that the information and choices of action are available to them. My discussion on the demobilization of law and the creation of a bogus war "reality" is also rooted in the insight provided by political-opportunity models and framing analysis. In this closing chapter, however, I highlight some contrarian lessons in the spirit of Kuhn, who credited anomalies with promoting scientific progress.[18]

To bring collective killings into collective-action scholarship, a point of departure is the extraordinary nature of these episodes – a type of collective action that should not have been tolerated by any state government, community, or living soul. In other words, it is the nature of the event that represents the most important aspect of the puzzle. One should not start with the strategic choice as settled and then move on to look

[17] Javier Auyero, *Routine Politics and Violence in Argentina: The Gray Zone of State Power* (New York: Cambridge University Press, 2007); Steven Wilkinson, *Votes and Violence: Electoral Competition and Ethnic Riots in India* (New York: Cambridge University Press, 2004); Roger V. Gould, *Insurgent Identities: Class, Community, and Protest in Paris from 1848 to the Commune* (Chicago and London: University of Chicago Press, 1995); Beth Roy, Some Trouble with Cows: Making Sense of Social Conflict (Berkeley: University of California Press, 1994); Ashutosh Varshney, *Ethnic Conflict and Civic Life: Hindus and Muslims in India* (New Delhi and Oxford: Oxford University Press, 2002); Gilles Kepel, *Jihad: The Trail of Political Islam* (translated by Anthony F. Roberts) (Cambridge, MA: The Belknap Press of Harvard University Press, 2002); Charles D. Brockett, "The Structure of Political Opportunities and Peasant Mobilization in Central America," *Comparative Politics* 23 (1991), pp. 253–274; Elisabeth Jean Wood, *Forging Democracy from Below: Insurgent Transitions in South Africa and El Salvador* (Cambridge, UK and New York: Cambridge University Press, 2000); Elisabeth Jean Wood, *Insurgent Collective Action and Civil War in El Salvador* (Cambridge: Cambridge University Press, 2003); see also Kevin J. O'Brien and Lianjiang Li, *Rightful Resistance in Rural China* (Cambridge: Cambridge University Press, 2006).

[18] Thomas S. Kuhn, *The Structure of Scientific Revolutions* (Chicago: University of Chicago Press, 1996). See also George Ritzer, *Sociology: A Multiple Paradigm Science* (Boston: Allyn and Bacon, 1974).

for resources and opportunities to explain why it happened. Instead, one must explain why this choice may be available to the actors in the first place. This explanation is less about the actors themselves and more about the environment, or a community, as a whole. The creation of a killing community results not only from the participants' strategic *mobilization* but also from a diverse set of *mobilizations* that are often in conflict with one another. That is, the nature of the collective action is an outcome not of one mobilization but rather an unintended consequence of a series of mobilizations.

Mobilization analysis that has often been practiced considers movement entrepreneurs, commonly in social-movement organizations (SMOs), as the main focus. The environment is not lost in the discussion but rather is viewed simply as opportunities from the SMO vantage point. The dependent variable is the emergence of a movement, or the occurrence of a collective-action event. The theory is more or less uninterested in the character of the collective action. Actors are treated as rational not only in the sense that they maximize their interests but also in that they are clear about their actions and purposively amass resources and create opportunities to succeed. However, this approach proves to be of little use in explaining why collective killings emerged as a tactical choice of collective action in China. In leading up to the collective killings, leaders at various levels of the state and villagers in the local communities were mobilizing entirely differently. The upper-level authorities in the Party Center and the provinces mobilized a bogus wartime "reality" but did not promote collective killings; in fact, they dispatched the army to intervene when their occurrence was revealed. Their goal was to solve the political problems in urban centers. For local cadres at the county and lower levels, that collective killings were an actionable tactic was not of their own making but rather a result of the long-standing discrimination policy against the so-called Four Types, the war rhetoric transmitted from the upper levels of government, and the acquiesce of the village onlookers. For the majority of villagers, collective killings may have been reprehensible, but they did not have any collective means to counter it.

Hence, two elements in the traditional mobilization analysis must be reconsidered. First is the assumption of purposive and strategic actors. I do not suggest that they are irrational in the sense that they act from emotion or on a whim that is inconsistent with their own interest. Instead, I suggest that the focus of investigation change to how the choice became available to them, a situation over which the actors have only minimal or no control. In a sense, by definition, collective killing is an irrational choice. The second element, related to the first, is that the analysis should not be limited exclusively to the direct participants. Rather, the scope should be extended to include a diverse set of actors who directly or indirectly contribute to the creation of a killing community. Especially, we should exonerate various state actors from the reification of "political opportunities."

The mobilization paradigm is inadequate in yet another larger sense. As pointed out herein, collective killings were an outcome of both state sponsorship and state failure. If the state is perceived as a vast mobilization machine in the political campaigns, its parts were not coherent. The upper-level directives were subject to diverging local interpretations, and the political campaigns often disabled other means of local state authority. The failure of social control represents a structural breakdown. To understand the nature of collective action, we should not only consider strategic mobilization by the actors but also the social conditions that may cause a vacuum in social control.

By the mobilization apparatus, I mean the vast network of the party–state personnel and mass activists. Leaders at various levels – central, provincial, county, township, and village – held conflicting interests and, as important, they could not communicate clearly with one another. For coherence and consistency, upper-level authorities exerted two types of control – organizational and informational – over lower-level actors.[19] Some local communities took seriously the Party Center's promoted frames of class struggle and war – a success of informational control – but failed to anticipate punishment for extreme violence, which only organizational control could produce. Moreover, in the heat of the Cultural Revolution, the two modes of control contradicted one another because war rhetoric undermined law-and-order organizational procedures. Indeed, the perpetrators were not punished until ten years later, well after the end of the Cultural Revolution.[20] The killers need not be isolated from the state machine; to the contrary, to the extent that individuals were close to the party–state, they were more likely to identify

[19] This is inspired by Franz Schumann's (1968) classic depiction of the party–state as consisting of organization and ideology. See Franz Schumann, *Ideology and Organization in Communist China* (Berkeley: University of California Press, 1968).

[20] To use an example familiar to a reader in the United States, the rhetoric "enemy combatants" in the war on terror by the Bush administration was taken to heart by soldiers, a success of informational control. That helped created incidents of failure of organizational control such as the Abu Ghraib prisoner abuses and the Haditha civilian killings during the Iraq War.

with the Party's frames. Therefore, the breakdown I refer to herein is structural rather than psychological. In summary, my community model lies between strategic mobilization and structural breakdown. From the vantage point of the state, collective killings were a result of both state sponsorship and state failure.

Traditional breakdown models suggest that social disintegration leads to discontent, which in turn leads to collective action. The empirical implication is that individuals who are isolated from mainstream social institutions are more likely to join a collective action. A generation of research under the rubric of a resource-mobilization and political-opportunity structure has mounted voluminous evidence to refute the most extreme claims of these models. However, recent breakdown theorists make two important points. First, although discontent may not be sufficient for mobilization, it is nonetheless a factor that should not be neglected. Aggrieved individuals need not be isolated from social organizational structures; when resources and opportunities are available, they are more likely than others to join a collective action.[21] Second, breakdown critics have skewed their focus on "routine" social movements with previously established SMOs, at the expense of spontaneous events of protests and riots.[22] Suddenly, imposed threat and disruption are believed to be sufficiently powerful to push otherwise unorganized individuals to act collectively. For protests like this, social strain facilitates the occurrence of collective action.

I hold the middle ground in adding a breakdown component to my community model. I distinguish two types of integration: informational and organizational. Collective-killing participants are highly integrated in terms of information, by virtue of their organizational affiliations, or are otherwise fully subject to the predominant framing discourse. They are not an isolated group of individuals with lower social status. However, collective killing takes place in a gap of organizational integration. This is not about a lack of organizational affiliations as much as it is about a failure of disciplinary control over otherwise organized actors. Such an organizational gap is reminiscent of the social disintegration identified by classic breakdown models, but there is a key difference. The breakdown in my model is *structural*, a condition in which actors evade discipline and punishment, whereas the classic models invoke psychological breakdowns

21 Ronit Lentin and Robbie McVeigh, *After Optimism? Ireland, Racism and Globalisation* (Dublin: Metro Eireann Publications, 2006).

22 Useem, 1998; Snow et al., 1998.

to link structural conditions to collective action. I identify a breakdown within the mobilization apparatus, whereas the breakdown in the debate is in the social structure. In Mao's China, such a distinction was not clear because the party–state conducted campaigns involving the entire society. Conceptually, however, this distinction is important if my model is to be applied to other cases. For the breakdown I am referring to here, what is "broken" is the linkage *between* the upper levels of government and the community at issue. In traditional theories, what is "broken" is the "normal" state of mind of actors *within* the community, who take unusual actions to address psychological needs.

Toward a Sociological Model of Genocide and Mass Killing

If research on genocide and mass killing has been dominated by the state-policy model, this is due in part to the fact that most theorists are political scientists trained in policy analysis. The utility of this model is not in doubt. For example, in the Chinese case of collective killings, the nature of the regime and policy from the Party Center were partly responsible. Yet, collective killings are often an unintended consequence of the policy makers. Between state policy and the occurrence of eliminationist killings lies a complex set of social processes. For this reason, sociologists have much to offer. Endless debates have been waged with regard to the definition of genocide. Much effort has been expended to interpret or revise the UN Convention on Genocide to identify current cases of genocide in international politics.[23] Conversely, my approach is concerned with fewer legal and political considerations than theoretical conceptualizations for social-scientific research. I emphasize key aspects of genocide and mass killing shared by historical episodes such as the Salem witch-hunt, the Jedwabne massacre, the lynching of blacks in the American South, the My Lai massacre, the Holocaust, and the Rwandan genocide. Throughout these events is the creation of a self-contained local community in which "atrocities in plain sight" become possible. This conception of the dependent variable also can be perceived as a special form of collective action resulting from a dual process of mobilization and social breakdown.

As stated at the beginning of this book, the social outcome of collective killings need not be a direct translation of state policy. Between

[23] Frank Robert Chalk and Kurt Jonassohn, *The History and Sociology of Genocide: Analyses and Case Studies* (New Haven, CT: Yale University Press, 1990), pp. 3–53; Helen Fein, *Genocide: A Sociological Perspective* (London: Sage Publications, 1993).

the state's genocidal policies or its lack thereof and the genocidal outcome are local conditions and localized processes that play the role of mediation. This logic of sorting out causality echoes the political-process model of social-movement research championed by McAdam.[24] It also resonates with the political-mediation model predicting social-movement outcomes, although in the latter case, Amenta et al. address the causal direction from collective action to policy changes.[25] Nevertheless, once we refuse to short-circuit the relationship between state policy and a specific social outcome and begin to focus on the mediating factors in between, a rich ground is opened up for sociological inquiry.

In the cases in which explicit eliminationist policies seem to be apparent (e.g., the Holocaust and the Rwandan genocide), massive numbers of deaths were possible only when these conditions and processes were in place. Fein showed that the project to exterminate Jews met various levels of success across Nazi-occupied countries due to differentiated social and political conditions, as well as varying levels of compliance by state leaders.[26] In the same vein, Straus documents regional variations in the Rwandan genocide under a single genocidal policy in 1994. He attributes the differential depth of the tragedy across communities to three factors: the impact of the civil war, the local composition of the party–state institutions, and the heightened process of ethnic categorization in the heat of state propaganda promoting killing.[27]

In the cases in which policies of explicit extermination seem to be absent, state policies such as discrimination against minority groups and stigmatization of so-called state enemies may take on a genocidal dimension and result in massive numbers of killings, by way of mediating factors in between. This is the main theme that my research attempts to

[24] Doug McAdam, *Political Process and the Development of Black Insurgency, 1930–1970*, Chicago, IL: University of Chicago Press ([1982], 2003).

[25] Edwin Amenta, *Bold Relief: Institutional Politics and the Origins of Modern American Social Policy*, Princeton, NJ: Princeton University Press (1998); *When Movements Matter: The Townsend Plan and The Rise of Social Security*, Princeton, NJ: Princeton University Press (2006); Edwin Amenta and Jane D. Poulsen, "Social Politics in Context: The Institutional Politics Theory and Social Spending at the End of the New Deal," *Social Forces* 75 (1996), pp. 33–60; Edwin Amenta, Neal Caren, and Sheera Joy Olasky, "Age for Leisure? Political Mediation and the Impact of the Pension Movement on U.S. Old-Age Policy," *American Sociological Review* 70 (2005), pp. 516–538; Edwin Amenta and Drew Halfmann, "Wage Wars: Institutional Politics, WPA Wages, and the Struggle for U.S. Social Policy," *American Sociological Review* 65 (2000), pp. 506–528.

[26] Helen Fein, *Accounting for Genocide: National Responses and Jewish Victimization during the Holocaust*, New York: The Free Press (1979).

[27] Straus, *The Order of Genocide*.

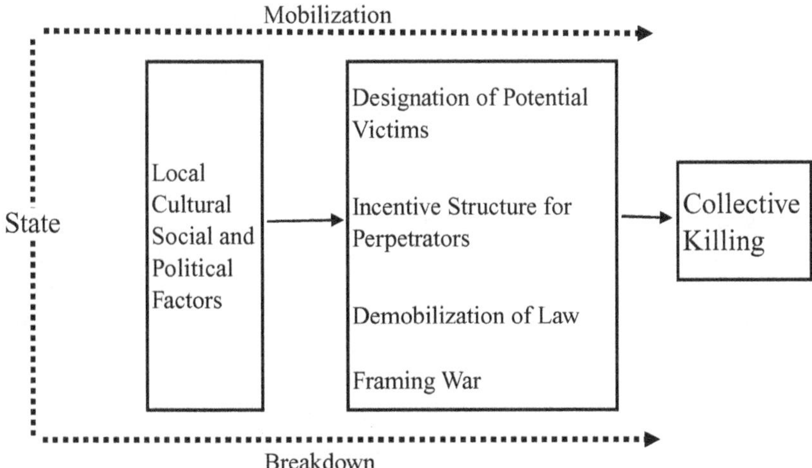

FIGURE 9.1. A sociological model of collective killings.

demonstrate. Building on the work of the previously mentioned scholars, Figure 9.1, a sociological model of collective killings, summarizes the theoretical ideas that guide my investigation.

As documented in Chapter 8, examples of cultural and social factors include saliency of clan institutions, geographical location, party organizational strength, trajectories of political process, and prior conflict. In previous chapters, I identify four intervening social processes: the designation of potential victims, an incentive structure for potential perpetrators, the demobilization of legal institutions, and wartime framing. State policy joins other cultural, social, and political factors to create these processes. Hence, state policy exerts indirect rather than direct effects in generating collective killings. In responding to the extraordinary political situation of the time, the Chinese state promoted the long-standing discrimination practices and exaggerated threats to the state. The mobilization efforts artificially constructed a war-time "reality." Meanwhile, local actors responded to the mobilization by ignoring preexisting moral and organizational constraints on violence. Hence, state breakdown went hand in hand with state mobilization andcollective killings ensued.

Methodologically, my use of the community as the unit of analysis – in contrast with the state-policy model that employs the national state[28] – makes it possible to collect and analyze systematic data on

[28] Nation-state can be seen as a type of community when appropriate.

subnational variations. My approach follows a long tradition in sociology of using jurisdictions such as precincts, counties, states, and census tracts as the unit of analysis.[29] Comparing subnational units has an added value: Because the units share the same political regime and central policy, these factors are implicitly controlled. More important, in China during the Cultural Revolution and in most instances of collective killings, most killing decisions took place at this local level; thus, they are imperative for our understanding. The patterns of variation forcefully speak to the need to go beyond national policy to explain genocide and mass killing.

Concluding Remarks: Neighbors in Mao's China and Beyond

In 1948, the UN passed the Convention on the Prevention and Punishment of the Crime of Genocide. Lemkin and other framers clearly had the Holocaust in mind when they defined genocide as an act of a nation-state to eliminate an ethnic or national group. Despite myriad variations and endless debates, the essential elements of the UN definition survive to this day. The UN Convention has achieved a poor record thus far in its enforcement, however, partly because rogue states are able to deny any explicit genocidal policy and partly because mass killings often take place within a state that does not have such a policy. To the extent that the community model holds true, these states should be held accountable for the indirect actions and overarching policies that generate potential targets of mass killings, including the creation of a bogus war situation and the destruction of legal institutions in communities. Hence, the burden of proof is lowered, and prevention measures may include

[29] See Edwin Amenta and Jane D. Poulsen, "Social Politics in Context: The Institutional Politics Theory and Social Spending at the End of the New Deal," *Social Forces* 75 (1996), pp. 33–60; Edwin Amenta, Neal Caren, and Sheera Joy Olasky, "Age for Leisure? Political Mediation and the Impact of the Pension Movement on U.S. Old-Age Policy," *American Sociological Review* 70 (2005), pp. 516–538; Edwin Amenta and Drew Halfmann, "Wage Wars: Institutional Politics, WPA Wages, and the Struggle for U.S. Social Policy," *American Sociological Review* 65 (2000), pp. 506–528. See also Sarah A. Soule and Y. Zylan, "Runaway Train? The Diffusion of State-Level Reform to AFDC Eligibility Requirements, 1950–1967," *American Journal of Sociology* 103 (1997), pp. 733–762; Sarah Soule and David Strang, "Diffusion in Organizations and Social Movements: From Hybrid Corn to Poison Pills," *Annual Review of Sociology* 24 (1998), pp. 265–290. See also Rory McVeigh, "Structural Influences on Activism and Crime: Identifying the Social Structure of Discontent," *American Journal of Sociology* 112 (2006), pp. 510–566; and Rory McVeigh and Juliana Sobolewski, "Red Counties, Blue Counties, and Occupational Segregation by Sex and Race," *American Journal of Sociology* 113 (2007), pp. 446–506.

helping weak states to police their local communities in a time of crisis. Even when a rogue state with a genocidal policy can be ascertained, the identification of social variables and processes can help devise measures to minimize the policy's impact short of regime change. As with Mao's China, abusive policies that can degenerate into genocide are rooted in the nature of the regime. To engineer a regime change is obviously a costly if not impossible approach to intervene.

To date, the central tenet of international intervention has been the criminal prosecution of rogue-state leaders. This is a legacy of the successful prosecutions of Nazi war criminals following World War II. Since then, however, this approach has met little success. Why? The conditions following the war – that is, a thoroughly defeated rogue state, an international consensus, a well-documented genocidal crime, a commanding authority by the international tribunal – simply did not repeat themselves. In comparison, when these conditions are absent – particularly during a wave of ongoing genocidal events (e.g., Darfur) – making genocidal accusations and prosecution attempts are not only ineffective but also alienates the state in question. If the community model is to some extent valid, an alternative approach should be proactive engagement. The international community would first suspend judgment on the policy at the state level and then devise measures to intervene with assistance of top state leaders. These measures may include bringing in peacekeeping forces, opening up the information flow, and disarming local militias. To make such engagements effective, a sociological analysis of genocide and mass killings is needed.

"These are differing evils, but they are the common works of man. They reflect the imperfection of human justice, the inadequacy of human compassion, our lack of sensibility towards the suffering of our fellows. But we can perhaps remember even if only for a time that those who live with us are our brothers; that they share with us the same short moment of life; that they seek as we do nothing but the chance to live out their lives in purpose and happiness, winning what satisfaction and fulfillment they can."[30] These words by Robert Kennedy were spoken in 1966, one year before the onset of the collective killings described in this book. Since then, the world has added a long list of "lack of sensibility towards the suffering of our fellows," including the unspeakable atrocities in Cambodia, Bosnia, Rwanda, and – more recently – Darfur. The commandment to "love thy neighbor" has been and will be broken time and again.

[30] Robert Kennedy's speech made to the young people of South Africa on their Day of Affirmation in 1966, cited in Edward Kennedy's eulogy of Robert Kennedy, 1968.

Past lessons are valuable, and Chinese lessons are no exception. The question then is this: Are we drawing the right lessons grounded in historical facts? One theme of this book is how the Chinese government buried information on the scale and depth of Cultural Revolution violence. The difficulty of obtaining data has partly contributed to a skewed history of the Cultural Revolution. As I note, the majority of published studies center on ideals and hidden group interests behind the mass conflict, whereas the consequences – particularly the violent impact – of the mass actions have been underappreciated. This oversight has contributed to the absence of a rigorous rebuke to a new intellectual current in contemporary China known as the New Left. As social problems, particularly the plight of the working class, in a reformed China grew in recent decades, a growing contingent of Chinese scholars has fashioned a Maoist critique of the current system. One of their intellectual foundations is the interpretation of the Mao era as a haven of egalitarian values and broad mass participation. For them, Mao's China is a lost paradise worthy of restoration. Indeed, reports are emerging that the ideas of these intellectuals are echoing in the streets, with worker protesters flashing Mao's portrait.[31]

Another tendency in reading China's recent past is premised on an intellectual shortcut: Many scholars attribute the violence under Mao to a simplistic cause: a criminal regime. Mao's regime was indeed criminal, as demonstrated abundantly in this book. However, this legalistic and moralistic approach obscures as much as it reveals. As I have shown, the nature of a regime and its central policies are only a starting point for uncovering useful historic lessons. Only when these specific details are documented and patterns charted can we have a real understanding of the criminal nature of Maoism. More important, only then will the Chinese lesson – soaked in so many innocent people's blood – be drawn for use beyond its borders.

[31] Cui Zhiyuan 崔之元. "Mao Zedong wenge lilun de deshi yu 'xiandaixing' de chongjian" 毛泽东文革理论的得失与 "现代性" 的重建 ["The Loss and Gain in Mao Zedong's Theory of the Cultural Revolution and the Reconstruction of 'Modernity'"]. *Zhongguo yu shijie* 2 (1997); Cui Zhiyuan 崔之元, *dierci sixiang jiefang he zhidu chuangxin* [第二次思想解放和制度创新](The Second Thought Liberation and Institutional Innovations) (Hong Kong: Oxford University Press, 1997); "中国同志向国际毛泽东主义同志紧急呼吁" ("An Appeal to the International Maoist Comrades from Chinese Comrades"), available at http://www.red-sparks.com/ssos.htm, accessed August 1, 2008; Zhang Qianfu 张倩夫, "郑州四君子" 纤夫刑满获释 – – 致全国全球思想同志友人感谢信" ("A Thank-You Letter to Comrades in the World: The 'Four Gentlemen of Zhengzhou' Released"), available at http://blog.dwnews.com/?p=32583, accessed August 1, 2007.

The democratic values and human rights in contemporary Western societies – that is, treating fellow human beings as equals regardless of race, religion, or political orientation – can be credited in important ways to lessons extracted from the Holocaust. "Never again!" has become a modern motto. At the same time, "never again" has not been our reality. Different versions of the Holocaust have invaded our lives and memories since the end of World War II. They challenge our conscience as well as our intellect. An urgent question for social-science scholars in the era of Bosnia and Darfur is this: Have we extracted the lessons from the Holocaust? Equally as important, can we adapt intellectually when confronting other cases of genocide and mass killing?

Appendix

Methodological Issues and Statistical Analyses

In this appendix, I provide greater detail regarding the quantitative analyses of collective killings across counties in Guangxi and Guangdong Provinces, as analyzed in Chapter 8. I use two dependent variables: that is, whether the county had collective killings (used in the bivariate analysis in Tables 8.3 and 8.4) and the number of deaths caused by collective killings (used in the Poisson regression models in Table 8.5 and Table A3 herein). The source for the first variable is described in Chapter 2. I read the narratives in the *xianzhi* (i.e., county gazetteers) and decided whether there were collective-killing events in a county based on the number of deaths (i.e., ten or more in a given event) and the manner of killings. To compute the number of collective-killing deaths, I first obtained the total number of deaths during the entire Cultural Revolution. I then subtracted the deaths caused by the earlier persecutions and those caused by armed battles.

My analyses are based on data from the 65 counties in Guangxi Province and 57 counties in Guangdong Province whose *xianzhi* are available (of 162 rural counties in 1965). My dataset thus includes more than three quarters of the counties, and there is no reason to believe that the missing counties are biased in any particular direction regarding killings or their covariates. Because some of the covariates have missing values, the total number of counties may be less than 122 in some of the analyses.

I read the entire volume of each *xianzhi* to compile relevant county characteristics as the independent or causal measures. Table A1 provides the definition of and expectations surrounding these measures and their summary statistics.

TABLE A1. *Description and Summary Statistics of Key Variables*

Name of Variable	Operationalization	Mean	SD	Min.	Max.	N
Dependent Measures						
Collective killing	1 = County reports to have collective killing, 0 = Other	0.57	0.50	0	1	122
Number of deaths	Number of collective-killing deaths	506.13	695.34	0.00	3914.00	118
Independent Measures						
Distance from provincial capital	Distance from provincial capital, unit: 100 km	1.98	1.01	0.29	0.48	118
Population density	Residents in thousands per km^2 in 1965	0.17	0.18	0.02	0.97	118
County revenue per capita	County government revenue per capita, unit: 1,000 *yuan*	1.76	1.18	0.45		114
Party members per thousand	Party members per thousand population	19.51	6.96	2.66	66.50	115
Previous armed battle	1 = County with armed battle; 0 = Other	0.62	0.49	0	1	122
Heterogeneous leadership	1 = With both native-born and outside secretaries, 0 = With only outside secretaries	0.62	0.49	0	1	114
50 percent or more minorities	1 = County with 50% or more minorities population, 0 = Other, Guangxi	0.26	0.44	0	1	122
Hakka County	In Guangdong: 1 = Pure Hakka; 0 = Mixed in Guangxi: 1 = Mixed; 0 = Non-Hakka	0.25	0.43	0	1	122
Control Measures						
Cultural Revolution account length	Number Chinese words recording the Cultural Revolution in *xianzhi*, Unit: 1,000 words	5.13	3.12	0.84	27.04	116
Guangxi	1 = County is in Guangxi; 0 = County is in Guangdong	0.53	0.50	0	1	122

TABLE A2. *Description and Summary Statistics of Key Variables*

	(1)	(2)	(3)	(4)	(5)	(6)	(7)	(8)	(9)	(10)
(1) Cultural Revolution account length	1.00									
(2) Guangxi	0.01	1.00								
(3) Distance from provincial capital	−0.04	0.27	1.00							
(4) Population density	−0.02	−0.35	−0.08	1.00						
(5) County revenue per capita	−0.05	−0.47	−0.15	0.41	1.00					
(6) Party members per thousand	−0.03	−0.25	−0.16	−0.01	0.54	1.00				
(7) Previous armed battle	0.17	0.17	0.16	−0.10	−0.27	−0.27	1.00			
(8) Heterogeneous leadership	0.08	−0.16	−0.02	0.28	0.18	0.08	0.10	1.00		
(9) 50 percent or more minorities	0.09	0.58	−0.14	−0.28	−0.30	−0.06	0.12	−0.09	1.00	
(10) Hakka county	0.00	0.12	0.16	−0.10	−0.22	−0.11	0.07	−0.10	−0.14	1.00

TABLE A3. *Poisson Regression Models Predicting Collective-Killing Deaths in Guangdong and Guangxi Provinces*

	Regression Coefficients			
Independent Variables	M1	Notes	M2	Notes
Intercept	5.369	***	4.826	***
Cultural Revolution account length	0.063	***	0.065	***
Guangxi	0.787	***	0.332	***
Distance from provincial capital			−0.031	***
Population density			−0.278	***
County revenue per capita			−0.322	***
Party members per thousand			0.033	***
Previous armed battle			0.819	***
Heterogeneous leadership			0.095	***
50 percent or more minorities			−0.360	***
Hakka county			0.197	***
−2Log Likelihood	80,782.830		55,075.992	
Number of counties	116		102	

Notes: ** $p < .05$, *** $p < .01$

The length devoted to describe the Cultural Revolution varies across *xianzhi* volumes. Among the Guangdong and Guangxi provincial counties, the length is positively associated with the number of deaths reported ($r = 0.20$). I use this measure as a control in my analyses to predict the number of deaths.

Table A2 shows the correlation coefficient matrix among the independent and control measures. Because all of the correlations are either weak or moderate, there is no potential multicollinearity problem.

Using collective-killing death counts as the dependent variable, the occurrence of deaths is treated as a Poisson process, fitting the Poisson distribution. With the mean and variance being 506.1 and 695.3, respectively, the problem of over-dispersion is minor.[1] I provide two main models. The first model includes control measures for the length of the accounts and the province. The second model includes each of the other causal measures described in Table A2 and discussed in Chapter 8. The coefficients for each measure are in the direction expected by the community model and are all significant at the 0.01 level. The odds ratios in Table 8.5 are based on models in Table A3. With the dependent

[1] J. Scott Long, *Regression Models for Categorical and Limited Dependent Variables* (Thousand Oaks, CA, and London: Sage Publications, 1997).

categorical measure of whether the county had collective killings, I also ran a series of logistic regression models (not shown); the patterns were similar to the results reported herein, although most coefficients are not statistically significant due to the more primitive nature of the dependent measures and the small sample sizes.

References

Amenta, Edwin. 1998. *Bold Relief: Institutional Politics and the Origins of Modern American Social Policy*. Princeton, NJ: Princeton University Press.

Amenta, Edwin. 2006. *When Movements Matter: The Townsend Plan and the Rise of Social Security*. Princeton, NJ: Princeton University Press.

Amenta, Edwin, Neal Caren, and Sheera Joy Olasky. 2005. "Age for Leisure? Political Mediation and the Impact of the Pension Movement on U.S. Old-Age Policy." *American Sociological Review* 70: 516–538.

Amenta, Edwin, and Drew Halfmann. 2000. "Wage Wars: Institutional Politics, WPA Wages, and the Struggle for U.S. Social Policy." *American Sociological Review* 65: 506–528.

Amenta, Edwin, and Jane D. Poulsen. 1996. "Social Politics in Context: The Institutional Politics Theory and Social Spending at the End of the New Deal." *Social Forces* 75: 33–60.

Andreopoulos, George J. (ed.). 1994. *Genocide: Conceptual and Historical Dimensions*. Philadelphia: University of Pennsylvania Press.

Annas, George J., and Michael A. Grodin (eds.). 1992. *The Nazi Doctors and the Nuremberg Code: Human Rights in Human Experimentation*. New York: Oxford University Press.

Arendt, Hannah. 2006. *Eichmann in Jerusalem: A Report on the Banality of Evil*. New York: Penguin Books.

Auyero, Javier. 2007. *Routine Politics and Violence in Argentina: The Gray Zone of State Power*. New York: Cambridge University Press, 2007.

Barnett, A. Doak. 1967. *Cadres, Bureaucracy, and Political Power in Communist China*. New York: Columbia University Press.

Baum, Richard. 1971. "The Cultural Revolution in Countryside: Anatomy of a Limited Rebellion," in *The Cultural Revolution in China*, edited by Thomas W. Robinson (pp. abc-de). Berkeley: University of California Press.

Beck, E. M., and Stewart E. Tolnay. 1992. "A Season for Violence: The Lynching of Blacks and Labor Demand in the Agricultural Production Cycle in the American South." *International Review of Social History* 37: 1–24.

Benford, Robert D., and David A. Snow. 2000. "Framing Processes and Social Movements: An Overview and Assessment." *Annual Review of Sociology* 26: 611–639.

Bernstein, Thomas P. 1984. "Stalinism, Famine, and Chinese Peasants: Grain Procurements during the Great Leap Forward." *Theory and Society* 13(3): 339–377.

Blossfeld, Hans-Peter, and Gotz Rohwer. 1995. *Techniques of Event History Modeling: New Approaches to Causal Analysis*. Mahwah, NJ: Lawrence Erlbaum Associates.

Boyer, Paul S., and Stephen Nissenbaum. 1974. *Salem Possessed: The Social Origin of Witchcraft*. Cambridge, MA: Harvard University Press.

Brockett, Charles D. 1991. "The Structure of Political Opportunities and Peasant Mobilization in Central America." *Comparative Politics* 23: 253–274.

Browning, Christopher. 1978. *The Final Solution and the German Foreign Office: A Study of Referat D III of Abteilung Deutschland, 1940–43*. New York: Holmes & Meier.

Browning, Christopher. 1992. *Ordinary Men: Reserve Police Battalion 101 and the Final Solution in Poland*. New York: HarperCollins.

Browning, Christopher. 2004. *The Origins of the Final Solution: The Evolution of Nazi Jewish Policy, September 1939 – March 1942*. Lincoln: University of Nebraska Press.

Brundage, W. Fitzhugh. 1993. *Lynching in the New South*. Urbana and Chicago: University of Illinois Press.

Cangwu. Party Ratification Office 苍梧整党办公室. 1987. "Zaocheng yanzhong houguo de 'sange huiyi'." 造成严重后果的 "三个会议" ["Three Meetings That Caused Severe Consequences"]. Unpublished documents (August).

Cao Shuji 曹树基. 1997. *Zhongguo yiminshi: Diwujuan* 中国移民史: 第五卷 [*China's Immigration History: Volume 5*]. Fuzhou, Fujian: Fujian renmin chubanshe.

Chalk, Frank, and Kurt Jonassohn (eds.). 1990. *The History and Sociology of Genocide: Analyses and Case Studies*. New Haven, CT: Yale University Press.

Chan, Anita, Richard Madsen, and Jonathan Unger. 1992 (second edition). *Chen Village under Mao and Deng*. Berkeley: University of California Press.

Chan, Anita, Stanley Rosen, and Jonathan Unger. 1980. "Students and Class Warfare: The Roots of the Red Guard Conflict in Guangzhou." *China Quarterly* 3 (September): 397–446.

Chang, Iris. 1997. *The Rape of Nanking: The Forgotten Holocaust of World War II*. New York: Penguin Book.

Chen Yangyong 陈扬勇. 2006. *Kucheng weiju: Zhou Enlai zai 1967* 苦撑危局: 周恩来在 1967 [*Weathering the Storm: Zhou Enlai in 1967*]. Chongqing: Chongqing chubanshe.

Chen Yiyuan 陈益元. 2006. *Geming yu xiangcun: Jianguo chuqi nongcun jiceng zhengquan jianshe yanjiu: 1949–1957, yi hunansheng lilingxian wei ge'an* 革命与乡村: 建国初期农村基层政权建设研究: 1949–1957, 以湖南醴陵县为个案 [*Revolution and Village: A Study on the Establishment of Grassroots Governance in the*

Countryside in the First Years of PRC, 1949–1957, The Case of Liling Xian]. Shanghai: Shanghai shehui kexueyuan chubanshe.

Chen, Yung-fa 陈永发. 1986. *Making Revolution: The Communist Movement in Eastern and Central China, 1937–1945*. Berkeley: University of California Press.

Cohen, Jean L. 1985. "Strategy or Identity: New Theoretical Paradigms of Contemporary Social Movements." *Social Research* 54(4): 663–716.

Conquest, Robert. 1986. *Harvest of Sorrow: Soviet Collectivization and the Terror-Famine*. New York: Oxford University Press.

Conquest, Robert. 1990. *The Great Terror: A Reassessment*. New York: Oxford University Press.

Constable, Nicole (ed.). 1996. *Guest People: Hakka Identity in China and Abroad*. Seattle: University of Washington Press.

Courtois, Stephane, Nicolas Werth, Jean-Louis Panne, Andrzej Paczkowski, Karel Bartosek, and Jean-Louis Margolin (eds. 1999). *The Black Book of Communism: Crimes, Terror, Repression*. Cambridge, MA: Harvard University Press.

Crook, Isabel, and David Crook. 1959. *Revolution in a Chinese Village: Ten Mile Inn*. London: Routledge and Kegan Paul.

Crook, Isabel, and David Crook. 1979. *Ten Mile Inn: Mass Movement in a Chinese Village*.New York: Pantheon Books.

CRRM. 1988. "Beijing daxue geming weiyuanhui shengli dansheng" 北京大学革命委员会胜利诞生 ["Victorious Birth of the Beijing University Revolutionary Committee"], *Renmin Ribao*, October 6, 1969, p. 373 in *Wenhua da geming yanjiu ziliao* 文化大革命研究资料 (中) [*The Cultural Revolution Research Materials*] Vol. 2., edited by Zhongguo renmin jiefanjun guofang daxue dangshi dangjian zhenggong jiaoyanshi 国防大学党史党建政工教研室. Beijing: Zhongguo renmin jiefangjun guofang daxue dangshi chubanshe.

Cui Zhiyuan 崔之元. 1997a. "Mao Zedong wenge lilun de deshi yu 'xiandaixing' de chongjian" 毛泽东文革理论的得失与"现代性"的重建 ["The Loss and Gain in Mao Zedong's Theory of the Cultural Revolution and the Reconstruction of 'Modernity'"]. *Zhongguo yu shijie* 2.

Cui Zhiyuan 崔之元. 1997b. *Dierci sixiang jiefang he zhidu chuangxin* [第二次思想解放和制度创新] (*The Second Thought Liberation and Institutional Innovations*). Hong Kong: Oxford University Press.

Dallin, Alexander, and George W. Breslauer. 1970. *Political Terror in Communist Systems*. Stanford, CA: Stanford University Press.

Danner, Mark. 2004. "Abu Ghraib: The Hidden Story." *The New York Review of Books*, October 7.

Ding Shu 丁抒. 1993. *Yangmou: "Fayou" qianhuo* 反右前祸 [*Open Conspiracy: Crisis before the Anti-Rightist Campaign*]. Hong Kong: Jiushi niandai chubanshe.

Ding Shu 丁抒. 2006. *Yangmou: Fan youpai yundong shimo* 阳谋: 反右派运动始末 [*Open Conspiracy: The Complete Story of Chinese Communist Party's Anti-Rightist Campaign*]. Hong Kong: Kaifang zazhishe.

Dower, John W. 1986. *War without Mercy: Race and Power in the Pacific War*. London: Faber.

Du, Xichuan, and Lingyuan Zhang. 1990. *China's Legal System: A General Survey*. Beijing: New World Press.

Duara, Prasenjit. 1988. *Culture, Power, and the State: Rural North China, 1900–1942*. Stanford, CA: Stanford University Press.

Dutton, Michael R. 1992. *Policing and Punishment in China: From Patriarchy to 'the People.'* New York: Cambridge University Press.

Dutton, Michael R. 2005. *Policing Chinese Politics: A History*. Durham, NC: Duke University Press.

Eisenhardt, Kathleen M. 1985. "Control: Organizational and Economic Approaches." *Management Science* 31: 134–149.

Emerson, Richard M. 1962. "Power-Dependence Relations." *American Sociological Review* 27: 31–41.

Esherick, Joseph W. 1987. *The Origins of the Boxer Uprising*. Berkeley: University of California Press.

Esherick, Joseph W., and Mary Backus Rankin (eds.). 1990. *Chinese Local Elites and Patterns of Dominance*. Berkeley: University of California Press.

Etzioni, Amitai. 1975. *A Comparative Analysis of Complex Organizations: On Power, Involvement, and Their Correlates* (second edition). New York: The Free Press.

Fein, Helen. 1979. *Accounting for Genocide: National Responses and Jewish Victimization during the Holocaust*. New York: The Free Press.

Fein, Helen. 1993. *Genocide: A Sociological Perspective*. Newbury Park, CA: Sage Publications.

First National People's Congress of the People's Republic of China. 1954. *The People's Republic of China Constitution*. Beijing: Foreign Language Press.

Fitzpatrick, Sheila. 1994. *Stalin's Peasants: Resistance and Survival in the Russian Village after Collectivization*. New York: Oxford University Press.

Forster, Keith. 1990. *Rebellion and Factionalism in a Chinese Province: Zhejiang, 1966–1976*. Armonk, NY: M. E. Sharpe.

Foucault, Michel. 1979. *Discipline and Punish: The Birth of the Prison*. New York: Vintage Books.

Freedman, Maurice. 1965. *Lineage Organization in Southeastern China*. New York: Humanities Press.

Freedman, Maurice. 1966. *Chinese Lineage and Society: Fukien and Kwangtung*. New York: Humanities Press.

Friedlander, Saul. 1997. *Nazi Germany and the Jews, Volume I: The Years of Persecution, 1933–1939*. New York: Harper Perennial.

Friedlander, Saul. 2006. *Nazi Germany and the Jews 1939–1945: The Years of Extermination*. New York: Harper Perennial.

Friedman, Edward, Paul G. Pickowicz, and Mark Selden. 1991. *Chinese Village, Socialist State*. New Haven, CT: Yale University Press.

Friedman, Edward, Paul G. Pickowicz, and Mark Selden. 2005. *Revolution, Resistance, and Reform in Village China*. New Haven, CT: Yale University Press.

Funnel, Victor. 1970. "The Chinese Communist Youth Movement, 1949–1966." *China Quarterly* (April-June): 105–130.

Gamson, William A. 1975. *The Strategy of Social Protest*. Homewood, IL: Dorsy.

Gamson, William A. 1992. *Talking Politics*. New York: Cambridge University Press.

Gamson, William A. 1995. "Construction Social Protest" in *Social Movements and Culture*, edited by Hank Johnston and Bert Klandermans (pp. 85–106). Minneapolis: University of Minnesota Press.

Gao, Hua 高华. 2000. *Hongtaiyang shi zenyang shengqide* 红太阳是怎样升起的: 延安整风运动的来龙去脉 [*How Did the Red Sun Rise over Yan'an?: A History of the Rectification Movement*]. Hong Kong: The Chinese University of Hong Kong Press.

Gao, Yuan. 1987. *Born Red: A Chronicle of the Cultural Revolution*. Stanford, CA: Stanford University Press.

Ge, Jianxiong 葛剑雄. 1991. *Zhongguo renkou fazhan shi* 中国人口发展史. Fuzhou, Fujian: Fujian renmin chubanshe.

Ge, Jianxiong 葛剑雄. 1997. *Zhongguo yiminshi: Dierjuan* 中国移民史: 第二卷 [*China's Immigration History: Volume* 2]. Fuzhou, Fujian: Fujian renmin chubanshe.

Ge Jianxiong 葛剑雄, Wu Songdi 吴松弟, and Cao Shuji 曹树基. 1997. *Zhongguo yiminshi: Diyijuan* 中国移民史: 第一卷 [*China's Immigration History: Volume 1*]. Fuzhou, Fujian: Fujian renmin chubanshe.

Geertz, Clifford. 1980. *Negara: The Theatre State in Nineteenth-Century Bali*. Princeton, NJ: Princeton University Press.

Goldhagen, Daniel J. 1996. *Hitler's Willing Executioners: Ordinary Germans and the Holocaust*. New York: Vintage Books.

Goldman, Merle, Timothy Cheek, and Carol Lee Hamrin. 1987. *China's Intellectuals and the State: In Search of a New Relationship*. Cambridge, MA: Harvard University Council on East Asian Studies.

Gould, Roger V. 1995. *Insurgent Identities: Class, Community, and Protest in Paris from 1848 to the Commune*. Chicago: University of Chicago Press.

Gould, Roger V. 1996. "Patron–Client Ties, State Centralization, and the Whiskey Rebellion." *American Journal of Sociology* 102(2): 400–429.

Gould, Roger V. 1999. "Collective Violence and Group Solidarity: Evidence from a Feuding Society." *American Sociological Review* 64(3): 356–380.

Gourevitch, Philip. 1998a. *We Wish to Inform You that Tomorrow We Will Be Killed with Our Families: Stories from Rwanda*. New York: Picador.

Gourevitch, Philip. 1998b. "The Genocide Fax: The United Nations Was Warned About Rwanda. Did Anyone Care?," *The New Yorker* (May 11) p. 42.

Gross, Jan T. 2001. *Neighbors: The Destruction of the Jewish Community in Jedwabne, Poland*. Princeton, NJ: Princeton University Press.

Guo Dehong 郭德宏, and Lin Xiaobo 林小波. 2005. *Siqing yundong shilu* 四清运动实录 [*Chroniclogy of the Four-Clean Movement*]. Hangzhou, Zhejiang: Zhejiang remin chubanshe.

GXWGDSNB. 1990. *Guangxi wen'ge dashi nianbiao* 广西文革大事年表 [*Chronology of the Cultural Revolution in Guangxi*]. Nanning: Guangxi renmin chubanshe. (Reprinted by Chinese Publications Services Center, Los Angeles, CA, 1995.)

Hai Feng 海枫. 1972. *Guangzhou diqu wen'ge licheng shulue* 广州地区文革历程述略 [*Mapping the Cultural Revolution Trajectory in Guangzhou Area*]. Hong Kong: Youlian yanjiu chubanshe.

Han, Dongping. 2000. *The Unknown Cultural Revolution*. New York: Garland Publishing.

Hannum, Emily. 1999. "Political Change and the Urban–Rural Gap in Basic Education in China, 1949–1990." *Comparative Education Review* (May): 193–211.

Harding, Harry. 1981. *Organizing China: The Problem of Bureaucracy 1949–1976*. Stanford, CA: Stanford University Press.

Harff, Barbara. 2003. "No Lessons Learned from the Holocaust? Accessing Risks of Genocide and Political Mass Murder since 1955." *American Political Science Review* 97(1): 57–73.

He, Jiangsui. 2006. "The Death of a Landlord: Moral Predicament in Rural China, 1968–1969," in *China's Cultural Revolution as History*, edited by Joseph W. Esherick, Paul G. Pickowicz, and Andrew G. Walder (pp. 124–152). Stanford, CA: Stanford University Press.

Hechter, Michael. 1975. *Internal Colonialism: The Celtic Fringe in British National Development, 1536–1966*. Berkeley: University of California Press.

Hersh, Seymour M. 1972. *Cover-Up: The Army's Secret Investigation of the Massacre at My Lai 4*. New York: Random House.

Hilberg, Raul. 1985. *The Destruction of the European Jews* (Vols. 1, 2, and 3). New York: Holmes & Meier Publishers.

Hinton, William. 1997. *Fanshen: A Documentary of Revolution in a Chinese Village*. Berkeley: University of California Press.

Hua Linshan 华林山. 1996. "Wen'ge qijian qunzhongxing duili paixi chengyin" 文革期间群众性对立派系成因 ["The Origins of Mass Factionalism during the Cultural Revolution"], in *Wenhuadageming: shishi yu yanjiu* 文化大革命：史实与研究 [*The Cultural Revolution: Histories and Research*], edited by Liu Qinfeng 刘青峰 (pp. 191–208). Hong Kong: Chinese University of Hong Kong Press, 1996.

Huang, Philip C. C. 1985. *The Peasant Economy and Social Change in North China*. Stanford, CA: Stanford University Press.

Huang Ronghua 黄荣华. 2006. *Geming yu xiangcun: Nongcun diquan yanjiu: 1949–1983, yi hubeisheng xinzhouxian wei ge'an* 革命与乡村：农村地权研究：1949–1983，以湖北省新洲县为个案 [*Revolution and Village: A Study of Land Property Rights, 1949–1983, The Case of Xinzhou Xian, Hubei Province*]. Shanghai: Shanghai shehui kexueyuan chubanshe.

Huaxian Zhi: Wenhua dageming zhi 华县志："文化大革命"志. Unpublished documents.

Hunan sheng Daoxian xianzhi bianzuan weiyuanhui bian 湖南省道县县志编纂委员会. 1994. *Daoxian zhi* 道县志 [*Dao County Gazetteer*]. Beijing: Zhongguo shehui chubanshe.

Hu Xizhang 胡希张, Mo Rifen 莫日芬, Dong Li 董励, and Zhang Weigeng 张维耿 1997. *Kejia fenghua* 客家风华. Guangdong: Guangdong remin chubanshe.

Jing, Jun. 1996. *The Temple of Memories: History, Power, and Morality in a Chinese Village*. Stanford, CA: Stanford University Press.

Johnson, Chalmers A. 1962. *Peasant Nationalism and Communist Power: The Emergence of Revolutionary China 1937–1945*. Stanford, CA: Stanford University Press.

Johnston, Hank, and Bert Klandermans (eds.). 1995. *Social Movements and Culture*. Minneapolis: University of Minnesota Press.

Kalyvas, Stathis N. 1999. "Wanton and Senseless?: The Logic of Massacres in Algeria." *Rationality and Society*, Vol. 11, No. 3: 243–285.

Kalyvas, Stathis N. 2003. "The Ontology of 'Political Violence': Action and Identity in Civil Wars." *Perspectives on Politics*, Vol. 1, No. 3 (September 2003): 475–494.

Kalyvas, Stathis N. 2006. *The Logic of Violence in Civil War*. New York: Cambridge University Press.

Kelman, Herbert C., and V. Lee Hamilton. 1989. *Crimes of Obedience: Toward A Social Psychology of Authority and Responsibility*. New Haven, CT: Yale University Press.

Kepel, Gilles. 2002. *Jihad: The Trail of Political Islam* (translated by Anthony F. Roberts). Cambridge, MA: Belknap Press of Harvard University Press.

Kiernan, Ben. 1985. *How Pol Pot Came to Power: Colonialism, Nationalism, and Communism in Cambodia, 1930–1975* (second edition). New Haven, CT: Yale University Press.

Kiernan, Ben. 2002. *The Pol Pot Regime: Race, Power, and Genocide in Cambodia under the Khmer Rouge, 1975–79* (second edition). New Haven, CT: Yale University Press.

Kuhn, Thomas S. 1996. *The Structure of Scientific Revolutions*. Chicago: University of Chicago Press.

Kuper, Leo. 1981. *Genocide: Its Political Use in the Twentieth Century*. New York: Penguin Books.

Kuper, Leo. 1985. *The Prevention of Genocide*. New Haven, CT: Yale University Press.

Ladany, Laszlo. 1992. *Law and Legality in China: The Testament of a China-Watcher*. London: Hurst & Company.

Lee, Hong Yung. 1978. *The Politics of the Chinese Cultural Revolution: A Case Study*. Berkeley: University of California Press.

Lemkin, Raphael. 1944. *Axis Rule in Occupied Europe*. Washington, DC: Carnegie Endowment.

Lentin, Ronit, and Robbie McVeigh. 2006. *After Optimism?: Ireland, Racism and Globalisation*. Dublin: Metro Eireann Publications.

Li Zijing 黎自京. 1996. "Zhonggong an cheng Mao baozheng haiguo yangmin: er qian liu bai wan ren cansi" 中共暗承毛暴政害国殃民: 二千六百万人惨死 ["The CCP Admission of Atrocities under Mao's Brutal Rule: 26,000,000 Deaths"]. *Cheng Ming* 228: 14–17.

Liu Ping 刘平. 2003. *Bei yiwang de zhanzheng: Xianfeng Tongzhi nianjian Guangdong tuke daxiedou yanjiu* 被遗忘的战争 – 咸丰同治年间广东土客大械斗研究 [*The Hakka–Punti War in Guangdong 1854–1867*]. Beijing: Shangwu yinshuguan.

Lubman, Stanley B. 1999. *Bird in a Cage: Legal Reform in China after Mao*. Stanford, CA: Stanford University Press.

Luo Xianglin 罗香林. 1971. *Zhongguo zupu yanjiu* 中国族谱研究. Hong Kong: Zhongguo xueshe.

Luo Xianglin 罗香林. 1979. *Kejia yuanliu kao* 客家源流考. Shijie keshu zonghui mishuchu.

Luo Xianglin 罗香林. 1992. *Kejia yanjiu daolun* 客家研究导论. Shanghai: Shanghai wenyi chubanshe.

Ma Jisen 马继森. 2003. *Waijiaobu wenge jishi* 外交部文革纪实 [*The Cultural Revolution in the Foreign Ministry*]. Hong Kong: Chinese University of Hong Kong Press.

Maass, Peter. 1997. *Love Thy Neighbor: A Story of War*. New York: Vantage Books.

Macfarquhar, Roderick. 1960. *The Hundred Flowers*. London: Stevens and Sons.

Macfarquhar, Roderick. 1974. *The Origins of the Cultural Revolution: Vol. 1, Contradictions Among the People, 1956–1957*. Oxford: Oxford University Press.

Macfarquhar, Roderick. 1983. *The Origins of the Cultural Revolution: Vol. 2, The Great Leap Forward 1958–1960*. New York: Columbia University Press.

Macfarquhar, Roderick. 1991. "The Succession to Mao and the End of Maoism" in *The Cambridge History of China, Volume 15: The People's Republic, Part 2: Revolutions within the Chinese Revolution, 1966–1982*, edited by John Fairbank and Roderick Macfarquhar (pp. abc-de). Cambridge: Cambridge University Press.

Macfarquhar, Roderick. 1997. *The Origins of the Cultural Revolution: Vol. 3, The Coming Cataclysm 1961–1966*. New York: Columbia University Press.

MacFarquhar, Roderick, and Michael Schoenhals. 2006. *Mao's Last Revolution*. Cambridge, MA: The Belknap Press of Harvard University Press.

Mann, Michael. 2000. "Were the Perpetrators of Genocide 'Ordinary Men' or 'Real Nazis'? Results from Fifteen Hundred Biographies." *Holocaust and Genocide Studies* 14(3): 331–366.

Mann, Michael. 2005. *The Dark Side of Democracy: Explaining Ethnic Cleansing*. New York: Cambridge University Press.

Mao, Zedong. 1962. *On Guerrilla Warfare*. New York: Prager.

Mao, Zedong. 1994. "Report on the Peasant Movement in Hunan" in *Mao's Road to Power: Revolutionary Writings 1912–1949 (Vol. II)*, edited by Stuart R. Schram (pp. 429–464). Armonk, NY: M. E. Sharpe.

Markoff, John. 1985. "The Social Geography of Rural Revolt at the Beginning of the French Revolution." *American Sociological Review* 50: 761–781.

Markoff, John. 1997. *The Abolition of Feudalism: Peasants, Lords and Legislators in the French Revolution*, University Park: The Pennsylvania State University Press.

Marx, Karl. 1959. "Eighteenth Brumaire of Louis Bonaparte" in *Marx and Engles: Basic Writing on Politics and Philosophy*, edited by Lewis S. Feurer (pp. abc-de). Garden City, NY: Doubleday.

Marx, Karl. 1978. "Manifesto of the Communist Party" in *The Marx-Engels Reader*, edited by Robert C. Tucker (pp. abc-de). New York: W.W. Norton Company.

Mazian, Florence. 1990. *Why Genocide? The Armenian and Jewish Experiences in Perspective*. Ames: Iowa State University Press.

McAdam, Doug. [1982] 2000 (second edition). *Political Process and the Development of Black Insurgency, 1930–1970*. Chicago, IL: The University of Chicago Press.

McAdam, Doug. 1998. "On the International Origins of Domestic Political Opportunities" in *Social Movements and American Political Institutions*, edited by Anne N. McFarland and Andrew S. Costain (pp. abc-de). Lanham, MD: Rowman and Littlefield.

McAdam, Doug. 1983. "Tactical Innovation and the Pace of Insurgency." *American Sociological Review* 48(6): 735–754.

McAdam, Doug, John D. McCarthy, and Mayer Zald (eds.). 1996. *Comparative Perspectives on Social Movements: Political Opportunities, Mobilizing Structures, and Cultural Framings*. New York: Cambridge University Press.

McAdam, Doug, Sidney Tarrow, and Charles Tilly. 2001. *Dynamics of Contention*. New York: Cambridge University Press.

McCarthy, John D., and Mayer N. Zald. 1977. "Resource Mobilization and Social Movements: A Partial Theory." *American Journal of Sociology* 82: 1212–1241.

McGovern, James, R. 1982. *Anatomy of a Lynching: The Killing of Claude Neal*. Baton Rouge: Louisiana State University Press.

McVeigh, Rory. 2006. "Structural Influences on Activism and Crime: Identifying the Social Structure of Discontent." *American Journal of Sociology* 112: 510–566.

McVeigh, Rory, and Juliana Sobolewski. 2007. "Red Counties, Blue Counties, and Occupational Segregation by Sex and Race." *American Journal of Sociology* 113: 446–506.

Meyer, David S. 1990. *A Winter of Discontent: The Nuclear Freeze and American Politics*. New York: Prager.

Meyer, David S. 1995. "Framing National Security: Elite Public Discourse on Nuclear Weapons during the Cold War." *Political Communication* 12: 173–192.

Meyers, Daniel. 2000. "The Diffusion of Collective Violence: Infectiousness, Susceptibility, and Mass Media Networks." *American Journal of Sociology* 106: 173–208.

Milgram, Stanley. 1963. "Behavioral Study of Obedience." *Journal of Abnormal and Social Psychology* 67: 371–378.

Milgram, Stanley. 1974. *Obedience to Authority: An Experimental View*. New York: Harper and Row.

Ministry of Civil Affairs, The People's Republic of China (ed.). 1998. 中华人民共和国民政部编. *Zhonghua renmin gongheguo xingzheng quhua, 1949–1997* 中华人民共和国行政区划 [*Jurisdiction Zoning of The People's Republic of China, 1949–1997*]. Beijing: Zhongguo shehui chubanshe.

Norton, Mary Beth. 2002. *In the Devil's Snare: The Salem Witchcraft Crisis of 1692*. New York: Alfred A. Knopf.

O'Brien, Kevin J., and Lianjiang Li. 2006. *Rightful Resistance in Rural China*. Cambridge: Cambridge University Press.

Oi, Jean C. 1989. *State and Peasant in Contemporary China: Political Economy of Village Government*. Berkeley: University of California Press.

Olzak, Susan. 1989a. "Analysis of Events in Study of Collective Action." *Annual Review of Sociology* 15: 119–141.

Olzak, Susan. 1989b. "Labor Unrest, Immigration, and Ethnic Conflict in Urban America, 1880–1914." *American Journal of Sociology* 94: 1303–1333.

Olzak, Susan. 1992. *The Dynamics of Ethnic Competition and Conflict*. Stanford, CA: Stanford University Press.

Ouchi, William G. 1977. "The Relationship between Organizational Structure and Organizational Control." *Administrative Science Quarterly* 22: 95–113.

Ouchi, William G. 1978. "The Transmission of Control through Organizational Hierarchy." *The Academy of Management Journal* 21: 173–192.

Ouchi, William G. 1979. "A Conceptual Framework for the Design of Organizational Control Mechanisms." *Management Science* 25: 833–848.

Pang Xianzhi 逄先知 and Jin Chongji 金冲及 (eds.). 2006. *Mao Zedong Zhuan 1949–1976*. 毛泽东传 1949–1976 [*The Biography of Mao Zedong 1949–1976*]. Beijing: Zhonggong zhongyang wenxian yanjiushi.

Perrow, Charles. 1979. *Complex Organizations: A Critical Essay* (second edition). Glenview, IL: Scott, Foresman and Company.

Perry, Elizabeth J. 2006. *Patrolling the Revolution: Worker Militias, Citizenship, and the Modern Chinese State*. Lanham, MD: Rowman & Littlefield.

Perry, Elizabeth J., and Xun Li. 1997. *Proletarian Power: Shanghai in the Cultural Revolution*. Boulder, CO: Westview Press.

Polonsky, Antony, and Joanna B. Michlic (eds.). 2004. *The Neighbors Respond: The Controversy over the Jedwabne Massacre in Poland*. Princeton, NJ: Princeton University Press.

Potter, Pitman B. 2003. *From Leninist Discipline to Socialist Legalism: Peng Zhen on Law and Political Authority in the PRC*. Stanford, CA: Stanford University Press.

Potter, Sulamith Heins, and Jack M. Potter. 1990. *China's Peasants: The Anthropology of a Revolution*. New York: Cambridge University Press.

Power, Samantha. 2002. *A Problem from Hell: America and the Age of Genocide*. New York: Basic Books.

Prunier, Gerard. 2007. *Darfur: The Ambiguous Genocide*. Ithaca, NY: Cornell University Press.

Qian Mu 钱穆. 1994. *Zhongguo wenhua shi daolun* 中国文化史导论 [*Introduction to the History of the Chinese Culture*]. Taipei, Taiwan: Shangwu yinshuguan.

Qu Jiang. 1982. Da xianzhi bangongshi, "Jixu 'wenhua da geming' yi xi buyi cu" 记叙'文化大革命'宜细不宜粗 ["The 'Cultural Revolution' should be narrated in detail, not in broad strokes"], *Sichuan difangzhi tongxun* 四川地方志通讯 [*Sichuan Local Gazetteers Newsletter*], 1: 7–9.

Ragin, Charles C. 1987. *The Comparative Method: Moving Beyond Qualitative and Quantitative Strategies*. Berkeley and London: University of California Press.

Ragin, Charles C. 2000. *Fuzzy-Set Social Science*. Chicago and London: University of Chicago Press.

Ritzer, George. 1974. *Sociology: A Multiple Paradigm Science*. Boston: Allyn and Bacon.

Rosen, Stanley. 1979. *The Origins and Development of the Red Guard Movement in China, 1960–1968*. Ph.D. Dissertation, Department of Political Science, University of California, Los Angeles.

Rosen, Stanley. 1982. *Red Guard Factionalism and the Cultural Revolution in Guangzhou (Canton)*. Boulder, CO: Westview Press.

Rosenthal, Bernard. 1993. *Salem Story: Reading the Witch Trials of 1692*. New York: Cambridge University Press.

Ross, Lee, and Richard E. Nisbett. 1991. *The Person and the Situation: Perspectives of Social Psychology*. Philadelphia, PA: Temple University Press.

Roy, Beth. 1994. *Some Trouble with Cows: Making Sense of Social Conflict*. Berkeley: University of California Press.

Rule, James. 1988. *Theories of Civil Violence*. Berkeley: University of California Press.

Rummel, R. J. 1990. *Lethal Politics: Soviet Genocide and Mass Murder since 1917*. New Brunswick, NJ: Transaction Publishers.

Schoenhals, Michael (ed.). 1996. *China's Cultural Revolution, 1966–1969: Not a Dinner Party*. Armonk, NY: M. E. Sharpe.

Schurmann, Franz. 1968. *Ideology and Organization in Communist China* (second edition). Berkeley: University of California Press.

Selden, Mark. 1971. *The Yenan Way in Revolutionary China*. Cambridge, MA: Harvard University Press.

Selden, Mark. 1995. *China in Revolution: The Yenan Way Revisited*. Armonk, NY and London: M. E. Sharpe.

Shirer, William L. 1967. *The Rise and Fall of the Third Reich: A History of Nazi Germany*. Greenwich, CT: A Fawcett Crest Book.

Shirk, Susan L. 1982. *Competitive Comrades: Career Incentives and Student Strategies in China*. Berkeley: University of California Press.

Short, Philip. 2005. *Pol Pot: Anatomy of a Nightmare*. New York: Henry Holt and Company.

Siu, Helen F. 1989. *Agents and Victims in South China: Accomplices in Rural Revolution*. New Haven, CT: Yale University Press.

Skinner, G. William. 1978. "Vegetable Supply and Marketing in Chinese Cities." *The China Quarterly* 76: 733–793.

Skinner, G. William. 1985. "Rural Marketing in China: Repression and Revival." *The China Quarterly* 103: 393–413.

Skinner, G. William. 2001. *Marketing and Social Structure in Rural China*. Ann Arbor, MI: Association for Asian Studies.

Skocpol, Theda. 1979. *States and Social Revolutions: A Comparative Analysis of France, Russia, and China*. New York: Cambridge University Press.

Smelser, Neil J. 1962. *Theory of Collective Behavior*. New York: The Free Press.

Snow, David A., and Robert D. Benford. 1992. "Master Frames and Cycles of Protest" in *Frontiers in Social Movement Theory*, edited by Aldon D. Morris and Carol McClurg Mueller (pp. 133–155). New Haven, CT: Yale University Press.

Snow, David A., E. Burke Rochford, Jr., Steven K. Worden, and Robert D. Benford. 1986. "Frame Alignment Processes, Micromobilization, and Movement Participation." *American Sociological Review* 51(4): 464–481.

Snyder, David, and Charles Tilly. 1972. "Hardship and Collective Violence in France 1830 to 1960." *American Sociological Review* 37: 520–532.

Solinger, Dorothy J. 1977. *Regional Government and Political Integration in Southwest China, 1949–1954: A Case Study*. Berkeley: University of California Press.

Solinger, Dorothy J. 1999. *Contesting Citizenship in Urban China: Peasant Migrants, the State, and the Logic of the Market*. Berkeley: University of California Press.

Solzhenitsyn, Aleksandr. 1974–1978. *The Gulag Archipelago, 1918–1956: An Experiment in Literary Investigation, I-VII*. New York: Harper & Row.

Song, Yongyi 宋永毅 (ed.). 2002a. *Wen'ge datusha* 文革大屠杀 [*Massacres during the Cultural Revolution*]. Hong Kong: Kaifang zazhishe.

Song, Yongyi (ed.). 2002b. *The Chinese Cultural Revolution Database* (CD-ROM). Hong Kong: Universities Service Centre for China Studies, Chinese University of Hong Kong.

Soule, Sarah, and David Strang. 1998. "Diffusion in Organizations and Social Movements: From Hybrid Corn to Poison Pills." *Annual Review of Sociology* 24: 265–290.

Soule, Sarah A., and Y. Zylan. 1997. "Runaway Train? The Diffusion of State-Level Reform to AFDC Eligibility Requirements, 1950–1967." *American Journal of Sociology* 103: 733–762.

Spence, Jonathan D. 1996. *God's Chinese Son: The Taiping Heavenly Kingdom of Hong Xiuquan*. New York: W.W. Norton.

Starkey, Marion Lena. 1969. *The Devil in Massachusetts: A Modern Enquiry into the Salem Witch Trials*. Garden City, NY: Doubleday & Co.

Straus, Scott. 2006. *The Order of Genocide: Race, Power and War in Rwanda*. Ithaca, NY: Cornell University Press.

Su, Yang. 1992. 苏阳 "Jingzu jizu huodong zhong de cunmin yu zuzhi – 1992 nian dui zhongguo xibei kongxing shancun de shidi diaocha" 敬祖祭祖活动中的村民与组织 – 1992 年对中 国西北孔姓山村的实地调查。*Shehuixue yu shehui diaochao* (February).

Su, Yang. 2003a. *Tumult from Within: State Bureaucrats and Chinese Mass Movement, 1966–71*. Ph.D. Dissertation. Stanford, CA: Stanford University.

Su, Yang. 2003b. "State Sponsorship or State Failure? Mass Killings in Rural China, 1967–68."Irvine: Center for the Study of Democracy, University of California, Irvine (Working paper).

Su, Yang. 2006. "Mass Killings in the Cultural Revolution: A Study of Three Provinces" in Paul Pickowicz, Joseph Esherick, and Andrew Walder (eds.), *China's Cultural Revolution as History* (pp. 96–123). Stanford, CA: Stanford University Press.

Sullivan, Andrew. 2005. "Atrocities in Plain Sight." *The New York Times*, January 13 Sunday Book Review.

Sutton, Donald S. 1995. "Consuming Counter-Revolution: The Ritual and Culture of Cannibalism in Wuxuan, Guangxi, China, May to July 1968." *Comparative Studies in Society and History* 7(1) (January): 136–172.

Tanigawa, Shinichi. 1999. "The Danwei and the Cultural Revolution: A Review Essay." *Ritsumeikan Journal of International Relations and Area Studies*, 14: 197–216.

Tarrow, Sidney. 1994. *Power in Movement: Social Movements, Collective Action and Politics*. New York: Cambridge University Press.

Thogersen, Stig, and Soren Clausen. 1992. "New Reflections in the Mirror: Local Chinese Gazetteers (*Difangzhi*) in the 1980s." *The Australian Journal of Chinese Affairs* 27: 161–184.

Tilly, Charles. 1964. *The Vendee*, Cambridge, MA: Harvard University Press.
Tilly, Charles. 1978. *From Mobilization to Revolution*. Reading, MA: Addison-Wesley.
Tilly, Charles. 2003a. *The Politics of Collective Violence*. New York: Cambridge University Press.
Tilly, Charles. 2003b. "Social Movement as Political Struggle" in *Encyclopedia of American Social Movements*, edited by Immanuel Ness (pp. abc-de). Armonk, NY: Sharpe Reference.
Tolnay, Stewart E., and E. M. Beck. 1995. *A Festival of Violence: An Analysis of Southern Lynchings, 1882–1930*. Urbana: University of Illinois Press.
Tolnay, Stewart E., and E. M. Beck. 1990. "Black Flight: Lethal Violence and the Great Migration, 1900–1930." *Social Science History* 14: 347–370.
Tolnay, Stewart E., Glenn Deane, and E. M. Beck. 1996. "Vicarious Violence: Spatial Effects on Southern Lynchings, 1890–1919." *The American Journal of Sociology* 102 (November): 788–815.
Unger, Jonathan. 1982. *Education under Mao: Class and Competition in Canton Schools, 1960–1980*. New York: Columbia University Press.
Unger, Jonathan. 2000. "Cultural Revolution in Villages." *The China Quarterly* 153 (March): 82–106.
Unger, Jonathan. 2002. *The Transformation of Rural China*. Armonk, NY: M. E. Sharpe.
Unger, Jonathan. 2007. "The Cultural Revolution at Grass Roots." *The China Journal* 57 (January): 109–137.
Useem, Bert. 1985. "Disorganization and the New Mexico Prison Riot of 1980." *American Sociological Review* 50: 677–688.
Valentino, Benjamin. 2004. *Final Solutions: Mass Killing and Genocide in the Twentieth Century*. Ithaca, NY: Cornell University Press.
Varshney, Ashutosh. 2002. *Ethnic Conflict and Civic Life: Hindus and Muslims in India*. New Haven, CT: Yale University Press.
Vermeer, Edward. 1992. "New County Histories: A Research Note on Their Compilation and Value." *Modern China* 18(4): 438–467.
Vogel, Ezra F. 1969. *Canton under Communism: Programs and Politics in a Provincial Capital, 1949–1968*. Cambridge, MA: Harvard University Press.
Walder, Andrew G. 1978. *Chang Ch'un-ch'iao and Shanghai's January Revolution*. Ann Arbor: Center for Chinese Studies of the University of Michigan.
Walder, Andrew G. 1986. *Communist Neo-Traditionalism: Work and Authority in Chinese Industry*. Berkeley: University of California Press.
Walder, Andrew G. 1987. "Actually Existing Maoism." *The Australian Journal of Chinese Affairs* 18: 155–166.
Walder, Andrew G. "Collective Behavior Revisited: Ideology and Politics in the Chinese Cultural Revolution." *Rationality and Society* 6 (3): 400–421.
Walder, Andrew G. "Cultural Revolution Radicalism: Variations on a Stalinist Theme" in *New Perspectives on the Cultural Revolution*, edited byW. Joseph, C. W. Wong, and David Zweig (pp. 41–62). Cambridge, MA: Harvard University Press.
Walder, Andrew G. 2000b. "Implications of Loss Avoidance for Theories of Social Movements." *Hong Kong Journal of Sociology* 1: 83–102.

Walder, Andrew G. 2002. “Beijing Red Guard Factionalism: Social Interpretations Reconsidered.” *Journal of Asian Studies* 61(2): 437–471.

Walder, Andrew G. 2006. “Ambiguity and Choice in Political Movements: The Origin of Beijing Red Guard Factionalism.” *American Journal of Sociology* 112: 710–750.

Walder, Andrew G., and Yang Su. 2003. “The Cultural Revolution in Countryside: Scope, Timing and Human Impact.” *The China Quarterly* 173: 74–99.

Wang Nianyi 王年_. 1988. *Da dongluan de niandai* 大动乱的年代 [*The Era of Great Turmoil*]. Henan: Henan renmin chubanshe.

Wang Shaoguang. 1995. *Failure of Charisma: The Cultural Revolution in Wuhan.* Hong Kong: Oxford University Press.

Wang Youmin 王友民. 2006. *Geming yu xiangcun: Jiefangqu tudi gaige yanjiu: 1941–1949, yi shandong junanxian wei ge'an* 革命与乡村: 解放区土地改革研究: 1941–1949, 以山东莒南县为个案 [*Revolution and Village: A Study on Land Reform in Liberated Area, 1941–1949, The Case of Luna County, Shandong*]. Shanghai: Shanghai shehui kexueyuan chubanshe.

Wang Youqin 王友琴. 2008. *Wen'ge shounan zhe: guanyu pohai, jianjin yu shalu de xunfang shilu* 文革受难者–关于迫害, 监禁与杀戮的寻访实录 [*The Victims of The Cultural Revolution*: Interviews on Persecution, *Imprisonment and Killing*]. Available at http://www.xindoor.com/zhuanyeziliao/ShowSoft.asp?SoftID=669; accessed August 26, 2008.

Watson, James L. 1975. *Emigration and the Chinese Lineage: The Mans in Hong Kong and London.* Berkeley: University of California Press.

Watson, James L. (ed.). 1984. *Class and Social Stratification in Post-Revolution China.* New York: Cambridge University Press.

Watson, James L., and Evelyn S. Rawski (eds.). 1988. *Death Ritual in Late Imperial and Modern China.* Berkeley: University of California Press.

Watson, Rubie S. 1985. *Inequality among Brothers: Class and Kinship in South China.* New York: Cambridge University Press.

Weber, Max.1958. “Politics as a Vocation” in *From Max Weber: Essays in Sociology*, edited by H. H. Gerth and C. Wright Mills (pp. 84–85). New York: Oxford University Press.

Weber, Max. 1978. *Economy and Society: An Outline of Interpretive Sociology.* Berkeley: University of California Press.

Wen Yuqiao 闻于樵. 2002. “Wen'ge 'qierwu jianghua': bujinjin shi Guangxi zaofan zuzhi de zhongjie” 文革七二五讲话: 不仅仅是造反组织的终结 [“July 25 Speech: Not Merely the Termination of Guangxi Rebel Organization”]. *Hua Xia Wen Zhai* [华夏文摘] vol. 287 (supplemental issue). Available at www.cnd.org, accessed August 11, 2008.

White III, Lynn T. 1991. *Policies of Chaos: The Organizational Causes of Violence in China's Cultural Revolution.* Princeton, NJ: Princeton University Press.

Whyte, Martin. 1974. *Small Groups and Political Rituals in China.* Berkeley: University of California Press.

Wilkinson, Steven. 2004. *Votes and Violence: Electoral Competition and Ethnic Riots in India.* New York: Cambridge University Press.

Wittfogel, Karl A. 1981. *Oriental Despotism: A Comparative Study of Total Power.* New York: Vintage Books.

Wood, Elisabeth J. 2000. *Forging Democracy from Below: Insurgent Transitions in South Africa and El Salvador*. New York: Cambridge University Press.

Wood, Elisabeth J. 2003. *Insurgent Collective Action and Civil War in El Salvador*. New York: Cambridge University Press.

Wu Songdi 吴松弟. 1997. *Zhongguo yiminshi: Disijuan* 中国移民史：第四卷 [*China's Immigration History: Volume 4*]. Fuzhou, Fujian: Fujian renmin chubanshe.

Xiao Donglian 肖东连, Xie Chuntao 谢春涛, Zhu Di 朱地, and Qiao Jining 乔继宁. 1999. *Qiusuo zhongguo: wen'ge qianshinian*, vols. 1, 2, 求索中国：文革前十年 (上，下) [*Exploring the Chinese Way: 10 Years before the Cultural Revolution*]. Beijing: Hongqi chubanshe.

Xu You-yu 徐友渔. 1999. *Xingxing sese de zaofan: hongweibing jingshen suzhi de xingcheng ji Yanbian* 形形色色的造反：红卫兵精神素质的形成及演变 [*Rebels of All Stripes: A Study of Red Guard Mentalities*]. Hong Kong: Xianggang zhongwen daxue chubanshe.

Xuan Ping. 1982. Chongqing shi shuili zhi bianji shi 重庆市水利志编辑室, "Zhide shensi de yipian wenzhang – 'Jixu "wenhua da geming" yi xi buyi cu' " 值得深思的_篇文章– "记叙'文化大革命'宜细不宜粗" ["An essay worth pondering – 'The "Cultural Revolution" should be narrated in detail, not in broad strokes"], *Sichuan difangzhi tongxun* 四川地方志通讯 [*Sichuan Local Gazetteers Newsletter*], 5: 40–41.

Yan Chongnian 阎崇年 (ed.). 1991. *Zhongguo shixian da zidian* 中国市县大字典 [*The Encyclopedia of Chinese Cities and Counties*]. Beijing: Zhonggong zhongyang dangxiao chubanshe.

Yang, C. K. 1959. *A Chinese Village in Early Communist Transition*. Cambridge, MA: The Technology Press.

Yang, Dali L. 1996. *Calamity and Reform in China: State, Rural Society, and Institutional Change since the Great Leap Famine*. Stanford, CA: Stanford University Press.

Yang, Guobin. 2000. "China's Red Guard Generation: The Ritual Process of Identity Transformation, 1966–1999." Ph.D. Dissertation, New York University.

Yang Kuisong 杨奎松. 2004. "Shanghai 'zhenfan' yundong de lishi kaocha" 上海"镇反"运动的历史考察 ["A Historical Examination of the Suppressing Counterrevolutionaries Campaign in Shanghai"]. *Huadong shifan daxuebao* 9.

Yang Kuisong 杨奎松. 2006. "Zhongguo 'zhenya fangeming' yundong yanjiu" 中国"镇压"反革命运动研究 ["Study on China's Suppressing Counter-Revolutionaries Campaign"]. *Shixue yuekan* 1.

Yang Li 杨立 (ed.). 1997. *Dai ci de hong meigui: Gudacun cenyuan lu* 带刺的红玫瑰：古大存沉冤录. Zhongong Guangdong chenwei dangshi yanjiushi.

Yu Luowen 遇罗文. 2002. "Beijing Daxing xian canan diaocha" 北京大兴县惨案调查 ["An Investigation of the Beijing Daxing Massacre"] in *Wen'ge da tusha* 文革大屠杀 [*Massacres in the Cultural Revolution*], edited by Song Yongyi 宋永毅 (pp.13–36). Hong Kong: Kaifang zazhishe.

Zhang Cheng 章成. 2001. "Daoxian da tusha" 道县大屠杀 ["The Daoxian Massacre"]. *Open Magazine* 开放杂志, July, August, September, and December issues.

Zhang Lianhe 张连和. 1998. "Wu jin Machun quan ting sha" 五进马村劝停杀 ["Five Visits to Ma Village to Dissuade Killings"] in *Nage niandia zhong de women*

那个年代中的我们 [*We as in That Era*], edited by Zhe Yongping 者永平 (pp. 398–404). Huhehot, Inner Mongolia: Yuanfang chubanshe.

Zhang Ning. 2008. "The Political Origins of Death Penalty Exceptionalism: Mao Zedong and the Practice of Capital Punishment in Contemporary China." *Punishment & Society* 10: 117–136.

Zhao Litao 赵力涛. 1999. "Jiazu yu cunzhuang zhengzhi (1950–1970): Hebei mou cun jiazu xianxiang yanjiu" 家族与村庄政治 (1950–1970): 河北某村家族现象研究. *Ershiyi shiji* 55 (October).

Zheng, Shiping. 1997. *Party vs. State in Post-1949 China: The Institutional Dilemma*. New York: Cambridge University Press.

Zheng, Xiaofeng 郑笑枫, and Shu Ling 舒玲. 1992. *Tao Zhu zhuan* 陶铸传 [*The Biography of Tao Zhu*]. Beijing: Zhongguo Qingnian Chubanshe.

Zheng Yi 郑义. 1993a. *Hongse jinianbei* 红色纪念碑 [*The Scarlet Memorial*]. Taipei, Taiwan: Huashi wenhua gongsi.

Zheng Yi 郑义. 1993b. "Guangxi chiren kuangchao zhenxiang: liuwang zhong ge qizi de di ba feng xin" 广西吃人狂潮真相: 流亡中给妻子的第八封信 ["The Truth about the Maddening Waves of Cannibalism in Guangxi: The 8th Letter from Exile to My Wife"], *Huaxia wenzhai* 华夏文摘 [*Chinese News Digest*], 15 (Supplemental Issue). Available at www.cnd.org, accessed August 23, 2003.

Zheng Yi 郑义. 1997. "Liangge wen'ge chuyi" 两个文革雏议 ["On Two Cultural Revolutions"]. *Huaxia wenzhai* 华夏文摘 [*Chinese News Digest*], 83 (Supplemental Issue): 1–14. Available at www.cnd.org, accessed August 23, 2003.

Zhengxi 郑正西, Guangxi tongzhi guan 广西通志馆. 1988. "'Cu' ji 'wenge' yu fenshi 'taiping'" "粗"记 "文革"与粉饰 "太平" ["Recording the 'Cultural Revolution' in broad strokes, and 'presenting a false picture of peace and prosperity'"]. *Sichuan difangzhi* 四川地方志 [*Sichuan Local Gazetteers*] 2: 13–14.

Zhong Wendian 钟文典. 2005a. *Guangxi kejia* 广西客家 [Guangxi Hakka]. Guilin, Guangxi: Guangxi shifan daxue chubanshe.

Zhong Wendian 钟文典. 2005b. *Fujian kejia* 福建客家 [Fujian Hakka]. Guilin: Guangxi shifan daxue chubanshe.

Zhonggong Xingning xianwei zuzhibu, Zhonggong Xingning xianwei dangshi ziliao zhengji yanjiu weiyuanhui bangongshi, Xingningxian Danganguan 中共兴宁县委组织部, 中共兴宁县委党史资料征集研究委员会办公室, 兴宁县档案馆合编. 1988. Zhonggong Guangdongsheng Xingningxian zuzhishi ziliao, Guangdongsheng Xingningxian zhengjuntongqun zuzhishi ziliao 中共广东省兴宁县组织史资料, 广东省兴宁县政军统群组织史资料. Unpublished documents.

Zhonggong zhongyang zuzhibu, Zhonggong Zhongyang renshibu 中共中央组织部人事部. 1999. *Zhongguo ganbu tongji wushinian: 1949–1998 nian ganbu tongji ziliao huibian* 中国干部统计五十年: 1949–1998 年干部统计资料汇编. Beijing: Dangjian duwu chubanshe.

Zhongguo renmin jiefangjun guofang daxue dangshi dangjian zhenggong jiaoyanshi 国防大学党史党建政工教研室. 1988. *Wenhua da geming yanjiu ziliao* 文化大革命研究资料 (上中下) [*The Cultural Revolution Research Materials*] Vols. 1–3. Beijing: Zhongguo renmin jiefanjun guofang daxue dangshi chubanshe (CRRM).

Zhou, Xueguang. 1993. "Unorganized Interests and Collective Action in Communist China." *American Sociological Review* 58: 54–73.

Zhu Jianguo 朱健国. 2008. Zhu Jianguo wenji: Guangdong weihe "fan difang zhuyi" 朱健国文集: 广东为何 "反地方主义", available at http://www.boxun.com/hero/zhujianguo/2_1.shtml, accessed August 20, 2008.

Zhu Zheng 朱正. 2004. *Fan youpai douzheng shimo*, vols. 1, 2. 反右派斗争始末(上, 下). Hong Kong: Mingbao chubanshe.

Zhulian yijia qikou de mingan 株连一家七口的命案. 1987. "The Causes for the Case that Killed Seven Family Members," Cangwu Party Ratification Office, July 31.

Zimbardo, Phil G. 1991. *Quiet Rage: The Stanford Prison Experiment* (video recording). Stanford, CA: Psychology Department, Stanford University.

Zuigao renmin fayuan yanjiushi 最高人民法院研究室. 2000. *Quanguo renmin fayuan sifa tongji lishi ziliao huibian: 1949–1998* (*Xingshi bufeng*) 全国人民法院司法统计历史资料汇编: 1949–1998 (刑事部分). Beijing: Renmin fayuan chubanshe.

List of Chinese *Xianzhi* (County Gazetters) Cited in the Text

Binyang xianzhi bianzuan weiyuanhui 宾阳县志编纂委员会 *Binyang xianzhi* 宾阳县志 [*Binyang County Gazetteer*]. Nanning: Guangxi renmin chubanshe, 1987.

Cangwu xianzhi bianzuan weiyuanhui 苍梧县志编纂委员会. *Cangwu xianzhi* 苍梧县志 [*Cangwu County Gazetteer*]. Nanning: Guangxi renmin chubanshe, 1997.

Dapu xian difangzhi bianzuan weiyuanhui 大埔县地方志编纂委员会, *Dapu xianzhi* 大埔县志 [*Dapu County Gazetteer*]. Guangzhou: Guangdong renmin chubanshe, 1992.

Debao xian difangzhi bianzuan weiyuanhui 德保县志编纂委员会. *Debao Xianzhi* 德保县志 [*Debao County Gazetteer*]. Nanning: Guangxi renmin chubanshe, 1998.

Du'an yaozu zizhixian difangzhi bangongshi 都安瑶族自治县地方志办公室. *Du'an Xianzhi* 都安县志 [*Du'an County Gazetteer*]. Nanning: Guangxi renmin chubanshe, 2002.

Gongcheng Yaozu zizhixian xianzhi bianzuan weiyuanhui 恭城瑶族自治县县志编纂委员会. *Gongcheng Xianzhi* 恭城县志 [*Gongcheng County Gazetteer*]. Nanning: Guangxi renmin chubanshe, 1992.

Guangdongsheng difangshizhi bianzuan weiyuanhui 广东省地方史志编纂委员会. 2001. *Guangdongsheng zhi zhonggong zuzhi zhi* 广东省志.中共组织志 [*Guangdong Province Gazetteers: The CCP Organizations*]. Guangzhou: Guangdong renmin chubanshe.

Guangdongsheng difangshizhi bianzuan weiyuanhui 广东省地方史志编纂委员会. 2004. *Guangdongsheng zhi zongsu* 广东省志.总述 [*Guangdong Province Gazetteers: The Summary*]. Guangzhou: Guangdong renmin chubanshe.

Hengxian xianzhi bianzuan weiyuanhui 横县县志编纂委员会. *Hengxian xianzhi* 横县县志 [*Hengxian County Gazetteer*]. Nanning: Guangxi renmin chubanshe, 1989.

Heping xian difangzhi bianzuan weiyuanhui 和平县地方志编纂委员会. *Heping Xianzhi* 和平县志 [*Heping County Gazetteer*]. Guangzhou: Guangdong renmin chubanshe, 1999.

Heyuan xian difangzhi bianzuan weiyuanhui 河源县地方志编纂委员会. *Heyuan Xianzhi* 河源县地方志 [*Heyuan County Gazetteer*]. Guangzhou: Guangdong renmin chubanshe, 2000.

Huaiji xianzhi bangongshi 怀集县志办公室. *Huaiji Xianzhi* 怀集县志 [*Huaiji County Gazetteer*]. Guangzhou: Guangdong renmin chubanshe, 2005.

Huaxian difangzhi bianzuan weiyuanhui 华县地方志编纂委员会. *Hua Xianzhi* 华县志 [*Huaxian County Gazetteer*]. Xi'an: Shannxi renmin chubanshe, 1992.

Huazhou xian difangzhi bianzuan weiyuanhui 化州县地方志编纂委员会. *Huazhou xianzhi* 化州县志 [*Huazhou County Gazetteer*]. Guangzhou: Guangdong renmin chubanshe, 1996.

Hunan sheng Daoxian xianzhi bianzuan weiyuanhui 湖南省道县县志编纂委员会. *Daoxian zhi* 道县志 [*Dao County Gazetteer*]. Beijing: Zhongguo shehui chubanshe, 1994.

Linggui xianzhi bianwei 临桂县志编委, *Lingui xianzhi* 临桂县志 [*Lingui County Gazetteer*]. Beijing: Fangzhi chubanshe, 1996.

Luchuan xianzhi bianzuan weiyuanhui 陆川县志编纂委员会. *Luchuan Xianzhi* 陆川县志 [*Luchuan County Gazetteer*]. Nanning: Guangxi renmin chubanshe, 1993.

Mengshan xianzhi bianzuan weiyuanhui 蒙山县志编纂委员会. *Mengshan Xianzhi* 蒙山县志 [*Mengshan County Gazetteer*]. Nanning: Guangxi renmin chubanshe, 1993.

Panyu shi difangzhi bianzuan weiyuanhui 番禺市地方志编纂委员会. *Panyu xianzhi* 番禺县志 [*Panyu County Gazetteer*]. Guangzhou: Guangdong renmin chubanshe, 1995.

Pingnan xianzhi bianzuan weiyuanhui 平南县志编纂委员会. *Pingnan Xianzhi* 平南县志 [*Pingnan County Gazetteer*]. Nanning: Guangxi renmin chubanshe, 1993.

Qujiang xian difangzhi bianzuan weiyuanhui 曲江县地方志编纂委员会. Qujiang xianzhi 曲江县志 [*Qujiang County Gazetteer*]. Beijing: Zhonghua shuju, 1999.

Tang Chuying 唐楚英 (ed.). *Quanzhou Xianzhi* 全州县志 [*Quanzhou County Gazetteer*]. Nanning: Guangxi renmin chubanshe, 1998.

Tiandong xianzhi bianzuan weiyuanhui 田东县志编纂委员会. *Tiandong Xianzhi* 田东县志 [*Tiandong County Gazetteer*]. Nanning: Guangxi renmin chubanshe, 1998.

Wuhua xian difang zhi bianzuan weiyuanhui 五华县地方志编纂委员会 *Wuhua Xianzhi* 五华县志 [*Wuhua County Gazetteer*]. Guangzhou: Guangdong renmin chubanshe, 1998.

Wuming xianzhi bianzuan weiyuanhui 武鸣县志编纂委员会. *Wuming xianzhi* 武鸣县志 [*Wuming County Gazetteer*]. Nanning: Guangxi renmin chubanshe, 1998.

Xianfeng xianzhi bianzuan weiyuanhui 咸丰县志编纂委员会, *Xianfeng xianzhi* 咸丰县志 [*Xianfeng County Gazetteer*]. Wuchang: Wuhan daxue chubanshe, 1990.

Xingning xian difang zhi bianxiu weiyuanhui 兴宁县地方志编修委员会 *Xingning xianzhi* 兴宁县志 [*Xingning County Gazetteer*]. Guangzhou: Guangdong renmin chubanshe, 1998.

Xinyi xian difangzhi bianzuan weiyuanhui 信宜县地方志编纂委员 *Xinyi xianzhi* 信宜县志 [*Xinyi County Gazetteer*]. Guangzhou: Guangdong renmin chubanshe, 1993.

Zhang Xiuqing 张秀清, *Chenghai xianzhi* 澄海县志 [*Chenghai County Gazetteer*]. Guangzhou: Guangdong renmin chubanshe, 1992.

List of Unpublished Chinese Documents on Wen'ge

Cangwu Party Ratification Office 苍梧整党办公室, "Zaocheng yanzhong houguo de 'sange huiyi'." 造成严重后果的"三个会议" ["Three Meetings That Caused Severe Consequences"].

Cangwu Party Ratification Office 苍梧整党办公室, "Zhulian yijia qikou de mingan" 株连一家七口的命案 ["The Causes for the Case that Killed Seven Family Members"], July 31, 1987.

GXWGDSNB, Guangxi wen'ge dashi nianbiao bianxie xiaozu 广西文革大事年表编写小组. *Guangxi wen'ge dashi nianbiao* 广西文革大事年表. Los Angeles, CA: The Service Centre for Chinese Publications, 1995.

Zhonggong Guangxi zhengdang bangongshi jimi dangan 中共广西整党办公室 [Guangxi Ratification Office]. *Guangxi Wenhua Da Geming Dashi Ji – 1968 nian* 广西文化大革命大事记 1968 年. Unpublished documents, 1987.

Zhonggong Nanning diwei zhengdang bangongshi 中共南宁地委整党办公室 [Nanning Ratification Office]. *Nanning diqu wenhua da geming dashi ji 1966–1976* 南宁地区文化大革命大事记 1966–1976. Unpublished documents, 1987.

List of Chinese Articles That Cite Unpublished Documents with Page Numbers

小平头: "青山遮不住, 毕竟东流去" – – "共特"封殺文革資訊阴谋破产记 Available at http://www.peacehall.com/news/gb/pubvp/2007/02/200702041005.shtml.

广西"反共救国团"冤案始末 – 文革机密档案揭密之一 Available at https://67.15.34.207/news/gb/kanshihai/shishi/2006/1101/172175.html.

广西融安大屠杀 – – 文革机密档案揭密之二 Available at http://www.xianqiao.net:8080/gb/7/1/6/n1581000.htm.

广西 "上石农总" 冤案始末 – – 文革机密档案揭密之三 Available at http://news.epochtimes.com/gb/7/3/8/n1639613.htm.

广西军区围剿凤山" 造反大军"真相 – – 文革机密档案揭密之四 Available at http://boxun.com/hero/2007/xiaopingtouyehua/63_1.shtml and http://boxun.com/hero/2007/xiaopingtouyehua/63_2.shtml.

广西文革人吃人事件揭密—文革秘档揭密之五 全文完 Available at http://www.64tianwang.com/Article_Show.asp?ArticleID=2319 六四天网》首发.

广西文革人吃人事件揭密—文革秘档揭密之五 (博讯2007年3月14日 转载) Available at http://boxun.com/hero/2007/xiaopingtouyehua/17_1.shtml and http://boxun.com/hero/2007/xiaopingtouyehua/17_2.shtml.

吴若愚: 中共机密文件记录的文革广西大屠杀 Available at http://www.boxun.com/hero/wenge/88_1.shtml.

晓明: 广西文革列传 Available at http://www.fireofliberty.org/oldsite/level4/issue3/4-wengeliezhuan-cover.htm.

Index

1911 Revolution, 86
1942 Yan'an Rectification Movement, 140

aboriginals, 79, 81–85, 90
"actually existing Maoism," 242
Amenta, Edwin, xvii, 17, 258, 260
Anti-Communist Army of Patriots, 40, 41
Anti-Communist Party Patriotic Army (ACPPA), 188, 203–208, 210, 215, 217, 230
Anti-Japanese War, 101, 109, 110, 216
anti-massacre committee, 203
Anti-Rightist Campaign, 119, 138, 140, 157, 163, 164, 273
anti-Semitic, 10
anti-Semitism, 14, 128, 246
April 22 or Four Twenty Two (FTT), 188, 189, 201–207, 210–212, 219, 225, 229
April 22nd Faction, 50, 61
Argentina, iii, 253, 271
armed battles, xiv, xvi, 37, 38, 41, 48, 50, 52, 142, 146, 174, 175, 200, 201, 209, 223, 224, 225, 232, 233, 235, 238, 239, 247, 265, 266
armed conflicts, 28, 195
Armenians, 97, 123
Asch, Solomon, 11
assassination squads, 40, 207, 215
atrocities, i, 5, 31, 35, 53, 59, 73, 75, 90, 92, 93, 131, 145, 193, 207, 218, 221, 225, 229, 242, 245, 257, 261
Atrocities in Plain Sight, 34, 242, 244, 245, 282
Auschwitz, 8

bad elements, 39, 40, 95, 117, 119, 129, 139
barricaded, 174
Beck, 246, 271, 283
Beijing, 25, 28, 40, 44, 45, 48–50, 53, 56, 59, 62, 72, 86, 87, 91, 138–140, 156, 161–163, 165, 167, 170–173, 175, 180, 183–185, 188, 190, 196, 198, 199, 201, 207, 208, 213, 223, 224, 248, 273, 274, 277, 279, 280, 284–288
Benford, Robert, 189
Binyang County, 3, 48, 64, 147, 148, 287
bivariate relationships, 230
black gangs, 172, 208
black groups, 40
black hands, 205, 207
border regions, 191, 199, 227, 251
bourgeois reactionary line, 26, 173, 176, 178
Boxer's Uprising, 86
Boyer, 5, 29, 245, 246, 272
breakdown, 19, 21, 22, 24, 64, 122, 222, 239, 243, 256, 257, 259
  recent breakdown theorists, 256
  traditional breakdown models, 256
Breslauer, George, 159
brigade, 39, 40, 43, 62, 64, 88, 118, 120, 209, 215, 216, 218, 219, 224, 248

Browning, Christopher, 128, 129
Bubei County, 61
Bush Administration, 246
bystander, 5, 6, 12, 13, 88

cadre, 58, 61, 75, 76, 78, 88, 107, 115–117, 131, 133, 134, 136, 139, 140, 145, 147, 148, 150, 155, 214, 218, 219, 224
cadre rectification, 138
Cambodia, 10, 97, 192, 261, 277
Cangwu, 31, 42–44, 55, 57, 58, 72–76, 88, 106, 117, 119, 120, 139, 145, 147–149, 163, 164, 167, 168, 177, 178, 193, 211, 213–219, 272, 287–289
Cantonese, 82, 83, 92
capital punishment, 158, 179–181
capitalist roaders, 54, 175, 208
capitalists, 99, 113, 116, 224
Central Military Commission, 178, 213
Central Military Committee, 48
chaos, 22, 157, 212
Chaozhou, 82, 83, 92
chronicle of major events (*dashiji*), 46
Chronology of the Cultural Revolution in Guangxi, 2, 58, 59
chuanlian. See Great Link-Up
Chusheng, 100
civil violence, 23
clan
  clan identities, 18, 32, 68, 69, 91
  clan tradition, 89, 92, 181, 226
  clan institutions, 79
class enemies, ix, xvi, 2, 12, 15, 17, 18, 33, 40, 41, 48, 50, 53, 56, 58, 60, 64, 68, 69, 75, 78, 95, 96–101, 103, 106, 108, 114–116, 118, 119, 121–124, 131, 140, 144, 148, 149, 151, 152, 157, 162, 185, 189, 190, 191, 194, 212–215, 219, 220, 222, 224, 235, 240, 251
  enemy class, 21, 29, 100, 106, 111, 114, 117, 123, 181
class struggle, 20, 21, 23, 27, 28, 33, 40, 62, 71, 76, 89, 93, 99, 101, 102, 112–114, 116, 119, 122, 123, 128, 142, 143, 147, 149, 150, 152–154, 165, 170, 176, 189, 190, 194, 212, 215, 219, 224, 233, 235, 247, 248, 251, 255
  class struggle doctrine, 212
Class-Struggle Education exhibitions, 204
classic breakdown models, 256
classic social movement agenda, 253
classicide, 8, 33, 99
cleansing the class ranks, 40
coercive, 114, 159
Cold War, 28, 279
collective action, 17, 19, 22, 23, 27, 127, 138, 141, 154, 159, 219, 243, 252, 253, 254, 255, 256, 257, 258
  character of collective action, 243
  emergence of collective action, 243
collective identities, 12, 14, 18–20, 22, 32, 36, 40, 62–64, 68–70, 83, 89, 91–93, 97, 123, 127, 128, 181, 223, 225, 229, 230, 233, 250
collective killings, i, xv, xvii, 2, 7, 9–21, 24, 27–42, 44, 48–50, 52–55, 60, 62–68, 70, 73, 75–78, 88, 91–94, 97, 109, 119, 124, 125, 127, 132, 133, 141, 142, 144, 149, 153, 154, 158, 160, 168, 175, 183–187, 190, 193, 203, 209, 217, 219–226, 229–233, 235–240, 242, 243, 245, 247–261, 265, 266, 268, 269
collective violence, 22, 23, 30, 89, 168
collectivization, 109, 114, 123, 134
commune, 3, 40, 43, 61, 62, 64, 77, 88–90, 95, 109, 118, 120, 125, 126, 145, 148, 149, 205, 207, 208, 214, 215, 218, 224, 248, 249
Communist countries, 8
communist revolution, 68
communities, xv, xvi, 4–7, 10–12, 14–21, 23, 24, 27, 29, 30, 31, 33, 34, 62, 67, 68–70, 82, 83, 85–87, 89, 93, 98, 101, 104–106, 109–111, 119, 120, 123, 124, 127–132, 142, 144, 150, 152, 154, 155, 159, 182, 187, 190, 191, 193, 207, 216, 219–225, 230, 231, 233, 234, 236, 240, 241, 244–246, 248–250, 253–261, 268
community model, 11, 14, 16, 18, 19, 21, 24, 30, 34, 62, 67, 98, 220–222, 225, 230, 231, 236, 240, 241, 243, 256, 260, 261, 268
community of killings, 255

Confucian, 80
Confucius, 81
conservative, 41, 46, 54, 62, 66, 174, 193, 210, 223, 226
conservative organizations, 198
conservative–radical thesis, 210
conspiracies, 18, 199
conspiracy groups, 33, 41, 58, 143, 191, 205, 208, 215
constitution, 116, 157, 160–164
contained politics, 19
contentious politics, 252
control measures, 236, 268
constructionist view, 97
Convention on the Prevention and Punishment of the Crime of Genocide, 7, 260
counter-guerrilla war, 192
 counter-guerrilla tactics, 193
 counter-guerrilla warfare, 192
counter-revolutionaries, 39, 40, 95, 116, 118, 119, 121, 180, 184, 188, 212, 224
counter-revolutionary, 29, 37, 77, 102, 116, 119, 121, 151, 166, 167, 181, 188, 198, 199, 200, 205, 206, 214, 215
County Archives, 73, 74, 76, 103
county gazetteers (*xianzhi*), 35
county leadership structure, 233
 heterogeneous leadership, 234, 239
County People's Armed Force Bureau (PAFB), 211
county revenue, 233
court-martial style, 160
covariates, 230, 265
Cultural Revolution Committee, 171
Cultural Revolution Leadership Group, 48

Dallin and Breslauer, 98, 114
Dallin, Alexander, 114, 159
Danwei, 142, 143, 282
Daoxian County, 47, 126, 151, 202
 Daoxian *xianzhi*, 47, 48, 288
Daoxian Massacre, 48, 53, 65, 68, 125, 142, 144, 146, 151–153, 184, 202, 216, 285
Darfur, xv, 261, 263, 280, 289
Daxing, 49, 285
death penalty, 158, 179, 180, 182, 286
decoupling, 24, 249
Dehuai, Peng, 156
demarcations, 14, 97
demobilization, 15, 16, 27, 28, 242, 248, 253, 259
 legal constraints, 15, 20, 33, 131, 155, 158, 186
demobilizing law, xviii, 33, 156
democide, 8
demotion, 134
Denmark, 59
dependent measure, 223, 236, 237
deterrent effect, 225, 250, 251
discrimination, 14, 76, 97, 98, 99, 187, 191, 254, 258, 259
distance from urban centers, 231
distinction between policy and policy outcomes, 250

Egypt, 253
El Salvador, 30, 253, 285
eliminationist killings, 12, 21, 24, 30, 97, 98, 187, 202, 225, 247, 257
eliminationist policies, 8, 258
Empress Dowager, 86
enablers, 13, 33, 127, 131, 144, 154
Enlai, Zhou, 118, 160, 175, 188, 196, 197, 207, 272
Etzioni, Amitai, 114, 159
execution
 executed, 32, 37, 39, 58, 161, 180, 181, 204, 205, 208, 217, 223
 executioners, 2, 4, 27, 88, 128, 150, 219, 239
 executions, 6, 29, 41, 53, 65, 77, 141, 154, 160, 177, 179, 180, 194, 225
 executions of captives, 223
extermination policy, 7, 187
extra-institutional politics, 24
extralegal, 7, 177

factionalism, 25, 77, 115, 174, 194, 212, 233, 234, 247, 251
factions, 6, 26, 28, 37, 39, 41, 62, 77, 190, 191, 193, 195, 197–201, 209–212, 225, 227, 235, 249
false, innocent, and wrongful cases, 42
famine of 1959–1961, 144
Fang, Fang, 117, 139
fault lines, 20, 93, 210, 211, 235

Fein, Helen, 14, 15, 257, 258
  "the universe of obligations," 15
Feng, Hai, 26, 31, 195, 197, 199, 200, 204, 205, 224, 235, 275
Fengkai County, 208
Fengshan County, 3, 41, 59, 60, 65, 188, 202
fenzi, 40, 107, 119–121, 153, 185
fieldwork, 70, 81
Final Solution, 10, 128, 129, 187, 191, 272
firearms, 39, 87, 102, 174, 183, 208
Five-Anti, 138
Four Types, 15, 16, 27, 29, 32, 33, 39, 40, 60, 62, 64, 65, 67, 95, 118–121, 126, 134, 146, 147, 150, 151, 153, 168, 181, 183, 193, 194, 202, 203, 207, 209, 210, 212–215, 217, 219, 229, 238, 240, 249, 254
Four-Clean, 116, 118, 275
framing, 6, 12, 16–19, 21, 22, 190, 220, 222, 228, 229, 235, 243, 252, 253, 256, 259
  attribution, 21
  diagnosis, 21, 118, 178, 190, 207, 219
  frame transformation, 189, 190
  framing action, 21
  master frame, 21, 189, 190, 220
framing war, ix, 33, 188
  war frame, 216
  warlike atmosphere, 238
freedom of speech, 161
French Revolution, 6, 30, 278
  Reign of Terror, 6
frontier, 79, 182
FTT. *See* April 22nd Faction
Fujian, 79, 82–85, 90, 272, 275, 285, 286
Fuzhi, Xie, 178, 184, 185

Gamson, William, 21, 189, 252
General Faction, 195, 197, 200, 211
genocides, i, xv, xvii, 2, 4, 6, 8–10, 12, 13, 16, 17, 30, 34, 69, 97, 129, 187, 191, 243, 245, 246, 257, 258, 260, 261, 263
geographical location, 246, 259
geographical variations, 12, 250
Gestapo, 11
"ghost and demons," 73
global mobilization. *See* state mobilization
GMD. *See* Guomindang (GMD)
Goldhagen, Daniel, 4, 10, 128
Gould, Roger, 69
Gourevitch, 6, 10, 97, 245, 275
Grasp Revolution, Promote Production (GRPP) headquarters, 176
Great Armed Battles, 195
Great Leap Forward, iii, 134, 144, 169, 272, 278
Great Link-Up, 173
great unity, 196, 197, 203, 211
Gross, Jan, 5, 11, 245, 246, 275
  Jedwabne, 5, 6, 10, 244, 245, 246, 275, 280
GRPP headquarters. *See* Grasp Revolution, Promote Production (GRPP) headquarters
Guangxi Problem, 200, 201
Guangxi University, 205, 207
Guangxi Wenge Dashi Nianbiao (GWGDSNB). *See* Chronology of the Cultural Revolution in Guangxi
Guangya High School, 196
Guangzhou, 26, 31, 43, 63, 84, 96, 104, 106, 117, 120, 138, 141, 164–166, 168, 178, 195, 197, 199, 200, 204, 205, 208, 211, 224, 235
guerrilla leaders, 116
guerrillas, 16, 192, 216
guest people. *See* Hakka
Guomindang (GMD), 71, 76, 204
Guoqing, Wei, 201
Gurr, Ted, 9
GWGDSNB. *See* Chronology of the Cultural Revolution in Guangxi

Hainan Island, 82
Hakka
  Hakka counties, 4, 84, 92, 94
  Hakka dialect, 4, 84
  Hakkas, 70
  non-Hakka, 92, 233
Han
  Hans, 82
  Han Chinese, 69, 79, 82, 91, 92, 233, 238
Han Dynasty, 82
Hannah Arendt, 9
  banality of evil, 9
Harrf, Barbara, 9
hidden treasures, 75, 107

Hilberg, Raul, 8, 10
The Destruction of the European Jews, 8
Holocaust, 4, 7–10, 15, 97, 128, 129, 187, 229, 243, 257, 258, 260, 263, 272, 274–276, 278
Hitler, 4, 7, 10, 128, 129, 275
Nazi, 5, 7, 15, 123, 128–130, 153, 187, 191, 192, 244, 246, 258, 261, 271, 272, 274, 281
Hong Kong, xviii, 25, 26, 28, 31, 42, 45, 50, 53, 79, 84, 101, 117, 138, 140, 141, 149, 157, 164, 193, 195, 196, 198, 201, 224, 227, 235, 251, 262, 273, 275–278, 282–285, 287
Universities Service Centre Library, 45
Huangpu [Whampoa] Military Academy, 101
Hubei Province, 54, 222, 226
hukuo, 132
Hunan, 1, 2, 4, 28, 31, 47, 48, 53, 56, 57, 99, 108, 114, 142, 151, 161, 179, 180, 184, 202, 215, 278, 288

ideological conviction, 130, 154
ideological terms, 130
indiscriminate beatings and killings (*luanda luansha*), 183–185
infidels, 12
informants, xvii, xviii, 2, 5, 31, 32, 36, 70, 75, 78, 89, 108, 120, 151, 153, 168
information flows, 186, 225, 261
Inner Mongolia, 28, 50, 53, 56, 57, 184, 199, 228, 286
institutional politics, 243
Iraq war, 245
Haditha, 23, 245, 246, 255

January Power Seizure, 174
January Storm, 178
Japanese, 16, 101, 109, 110, 192, 193, 216
Japanese War, *see* Anti-Japanese War
Jews, 5, 7, 8, 10, 12, 97, 123, 128, 153, 187, 191, 192, 244, 246, 258, 274, 276
Jiangxi, 47, 56, 76, 83, 85, 180, 199, 209, 228, 251
July 3rd Bulletin, 61
July 3rd Notice, 48, 200, 206, 207, 208, 209, 213
jurisdictions, 18, 28, 36, 42–44, 50, 53, 55, 62–64, 72, 74, 148, 150, 186, 193, 196, 198, 240, 260

Kai-shek, Chaing, 146
Kalyvas, Stathis, 194
Kennedy, Robert, 261
key-point units, 171
Khrushchev, Nikita, 162
killers, 4, 7, 8, 10, 13, 15, 18, 20, 23, 29, 30, 33, 73, 109, 127, 128, 129, 130, 131, 144, 152, 153, 154, 155, 217, 221, 224, 239, 244, 255
Korean War, 1, 117, 161, 216
Kuhn, Thomas, 253

Ladany, Laszlo, 160, 161
land reform, xiv, 31, 40, 75, 100, 104, 107, 161, 284
rectification, 102, 103, 107, 114, 116, 139, 140
Land Reform Rectification campaign, 75
landlords, 1, 2, 3, 31, 39, 40, 57, 58, 68, 70, 71, 75–77, 89, 95, 96, 98–102, 104–113, 115–121, 126, 133, 139, 151, 152, 156, 161, 172, 181, 194, 208, 209, 212, 215–218, 224, 244
law and order, 23, 244, 255
lawlessness, 156
leadership cleavage, 235
leftist deviations, 182
legal institutions, 168, 177, 186, 222, 242, 259, 260
legal mode, 158
legal system, xviii, 12, 157, 159–162, 164, 167, 178
legalistic and moralistic approach, 262
Lemkin, Raphael, 7, 260
Lenin, 179
li, 1, 101
Lingnan, 79, 81–83
Lingui County, 62, 64
Little Red Book, 79
Liu Xiaoyuan, 4
local and outside cadres, 234
local political processes, 251
localism, 234
anti-localism, 235
Los Angeles, 58, 184, 201, 244, 275, 280, 289
lull of mobilization, 141

lynching, 7, 244, 257
lynch mob, 7, 58
lynchings, 65, 246

Maass, Peter, 3
Love Thy Neighbor, 3
Mandarin, 82
Mann, Michael, 6, 10, 97, 98, 123, 128, 129, 159, 192
Mao, i, iii, ix, xvi, xviii, 4, 21, 25, 27–29, 32–34, 37, 45, 70, 77, 78, 80, 87, 90, 95, 96, 100, 101, 109, 113, 114, 123, 125, 127, 131–133, 138–140, 144, 145, 149, 152, 154–156, 158–164, 168, 172, 173, 175, 176, 178–180, 182, 184–186, 192–194, 196, 198, 201, 204, 210, 212, 213, 219, 222, 242, 247, 249, 257, 260–262, 272, 273, 277, 278, 280, 283, 286
Maoist, xvi, 17, 20, 26, 29, 33, 113, 123, 140, 153, 159, 176, 180, 181, 186, 193, 262
Maoism, 127, 158, 242, 247, 262, 278, 283
mass action, 25–27
mass campaign, 138, 155, 157–159, 165, 168, 175, 176, 207, 250
mass dictatorship, 40, 60, 214, 217
mass factions, 174
mass justice, 160, 175, 177
mass killings, i, xv, xvii, 2, 4, 6, 9–15, 33, 34, 38, 49, 63, 77, 97, 98, 123, 129, 147, 191–193, 203, 215, 219, 243, 247–249, 257, 260, 261, 263
mass movement
mass campaigns, 26, 100, 101, 138, 140, 142, 157, 160, 168, 175, 176, 182, 186, 240, 249
political campaigns, 26, 71, 99, 115, 155, 164, 168, 171, 239
May 16 Notice, 171
Mazian, Florence, 15, 17, 97
McAdam, Doug, iii, xvii, xviii, 12, 19, 20, 22, 127, 141, 142, 252, 258
McAdam tactical innovations, 23, 187
McCarthy, John, xvii, 20, 252
McPhail, Clark, 22, 23
Mengshan, 31, 41–44, 73–75, 82, 88, 106, 109, 164, 176, 216, 288
Mengshan County, 42, 44
Meyer, David, xviii, 20
Milgram, Stanley, 11, 128
Milgram experiment, 11, 128
militias, 1, 10, 12, 15, 27, 31, 33, 39, 41, 58, 60, 61, 65, 67, 68, 71, 76–78, 86, 95, 103, 115, 120, 121, 125–127, 130–132, 145, 146, 148, 150–154, 167, 168, 176, 177, 202, 203, 207, 209, 214, 215, 217, 218, 224, 229, 244, 261
Ming, Xiao, 59, 193
Minnan, 82
Minority at Risk, 9
misfits, 130
mobilization apparatus, 19, 21, 23, 255, 257
mobilization paradigm, 252
mobilization regime, 33
moral constraints, 190
multiple regression, 223, 230, 233, 236
multivariate analysis, xv, 236, 239
regression analyses, 222, 236
My Lai Massacre, 9, 245

Nanning, 28, 39, 41, 43, 44, 47–49, 57–60, 62, 72, 74, 83, 106, 118–120, 125, 147, 148, 164, 167, 173, 176, 177, 178, 184, 201–205, 207, 208, 211, 213, 216, 223–225, 231, 244, 275, 287–289
National People's Congress (NPC), 161, 163, 274
national security, 191, 199, 227, 251
Nationalist Party. *See* Guomindang (GMD)
nation-state, 8, 9, 16, 243, 250, 260
Nazi Germany, 5, 15, 123, 187, 191, 192, 274, 281
neighbors, xv, 1, 2, 5, 11, 29, 30, 69, 103, 108, 115, 151, 154, 243–246, 260, 275, 280
"Never again!" 263
New Left, 262
Ning, Zhang, 158, 179, 180, 182, 286
Ningming, 3
Nissenbaum, 5, 29, 245, 246, 272
normative, 159
NPC. *See* National People's Congress

"old thoughts, old cultures, old customs, and old habits," 172
One Hundred Flowers Bloom, 163

ordinary men, ix, 33, 125, 127, 128, 129, 130, 144, 154, 272, 278
organizational control, 23, 114, 158, 164, 232, 255
organizational hole, 256
organizers, 13, 20, 23, 30, 33, 69, 88, 127, 130–132, 142, 144, 147–149, 153–155, 209, 224
Ouchi, William, 158
outcasts, 130, 156

PAF. *See* People's Armed Forces Office (PAF)
PAFB. *See* County People's Armed Force Bureau (PAFB)
PAFD. *See* People's Armed Force Department
 paradigm, 21, 22, 252, 253, 255
paradox of state sponsorship and state failure, 249
Party Center, 37, 48
Party organizational strength, 236
party bureaucratic mode, 158
party-state, 20, 23, 26, 67, 88, 113, 157, 160, 166, 170, 176, 210, 255, 257, 258
patterns of killing, ix, 221
peaceful land reform, 107, 116, 139
Pearl, 79
Pearl Delta, 79
People's Armed Forces Department, 41, 145, 150, 176, 177, 202, 203
People's Armed Forces Office (PAF), 60
People's Court, 122, 161, 162, 165, 217
People's Court Organization Law, 161
People's Daily, 138, 172, 175, 212
"people's enemy," 98
People's Procuratorate, 161, 162
people's tribunal, 160
perpetrators, xvi, 4, 6, 7, 9, 10, 12, 13, 20, 23, 30, 31, 38–40, 60, 62, 65–67, 69, 93, 97, 98, 108, 127–131, 153–155, 157, 184, 220, 245, 255, 259
PLA, 47, 185, 200
pogrom, 5, 11, 39, 40, 62, 64, 109, 246
 pogroms against the so-called four types, 39, 62, 64, 151, 244
 political witch-hunt, 39, 40, 53
Poland, 5, 128, 244, 245, 246, 272, 275, 280
 Polish, 6, 11
political mediation model, 258
political opportunities, 243, 255
political-opportunity structure, 19, 20, 256
political process model, 258
political witch-hunt, 39, 40, 53
politicide, 8, 9
Poor and Lower Middle Peasants' Supreme Tribunal, 61
Poor Peasant Association, 112
population density, xvi, 230, 233, 237, 239, 240
post-Cultural Revolution investigations, 3, 36
power holders, 26, 150, 174, 176, 178, 235
power seizure, 157, 175–178
preexisting factionalism, 251
prior conflict, 227, 259
proletarian dictatorship, 179
protest, 13, 22, 23, 61, 126, 142
province gazetteers (*shengzhi*), 35
provincial differences, 226
PSD. *See* Public Security Department (PSD)
psychological breakdowns, 256
Public Security Department (PSD), 150
Public Security Ministry, 177, 178
purges, 170
purposive and strategic actors, 252, 254

Qin Dynasty, 32, 79, 82
Qing Dynasty, 84
Qinghai, 28, 53, 56
Qingzhou Prefecture, 59, 60
Quanzhou, 3, 39, 62, 64, 65, 125, 126, 142, 202, 208, 215, 244, 288
 Quanzhou County, 3, 39, 40, 125, 202, 208, 244, 288
quotas, 99, 100, 106, 163, 210

realist view, 98, 99, 124
Rebel Organization, 189, 201, 284
rebellious, 86, 123, 174, 177, 193, 200
Red Flag, 50, 195, 197, 198, 199, 200, 205, 206, 210, 211, 212, 215
Red Guards, 2, 25, 26, 71, 73, 96, 156, 172–174, 196, 198, 199, 201, 210, 227, 251, 272, 280, 284, 285
remunerative, 159
resource mobilization, 19, 20, 21, 256
restoration to capitalism, 113
retaliation, 229

revolutionary committees, 18, 28, 37, 38, 50, 52, 67, 148, 178, 196–198, 219, 227, 247, 248
rich peasants, 3, 39, 40, 68, 76, 95, 99–102, 104–113, 116–120, 126, 139, 156, 181, 194, 208, 212, 215, 216, 224
Rightists, 43, 163, 164, 169
rivers, 2, 70, 71, 75, 79
rogue states, 24, 260
Rongxian County, 3, 183, 202, 204
rule of law, 157, 159, 166
Rule, James, 23
rural communities, 190, 191, 219, 222, 224, 225, 240
rural–urban differences, 223
Rwanda, xv, 6, 14, 69, 123, 245, 261, 275, 282, 289
  Rwandan, 10, 16, 97, 257, 258
Rwandan genocide, 5, 191
  Hutus, 6, 10, 14, 97, 245
  Tutsi, 6, 16
  Tutsis, 6, 14, 97, 123, 191, 245

sabotage acts, 189
Salem witch-hunt, 5, 29, 244, 245, 246, 257, 272, 279, 281, 282
scapegoat, 207
Scarlet Guards (*chi wei dui*), 174
Second World War, 7, 16, 261, 263
Security Bureau, 77, 165, 177. *See* demobilizing law
self-contained environment, 244
Shannxi, 118, 145, 177, 194, 288
Shaoqi, Liu, 140, 156, 162, 175
Sheng, Kang, 188, 205, 207
Shrief, Muzafer, 11
Shu, Ding, 164
"Smash Four Olds" campaign, 172
Smelser, Neil, 17
SMOs. *See* social movement organizations
Snow, David, xvii, xviii, 17, 21, 189, 252
social control, 157, 158, 167, 177, 179, 181, 250, 255
  modes of control, 158, 255
social mobility, 27, 33, 242
social movement, i, xvii, 6, 19, 21, 186, 243, 252, 253, 256, 258
social movement organizations, 254
socioeconomic factors, 231
Solzhenitsyn, Aleksandr, 187
South China, 68, 80, 90, 142, 217, 281, 284
Soviet Union, 97, 98, 168, 187, 191
"speaking bitterness," 107
squares, 2, 70, 71, 75, 174
Stalinist crimes, 162
Stanford, i, iii, xvii, xix, 11, 25, 45, 48, 80, 81, 110, 114, 128, 134, 149, 156, 157, 159, 166, 170, 199, 234, 240, 273–277, 280, 282, 285, 287
state breakdown, 221, 222, 238
  global breakdown, 222
State Council, 48, 160, 213
state failure, 25, 26, 170, 194, 248, 282
state mobilization, 27, 221, 222, 238, 259
  global mobilization, 222
  local mobilization, 222
state of anarchy, 156
State Security Bureau, 73
state sponsorship, 6, 7, 25, 26, 170, 194, 248, 282
state-policy model, 7, 9, 10–12, 24, 30, 127, 187, 219, 221, 236, 238, 243, 250, 257, 259
statistics, 35, 37, 44, 49, 52, 53, 57, 59, 66, 78, 82, 135, 143, 144, 165, 167, 171, 180, 182, 215, 265
strategic mobilization, 19, 22, 24, 243, 254–256
Straus, Straus, xv, 14, 69, 258, 282, 289
street battles, 195. *See also* armed battles
structural breakdown, 19, 24, 255, 256
struggle education exhibitions. *See* Class-Struggle Education exhibitions.
struggle sessions, 102, 133, 164, 173, 181
subethnic, 14, 32, 69, 70, 81, 82, 83, 85, 233, 250
subnational variations, 260
suddenly imposed threat and disruption, 256
suicide, 54, 103, 108, 119, 120
Suppress Antirevolutionary Campaigns, 138
supreme leader, 243
Supreme People's Court, 162
surname, 14, 68, 69, 85, 87, 93, 101, 102, 225
surveillance, 4, 99, 109, 111, 120, 121, 123, 164, 191, 194, 209, 229

tactical innovation, 141, 142, 155
Taiping Uprising, 86
Taiwan, 59, 65, 66, 76, 80–82, 100, 102, 109, 120, 121, 125, 126, 147, 152, 193, 205, 280, 286
Tang Dynasty, 82
Tarrow, Sidney, iii, 12, 19, 20, 252, 282
"ten years of turmoil," 157
terrorists, 12
threat, 11, 17, 19, 39, 64, 97, 98, 103, 114, 123, 124, 148, 190, 191, 204, 206, 213, 215
"Three-All Policy," 193
Three-Anti, 138
Three-Family Village, 172
Tiananmen Square, xvi, 73, 172, 173
Tiandeng County, 61
Tianhui, Huang, 4, 39, 125, 126
Tibet, 199, 228
Tilly, Charles, iii, 12, 19, 20, 30, 127, 149, 150, 252, 279, 282
Tolney, 246
torture, 107
totalitarianism, 158
traditional mobilization analysis, 254
trajectories of political process, 259
Turkey, 123
two types of integration, 256
Type 1 provinces, 229

UN. *See* United Nations
UN Convention of Genocide, 257
unarmed civilians, 32, 41, 191
unit of analysis, 9, 12, 259
United Headquarters, 61, 188, 200, 202, 204
UHQ, 61, 188, 201, 202, 203, 204, 205, 211, 212
United Nations (UN), xv, 7, 8, 32, 72, 73, 260, 275
United States, i, vi, xvi, 7, 23, 28, 74, 141, 168, 245, 255
unnatural causes, 37, 38
unnatural deaths, 40, 43, 95, 148, 214
unsanctioned killings, 157
urban communities, 18, 223
U.S. Army, 9, 245

Valentino, Benjamin, 8, 9, 13, 15, 38, 97, 123, 129, 130, 159, 192, 193, 283
Varshney, Ashutosh, 69, 253
victims, xvii, 2, 3, 5, 8, 12–14, 16, 20, 27, 30–32, 36, 39–42, 47, 48, 60–68, 73, 74, 93, 96, 97, 119, 123, 125, 126, 131, 132, 138, 152–154, 181, 187, 191, 193, 194, 204, 207, 215, 217, 223, 229, 244, 259
Vietnam, 28, 201, 202, 245
  Vietnamese, 9, 245
Vietnam War, 201
vigilante, 86
Vogel, Ezra, 116, 234
  Canton under Communism, 116

Walder, Andrew, xvii, xviii, xix, 2, 37, 38, 45, 138, 143, 282
Wang Shangguang, 210
wartime, 12, 13, 16, 21, 28, 33, 114, 129, 143, 165, 190, 191, 225, 238, 254, 259
war frame, 191, 219, 220, 240
weilongwu, 85, 101
Western democracies, 252
work-teams, 88, 89, 170, 171
World War I, 191
World War II, 5, 272
Wuhan Incident, 198, 227
Wuhua County, 43, 77, 106, 120, 166, 175, 209, 211, 216, 217, 244, 288
Wuzhou City, 74, 202

Xiao Pingtou, 59, 188, 193, 202, 204, 205, 206
Xiaoping, Deng, 77, 140
Xi'nan Guanhua, 82
Xingning County, xiv, 43, 76, 77, 95, 96, 103, 104, 106, 164, 168, 209, 211, 216, 288
Xinjiang, 56, 196, 199, 228

Yangchun, 49, 57
Yangtze, 79
Yao, 82
Yao village, 82
Yaobang, Hu, 42
Yellow River, 79
Yi, Zheng, 47, 48, 59, 65, 66, 73, 74, 109, 125, 126, 147, 152, 193, 286
Yongsheng, Huang, 197, 198, 200, 201, 205

Yongyi, Song, xviii, 28, 42, 53, 73, 193, 282
Youyu, Xu, 198, 199, 201, 227, 228
Yuan Dynasty, 79, 84
Yulin Prefecture, 60
Yunnan, 28, 47, 53, 56

Zald, Mayer, 20, 252, 279
Zhang Cheng, 31, 47, 48, 53, 64, 65, 66, 68, 125, 145, 146, 147, 151–153, 184, 202, 215, 216, 285
Zhen, Peng, 156, 161, 280
Zhongshan University, 195
Zhu, Tao, 116, 138, 139, 140, 286
Zimbardo, Phillip, 11
Ziyang, Zhao, 42, 116, 139

CPSIA information can be obtained
at www.ICGtesting.com
Printed in the USA
LVHW012027271220
675133LV00001B/57